THE CHILDREN'S SONGBOOK COMPANION

PAT GRAHAM
MARY GOURLEY
TRUDY SHIPP
LINDA STEWART

Illustrated by

NINA GROVER

The Children's Songbook Companion
This work is not an official publication of The Church of Jesus Christ of Latter-day Saints.
The views expressed herein are the responsibility of the authors and do not necessarily represent the position of the Church.

Printed in the United States of America

10 9 8 7 6 5 4 3 2 1

CONTENTS

PREFACE

This book contains a gold mine of ideas to help you be more effective in teaching the songs in the *Children's Songbook* and to have more fun doing it. What a wonderful opportunity you have to teach the gospel of Jesus Christ through these inspired songs.

We have divided the book into two parts. Part One explains what you need to know in order to teach a song successfully and explains the method we used to develop the lesson plans included in Part Two. We have great confidence in the method demonstrated on the "How to Teach a Song to Children" video cassette (53005) and have used the steps outlined in that video. You will find those steps invaluable for creating plans of your own.

You might teach a particular lesson plan from Part Two on only one occasion, but sing the song many times. As you review the song with the children and reinforce the concepts you are teaching, Part One will give you the additional attention-getters and teaching tools you need to keep the children involved and strengthen the original teaching.

Part Two contains a lesson plan for each song in the *Children's Songbook,* with countless ideas to add variety, interest, and fun to your singing time. As you study these ideas, we hope your vision of children's music will expand. As you implement the ideas, you will feel great joy in helping children internalize the gospel principles taught in the songs.

We hope that as you practice the ideas given here you will grow in confidence and in your ability to help children learn and feel joy through the music of the gospel. As President Hugh B. Brown said, "As you give of yourself and of your talents, even as the flower breathes its fragrance into space, so shall God speak through you, and through your eyes smile upon these little ones" (*Primary Music Guide,* 1967). How rewarding it will be for you to see truth and testimony come alive in others because of your best efforts!

♪ ABOUT THE AUTHORS

In 1984 a Primary General Board Ad Hoc Committee was called to help with the preparation of the 1989 *Children's Songbook*. Pat Graham, already the General Primary Music Chairman, was asked to head up that committee. She devoted countless hours to the project and has said, "I wish every child in the world could grow up singing the songs in the *Children's Songbook*." Three committee members who responded to Pat's leadership are Mary Gourley, Trudy Shipp, and Linda Stewart. All three were serving as ward or stake Primary music leaders when they were called to the Committee. They assisted with the selection of the songs to be included in the *Children's Songbook*, helped to choose the scriptures for each song, determined the topics addressed in each song for indexing, and made suggestions for the content of the artwork. They also prepared a lesson plan for each song in the book—a project that was initially being considered for release along with the 1989 Songbook. Difficulties in translating the ideas into other languages sidetracked the project. Only now, with the release of this *Children's Songbook Companion,* has this incredible collection of ideas—vastly expanded and improved—become available.

The information that follows will alert you to the wealth of experience and diversity of backgrounds of those involved in the creation of both the *Children's Songbook* and the *Children's Songbook Companion.*

Patricia Kelsey Graham

Pat said she grew up on a piano bench. She played for weekday Primary when she was ten and became ward organist at fourteen. She spent many years as Jr. Sunday School coordinator, Young Women president, and Relief Society president, then was called to the Primary General Board where she served from 1980–1988. "Everything I know how to do I learned through my service in the Church," Pat explains. However, she did supplement that experience with a BA in Elementary Education from BYU and a Masters of Education from the University of Utah where she currently teaches in the Preparatory Division of the Music Department.

She has taught private piano since 1962, wrote the Sharing Time page in the *Friend* magazine for many years, and is the composer and author of five Primary songs, as well as the books *Sing Out! Songbook*, *Sing about Families*, and *Fun and Games*.

Pat and her husband, G. Robert Graham, live in Salt Lake City and are the parents of six children and grandparents of five.

Mary Curtis Gourley

Music has always been an important part of Mary's life. Her innate musical talents were first cultivated by attending professional performances with her family and listening to her father play violin. Mary began studying piano as a child and has become an accomplished pianist. She studied music at Brigham Young University.

Mary loves to teach as well as learn. She is a private piano instructor and has her own sewing school for young children. Her musical experience includes service in every ward and stake Church music position—pianist, organist, choir conductor, and music chairman. Positions as Young Women president and Relief Society Homemaking counselor have added variety along the way.

She enjoys playing golf and being in the mountains, especially at the family cabin. Mary and her husband, Michael H. Gourley, have five children and eight beautiful grandchildren who are Mary's pride and joy. Mary loves her family and has dedicated her life to the gospel.

Trudy Swenson Shipp

Trudy grew up in Portland, Oregon, where at age fifteen she accepted her first calling in the Church as Primary chorister. Over the years she was repeatedly called to be Primary chorister and it became her favorite calling—one to which she lends a tremendous amount of creativity and energy. Trudy enthusiastically says, "I love the Primary songs of the Church!" She has also been ward and stake Primary and Young Womens president, but is always happiest when she gets back to teaching the songs of the gospel to Primary children.

Trudy lives in Sandy, Utah, with her husband, Bill, and their youngest son, Michael. Her older children, Adam, Mindy, and Ryan, attend BYU. Trudy graduated from BYU in Elementary Education and enjoys quilting, reading, playing the piano, singing, keeping the family scrapbooks up to date, and being in the great outdoors. Her statement "I love life!" characterizes this bubbly, vivacious lady.

Linda Call Stewart

Linda has served as ward or stake Primary music leader for nearly twenty years and has worked in all auxiliaries. She is a picture expert who knows every picture in the meetinghouse library. She loves Primary songs and says they are a big part of her life. "I have loved learning and teaching the gospel through the words of the beautiful Primary music," she says. "I always feel a special sweetness when I hear the children singing."

Linda is a dedicated homemaker and mother, and works as an executive assistant for a financial consulting firm. She lives in Midvale, Utah, but enjoys spending time in Oakley at the cabin her husband and family built. She and her husband, Lynn J. Stewart, are the parents of seven children and grandparents of four. Linda enjoys children of all ages—her Primary children, and especially her own children and grandchildren.

Nina Grover

Nina received a degree in Fine Arts and Graphic Design from the University of Utah and has put her art talent to good use ever since. She said, concerning her involvement with this project, "My patriarchal blessing tells me that I have been given a gift to communicate with children through my art. I am glad to use my gift on a project that will help children understand the gospel." Nina has great love for the Primary, has served in ward and stake Primary presidencies, and was an assistant designer for the *Friend* magazine. She has also illustrated *Songs for a Mormon Child; Books 1, 2, and 3 of Stories to See and Share, Articles of Faith Workbooks,* and many coloring books.

Nina and her husband, Gary, live in Salt Lake City and are the parents of four sons.

♡♡ ACKNOWLEDGMENTS ♡

Have you ever wondered who made up the actions to "Book of Mormon Stories" or who first thought of using a paper plate with a smile and a frown to turn upside down while singing "If You Chance to Meet a Frown"?

Sometimes a great idea occurs independently to several people in different places in the world! This book is a compilation of ideas that have grown out of our study of each of the children's songs as well as ideas we have seen others use successfully. So we say a simple, heartfelt thank you to all of you who may have contributed to this book through your creativity.

We particularly acknowledge the influence of four women who have, over many years, taught and demonstrated the rote teaching method: Susan Hobson Kenney, professor of Music, Brigham Young University, former member of the Primary General Board, and former member of the General Music Committee of The Church of Jesus Christ of Latter-day Saints; Vanya Yorgason Watkins, music television teacher, composer, Brigham Young University faculty member, former member of the Primary General Board, and former member of the Church's General Music Committee; Patricia Haglund Nielsen, composer, former member of the Primary General Board, and formerly on the music faculty at BYU; and Ruth Muir Gardner, piano teacher, composer, and former member of the Primary General Board.

We appreciate Elaine Rich Anderson, Jill Christensen Rawstorne, and Jill Stallings Summerhays for their field testing and valuable suggestions. We are grateful for our husbands who have understood our obsession with this project and encouraged us to pursue our dream.

We appreciate our editor, Darla Isackson, as well as Jennifer Utley, Rebecca Porter, and all the capable staff at Aspen Books who have made the dream a reality.

Pat ♪ Mary ♪ Trudy ☺ Linda ♡

Introduction

The Importance of Music for Children

Music Helps You Remember

How long has it been since you were a child in Primary? Do you think you could still sing "'Give,' Said the Little Stream"? As you begin humming the tune, the words automatically come back to you. The melody stimulates recall, and the words help you remember the melody. Those who produce TV commercials and jingles certainly rely on this fact!

Some researchers have found that we remember only a small percentage of what we hear in lecture form. Recall increases when stories or visual aids are included. But if we teach a child a song and they memorize it, they will recall most of it indefinitely (*Spectrum*, May 5, 1982, Bascom, Hanks).

As a teacher, you can also make good use of this principle. Try to have each child memorize the words and music to the Primary songs, rather than read them from a word chart. Try to have the children singing every possible minute.

> The music in my heart I bore
> Long after it was heard no more.
> —William Wordsworth

Music Helps You Feel Truth

Appropriate, beautiful music can refine, elevate, and enlarge a child's nature. Through music, children have the opportunity to internalize nearly every principle of the gospel.

Truth in a musical setting can play a vital role in developing a child's testimony of gospel principles as it often teaches the heart as well as the mind on a deeper level than the word alone does. Elder Boyd K. Packer has stated, "We are able to feel and learn very quickly through music . . . some spiritual things that we would otherwise learn very slowly" ("The Arts and the Spirit of the Lord," *Ensign* Aug. 1976, p. 61).

When you sing "I Am a Child of God," you might feel a warm swelling inside that says, "Yes, I *am*." When you sing "I Know My Father Lives," you can feel the whisperings of the Spirit confirming that he *does* live. Children have these feelings, too, and leaders have the wonderful opportunity of helping to identify them. When tears run down your cheeks, say, "Boys and girls, do you feel that warm, sweet feeling? That is the Holy Ghost telling us that what we are singing about is true."

Elder Dallin Oaks has said, "Our sacred music prepares us to be taught the truths of the gospel . . . we . . . need to keep singing that we may draw ever closer to Him who has inspired sacred music and commanded that it be used to worship Him" (*Church News*, Oct. 8, 1994, p. 8).

PART ONE

Teaching Children through Music

For generations, children have learned to sing by rote. That is, they hear a song and repeat it; they listen and imitate. Learning depends on listening rather than reading. You probably know more Primary songs than hymns by heart, even though you may not have sung Primary songs for many years yet sing hymns every week. The difference is that you learned the Primary songs by rote, whereas you read the hymns and are seldom required to memorize them.

Even before children are old enough to fully know the meaning of the words, they are able to sense the spirit of a song. A very little girl once said, "I love our Primary songs—they make me feel Heavenly Father-like."

We can learn the words of songs by listening, or we can read them without thinking. However, the reason for music in the Church is to help us understand the principle we are singing about. The Apostle Paul wrote, "I will sing with the spirit, and I will sing with the understanding also" (1 Cor. 14:15).

Learning by rote gives a child an opportunity to listen, to feel, and to understand the song in a powerful way. This manual has been written to help you teach in such a way that words can become meaningful principles.

> *THE SINGERS*
> *God sent his singers upon earth*
> *With songs of sadness and of mirth*
> *That they might touch the hearts of men*
> *And bring them back to heaven again.*
> *—Henry Wadsworth Longfellow*

 PREPARING TO TEACH

As a teacher, you can have a great impact on children's attitudes about singing and about the gospel. Being prepared spiritually is vital preparation to teaching and results from studying the scriptures regularly and keeping the commandments. Bearing testimony of a principle is most effective when you are living that principle. As you prepare and ask for God's help in reaching the children, you will feel directed in both your planning and your teaching.

"The Lord does not ask us about our ability, but only about our availability.
And then if we demonstrate our dependability, the Lord will increase our capability."

–Neal A. Maxwell, Conference Report–Denmark,
Finland, Norway, & Sweden Area Conference, 1974, p.12

LEARNING THE SONG

You should do two things to prepare to teach a song: (1) learn the song and (2) become familiar with the lesson plan you have chosen from Part Two of this book. If you are teaching a song not in the *Children's Songbook*, you may create your own plan using the questions below as your guide (also see *Children's Songbook*, p. 300).

The answers we gave to these questions as we analyzed each song in the *Children's Songbook* became the basis for the lesson plans included in this book. You may also want to copy the worksheet "How to Learn a Song" on p. 13, fill it in for each song you are going to teach, and use it along with the lesson plans in Part Two.

Study the Words

You can do this even *before* you sing a note or hear it played on the piano. Here are some questions that you should answer:

1. What **message** do I want the children to learn from singing this song?
   Read the words and rephrase them into a simple statement. Then ask yourself, "What is the message of this song?" Your lesson plan should focus on helping the children understand the message or main idea of each song.

2. What **words** will I need to explain or pronounce?
   Notice the words or phrases that you think the children may not understand. Be sure you have a clear definition of these words as used in the song.

3. What **key words** or **phrases** will help the children learn the song quickly?
   Key words can be (1) important words, (2) rhyming words, (3) words to define, or (4) the order of words. Key phrases or groups of words can outline the text and help you learn the order of ideas. Especially notice phrases that are alike or different in a memorable way.

4. What **visual aids** or **actions** do the words suggest?
   Think of pictures or objects that might clarify the message for the children. These could be used to start the song. Perhaps the words lend themselves to simple actions.

5. What **personal experience** could I relate that would express my feelings or bear testimony of the song's message?
   You can communicate through the Spirit by sharing short personal experiences, bearing your testimony of a principle, or sharing someone else's experience.

Study the Music

After you have studied the words, study the music. Though you will also want to hear the music by playing it yourself, allowing someone to play it for you, or listening to a tape recording, you can learn much just by looking at the notes. Ask yourself these questions:

1. What is memorable about the **melody**?
    You can read the music notes like a dot-to-dot picture to find the shape of the melody. Look for unusual intervals (skips) and repeated notes or patterns. Notice the highest and lowest note.

2. What **rhythm patterns** make the song interesting?
    Look for repeated or unusual rhythm patterns. Watch for quick notes or especially long notes. Discovering patterns in the rhythm of the song will help you remember it accurately and teach it correctly.

3. What **dynamic markings** are given to create mood, tempo, or musical emphasis?
    For information on descriptive words, volume, and tempo markings, see *Children's Songbook,* pp. 301–4.

4. What is the **form** of the song?
    Which lines or phrases are alike and which are different? (Example: AABA)

Now you know much more about the song than you will ever teach. What you present to the children will be as Hemingway stated, "the tip of the iceberg," or the most relevant ideas that have occurred to you as you learned the song. The additional information provides enrichment possibilities and strength to your presentation.

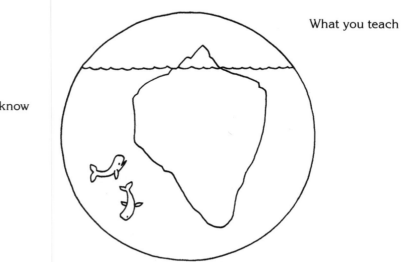

What you teach

What you know

How to Learn a Song Worksheet

FOR _____

Study the Words

1. What **message** do I want the children to learn from singing this song?

2. What **words** will I need to explain or pronounce?

3. What **key words** or phrases might help the children learn the song quickly?

4. What **visual aids** or actions do the words suggest?

5. What **personal experience** could I relate that would express my feelings and bear testimony of this message?

Study the Music

1. What is memorable about the **melody**? (repeated patterns, shape, unusual intervals)

2. What **rhythm patterns** make the song interesting?

3. What **dynamic markings** are given to create mood, tempo, or other musical emphasis?

4. What is the **form** of the song?

Developing a Plan

"If ye are prepared ye shall not fear."
—D&C 38:30

Putting the Plan Together

1. **MESSAGE** (What do I want the children to learn and remember?)

   Now that you have learned the song and have stated the message you are going to teach, you are ready to study the lesson plan given or develop a plan of your own. A short formula for each of our lesson plans is: get the children's attention, ask questions to help them listen to the song, and plan reasons to have them repeat the singing.

   When we studied the words of the song, we answered this question: "What do we want the children to understand and remember by learning this song?" Our answer is the focus of the plan. The following explanations describe the function of each part of the lesson plan.

2. **ATTENTION-GETTER** (In what catchy way do I start my presentation and capture the children's interest?)

   Perhaps you will recall that as a child someone asked you to listen quietly for a pin to drop. Even now as you think about it, you can feel the intense silence while everyone anxiously strained to hear the tiny sound. That was a simple and effective means of getting your attention.

   An attention-getter is needed when you first introduce the song and every time you review it. To be effective, an attention-getter should set the stage for learning and be relevant to the message. It should create an exhilarating teaching moment when you sense that everyone is with you. The following ideas are just as simple as dropping the pin and can be adapted for use as attention-getters for many songs.

   - Object or Picture. Simple objects, such as a picture of your family or an apricot twig in bloom, can be used effectively. You could put the item behind your back and give clues to help the children guess the object.
   - Key Words. These can be put under chairs, on a magnet board, around the room, or on headbands. The children listen to the song then arrange the key words in order.
   - Scrambled Word. Choose an important word from the song and scramble it. The children must listen to the song to unscramble the key word.
   - Riddle. Challenge the children to guess who a song is about as you sing the words and hum the answer. Examples: Jesus, mother, our bishop.
   - Question. Ask the children any question that would lead into the song.
   - Quotation. Share a statement made by a church leader or the song's composer.
   - Lyrics. Recite the lyrics as a poem.
   - Story. Briefly share a personal experience or story that relates to the song.
   - Scripture. Read a scripture about the song's message. Have the children guess what song it relates to.
   - Testimony. Relate the way you gained your personal conviction of the gospel principle you are teaching.
   - Whisper. Sometimes just a whisper is all you need to get the children's attention.
   - Draw a Mental Picture. Through descriptive detail, help the children to feel a part of the setting of the song.
   - Sense. Use stimulating activities that allow the children to see, smell, hear, taste, or feel something relating to a song.
   - Actions. Without introduction, sing the song with appropriate actions or sign language.
   - Chalk Talk. As you sing, draw simple chalk figures illustrating the lyrics.

3. **QUESTIONS FOR LISTENING EXPERIENCES** (How do I get the children to listen to the song so they can learn what it means?)

After getting their attention, ask a question that the children can answer by listening to the song. Listening to discover an answer allows *every* child to be involved, not just the few who can guess what the teacher means. Permanent learning is often discovery oriented. Don't tell the children if they can find out for themselves.

Even though today's children are very visually oriented, children also learn by listening. They imitate what they hear. Helping a child learn to listen for answers may be the most important teaching you can do. It is preparatory to the spiritual listening that will develop as the child learns to recognize and follow the still, small voice of the Holy Ghost. For example, you might ask children to listen for—

- *Key words*
- *Rhyming words*
- *Answers to questions about the text*
- *Correct order of random-order pictures*
- *How many times a particular word or phrase is sung*
- *Words on the highest or lowest note in the song*
- *Repeated melody or rhythm patterns*

For children to learn by listening, they must think. An involved, thinking child is a productive rather than a disruptive child.

4. **SINGING EXPERIENCES** (How can I give the children an opportunity to join in?)

When the children have heard the song several times, they are ready to join in. As the children discover the answers to the questions you ask, invite them to sing that phrase with you. Then ask another question that directs their listening to the next part you want to teach. Encourage the children to sing the phrases they know each time you sing the song to them. If the children do not join in the singing, it may be that they haven't heard the song enough times.

To keep the children's interest as you repeat the singing, give *specific* instructions for repeating and improving the singing. Rather than saying, "That wasn't very good, let's do it again," or "I can't understand your words; sing it better this time," you might say:

- "Let's sing again and check to see if we have the pictures (or key words) in order."
- "Can you keep your eyes on me for the whole song?"
- "Which do you think matches the message—to grow in volume or to soften on these words?" Sing the song using varying dynamics.
- Ask the children to do one of the following: (a) begin with the very first word; (b) observe cutoffs; (c) sustain long tones on a vowel sound; (d) sing whole phrases before taking a breath; (e) articulate consonants together.

To conclude your presentation, compliment the children, comment on the feelings that have come from the music, and bear testimony to the message of the song.

5. **ENRICHMENT.** (How can I make this song more meaningful and memorable to the children?) This part of the plan includes suggestions for singing and reviewing after the children understand the song. These ideas are specific to each song. General enrichment ideas are explained in the section "Ideas for Reviewing a Song," pp. 29–40.

♪ *About the Song*

These stories and insights are a compilation of personal experiences and interviews during the five years Pat Graham served as chairman of the Primary General Board Music Committee. Some information was previously written for her Sharing Time pages in the *Friend* magazine

(1984, 1985, and 1986) and some of it she recorded as she was invited to speak about the songbook. The natural coincidences and little miracles that occurred during the preparation of the *Children's Songbook* reaffirmed the songbook committee's testimonies of the importance of using music to teach children the gospel. The authors share these accounts with the hope that readers might be strengthened as they have been.

6. **MATERIALS** (What items do I need?)

Each lesson plan includes a list of materials needed. Most have visual aid and illustration ideas. Many resources (available from your distribution center) may be in your meetinghouse library:

- Pictures. It is helpful to have your own copy of the *Distribution Center Catalog* to use as a visual and numerical picture reference. Since the catalog is periodically updated, all the picture numbers referred to in this book may not be in the current catalog, but the picture may still be available in your meetinghouse libraries. Be alert to opportunities to gather pictures about to be discarded. They are perfect to collect as well as to cut and paste to make collages and other visual aids.
- Primary course manuals
- Beginning Course Visual Aids Kit (31269)
- Visual Aid Cutouts, 10 sets (33239, 33242 through 33250)
- Church magazines
- Larger pictures, charts, maps
- *Primary Sharing Time Resource Manual* (33231)
- *How to Teach a Song to Children* (videocassette 53005)
- *How to Conduct a Hymn* (videocassette: *Music Training* 53042)
- Conducting Course (manual and audiocassette, 33619)
- Reversible flannel/write-on board. (One side is a flannel board. The other is a hard white surface designed for use with erasable markers.) 16" x 24" (80346); 24" x 32" (80347)
- Five-line chalk holder (33131)
- Recordings of all the songs in the *Children's Songbook* (cassette 52428, disc 50428).

Using the Illustrations

1. Permission to enlarge the line drawings as needed for teaching is given with the purchase of this manual. Do so with a copy machine (continue to enlarge each enlargement until you get the size you need) or an opaque projector (available at public libraries).
2. Outline in black and color vividly. Colored pencils are good for shading.
3. Rather than coloring, you may find it faster to reproduce on pieces of colored paper.
4. Use rubber cement or a glue stick for mounting—water-base glue wrinkles paper.
5. Laminate, especially if children will be handling the pictures.

EVALUATING WHILE YOU PRACTICE THE PLAN

Now that you understand the purpose of each part of the lesson plan, you can begin to practice the attention-getter and questions. Prepare in front of a mirror to see if you are animated and clear in your delivery, or try your plan with a small group of children.

Evaluate your plan against the checklist below:

1. Sing the whole song as the children listen.
2. Sing the song for the children without the piano whenever possible.
3. Teach the words and melody together. Avoid isolating the words or chanting them without the music.

4. Invite children to join in on parts of the song as you sing the whole song.
5. Always sound a beginning pitch for the children before asking them to sing.
6. Word your questions so that the children can answer them by listening to the song.
7. Don't tell the children an answer if they can discover it.
8. Involve the children mentally or physically.
9. Plan meaningful reasons to repeat the singing.
10. Adapt the lesson plan to fit the ages and interests of the children you teach.
11. Make sure visual aids do not detract from the gospel message of the song.
12. Work as a team with your accompanist.
13. Plan and calendar the songs you will teach and review weekly, monthly, and annually.

IMPROVING YOUR SKILLS

This is a true story:

> One Sunday morning, everyone in Primary was waiting to begin singing, but there was no music leader. Someone asked the teacher on the front row to please lead the opening song. The frightened teacher faced the children and somehow helped them start and end together. She had never sung in front of anyone before and did not know how to conduct. But she smiled and she tried. Two weeks later she was called to be the Primary chorister.

Only if this had happened to you could you fully appreciate this person's overwhelming feeling of inadequacy. A great deal is expected of someone in this assignment. A music leader needs (1) basic teaching skills, (2) music skills for singing and conducting, (3) organizational skills for calendaring and planning, and (4) the flexibility to adjust plans to fit the available singing time.

Singing time may sometimes feel more like crowd control as you try to keep the interest of various ages of children while you fit your fifteen-minute plan into the five minutes that are left! Remember that others have survived this scenario. Your goal should be to grow one step at a time by improving your skills. Then you can use music as an effective means of teaching the gospel to children. If the former teacher from the front row could do it, so can you!

TEACHING

> *"Every human being is trying to say something to others;*
> *Trying to cry out, I am alive; notice me! speak to me! listen*
> *to me! confirm for me that I am important: that I matter!"*
> —Marion D. Hanks

As a Primary chorister, you are also a teacher. What you do during singing time can greatly influence the children's attitudes about music, the gospel, and themselves. Older children especially are searching for self-identity. Here are some pointers that will help you meet their needs:

• *Care about the children* as a group and individually. Although it may seem difficult to meet the needs of all the children at the same time, remember that all children need to be loved and recognized.

• *Know the children's names.* Call each child by name. Everyone loves to hear their name spoken. This simple effort is an effective way to give each child recognition.

• *Reinforce good conduct* instead of pointing out inappropriate actions of misbehaving children. Recognize positive effort rather than giving attention to misbehavior. Children often behave according to their feelings about themselves, and your response may help them to see themselves in a more positive way.

Here are some encouraging statements that will reinforce good conduct:

- *You're really working hard today.*
- *That's the best you have ever done.*
- *Now you've figured it out.*
- *That's quite an improvement.*
- *I knew you could do it!*
- *You are learning fast.*
- *Good for you!*
- *One more time and you'll have it.*
- *You haven't missed a thing.*
- *Fantastic!*

• *Adapt your plan to fit the age group.* Many techniques can be successful with all children. However, understanding the characteristics of each age group will help you adapt your teaching plan to appeal to the children you teach.

Younger children find challenge and interest through movement. Therefore, look for ways to have very young children move as you teach them songs. For example, you might use action songs or help the children act out the words of a song. You could help the children respond to musical rhythms. Challenge them to pat their laps, shoulders, heads, tummies, or fingertips to the beat of a song; to swing their arms to the beat of the song or move their arms with you as you trace phrases in the air. Invite the children to copy you as you pitch lead. Younger children are good imitators and will try to do anything you do. Do not expect them to perform perfectly, for they are just learning how to control body movement.

Use pictures to help children explore ideas in the song, since many will not be able to read.

Because young children love repetition, repeat the song many times, especially if movement is involved. Avoid talking about the song, just sing it over and over again.

Little children respond most easily to your voice, and so it may be helpful to add the accompaniment only after they know the song.

Older children find challenge and interest through both thinking and moving. Challenge the older children mentally *and* physically. They respond well to riddles and questions that encourage them to search for answers. Older children may learn to conduct while singing, which can provide them additional interest and valuable training.

You might also challenge their listening skills. Many older children love to read, and they enjoy word cards used as clues to learn a song. Avoid writing all the words to a song on a chart. Instead, ask questions that challenge the children to listen. Questions can involve the following:

Words:	"What three things am I thankful for?"
Rhythm:	"Pat the beat on your lap as I sing." "How many beats are in the first phrase?" "What words occur on this rhythm?"
Melody:	"When you hear this melody, raise your hand."
Form:	"How many times do you hear the first line repeated in the song?"
Other:	"Would the song express the words better if we sang it soft or loud?"

SINGING

As a music leader, you can help children enjoy singing. Your call to serve might have been prompted because you love music or children, or because of your testimony. You may feel unprepared because your music background consists only of singing lullabies to your own children. Perhaps you were even told at some time in your life that you sang off pitch and were asked whether you would like to hold the poster instead of sing. Because singing can be very personal, it is often difficult to overcome feelings of inadequacy. Children, however, will rarely criticize your voice. If you are enthusiastic, they will like what you do! The following suggestions may help you improve your personal vocal ability and increase your understanding of how to help children improve their singing.

I Shall Be Glad

I shall be glad if sometime in the future
Some heartened one shall come to me and say:
"The little song you sang when I was weary
Showed me a better and a clearer way."
I shall rejoice and thrill through all my being
If somewhere, sometime, in the days to be
I shall find one with eager heart to tell me
The song I sang gave him new eyes to see.
(From Katherine Edelman, "Friendly Thoughts Hallmark Treasures")

Developing a Singing Voice

Most happy children learn to sing as naturally as they learn to speak. The most important thing you can do is to provide positive singing opportunities. With your help, children can be encouraged to find joy through singing, regardless of the degree of their natural singing ability.

Tone

Singing should never be so loud that quality is lost. A good rule to follow is "Never louder than beautiful." Encourage children to project the tone by suggesting that they try to sing through a hoop (your arms held in a large circle) or to a particular spot on the wall behind you, such as a clock. The idea is to project the tone mentally first, and the physical tone will naturally follow.

Sometimes boys want to imitate men's low bass voices. Encourage them to sing in their head voice until their voice change is complete.

Posture

Have children slump over and sing. Then have them sit with their heads tilted back and sing. Finally, have them stand or sit and sing with backs straight and their chins level. Once they have experienced the difference these postures make, you might say (referring to the last position), "This is the best way to sit (or stand) when you sing." Good posture helps breathing and tone.

For a performance, you may want to have the children sit forward on the edge of their seats with both feet firmly on the floor. Tell them that you have a pretend rope tied around their waists, and when you give the signal, you will "pull" them forward. (This is sometimes preferable to the noise of standing.) Occasionally, tell the children to relax and let their backs touch the chairs while you give instructions. Then "pull" them forward into the correct singing posture again.

Breathing

Children can increase their breath control when singing if you will show them how. Your ribs should go out as you breathe deep down and fill your lungs to capacity. Ask the children to place their hands at the bottom of their rib cages and feel them open as they inhale. After a deep breath, have them sustain a soft "oo" and see how long they can continue to exhale.

Decide with the children the breaks that would make the words have the most meaning, then practice breathing together in those places. One way to practice is to trace the phrase in the air, breathing only at the beginning and the end. Another idea is to begin the phrase with both arms together high overhead and make a circle out and down, ending low in front of the body as the phrase ends. As the children raise their arms to begin the next phrase, they are automatically encouraged to breathe from their diaphragms.

Diction

By paying attention to vowels and consonants, you can achieve a beautiful sound that is easy to understand. Instruct the children to pronounce the vowels uniformly and to sing on the vowel as long as possible, then make the consonants definite and precise. A basic rule is to put the last consonant on the next syllable (for example, sing *gospel* as go-spel, not gos-pel). Consonants such as "*s*" can become a repeated sound in a group (s-s-s-s) unless you direct exactly when it should be sung. Be careful not to anticipate consonants at the end of a word or syllable so that you sing them too soon.

Pitch

Many children under age eight have difficulty singing on pitch. When some children are not matching the melody, you might practice small phrases unaccompanied and have the children as a group match your voice one note at a time. Never single them out, but encourage them as a group to listen to the way they sound. Make sure the children understand that they can improve rather than feel they have failed. Maturation and correct practice will almost always bring improvement.

Generally, if you can think the pitch, you can sing it. Suggest that they think of hitting the high notes from above like a basketball shot. The ball first must go above the rim in order to get to its destination. Sing down to the high notes rather than sliding up to them (be an organ, not a slide trombone). Approach high notes like you would throw a ball—with your whole body and plenty of energy. Think high on repeated notes and descending passages to avoid going flat.

Harmony

Two-part songs provide an opportunity for children to sing in harmony. Teach everyone part one and part two, then divide the children into two groups. A music leader for each group gives support. Descants (a part above the melody that has its own words) and ostinatos (a repeated pattern that can be created from an idea in the song) could be sung by a small group of children or all the girls or all the boys. A cappella round singing also helps build confidence in singing two or more parts together and provides a challenge to the older children.

CONDUCTING

Following the Leader

To some extent, you will probably get whatever you expect from the children. If you do things that require their attention, they will probably focus on you. If you are totally predictable, their eyes may wander. When you direct children to sing with expression, you can unite them in their singing. Expressive singing brings feeling and the spirit of testimony to the song, and should be your highest goal, but practicing good singing techniques is also important:

1. Encourage the children to watch you and begin together. Test their watching by asking them to sing only the first word of the song at your signal. If all do not sing, try it again until all are watching and singing the first word. Then go on with the rest of the song.
2. Cut off in different places to test if children are watching you.
3. Give children signals for singing louder, softer, faster, slower, cut off. Direct the song using the signals and check the children's responses.
4. Practice singing correct vowel sounds in words. Stop on a certain word and sing only the vowel sound, holding it until there is a unity of sound.
5. Practice ending consonants.
6. Challenge the children to sit tall without leaning against the backs of the chairs for one whole verse or song.
7. Sing a long phrase without taking a breath. Try singing a whole song without taking a breath.
8. Challenge the children to watch you without looking away for one line of the song. Then try two lines, then the whole song.

There are two ways to conduct children's music—by pitch leading or by standard beat pattern.

Pitch leading consists of using your hand as a visual aid showing the direction the melody moves. Your conducting hand should be horizontal, palm down. Move your hand up when the pitch rises, down when the pitch lowers, and at the same level for repeated notes.

You can also show the rhythm or duration of the notes by the length of time your hand stays in the same position. In this way, pitch leading teaches both the direction and the rhythm of the melody. When children sing with confidence, you may combine or replace this method with standard beat patterns.

Standard beat patterns help the music flow smoothly. Look at the top number of the time signature to determine the number of beats you should conduct in each measure. For help in basic conducting techniques and beat patterns see: *How to Conduct a Hymn* on *Music Training Video* [53042]; *Hymns* pp. 383-85, and *Children's Songbook*, p. 301.

Use a mirror and practice these beat patterns until you feel secure. Appropriate conducting should help the children start together, stay together, end together, and sing with expression.

Calendaring

Plan and calendar your teaching time so that children will feel the pleasure of completely knowing a variety of songs. You will want to allow time for prayer songs, seasonal or weather-related songs, baptism and birthday songs, activity and other fun songs for a change of pace, and songs that reinforce a principle being taught.

You could make a pencil tally on a copy of the contents page each time you sing a song so that you keep track of how often you use it. Otherwise, you may sing one particular song ten times during the year, and leave out another of the children's favorites altogether!

Notify your accompanist of your monthly and weekly plan to allow her to prepare adequately.

Even the best plans will not always fit the actual time you may have. You will need to be flexible in order to shorten your presentation on one Sunday or add songs on another. Record which verses you actually teach each week so that you will know where to start the following week. You will need to be prepared with several optional songs and activities to use when you are given more time than you planned.

Working with Your Accompanist

The way a song is played influences the way children will sing it. The pianist is a support to both the music leader and the singers. Instruct your pianist to prepare to do the following:

• *Play the melody alone* as the children learn the song or give occasional pitches at any point in the music leader's presentation.

• *Practice the entire accompaniment for accuracy* of notes and rhythm, including introductions.

• *Use the fingering* or write her own and decide whether to play optional octaves and other cue notes.

• *Play the song with musical expression.* Usually it is musically correct to shape the phrases by increasing the volume as the melody rises and decreasing as the melody descends. A metronome can help in practicing the correct tempo of the song.

• *Help the singers observe the phrasing.* The pianist should follow the words in each verse and release the hands and pedal briefly at the phrase end and other breathing places that the music leader has planned. This will help to emphasize the important words.

Your pianist should always work closely with you in order to be well prepared. It is advisable to help her prepare a notebook with a monthly plan, listing the songs—and their order—for each Sunday. Suggest that she insert sheets of paper or post-it notes in the songbook to mark each page you are going to be singing that day so she can quickly move from one song to another.

TEACHING A SONG

In order to effectively learn by rote, children must actively listen to the song several times. The things you have learned about the song will provide the springboard for your teaching ideas. Here are some great ways to add interest and variety to your presentation:

TEACHING WITH MUSICAL IDEAS

Often the music reinforces a gospel message. By paying attention to the music, children will learn the song faster and will feel the message more deeply. Following are suggestions for helping children learn a song while noticing musical ideas.

Melody

Pick a small word phrase from a song and make a picture of the melody that goes with the words. For example, you might select "teach me all that I must do" from the song, "I Am a Child of God." A melody picture may be represented in any of the following ways:

Line contour of melody:

Short lines indicating high and low notes:

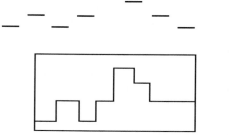

Melodic shape piece:

Traditional notes indicating high and low notes:

Exact representation of the melody on a staff:

Sometimes the subject of the song could allow the short melody lines to be substituted by pictures such as leaves, snowflakes, and flowers. In the song, "I Am Like a Star," the melody might be represented this way:

Show the melody picture to the children, and hum it two or three times so they will know the sounds it represents. After humming it, sing the entire song and do any of the following:

1. Ask the children what words occur on that melody line.
2. Ask how many times the melody occurs. Ask what the different words are if the melody pattern occurs more than once.
3. Trace the melody pattern with your hand and invite the children to do the same. Or have the children stoop or stretch to show the up and down direction of the melody (body pitch leading).
4. Sing the whole song; then ask the children what word comes at the highest point or the lowest point of the phrase. If they can read, have them put wordstrips at the highest and lowest points of the melody picture.
5. After the children know the song, ask them to sing the song out loud excluding the melody phrase. They should sing that phrase in their minds only. The accompanist could play just that melody phrase when it comes in the song.
6. Have a child play the melody pattern on melody bells, pipe chimes, or a xylophone while all the children sing it.
7. If appropriate, show several melody pictures from the song. Hum each picture and then ask the children to determine the correct order of each melody picture by listening to the song.
8. Teach the children to hear the difference between a major and minor triad. Have children listen to determine if the song is in a major (happy) or minor (sad) key.

Rhythm Patterns

Pick a small word phrase from the song and make a picture of the rhythm. For example, in the song "Dare to Do Right," the rhythm of the first phrase may be represented in the following ways:
Dashes representing long and short sounds

———— —— ———— ————————

Traditional note stems and heads

Clap or tap the pattern two or three times and then ask the children to clap it so they feel the rhythm they are seeing. Then sing the song using any of the following ideas:

1. Ask children what words occur on that pattern. *[Dare to do right, dare to be true.]*
2. Ask how many times the pattern occurs. *[Five times.]*
3. Ask children to clap the pattern when it occurs in the song as you sing it.
4. Play the pattern by tapping on crossed pencils (or use fingertips in the same way) each time it occurs.
5. Sing the entire song aloud—except the pattern, which the children should sing in their minds.

Other ways to teach rhythmic patterns might include the following:

1. Tap the beat of the song. Rather than clapping, use finger or lap tapping.
2. Help the children determine whether the song has a feeling of two beats or three beats.
3. Clap strong beats and tap weak beats.
4. Determine what important words come on strong beats in the song.
5. Create a physical movement for the children to make on rests or on certain phrases in the song.
6. Ask some classes to step the beat of the song while other classes clap the rhythmic pattern. Older children may enjoy the challenge of stepping the beat at the same time they clap the rhythm pattern.
7. As the children tap the beat, ask them to determine a beat that has two words or syllables on it.
8. Teach the children to conduct the song using traditional conducting patterns (see *Children's Songbook*, p. 301). Consider letting them use new, unsharpened pencils as batons. You could also prepare the finger puppets illustrated. Invite a child to direct the music by putting their pointer finger through the hole in one of the puppets. Or you could enlarge the puppet on a posterboard and have a child put an arm through the hole to conduct.

Dynamics

The markings that have to do with volume and tempo enhance the feeling of the song. Help the children become aware of these expressive qualities.

Consider showing children various musical signs such as crescendo ◁, rest ⅄, ritardando (rit.), fermatas ⌒, diminuendo ▷. Hold up any one of the signs at an appropriate place in the song and see if the children can determine what that particular sign means. Once they know what a sign means, ask them to do what it says whenever you hold it up. After several weeks, when children have discovered what the signs mean, use more than one during a song. Occasionally let children hold the signs and decide when to raise them up.

Try singing a phrase of repeated words with different dynamics. Ask the children which dynamics they think best express the words and feeling of the song.

Form

The form of a song is determined by phrases. Phrases can be represented by drawing a slightly curved line from the beginning of the phrase to its end. The length of a phrase is often determined by where the commas, periods, or other punctuation marks fall.

Use the following activities to help the children understand the form of the song:

1. Ask the children to listen to the song and count the number of phrases.
2. Draw the phrase lines on a chalkboard as you sing the song.
3. Ask children to trace the lines in the air as you sing.
4. Sing certain phrases more softly than others.
5. Ask what words come at the end or beginning of each phrase.
6. Consider asking different groups of children to sing different phrases. For example, boys could sing one, girls another, and teachers another. You could also use other categories such as age groups or colors of clothes, shoes, hair, or eyes.

7. Try singing one phrase out loud and the next in your mind. Let the children know how to sing by signaling to them with your hand: pointing to them or opening your fist means to sing aloud; closing your hand means to sing in their minds. This will also encourage them to watch you.

8. Draw the phrase lines on a chart. Mark spots in each phrase and ask the children what word occurs at the mark. Trace the line carefully so your finger lands on the mark just as you sing the intended word. If children can read, place word cards on the phrase line as they answer. See lesson plan #12, "A Child's Prayer."

Instruments

1. Rhythm instruments, resonator bells, and other instruments may be used to involve the children in Primary but are not appropriate for sacrament meeting.

2. You might occasionally invite someone who plays the violin, flute, or other instrument to play one of the children's songs. Ask the children if they can identify the song by its melody. The guest might also play as the children sing.

3. Try to help the children notice special effects created by the accompaniment. For example, ask the pianist to play the optional left-hand octaves in "My Country" or "Called to Serve." Help the children notice how that bass line adds to the majestic effect of the song. Challenge them to listen to the accompaniment as they sing.

TEACHING WITH MOVEMENT

Movement is a powerful learning tool, especially for very young children. Moving to the music will often help them focus on the ideas in the song. In our desire for order, we sometimes expect children to learn while they sit still, fold their arms, and listen; yet children learn more quickly and remember more when they are allowed to move. It would be ideal to include moving and doing in all instruction.

Actions

Include some kind of action song whenever possible (see the index in the *Children's Songbook*). Or encourage the children to help you plan actions to a song you wish to review.

Sign Language

Sign language adds meaningful movement to a song. If any of the children in your Primary know the signs, invite them to demonstrate to the other children.

Teach the signs as you teach the song. For example, sing the song "Search, Ponder, and Pray" as you sign all the words you intend to use. Ask the children if they can determine what the sign is for a particular word in the song by watching and listening. Continue with other key words, singing the song each time you ask. It is not necessary to sign every word.

Dramatization

The words in a song can seem to come alive if children have the opportunity to act them out. You might ask children to listen to the song and act it out extemporaneously. If costumes are used, keep them simple. Sometimes a single prop will help express a song's message. The following ideas might be helpful.

1. **Acting and Pantomime:** Invite children to pretend to be different characters and act out what they are singing. You will need no costumes or props. Assign each child a part and then tell them to listen to the song to know what to do. Try this with various verses of "Book of Mormon Stories," "Pioneer Children," or "Saturday."

2. **Simple Costumes:** In the song "A Happy Family," use an apron to represent mother, a tie for father, a jacket for brother, a hair ribbon for sister. You might put simple costume items on some children and ask the others to determine who each person represents. For example, "I Hope They Call Me on a Mission" might be represented by a man's suit coat, tie, scriptures, and missionary name tag.

3. **Puppets:** Make simple puppets from socks, paper sacks, or paper plates. A garden glove with a face on each finger could also be used. Finger puppets are fun with songs such as "A Family Tree" or "In the Leafy Treetops." Sack puppets could be used with songs such as "The Nativity Song" or "Follow the Prophet."

4. **Instant Costume:** Using heavy cardboard, make large pictures of objects in a song. Cut a circle in the center of each picture so a child's face can fit through. As the song is sung, children can stand behind the pictures and place their faces in the holes. Examples: "I Am Like a Star" (child's smiling face in a star); "A Happy Family" (posters with hair styles of family members; children hold hands at the end); "In The Leafy Treetops" (tree, birds, flowers, sun).

TEACHING WITH VISUALS

You are your own best visual aid! You do not need to compete with television to entertain children, but you should become expert in providing sincere, spiritual instruction. Having the children explore the song visually can promote interest and increase learning. Visual teaching methods can range from objects to word-oriented visuals. How you will use visuals in your teaching will depend on your skills as well as on the ages of children you teach.

Wordstrips, Word cards, and Letters

Wordstrips can be used effectively to teach a song, especially if you let the children discover what the words are by listening to the song. The following examples may be helpful:

1. **Key Words:** Write key words for a song on cards. Show the cards to the children and ask them to put the words in order as they listen to the song. Invite the children to join you in singing only the key words while you sing the complete song.

2. **Rhyming Words:** Ask children to identify rhyming words as they listen to the song. Invite children to sing only the rhyming words as you sing the whole song.

3. **Mystery Words:** If a song tells a story, put up word cards such as WHO? WHAT? WHY? WHERE? and WHEN? Ask the children to answer the questions when they have listened to the song. Ask different classes to sing the part in the song that answers a particular question. (Example: To whom did Jesus come? [John the Baptist])

4. **Important Words:** Print the important words of a verse or chorus on index cards and put them in an envelope. Challenge some children to pin the words in order on the cork board while you sing the song. Repeat the song as many times as necessary. Check to see if the words are in order by inviting everyone to sing with you.

5. **Hide the Letters:** Cut large letters to spell a word. Tape the letters under various chairs in the room. Ask the children to find the letters and try to spell a word as you sing the song about it.

6. **Scrambled Letters:** Put letters of a word on a chart in mixed order. Ask the children to determine what the real word is by listening to the song. Example: SLOPEG—Gospel ("I Want to Live the Gospel.")

Pictures

Avoid combining sacred messages with secular pictures. Children need to know that everything you show them is correct and true. Cartoon characters, faces on inanimate objects, and rebus (pictures substituted for words) generally lead away from the actual message. See if you can decode the following rebus example:

It takes longer to process a rebus than to read the actual word, and until age nine or ten children are not usually able to grasp the hidden meaning. A rebus may save space on a chart, but a picture of the real item would be more efficient for teaching the message.

The following suggestions give many ways to interest children with pictures.

1. **Mental Imagery:** Stimulate children's imaginations by asking them to close their eyes and think of what you describe. As you finish the description, begin to sing the song.
2. **Chalkboard Art:** Draw stick figures or other simple shapes on the chalkboard as a song is sung.
3. **Children's Art:** Ask the children to draw a picture of what they hear in the song, or assign children particular things to draw. Mount the finished pictures on poster board and use them when reviewing the song. A simple way to mount pictures is to cut slits in a piece of posterboard so that you can slip pictures into the corners rather than use tape. This will give a nice, mounted look and help the picture stay on an easel. You can use the poster frame over and over. You could also cut a one-inch rectangle and glue it on the outside edge of three sides to form a frame pocket. Several pockets could be connected to form an accordion book.

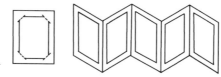

4. **Meetinghouse Library Pictures:** Your meetinghouse library has a wonderful assortment of appropriate pictures. Be familiar with the catalog listings and those already in the file.
5. **Picture File:** Collect pictures from calendars, coloring books, Church magazines, and similar sources. Categorize them in a file for future use.
6. ***Children's Songbook* Pictures:** Use an opaque projector to enlarge the illustrations in the songbook. Some copy machines will print clear color enlargements.
7. **Room Pictures:** Place pictures for a song around the room. As you sing the song, walk and point to the appropriate pictures. Then ask children to point to the pictures as they listen to the song.
8. **Random Order:** Show the children pictures in random order that represent ideas in a song. Ask them to arrange the pictures in correct order after listening to the song.
9. **Clothesline:** Select key words or pictures for a song and hang them in random order on a rope with clothespins. Ask the children to listen to the song and then arrange the words or pictures in sequence.
10. **Flip-Charts:** Mount pictures and create a flip-chart to show as the song is being sung.
11. **Box:** Attach pictures to all four sides and the top and bottom of a square box. Turn the box as the song is sung.
12. **Roller Box:** Obtain a roll of paper from a craft store or a butcher shop. Place drawings that the children have previously made on the paper in correct order. Unroll the paper as the song is sung. Or you could attach each end of the paper to dowels and roll it up. The roll can be placed in a box to create a screenlike presentation.

13. **Puzzles:** Create a large picture representing a particular song. Cut it into five or more puzzle pieces. Give each piece to a different child. Ask the children to listen to the song and then guess what the puzzle picture will be. After the children have made their predictions, sing the song again, and ask the children to put the puzzle together.

14. **Figures on Sticks:** Attach craft sticks onto pictures or word cards. Either have the children hold them, or place them in a styrofoam or clay base or a pot full of dirt. You could make a set of reusable picture holders by laminating four or five nine-inch posterboard circles and attaching sticks to them. You can easily tape laminated cutouts to the circles and then remove them for another song.

15. **Flannel Board:** Make wordstrips or picture cutouts to place on a flannel board as the song is sung; or place them in random order on the board before the song is sung and ask the children to place them in their correct sequence after listening to the song. As the children learn the song, remove the pictures or wordstrips one at a time to test the children's memory.

16. **Reversible Flannel/Write-On Board:** Available at the Church distribution centers. One side is a flannel board; the other side is a hard white surface designed for use with erasable markers.

17. **Dry-Erase Boards:** Make a dry-erase board from a laminated poster board or a slick white "shower board" that can be purchased at hardware stores. Use dry-erase markers only, and wipe off markings with a dry cloth.

18. **Magnetic Board:** Make a magnetic board to eliminate taping and to allow you to rearrange your visual aids easily. Obtain a piece of sheet metal and crimp the edges. (Some sheet metal shops will crimp the edges for you.) Cover the sheet metal with white contact paper on one side and royal blue on the other. Wrap a two-inch wide strip of heavy tape around all four edges. Purchase magnetic tape at the craft store, snip off a small amount, and attach it to the back of your visual aid.

Objects

1. **Relevant Items:** Place relevant objects in a sack or box. For example with the song "Saturday," you might place a duster, clothes brush, shampoo, and similar items in a box. As the song is sung, invite children to take out the appropriate objects.

2. **Sense Objects:** As an attention-getter, use objects that children can feel, smell, or taste.

TEACHING WITH AUDIOVISUAL EQUIPMENT

Opaque and Overhead Projectors

Sometimes it is enjoyable to help older children to learn a song by allowing them to "read" it. For example, the holidays bring many wonderful songs but not enough time to teach them to the children by the rote method. By using an opaque projector, you can simply lay your songbook on the projector, and the song will project up on the screen or wall large enough for all to see. The children can then sing directly from the music. Because the lights must be turned off, ask the pianist to bring a piano light. Christmas, Easter, and Thanksgiving are good times to read songs. Because you are not teaching in the usual way, be sure to emphasize the message. Overhead projectors can be used in a similar way but require preparing a transparency of the music ahead of time.

Tape Recorder

1. Rather than singing the song for the children, play a recording of it. All of the songs in the *Children's Songbook* are available on cassette tape and disc. Because repeating the song is important, you may wish to record the same song several times so you will not have to rewind each time you repeat the song.

2. Record the children singing. Play it back for them and help them evaluate their own performance. List any problems the children notice and then practice improving those parts. Record the song again and listen for improvements. Save the tape and play it on another day as a surprise for the children.

3. Record the bishop or another ward leader reading a scripture that pertains to a song the children are learning.

4. Invite the children to sing solo phrases on a tape recording of a song they know well. Perhaps a different child could sing each phrase. Encourage them to participate, but do not force any child to sing alone. Play the recording back without evaluating, and praise the efforts of each child.

IDEAS FOR REVIEWING A SONG

We all love to sing when we know a song by heart, but even well-learned songs need to be reviewed regularly. Involve the children in many ways while you help them enjoy their favorites.

HAVING FUN WITH GAMES

We want all the children to enjoy the singing equally, so we have avoided giving game ideas requiring competition. Children often feel too much competition in other areas of their lives and we don't want to have winners and losers at Primary—all the children are winners! Competitive games are also avoided because they often cause irreverence.

Guess My Song

1. **Hum:** Hum the melody and ask the children to guess the song. Then sing it together. Or whisper the name of the song into a child's ear and let him hum it to the children.

2. **Melody Picture:** Show a melody picture and hum it, or show a rhythm pattern and clap it. Ask the children if they can identify the song from which the pattern came. This is easier when a list of songs is given to choose from.

3. **Name That Tune:** Ask the pianist to play the first three notes of a song. See if the children can guess the song. If not, play the first four notes, then the first five, and so on until the children have guessed the song. Then sing it together.

4. **Name That Song:** Select five songs. Write one line from each song on a strip of paper and place the strips in a basket or box. Invite one child at a time to draw out a slip and read it to the other children and then guess which song the line is from. Accept first lines or titles. Then sing that song.

5. **Name That Word:** Ask the pianist to play a song the children know, stopping at some point. Have the children guess the word she stopped on.

6. **Song Pictionary:** Invite a child to the front. Whisper a song title in his ear. Let him draw a picture to represent the song. The other children raise their hands when they think they know which song it represents.

7. **Charades:** Divide the children into groups and let them act out songs for the rest of the children to guess.

8. **Crossword Puzzle:** Create a crossword puzzle. Ask one question per song to get the answers needed to fill in the spaces of the crossword puzzle. As each is placed on the puzzle, sing the song it represents.

9. **Scrambled Letters:** Scramble cutout letters or words and have older children unscramble them to complete the word or words in a song title. For example: "Okob fo Romonm Rotssie" ("Book of Mormon Stories").

10. **Word Search:** Make a poster. Hidden in the maze of letters are the titles of songs. When a child finds a title, all the children sing the song.

11. **Sing-a-Song Match-Up:** Have the children look at a list of songs printed on the chalkboard and try to match each song with a picture or object that represents the song. After they have matched a song with either its picture, object, or flannel board figure, invite them to sing the song it represents.

12. **Antonyms:** The object of the game is to guess the correct song title; however, words in the title of the songs are stated in an opposite way. Examples:

"Laban's Cowardice". . . . . "Nephi's Courage"
"When I Stay Home" . . . ."When I Go to Church"
"Mislead Me to Run in the Dark" . . . . . . "Teach Me To Walk In the Light"
"An Unhappy Person" . . . ."A Happy Family"
"Doubt" . . . ."Faith"

13. **Who or What Am I?** A child chooses a paper out of a basket and reads aloud. The children solve the riddle and the song is sung. Example:
I am a special part of our family.
I cook for you and tuck you in bed at night.
Who am I? ("Mother Dear")

Who Sings?
1. **Inner Hearing:** Invite children to sing the first and last word of the song aloud and the rest of the song in their minds while you lead. If they concentrate, they will all end on the last word together. Try singing just one phrase of the song in inner hearing and the rest of the song out loud. Consider tapping the words while singing in inner hearing, or indicate "stop" and "go" with a closed or open fist.

2. **Stop and Go Signs:** Prepare stop and go signs and mount them on craft sticks. (Or mount them back-to-back on one stick.) Invite the children to sing or stop as you indicate. (The pianist should continue to play when the stop sign is shown.)

3. **Craft Stick Characters:** Mount a character on a craft stick to indicate *how* the children are to sing or *which children* are to sing. Here are some examples:

Boys sing | Girls sing | Lulu—loo
Humphrey —hum | Wordsworth —words | Shherie —soft

4. **Cube Toss:** Cover a box with paper. On each of the six sides, draw or tape a picture direction for how to sing the song (for example, a lamb for quiet singing, a bee for humming, a whistle, a boy for boys only, a girl for girls only, a child leading the music, a note with a line drawn through it for singing a cappella). Toss the cube in the air and follow whatever direction ends up on top of the cube.

5. **Game Board Fun:** Prepare a game board similar to the one illustrated. On each space, write the directions for who should sing, such as those wearing buttons or white socks, all children wearing brown or black shoes, every other person, all children with brown eyes or blonde hair, all children wearing blue or green, or children who brought their

scriptures. Have children spin to determine the number of spaces to move.

6. **Sing with Color:** Hold up one of several pieces of colored construction paper and ask the children wearing that color to sing.

7. **Suggestion Box:** Write the following direction statements on separate pieces of paper. Fold each paper and place it in a box or container. Ask a child to select one of the papers, then to follow the directions. Fill in the blanks with a song of your choice in the following direction statements:

   • Clap the beat while singing_____.
   • Sing _____. Boys sing the first phrase, girls the second, teachers sing the third phrase, and everyone sings the fourth phrase.
   • Clap the rhythmic pattern while humming _____.
   • Hum the first verse of _____. Then sing the second verse.
   • Blazers and the CTR B classes clap the beat; the Merrie Miss and CTR A classes sing; all others hum the song _____.
   • Blazers help the Sunbeams go to the front of the class and sing _____.
   • Conduct the beat pattern while singing _____.

8. **Winter Fun:** Using blue posterboard, prepare a winter scene with white mountains and a blue lake. Use butcher paper sprinkled with glitter for the mountains to make the "snow" glisten. On the smallest hill, put a small sign that says "Humming Hill." In the valley place a sign saying "Rest Area." On the mountain put a sign saying "Avalanche Pass." On the lake make a sign that says "Thin Ice." Prepare a figure (skier or sleigh rider) and attach it to the end of a dowel. Move the figure to the various ski areas at unexpected times during the singing. Instruct the children to follow the directions on the signs.

Avalanche Pass . . . . . .Sing
Humming Hill . . . . Hum
Thin Ice . . . . .Whisper Sing
Rest Area. . . . . Piano Only

MAKING THE MOST OF CHOOSING TIME

You will want to have some control over which songs the children may choose so you can plan a purpose for singing and your accompanist can adequately practice. Following is a collection of ideas that will involve children in choosing and also give structure to the review. Be sure to save one song that will lead to a reverent conclusion.

Seasonal and Holiday Ideas

Because of the natural interest that children have in holidays and changing seasons, you can take advantage of special times of the year to motivate the children to enjoy reviewing songs that they already know. Consider some of the following ideas:

1. **Seasonal Choosing Time:** Put song titles on the back of seasonal objects such as snowflakes, hearts, shamrocks, eggs, flowers, birds, fish, flags, apples, or bells.

2. **A Song a Season:** Make a circle on posterboard and divide it into four pieces. Put a picture in each of the spaces to represent each season. Use a spinner to find out which season you will sing about next.

3. **Pin the Tail on the Season:** Prepare a poster depicting the four seasons. Say, "Heavenly Father has given us beautiful seasons. Let's sing about them." Blindfold a

child. Turn him around, direct him toward the poster, and help him pin a badge on the poster. Remove the blindfold and direct the selected song for that season.

4. **New Year's Resolutions:** Write some resolutions for the New Year on slips of paper. A child chooses one from a basket and reads both the resolution and the accompanying song: be kind ("Kindness Begins with Me"); be a missionary ("I Hope They Call Me on a Mission"); regularly read the scriptures ("Search, Ponder, and Pray"). Consider ringing in the New Year with resolutions by putting the song titles on bells.

5. **Snowman:** Build a snowman by preparing separate body circles and costume pieces. Write song titles on the back of each piece.

6. **Love-a-Lot Hearts:** Cut a large heart from posterboard. In the center write "Love-a-Lot." Tape smaller hearts to the large one. Tell the children that you love each one of them a lot and that you love each song you will be reviewing a lot too. Have a child choose one of the hearts. The song title is on the back.

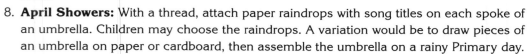

7. **Let's Go Fly a Kite:** Prepare small paper kites with song titles on the back. Or prepare a large kite with a ribbon tail; tie bows on the tail with song titles on bows.

8. **April Showers:** With a thread, attach paper raindrops with song titles on each spoke of an umbrella. Children may choose the raindrops. A variation would be to draw pieces of an umbrella on paper or cardboard, then assemble the umbrella on a rainy Primary day.

9. **Tree Choosing:** Prepare a large, brown poster-sized tree without leaves. Prepare a large piece of green posterboard to represent the leaves. Pictures of apples, birds, blossoms, fruit, or children playing in the tree could be chosen from the tree.

10. **Hats Off to Mothers:** This poem and visuals can be used as a Choosing Time. Write song titles about mothers on the hats. This can also be used as a Mother's Day program. (See *Friend*, May 1983, p. 43).

Hats Off to Mothers

1. *My mommy's a nurse who fixes and patches*
   All of my hurts and my sores and my scratches.
2. *My mother's a chef who fixes each dinner*
   Fit for a king—a blue-ribbon winner!
3. *My mom's a chauffeur who drives pretty slow*
   But gets me to places where I need to go.
4. *My mom's a detective, and no one is greater*
   At getting the truth from me sooner or later.
5. *My mommy's a gardener and works really hard,*
   Planting and weeding and grooming our yard.
6. *My mother's a maid—at least that's what she said—*
   'Cause she cleans up the house and makes every bed.
7. *My mother's an angel—a queen in disguise—*
   Who teaches the gospel with tears in her eyes.
   Today take these hats off, and please wear no other.
   Let me do your work, to show I LOVE YOU, MOTHER!
   (Janice Gardiner Wright, *Friend*, May 1983, p. 43.)

11. **Father's Day Puzzle:** This poem and puzzle can be used for a Father's Day program or Choosing Time (see *Friend*, June 1984, p. 37). Put a song title behind each puzzle piece.

Father

1. You're HEAD of our whole family.
2. You SEE to all our needs.
3. You LISTEN and HEAR with love.
4. You SMILE and PRAISE good deeds.
5. You SHOULDER your own heavy loads,
   And share our burdens too.
6. ARMED with patriarchal power,
   God blesses us through you.
7. Your strong HANDS hold our smaller ones
   When calming childish fears
   Or TOUCH to gently reassure
   And wipe away our tears.
8. As you WALK forth in righteousness,
   We want to follow you.
9. And on our KNEES we humble pray
   To God, just as you do.
10. We're walking in your FOOTSTEPS,
    Secure in loving care.
    God bless you fathers, everyone,
    Is our most humble prayer.
    (Mary Jane Davis, *Friend*, June 1984, p. 37.)

12. **Build a Flag:** Laminate a white posterboard. Cut seven red stripes and make a field of blue with silver stars on it. Place patriotic song titles on the back of each stripe, and tape them to the posterboard.

13. **Raise the Flags:** Purchase six small flags and place them in a styrofoam base. Write song titles on the back of each flag.

14. **Going Fishing:** Put song titles on the back of fish drawn on posterboard or other sturdy paper. Attach a paper clip to each fish and let the children go fishing with a stick, string, and magnet. The fish could be placed in a real fish bowl.

15. **Covered Wagon Choosing:** Draw a large covered wagon with removable parts, such as wheels, rope, barrel, lantern, and water jug. Put the parts on the covered wagon as the children choose them to complete the picture. Write the titles on the back of each part.

16. **Church History Sites:** Enlarge the map of the United States in 1847 that can be found in your triple combination (between the D&C and Pearl of Great Price). Draw the trail of the pioneers on the map. Draw Church history sites on small signs to place on the trail, and have the children post the signs in order on the map. Sing the song indicated on the back of the signs.

17. **What the Pioneers Saw from Their Covered Wagons:** Color and cut out a covered wagon and a picture wheel with the four pictures as illustrated on page 221. Mount them on heavy paper. Remember to cut out the window of the covered wagon along the broken lines. Place the picture wheel behind the covered wagon and attach it with a brad fastener through the center. As you turn the wheel, read the description of each scene and then sing the appropriate song. (See *Friend*, July 1984, p. 37.)

Scene 1:   You might have climbed mountains and crossed rivers. You would have been glad to have water because of the dust and heat. Song: "Covered Wagons." (See song for illustration on p. 239)

Scene 2:   You might have seen a buffalo herd thundering across your path. The buffalo would have provided meat for meals and hides for coverings, and your fire would have burned brightly with buffalo chips. Song: "Westward Ho."

Scene 3:   If you had watched patiently, you might have seen small animals hiding among the bushes. Perhaps you would have picked wild berries. How grateful you would have been for something good to eat! Song: "Little Pioneer Children."

Scene 4:   Sometimes from your wagon seat your view would have looked like a beautiful painting, with tall trees silhouetted against a flaming sunset. Heavenly Father created a beautiful world for each of us to enjoy. Song: "Whenever I Think about Pioneers."

18. **Count Your Blessings:** Draw a large cornucopia with the words "Count Your Blessings" on it. Cut out pictures of fruit and place the song titles on the back of each piece. Put them in the cornucopia. This can also be done with real fruit and a wicker cornucopia.

19. **Pilgrims:** Enlarge a picture of the Mayflower. Draw and cut out small pilgrim boys and girls, write song titles on the back of the figures, and place them on the ship.

20. **Christmas Choosing:** Prepare a poster-sized Christmas tree or wreath. Decorate it with ornaments on which song titles are written. Use Christmas symbols (star, shepherd's crook, bell, wreath, the color red, gift, candle) and briefly explain the meaning of each. Ornaments with song titles could also be placed on a small artificial tree or the names of songs could be placed inside gift boxes at the base of a tree.

Props and Posters

Great teaching power can be generated by using some simple objects that you already have or can make relatively easily. The following examples can be used or adapted to maintain the interest of children of all ages.

1. **Grab Bag:** Place one object for each song in a bag. Let a child come up, put a hand in the bag, pull out an object, and guess which song it represents.

2. **Pick-a-Pocket:** Wear an apron that has several pockets and let children choose song titles from each pocket.

3. **Musical Mailbox:** Place envelopes in a mailbox. Tell the children to come up and see if there is any musical mail today. The child opens the letter and reads the title to a song that is to be sung. Seasonally adapt this idea to Christmas cards or valentines.

4. **Noah's Ark:** Draw an ark. Make pairs of animals with song titles on their backs. Let a child choose a pair of animals and place the animals wherever they want on the ark.

5. **Scoop It Up!:** On a posterboard draw an empty ice cream cone. Let the children pick a flavor (different colors) of ice cream, read the song title on the back of each scoop, and add it to the cone.

6. **Topic Toss:** On each side of a six-sided cube, write a topic from the index of the *Children's Songbook*, such as families, Book of Mormon, prayer, Jesus Christ, love, or seasons. Invite a child to toss the cube and then select a song that fits in the category on the side which lands face up.

7. **Children's Art:** During the week ask some children to draw pictures of songs you wish to review. Write the titles of the songs and the name of the artist on the pictures. Place all the pictures in a box. On the review day, select pictures from the box and display them while singing the song.

Gospel Themes

You might try building your song review around a particular gospel theme, as in the following examples.

1. **Circle of Love:** Cut a circle out of a poster-board. Cut out another circle the same size, then cut a pie-shaped piece out of the second circle and place it on top of the first, fastening them together in the center with a brad. Put pictures depicting love on the first circle so that when the top spins, the pictures on the underneath circle show. Have a child spin the spinner board and then all sing the song it represents. This idea could be used with any gospel theme.

Name of Song:	Picture # and Name:
"Jesus Said Love Everyone"	62541 Jesus Healing the Nephites
"Families Can Be Together Forever"	62307 Family with a Baby
"Love One Another"	62467 Christ and the Children
"The Hearts of the Children"	62559 Young Couple Going to the Temple
"Love Is Spoken Here"	62317 Sharing the Tricycle
"Reverence Is Love"	62200 Class Prayer

2. **Put on the Whole Armor of God:** Using the scripture from Ephesians 6:13–17, prepare a picture of a modern boy and place it on a shield. Using silver posterboard, make cutouts of the parts of the armor talked about in the scripture. As you read the scripture to the children, put each piece of armor on the boy. Sing songs to represent the principles taught.

3. **Sing of Our Ancestors:** Prepare a simple pedigree chart. Cut and color separate pictures of a child, two parents, and four grandparents. Place the titles of songs on the back of each of the ancestors and have a child choose one. The songs could represent principles taught to us by our parents or grandparents, such as keeping the commandments, paying tithing, and showing kindness. You may want to use "The Hearts of the Children" to introduce this theme.

4. **I Will Pay My Tithing:** Cut out ten brown circles representing pennies. Draw a large piggy bank on posterboard or cardboard with a slit for the pennies to drop through. Place an envelope on the back of the slit to catch the pennies. Review what one-tenth is and how we can put nine pennies in our banks, but we will place the tenth in an envelope to give to the bishop for tithing. One at a time drop the other nine in the bank and sing the songs written on the backs.

5. **Family Night:** Prepare cutouts of things you do at your family home evening (pray, sing, learn the gospel, play games, work together, have treats, etc.). Place the cutouts on a posterboard and draw around the outline of each to make a simple puzzle. Take the cutouts off and place them on a table. The children could tell something they do at family night and put the matching picture on the posterboard outline. Sing a related song for each cutout.

6. **Scripture Match:** Below each song in the *Children's Songbook* is a corresponding scripture. On individual slips of paper, write a scripture from each of the songs you have selected to sing. Place the papers in a bowl or basket. Have a child choose a paper, read the scripture aloud, and guess what song the verse matches. There may be more than one good choice. Sing the corresponding song.

Fun with Favorites

Showing an interest in what the children want to sing can be an effective way of building your relationship with them as well as reviewing songs. Here are a few innovative ways to do this.

1. **Primary Hit Parade:** During class time on a previous week, let each class vote on their favorite songs. Tabulate the "Top Five Favorites" and have a "Favorite Hits Countdown." Begin with the number five song. Tell something about the song or the author who wrote it and then sing. Repeat until you count down to the number one favorite.

2. **Crack That Song:** Next time you crack walnuts, save any shells that split in half. Glue the shells back together with a song title inside and have a child come to the front and crack the nut into a bucket or sack. The children will be surprised and excited to find the titles inside. This idea could be adapted to homemade fortune cookies by substituting song titles for fortunes.

3. **Bubble Gum Choosing:** Draw and color a bubble gum machine on a piece of posterboard. Cut out colorful removable circles for the gum balls. Write song titles on the back of the circles. A variation would be to draw a large flower with song titles on the back of each petal, then have the children pick petals off the flower.

4. **Ball Toss:** Use a numbered velcro target board and a velcro ball. When the ball hits one of the numbers, the corresponding song from your list is then sung.

5. **Hide the Note:** Hide musical notes with song titles around the room. Choose a child to look for one. Sing the song when it is found. Then choose another child. For variety, you could use stars, shamrocks, flowers, etc. You can also play "hot and cold." While one child leaves the room, another child hides a note. When the first child returns, the children sing louder as the child gets closer to the note, and softer when farther away.

6. **We Can Write Songs:** Draw a music staff on the chalkboard. Above the staff write "We Can Write Songs." Ask a child to select a cutout note that has a song title written on it. If the majority of the children are able to remember the song and join in the singing, invite the child to place the note on the staff (on a line or a space) beneath one of the syllables. Repeat until all four notes are on the staff. Have the accompanist play the melody that the children have "composed" and have the children sing the words "We Can Write Songs" to their melody. (See *Friend*, Oct. 1985.)

7. **It's Time to Sing About _____:** Draw any kind of clock. Above the clock write "It's time to sing about_____." Make a slit on two sides of the base of the clock. Prepare a wordstrip that tells what the theme of the singing time will be for the day. Slip that wordstrip through the slits. Use the topical guide in the back of the *Children's Songbook* for possible themes (family, prayer, service, etc.).

8. **Book of Mormon Journey:** (See *Friend*, Oct. 1988, p. 46.) Make a marker and place it at the starting point on the map. Draw a representation of the Liahona and make eight copies of it. Write the name of a song and a question about it on the back. Attach a craft stick to each Liahona and stand them in a piece of styrofoam. One child is selected to choose a Liahona and read the name of the song and the question about it. The child should sing through the song in his mind to find the answer. If the child can't answer, he may choose another child to help him. He then moves the marker to the next point on the map and everyone sings the song. Another child comes forward to take a turn. Here are some sample song titles and questions. The answers are given here but should not be printed on the Liahonas:

Start (Place your marker on. . .)

    1. Jerusalem then sing:

        "Book of Mormon Stories": The Lamanites were given this land if they did what? [Lived righteously] move to . . .

2. Wilderness:

"**Called to Serve**": Whom are we called to serve? [Heavenly King of Glory, or King]

3. Building the Boat:

"**The Golden Plates**": Where are the stories from the golden plates retold? [In the Book of Mormon]

4. Crossing the Ocean:

"**Nephi's Courage**": Why did Nephi have the courage to go and do what the Lord commanded? [Because he knew that the Lord provides a way]

5. The Land of Bountiful:

"**Keep the Commandments**": What are two blessings we receive from keeping the commandments? [Safety and peace]

6. The Savior Appears:

"**We'll Bring the World His Truth**": Why have we been saved for these latter days? [To build the kingdom in righteous ways]

7. Moroni Buries the Plates:

"**Books in the Book of Mormon**": How many books are there in the Book of Mormon? [Fifteen]

8. The Book of Mormon is Published:

"**I Am a Child of God**": What do I have to do to live with Heavenly Father once more? [Learn to do his will]

Finish!

SINGING A STORY

Songs can be arranged in an order to tell a story or develop a theme. The words of the songs tell most of the story, and the music director need add only a brief narrative for continuity. A sing-a-story can be developed by using the topical index at the back of the *Children's Songbook*. Choose a topic and select songs from those listed under that topic. Make a sing-a-story book from heavy paper using one picture on each page to introduce the song to be sung. Here are some "sing-a-story" examples:

Love One Another

Objective: To teach the children the importance of loving *all* of Heavenly Father's children.

Narrator: Jesus has told us to love everyone the same way he did.

Song: "Love One Another" Picture: 62467 Christ and the Children

Narrator: It's easy to be kind to our best friends. But if you want a friend, you must be a friend, too.

Song: "Friends Are Fun" Picture: 62523 Jumping Rope

Narrator: Children who may be a little different than we are, are also Heavenly Father's children. We need to show our love to them as Jesus has asked us to.

Song: "I'll Walk with You" Picture: A handicapped or foreign child

Narrator: Children can lead out in showing friendship and love to everyone.

Song: "Kindness Begins with Me" Picture: 62317 Sharing the Tricycle

Narrator: All children deserve our love and kindness, for we are all children of our Heavenly Father.

Song: "I Am a Child of God" Picture: 62276 God's Care by Night

Sing-a-Story of Easter

An Easter program could be given with the children reading the narrator's parts. (See the *Friend*, March 1986, p. 38.)

Song: "Tell Me the Stories of Jesus"

Narrator: The Easter story is a story of love. Heavenly Father loves us so much that he sent his Son to earth to atone for our sins. Jesus loves Heavenly Father and was willing to obey him. And Jesus loves each one of us. He gave his life so that we may be forgiven when we do something wrong and then repent.

Song: "He Sent His Son"

Narrator: "Greater love hath no man than this, that a man lay down his life for his friends" (John 15:13).

Song: "Love One Another"

Narrator: Jesus died and was resurrected, which means that he lived—and lives again.

Song: "Did Jesus Really Live Again?"

Narrator: "He is not here: for he is risen" (Matthew 28:6).

Song: "Jesus Has Risen"

Narrator: Many people saw Jesus after he was resurrected. However, we do not need to see him to know that he lives. As we keep the commandments and remember Jesus, we feel good. And that good feeling is the beginning of a testimony.

Song: "Keep the Commandments"

Narrator: A testimony of Jesus means that you accept the divine mission of Jesus Christ, embrace his gospel, and do his works.

Song: "I Want to Live the Gospel"

Narrator: For a long time the world was in darkness; there was no spiritual light upon the earth. When Joseph Smith saw the Father and the Son, the world was awakened and the priesthood was returned to earth.

Song: "On a Golden Springtime"

Narrator: We are blessed to have the gospel restored in our day. As we learn more about the teachings of Jesus and try to live as he taught, our testimonies will grow.

Song: "I'm Trying to Be Like Jesus"

Sing-a-Story of Thanksgiving

Make a large picture book using half a posterboard for each cover and butcher paper pages inside. Write *Harvest Time* on the cover and draw some pumpkins and corn stalks. Display the pictures listed below and read the story to the children. Let them fill in the blanks by choosing the picture that best completes the statement. After they fill in the blank, they sing the song and you tape the picture into the book. There are more songs than you may have time to sing.

Suggested pictures and songs:
1. *Mayflower* . . . . (story only)
2. Cabin . . . . "Home"
3. Fruits and vegetables . . . . "The Prophet Said to Plant a Garden"
4. Fall leaf . . . . "Autumn Day"
5. Pilgrims. . . . .(story only)
6. Feasting. . . . . "A Song of Thanks"
7. Indians . . . ."Book of Mormon Stories"
8. Turkey. . . . ."Thanksgiving Round"
9. Prayer. . . . . "Thank Thee, Father"

1. The pilgrims came to America on the (1) .
2. They needed a place to live so the pilgrims built log (2) .
3. They worked very hard planting and harvesting (3) .
4. The first Thanksgiving was celebrated in the (4) .
5/6. The (5) set aside this special day for (6) and thanking God.
7. More than eighty friendly (7) came to the feast.
8. The Indians brought wild (8) and venison to share.
9. Three days were spent in feasting and (9) .

Sing-a-Story of Christmas

Display the picture that represents each scripture, read the verse, and then sing the song.

Picture #	Picture Name	Scripture	Song
62370	Samuel the Lamanite on the Wall	Helaman 14:2	"Samuel Tells of Baby Jesus"
62119	Flight into Egypt	Luke 2:1, 4–5	"When Joseph Went to Bethlehem"
62495	The Nativity	Luke 2:7	"Away in a Manger"
62217	The Announcement of Christ's Birth to the Shepherds	Luke 2:8, 9–10	"Stars Were Gleaming"
62116	The Birth of Jesus	Luke 2:11	"The Nativity Song"

MOTIVATING THE SINGER

Reviewing

The following ideas can help you get the children's attention and then maintain their interest while reviewing a number of songs for a program.

1. **Dot-to-Dot:** Enlarge a dot-to-dot picture from the *Friend* to posterboard size. Laminate it if you wish to reuse it, and use a marker that can be erased to connect the dot-to-dot picture. As the children's singing improves, connect more dots.

2. **Mission Excellence:** Glue cutouts of planets lined up vertically to the top of a black posterboard. Number the planets, one for each song to be reviewed. Write **Mission Excellence** at the top. Prepare a small cutout of a rocket ship that will move from planet to planet as each song is reviewed. If the children sing all the songs, they will achieve **Mission Excellence**.

3. **Pioneer Trek:** Draw a large United States map on a posterboard. Trace the approximate pioneer trail and then carefully cut the trail with a razor blade. Make a covered wagon with a flap taped to the back. Put the flap through the slit. Move the wagon along the trail. As each song is reviewed, move the wagon to the next town.

4. **Basketball:** On a posterboard, draw a picture of children playing basketball. Glue one half of a clear plastic drinking cup to the spot where the basket would be. Use a ping pong ball and paint it to represent a basketball. Glue a magnet to one side of the ball. As a song is successfully reviewed, let a child use a strong magnet on the back of the poster board to "move" the ball through the cup basket.

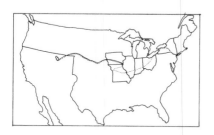  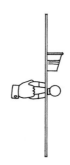 

Fold Line

Tab

Motivating Participation

Singing meters can be used to motivate the children's participation. The goal is to have all the children singing. The meter should be used sparingly and not to measure volume. It indicates participation and should encourage beautiful rather than loud singing.

1. **Worm Your Way Out:** Make a large apple the size of a red poster board. Cut a circle big enough for your hand to fit through. On the back, attach a square of red fabric as the flap over the circle. Make a worm puppet by attaching two eyes to the toe of a green sock. Pull the sock onto your arm and "worm" your way out of the hole as all the children participate. This idea could be adapted to be the trunk of an elephant.

    String meters (ideas 2–5) are made by cutting a slit in the top and bottom of a posterboard. Thread, string, fishing line, or ribbon through the slits and tie it in back to make a continuous loop. Tape an object to the front side of the loop and move up or down to indicate the level of the children's participation.

2. **Thermometer:** Prepare a singing thermometer by cutting slits in the top and bottom of a heavy posterboard. Make a complete circle loop out of ribbon—one half red and the other half white. When the children sing well, bring the red to the front of the poster and move it up as if the temperature is rising.

3. **Sing the Sun Up:** Place a sun on transparent thread behind a brown mountain. When the children sing all the words, bring the sun from behind the mountain; the sun rises in response to the level of participation.

4. **Put Father's Bow Tie in Place:** Prepare a picture of a father the size of a posterboard. Attach a bow tie to transparent thread and raise the bow tie to its proper place when the children follow your directions.

5. **Raise the Flag:** Draw a flag pole with a boy standing by it on the posterboard. Attach the fabric part of a small flag to the transparent thread so the flag can be raised as the children perform well.

PART TWO
LESSON PLANS

My Heavenly Father

It is important for a child to understand his relationship to our Heavenly Father.
Songs on prayer, thankfulness, and reverence.

I AM A CHILD OF GOD

MESSAGE: I am my Heavenly Father's child. I have many blessings and many needs. I need parents, teachers, and others to help me learn what I must do to live with him someday.

ENRICHMENT IDEAS:

1. Read the following quote:

   "Several years ago, before Spencer W. Kimball became president of the Church, he was visiting a conference in California where Primary children sang this song. Later, he said to a visiting Primary General board member, 'I love the children's song, but there is one word that bothers me. Would Sister Randall mind if the word *know* were changed to the word *do*?'

   "The change was made, for President Kimball had pointed out a very important truth—that while it is important to know what is right, it is more important to do what is right. Only in this way can we be sure of returning someday to our heavenly home to live always with our Father, his Son Jesus Christ, and our loved ones." (Robert D. Hales, "I Am a Child of God," *Friend*, Mar. 1978, pp. 7–9.)

2. Teach the harmony line (obbligato) to a group of older children.

3. Use the "*I Am a Child of God*" Coloring Songbook, Aspen Books, 1991.

♪ *About the Song*

In 1957, Naomi Randall called Mildred Pettit who had served on the Primary General Board and asked if she would help with the music for a new song to be written for Primary conference. Sister Randall agreed to write the words and send them to Sister Pettit in California. That night, Sister Randall prayed for help to find the right words for the song. Hours later she awakened and wrote the words for three verses. Then she thanked Heavenly Father for helping her.

Sister Pettit also wanted to have the music the way the Lord wanted it. She felt that she knew how the melody was supposed to go, but she worked on the closing phrase over and over and had her children sing it many times until she was satisfied it was right. The two women worked on the chorus together, and within a week the song was completed.

Camilla Kimball referred to the song as "the gospel in a nutshell." (Young Women Conference, Mar. 28, 1981, Salt Lake Tabernacle.)

MATERIALS:

Pictures: V.1, children from different lands

Word cards: V.3, BLESSINGS, STORE, WILL, MORE

ATTENTION-GETTER:

Hold up pictures of children from many lands.

- *Do you think these children have the same father? We can tell they have different fathers because they come from different lands. But these children do have another father who is the same. Who is he?* [Heavenly Father]

Explain that Heavenly Father is the father of all of our spirits and he loves us very much.

- *I have a testimony that Heavenly Father is the father of my spirit and that . . .* (Sing) *I am a child of God.*

LISTENING AND SINGING EXPERIENCES:

Use questions and statements similar to those listed below to encourage the children to listen. As children discover answers, invite them to sing that part of the song with you. Add one phrase at a time to the ones already learned. Teach the chorus first.

Chorus:

- *Where do I want to live someday?* [With him]
- *What do I want help to find?* [The way]
- *The song says "teach me" something very important. What is it?* [All that I must do]

Verse One:

- *Who sent me here?* [He, God, Heavenly Father] Clue: Tell the children that the answer is on the highest note. As you lead, accentuate the word "he."
- *What has Heavenly Father given me?* [An earthly home with parents kind and dear]

Verse Two:

- *Because I am a child of God, my needs are very important. The song uses another word instead of important. What is it?* [Great]
- *What do I want to understand?* [his words]

Explain that we learn his words through prayer, scriptures, and the prophet.

- *What word rhymes with great?* [Late]

Verse Three:

Challenge a child to put the word cards in the correct order as you sing. Then sing the verse again to check the order of the cards.

Verse Four:

- *What glory has Heavenly Father promised me?* [Celestial]
- *What must I do to earn celestial glory?* [Endure]

Bear your testimony that of all the many blessings Heavenly Father has given us, the greatest is the blessing of living with him and our families forever.

I LIVED IN HEAVEN

MESSAGE: Because Heavenly Father loves us, he gave us a wonderful plan to help us be like him and return to his presence.

ATTENTION-GETTER:

Briefly tell how blessed you feel to live in your beautiful part of the world.

- *A long time ago, I lived in a more beautiful place, and so did you. As I sing, listen then tell me where it is that I used to live a long time ago. Sing the entire verse. [In heaven]*

LISTENING AND SINGING EXPERIENCES:

Verse One:

- *When we sing about heaven, the melody flows gently up and down.* Sing the first line again while moving your hand to follow the melodic direction, starting the phrase lower and ending higher like this:

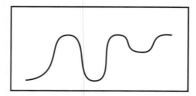

Invite the children to sing this phrase with you.

- *Listen as I sing to see if the second line has the same melody. [Yes]* Demonstrate in the same way and sing the second line. Invite the children to sing both lines.
- *What did Heavenly Father present one day? [A beautiful plan]*
- *This next line sounds a little different than the first two, but listen as I sing it and see if it, also, flows up and down like the other two lines. [Yes]*

Invite the children to join you in singing this line until they are secure with the melody.

- *This plan told us that we would come to earth to get a body and that after we left the earth we would be resurrected and live with Heavenly Father forever. But the song does not use the word "forever." There is another word in the last line that means forever. What is that word?* Sing the third and fourth lines again. *[Eternal]*

Sing the last two lines with the children.

Invite the accompanist to play as everyone sings the first verse.

Verse Two:

- *When Heavenly Father said he needed someone to give his life for his children, what did Jesus say? ["Father, send me, and the glory be thine."]*
- *Listen to find a word that rhymes with "thine." [Divine]* Explain that Satan wanted all the glory for himself.
- *If Jesus would give his life for us, what was the great blessing that would be ours? [We all could return there (to Heavenly Father) above.]*

Verse Three:

- *Who is waiting for us in heaven? [Heavenly "Father"]*
- *What did Jesus' sacrifice give us hope of? [A wonderful life yet to be]*
- *What two things did Jesus conquer? [Evil and death]*
- *What is another name for Jesus that begins with the letter "M"? [Messiah]*

ENRICHMENT IDEAS:

1. Write the words WHERE, WHEN, WHAT, and WHO on cards or on the chalkboard. Ask the children the following questions.

   - *WHERE did I live? [In heaven]*
   - *WHEN did I live there? [A long time ago]*
   - *WHAT did I do besides live there? [Loved there]*
   - *WHO lived there with me? [People I know]*

2. Divide the children into three equal groups to show the children what 1/3 looks like. Point out that 1/3 of Heavenly Father's children did not choose Heavenly Father's plan and could not come to earth. We know that we did choose Heavenly Father's plan because we're here on earth!

3. Have the children look for rhyming words.

4. Use the picture titled "The Eternal Family through Christ," by Judith Mehr, *Ensign*, Dec. 1988, pp. 24–25.

5. Younger children will enjoy swaying gently to the rhythm, or imitating you as you move your hand up and down to follow the direction of the melody.

♪ *About the Song*

Janeen Brady was asked to write a song about heaven that would explain Heavenly Father's plan. When this song was completed, she described it as a ballad—a story song—and said that it is a true story.

I KNOW MY FATHER LIVES

MESSAGE: I know through the whisperings of the Spirit that my Heavenly Father lives, loves me, and sent me here to earth. My faith in Heavenly Father will help me live his plan.

ENRICHMENT IDEAS:

1. Have the children whisper-sing the words *"the Spirit whispers this to me and tells me it is true."* Or you could challenge them to sing this phrase in one breath, emphasizing the importance of that statement.

2. Use the arrangement of this song from the hymnbook (no. 302), or invite two people to play the duet accompaniment as described on the bottom of page 5 in the *Children's Songbook.*

3. Explain that the Holy Ghost doesn't whisper in your ear. He gives you ideas in your mind and a warm feeling in your heart.

♪ *About the Song*

Reid Nibley, a concert pianist and Brigham Young University faculty member, was asked to write a song about testimony for the *Sing with Me* collection. He said he wrote quickly because as he started thinking of how a child would express a testimony, the words and music came at the same time. The song was very short and simple. Brother Nibley is a very knowledgeable musician, so he began adding notes. It became more and more complicated. He said, "Thank goodness I had a big eraser!" He erased all the unnecessary notes, and when he finished, the song was just as he had written it the first time! (*Friend,* Oct. 1985, p.15.)

Because the song is in the hymnbook, Brother Nibley was asked to make a different arrangement for this songbook. He chose to write a duet accompaniment for this version of his song. This is one of the few songs in the book which does not have the melody in the accompaniment.

ATTENTION-GETTER:

Invite three or four children to come to the front of the room. Whisper to each one of them, "I know that Heavenly Father loves you." Then whisper to the entire Primary:

- *I know my Heavenly Father loves me. As I sing, listen for the way I know he loves me.* Sing the song. [*The Spirit whispers this to me.*]

LISTENING AND SINGING EXPERIENCES:

Continue singing the song, directing the children's listening with questions and statements similar to the following:

Verse One:

- *What does the Spirit tell me?* [*It is true.*]
- *We sing "and tells me it is true" two times because it is so important. The first time the word "tells" is on a high note.*

Invite the children to sing the last two phrases.

- *We know that Heavenly Father lives and loves us. Listen carefully and see which word occurs on the highest tone.* [*Loves*] *Sit up tall in your seat and sing the whole song. Be careful to sing the words "love" and "tells" on pitch.*

Verse Two:

- *Why did Heavenly Father send me here to earth?* [*To live his plan*]
- *How do I know I can do it?* [*The Spirit whispers that I can.*]

Bear your testimony of the message and tell the children that as they sing the words of this song, they are bearing testimony also.

THANKS TO THEE

MESSAGE: Wherever we are, we may thank our Heavenly Father for our blessings and ask for his guidance and protection.

MATERIALS:

Picture: (An Eleven-year-old Kneeling in Prayer 62218)

Word cards: AWAY, PRAY, SIGHT, RIGHT, FAMILY TOO, LOVE AND DO, ME, THEE

ATTENTION-GETTER:

- *Imagine that you are camping with your family. You go for a hike by yourself, and you suddenly realize that you can't find your way back to your campsite and family. What could you do?* Let children respond.

Hold up a picture of a child kneeling outdoors.

- *This boy was lost in the woods, but he knew that no matter where he was, Heavenly Father would hear his prayers and help him. What a blessing it is to be able to pray to Heavenly Father.* Sing the song for the children.

LISTENING AND SINGING EXPERIENCES:

Pass out the cards of rhyming words to eight children and challenge them to stand in the correct order as you sing. Repeat the song until they have it correct.

Sing the first line again asking the children to find the two rhyming words. Post the word cards AWAY and PRAY.

Ask the children to sing that phrase with you, guiding them with pitch leading.

- *Listen to discover two things that I ask for. [Keep me safely in thy sight; help me choose and do what's right.]* Post the word cards SIGHT and RIGHT. Have the children join you on this line and then add it to the first line.

- *As I sing, notice the things I am thanking Heavenly Father for. [Home and family too, many things to love and do]*

Post the word cards FAMILY TOO, and LOVE AND DO. Teach through repetition and add to first and second lines.

- *Because Heavenly Father is very good to me, what do I say to him? [Heavenly Father, thanks to thee.]*

Explain that the word "thee" is a respectful word meaning "you" that we use when talking to Heavenly Father. Post the word cards ME and THEE.

Sing the song with the children, referring to the word cards. Then remove the word cards one by one as the children become confident with the song.

ENRICHMENT IDEAS:

1. Sing just the first two measures and tell the children that this melody is repeated two more times. Have them raise their hands when they hear that melody as you sing the entire song again.

2. Have the children listen for prayer language words. *[Thy (your), thee (you), art (are)]*

3. Have the children sing every other measure. You sing the first measure; the children sing the second, and so forth.

I THANK THEE DEAR FATHER

MESSAGE: I thank Heavenly Father for his goodness and blessings. I ask him to help me be kind and obedient.

ENRICHMENT IDEAS:

1. To feel the "long-short" rhythm of the song have the children finger tap in rhythm as you sing.

2. Have the children raise their hands or fold their arms when they hear a prayer language word. *[Thee, thy]*

3. Have the children draw pictures of what they are thankful for. Use these pictures as the children sing the song.

4. Briefly discuss the four parts of prayer. (See "What Shall I Say When I Pray?" *Friend*, June 1985, p. 45.)

5. Assemble a scene with pictures as the song is reviewed.

MATERIALS:

Word cards or pictures to illustrate the following key words: GOODNESS, MERCY, KINDNESS, LOVE, HOME, FRIENDS, PARENTS, EVERY BLESSING.

Melody picture:

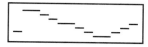

ATTENTION-GETTER:

- *Heavenly Father is so good to each of us. What is something Heavenly Father has given to you? [Friends, parents, homes, etc.]*

- *We have so many blessings that we can't name them all. What do you say to someone who has given you something? [Thank you.]*

- *Listen to the words I sing to thank our Father in Heaven and count how many times I sing them. [I thank thee—2 times.]*

LISTENING AND SINGING EXPERIENCES:

- *I sang about eight things that we are thankful for. Listen to see how many of them you can name. [Goodness, mercy, kindness, love, home, friends, parents, every blessing]*

Post word cards or pictures as the words are given, repeating until the list is complete. Have the children put them in the correct order.

- *The melody of the first line can be heard another time in the song, with a different last note. Raise your hand when you hear the repetition, and be ready to tell me the words you hear. [I thank thee for home, friends, and parents so dear.]*

Show the melody picture of the last phrase. Hum it as you point to each pitch level, then ask the children to tell you what words occur on that phrase. *[And for every blessing that I enjoy here]*

FATHER, WE THANK THEE FOR THE NIGHT

MESSAGE: We thank our Heavenly Father for the beauties of the day and night and for his loving care.

MATERIALS:

Old Testament

Pictures: night (62276), (Children Looking at Spring Flowers 62270), rest—child in bed (62498), a family blessing the food (62223), a parent and child (62205), a nature scene (62317)

ATTENTION-GETTER:

- *In Psalm 33:5 we read, "The earth is full of the goodness of the Lord." Will you say that scripture with me?*

Let the children repeat it back to you.

- *The earth is full of the goodness of the Lord. It is important for us to appreciate and thank Heavenly Father for making this earth so beautiful. One way to thank him is to sing a song of thanks to him. As I sing, listen for six things that we can give thanks for.*

As you sing, post the pictures in random order.

LISTENING AND SINGING EXPERIENCES:

- *What blessings can we thank Heavenly Father for? [Night, pleasant light, rest, food, loving care, all that makes the day so fair]*

Sing the song several times so the children can name all six things.

Invite a child to arrange the pictures correctly as you sing.

Invite the children to sing with you as you refer to the pictures.

ENRICHMENT IDEAS:

1. Write the last word of each phrase on a wordstrip to remind the children of the main ideas. *[night—light, care—fair]*

2. Ask the children to tell which of God's creations make the day so fair for each of them.

3. Use pictures drawn by the children.

4. Draw a fermata ⌒. Show its meaning by holding the note extra long to make sure that the children are watching you.

5. Connect the six pictures to make an accordion that can stand alone on the top of the piano or a table. Put three pictures on each side of the accordion to make it easier for you to hold.

CAN A LITTLE CHILD LIKE ME?

MESSAGE: Even though I am young, I can thank my Heavenly Father through my words and my actions.

ENRICHMENT IDEAS:

1. Add dynamics to the chorus. Encourage the children to begin softly and gradually raise their voices toward heaven.

2. Invite half of the children to sing the question on the first line, the others to sing the answer on the next two lines. Have both groups sing the chorus together. Trade parts.

3. Review this song using key words. Remove a few with each repetition.

4. Review using pictures such as the following: (I Can Dress 62312), (Bedside Prayer 62217), good and true (Sharing the Tricycle 62317), patient and kind (Children Playing with Blocks 62212) or (Waiting Our Turn 62316), (Jesus the Christ 62572), do your part, (Class Prayer 62200).

ATTENTION-GETTER:

Invite a child to stand before the group and ask him the following questions:

- *Can you tie your own shoes?*
- *Can you make your own bed?*
- *Can you drive a car?*
- *Can you type on a computer?*
- *Can you swim across the ocean?*
- *We have discovered some things that (child's name) can do and some things he cannot do. I have one more question that I would like you to ask yourselves. Listen as I sing to tell me what that question is.* Sing the entire song for the children. *[Can a little child like me thank the Father fittingly?]*

LISTENING AND SINGING EXPERIENCES:

Sing the song several times directing the children's listening by asking questions such as the following with each repetition:

- *What is the answer to the question "Can a little child like me thank the Father fittingly?"* [Yes]
- *Yes, we can thank our Father in Heaven fittingly, or in the proper way. As I sing, please find out what we can say.* Sing the chorus to the children. *[Father, we thank thee.]*
- *How many times do I sing "we thank thee?"* Sing the chorus again. *[Three times]*
- *The third time, we add two important words to the name of our Father. What are they?* Sing just the chorus with the children. *[In Heaven]*
- *In the first part of the song, you'll hear four things that we can be in order to thank our Father. The four things come after we sing "Yes, oh yes." Can you listen and find all four?* Sing the verse, and invite the children to join you on the chorus. *[Good, true, patient, kind in all you do]*
- *Now listen for three things that we should do.* Sing the verse and invite the children to join you on the chorus. *[Love the Lord, do your part, learn to say with all your heart]*
- *The rhythm on "do your part" and "all your heart" is the same as the rhythm on "fittingly."* Tap the long-short-long rhythm ♩. ♪♪ ♩ with the children.

Sing the whole song together, adding the accompaniment.

- *We have a scripture that says: "Thou shalt thank the Lord thy God in all things" (D&C 59:7). I'm sure Heavenly Father especially enjoys it when we give thanks through such beautiful singing.*

THANK THEE FOR EVERYTHING

MESSAGE: We thank Heavenly Father for all the beauty and variety in his good world.

MATERIALS:

Pictures: nature

ATTENTION-GETTER:

Display a variety of nature pictures from magazines or calendars showing deserts, mountains, plains, etc.

Lead a discussion on how different each part of the world is, yet how each part is beautiful.

- *I know a song about our good world. As I sing the song, listen to discover where beauty is found. [Everywhere in thy good world]*

LISTENING AND SINGING EXPERIENCES:

- *Listen as I sing and count how many times I sing "in thy good world." [Three times]*
- *The melody of these phrases is the same two of the times we sing it and different one time. Find out which time the melody is different as I sing. [The second]*

Sing the entire song, having the children join you each time you sing "in thy good world."

Explain that the word "thy" is used because this song is a prayer to our Heavenly Father.

- *What do we ask Heavenly Father to hear us sing? [Praises to thee]*
- *The melody on the first line is repeated. What words are sung on that melody? [Skies may be gray or fair; Trees may be green or bare.]*

Tell the children that Heavenly Father's beauty is everywhere, and we should thank him for everything in our good world.

ENRICHMENT IDEAS:

1. On a music staff, draw the descending scale as shown on the second line of the song. Sing and point out that this scale moves down for eight tones. Invite the children to pitch lead this octave with you.

2. Let the children share what they think is the most beautiful part of the world.

3. The following word card and pictures could be attached to craft sticks for children to hold: PRAISES, child singing, child praying and the world in background, skies gray and fair, trees green and bare, flower scene, world.

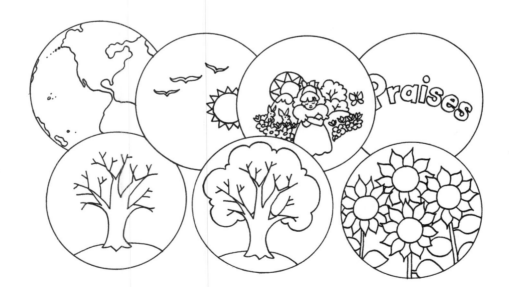

I'M THANKFUL TO BE ME

MESSAGE: At night I close my eyes and see the many blessings God has given me. These blessings make me thankful to be me.

ENRICHMENT IDEAS:

1. Make a simple poster of a boy in bed with the blessings he is thinking of above him as illustrated.

2. Invite children to read the following scriptures: Psalms 92:1; 24:5; 50:14; Alma 34:38; Rev. 7:12.

3. Pictures: (Bedside Prayer 62217), friends (62215 or 62523), teachers (62200), family (62307).

4. Be sensitive to children who do not have the typical family pictured. Discuss the many others who care about them (neighbors, relatives, home teachers, bishop, etc.).

MATERIALS:

Pictures: friends, teachers, and family

ATTENTION-GETTER:

- *I have so many blessings. What are some of your blessings?* Invite the children to name as many blessings as they can in thirty seconds. Let the children respond.

- *I like to think about all of the many things I'm thankful for that God has given me. As I sing a song for you, listen to discover one special time when I think about my blessings. [At night when I'm alone in bed]*

LISTENING AND SINGING EXPERIENCES:

Each time you sing this song, ask the children a question similar to the following:

- *When I close my eyes, what do I see? [The many things I'm thankful for that God has given me]* Point out the repeated notes in this phrase.

- *What people do I see that I am thankful for? [My friends, teachers, and others who love me]* Sing as many times as necessary to elicit all three answers. Post a picture to represent each response.

- *How do these blessings make me feel? [So thankful to be me]*

- *When I think of all the many things that Heavenly Father has given me, I am very thankful to be me. And I'm very thankful that you are you! Heavenly Father loves us very much.*

A CHILD'S PRAYER

MESSAGE: Heavenly Father really hears my prayers. I feel close to him when I pray.

MATERIALS:

Phrase charts as given in the song presentation

Word cards V.1: HEAVENLY FATHER, HEAVENLY FATHER, FATHER, THERE, PRAYER, AWAY, PRAY, NOW, AGO, ME, THEE, HEAR, ANSWER, HEAVEN, CLOSE, AROUND, JESUS, SUFFER THE CHILDREN, COMING; V.2 (as shown in the lesson plan)

Melody picture

ATTENTION-GETTER:

• *As I sing, tell me to whom you think the child is speaking. [Heavenly Father]* Sing verse one, humming when the words "Heavenly Father" or "Father" are mentioned.

LISTENING AND SINGING EXPERIENCES:

Verse One:

• *Listen again and tell me how many times I sing Heavenly Father's name? [Three times]*

Draw on the chalkboard eight phrase lines without the words, representing every four measures of the song:

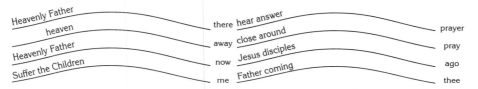

• *These lines represent the eight phrases in this song. Listen carefully and help me find out where to place Heavenly Father's name.* Sing and follow the phrase lines with your hand. Invite a child to place the first three word cards.

To discover the ending word of each phrase, pass out the next eight word cards. Challenge eight children to post word cards as you sing the song once again. Repeat to check answers.

Hand out the remaining word cards to eight children. Challenge the children to post the word cards as you sing the song again.

Invite the children to sing the song referring to the chalkboard. With each repetition invite a child to remove two or three key words.

Share an experience about a personal prayer that was answered.

Verse Two:

Make four melody pictures as illustrated (without the words) and post in random order. Have the children place the pictures in the correct order as you sing. Sing again to check answers.

• *Which of the phrases are exactly alike? [One and three]*

• *As I sing the song again, listen for a word in the second phrase that means Heavenly Father's love is all around me. [Surrounds]*

• *Phrase three sounds exactly like phrase one. Listen to hear two things that Heavenly Father does for his children. [Hears my prayers, loves his children]*

• *Heavenly Father loves his children so much. The kingdom of heaven is filled with his love. Listen as I sing the last phrase and find an important word that is sung two times. [Kingdom]*

Invite the children to sing the entire verse with the accompaniment. Bear your testimony that Heavenly Father does hear and answer the children's prayers.

ENRICHMENT IDEAS:

1. *Jesus told the disciples to allow or permit the children to come to him. The song doesn't use the word allow. Listen to find the word that Jesus used. [Suffer]*

2. Ask the children if they can find a one-syllable word that is sung on two notes. *[Child's—eighth measure.]* Challenge them to stay on the vowel "i" for both notes, adding the "ld's" just before singing the word "prayer."

3. Invite the teachers to sing the first word of each phrase and the children to sing the rest. *(Pray, speak, you, His love, He, He, of such.)* Then change parts.

4. When both verses are well learned, divide into two groups and sing the verses together.

♪ *About the Song*

There was some concern from the Correlation Committee about the lack of prayer language in the text of this song. However, "Thee" and "Thou" seemed too formal and not at all childlike (Father, art thou really there? And dost Thou hear and answer ev'ry child's prayer?). Janice Perry, the composer, said she had a strong feeling that this is as a child would express himself, and is more a song about a small child praying than it is a song to teach prayer language. The decision was made to leave it as it was.

Pray he is there, speak he is list 'ning.

You are his child, His love now sur rounds you.

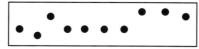

He hears your prayers, he loves the child ren

of such is the king dom, The king dom of heav'n.

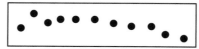

Melody pictures

I PRAY IN FAITH

MESSAGE: When I pray in faith to Heavenly Father, he hears and answers me. I address my Heavenly Father, thank him for my blessings, ask him for things I need, and then I close in the name of Jesus Christ.

ENRICHMENT IDEAS:

1. Use wordstrips *(Dear Heavenly Father, thank him, ask him, Amen)*. Explain that these important words help us remember the order of the words in the song and also the four important parts of prayer.

2. Explain to the children that saying "Amen" at the end of prayers given by others means that you agree with the prayer. It then becomes your prayer, too.

3. Use pictures showing times when we can pray: (Bedside Prayer 62217), outside prayer (62218), blessing food (62223), (Family Prayer 62275), (Classroom Prayer 62200), (Morning Prayer 62310).

4. See Prayer house story and pictures, *Sharing Time Resource Manual*, p. 103.

♪ *About the Song*

This song was requested in order to teach the parts of prayer and was written as a two-part song in an effort to interest older children.

ATTENTION-GETTER:

• *Imagine that your very best friend moved far away from you. You miss your friend so much and you want to keep in touch. How would you communicate with your friend? [Phone calls, letters, cassette tapes, etc.] There is someone else you love who you can keep in touch with through prayer. Who is this? [Heavenly Father]*

LISTENING AND SINGING EXPERIENCES:

Teach the song phrase by phrase, inviting the children to add each phrase as they learn it.

Verse One:

• *Listen as I sing to tell me when Heavenly Father will hear and answer me. [When I pray in faith]* Sing verse one.

• *To whom do we speak when we pray? [Heavenly Father]*

• *How often do we kneel to pray? [Every day]*

  Sing verse one again, asking the children to notice which two words are sung on the quickest notes. *[When I]*

Invite the children to join you in singing the first verse as you pitch lead.

Verse Two:

• *What do you say to begin a prayer?* Let children respond. *Listen as I sing to hear the words we use to begin a prayer. [Dear Heavenly Father]* Point out the rise and fall of the melody of this phrase.

• *What do I thank Heavenly Father for? [Blessings he sends]* Demonstrate the dotted rhythm on the words "thank him" by tapping as you sing.

• *What do we humbly ask him for? [Things that I need]* Tap the rhythm to this phrase.

• *Which word gets the dotted rhythm? [Humbly]*

• *How do we close our prayers? [In the name of Jesus Christ, amen]* Invite the children to tap the rhythm of this phrase with you.

When the children know both verses well, divide them into two groups and sing the verses together. Have another conductor lead one of the groups.

IF WITH ALL YOUR HEARTS

MESSAGE: If we seek Heavenly Father with all our hearts, we will surely find him.

MATERIALS:

Word cards: ALL, SURELY, TRULY, FIND, SEEK, GOOD, EVER, SAITH

ATTENTION-GETTER:

Play a game of "Hide and Seek." Hide a child somewhere in the Primary room. Ask another child to first look for the hidden child with no effort and then a second time with all his heart. When the child has been found say: *If you want something with all your heart, then you work very hard to get it. I know a song about seeking with all your heart. As I sing, listen and see who we're trying to find.* Sing the song.

LISTENING AND SINGING EXPERIENCES:

Sing the song several more times, asking one of the questions with each repetition.

- *Whom should we seek with all our hearts?* [God, him, Heavenly Father]

- *If we seek God with all our hearts, what will happen?* [We shall surely find him.]

- *Joseph Smith actually saw Heavenly Father and Jesus. Most of us won't have the chance to see God here on earth. But we can find him by feeling his love.*

Post the word cards in random order. After you sing the song, have the children put the words in correct order. Sing again to check the answers.

Invite a child to remove two word cards. Sing the song to check memory. Continue in the same way, inviting other children to remove cards.

ENRICHMENT IDEAS:

1. Make illustrations of the slurs (two notes for one word) as shown. Invite the children to sing and select the right word to go with each illustration. Pitch lead as you sing.

saith   our   saith   our

2. Introduce the melody with a flute or violin. Invite the children to hum the melody as the song is repeated.

3. Discuss and show pictures of ways in which we seek our Heavenly Father—prayer (62310), reading scriptures (62521), obeying his commandments, attending church. The following scriptures may be helpful: Matt. 7:7; James 1:5; D&C 88:63.

4. Play a recording of "If With All Your Hearts" from the oratorio *Elijah*. (Check with your local library.) Explain that the composer, Felix Mendelssohn, was a famous German musician. He and Joseph Smith lived during the same time.

5. The language in this song is the kind we use in prayer and that we find in the scriptures. This language shows respect for Heavenly Father. Explain that "ye" means "you"; "thus" means "this" or "so"; "saith" means "said."

6. Show the picture: (The First Vision 62470). Discuss other ways in which Heavenly Father answers us.

CHILDREN ALL OVER THE WORLD

MESSAGE: Our Heavenly Father knows and loves his children all over the world. He hears and understands each of our prayers.

ENRICHMENT IDEAS:

1. Make an eighth rest chart and hold it up so the children can learn to observe the rests after "loves them, loves them."

2. Instruct several children to use finger cymbals or a triangle following the words "loves them," "loves them," and "every one."

3. Use simple costumes from the countries mentioned or have children hold up large poster "costumes."

4. Have children representing each country hold the phonetically spelled word card out of sequence and have the children listen to discover the proper order.

5. Use pictures showing the world (62196) and prayer (62218, 62310).

♪ *About the Song*

The words for "thank you" are printed phonetically where they occur in the song to help you pronounce the words correctly. If you've ever conducted this song, you will know why!

Every song has an introduction marked with brackets. Sometimes the introduction is a little bit of the beginning and a little bit of the end of the song. This one is tricky to find. The pianist would play the complete first line (inside the brackets) and then jump down to the 3rd line and play inside the brackets over the words "own special way." Some pianists like to mark the brackets in red so they can easily find them.

MATERIALS:

Word cards with the phonetic spellings for "thank you" in six languages. (See p. 17, the *Children's Songbook.*) The words could be written on international flags or pictures of children from around the world.

Word cards: HEARS, UNDERSTANDS, KNOWS, LOVES

ATTENTION-GETTER:

Greet the children by saying, *"Kansha shimasu."*

- *Can you understand this word? It is a Japanese word. Do you think that Heavenly Father understands this word? How many languages does Heavenly Father understand? His children live in every part of the world and speak many different languages, but he understands each of us when we pray. I know a song that says something in several languages. Listen for what that something is.* Sing the song to the children. *[Thank you.]*

LISTENING AND SINGING EXPERIENCES:

Sing the song several times, using questions and statements similar to those listed below. As children discover answers, invite them to sing that part of the song with you. Add each phrase to the ones already learned.

- *What do these words mean? [Thank you.]*
- *Now listen and count how many foreign languages I sing. [Six]*

Have six children come forward and hold up the six phonetically spelled words for "thank you."

Help the children practice pronouncing the words. Invite the children to join you in singing them.

- *Where are tender voices heard? [All over the world]*
- *What do Heavenly Father's children all over the world do at the end of day? [Kneel and pray]*
- *What does each child say in his own special way? [Thank you.]*
- *Who hears them? [Heavenly Father]*
- *What else do we learn about Heavenly Father? [That he knows, loves, and understands the language of every person]*

Bear testimony that Heavenly Father loves all his children, no matter where they live or what language they speak.

I NEED MY HEAVENLY FATHER

MESSAGE: My Heavenly Father wants me to be happy and will help me to choose the righteous way.

MATERIALS:

A box with a mirror inside

A melody picture drawn on the chalkboard

ATTENTION-GETTER:

Walk among the children, holding a box with a mirror in the bottom. Tell them you have something you want them to see. Have several children peek inside and not tell anyone else what they see.

Comment on the children's happy, smiling faces as they looked in the box and saw their own reflections.

• *I love to see your happy faces, and so does your Heavenly Father.*

Express your assurance that he loves each one of us and wants us to be happy. Immediately sing the song.

LISTENING AND SINGING EXPERIENCES:

• *Heavenly Father wants us to be happy. Listen for what else Heavenly Father wants us to do. [Choose the righteous way.]*

Have children join in singing these phrases.

Show the melody picture to the children as you hum the melody for "He wants me to be happy." Ask them what words go with that melody.

• *How many times does the melody occur? [Two times]*

• *What word comes on the highest part of the melody? [Be]* Encourage them to sit tall and listen so that the pitch will be in tune.

• *Is the melody the same or different each time "choose the righteous way" is sung? [Different]*

Invite children to sing, noticing the difference.

Tell the children that choosing the righteous way includes doing what is right, helping each other, and so forth.

ENRICHMENT IDEAS:

1. Post the word cards NEED, HELP, HAPPY, and CHOOSE in random order. Ask the children to discover the correct order. Then ask children, *"Who do I need?" "When do I need him to help me?" "Who does he want to be happy?" "What does he want me to choose?"*

2. Have a child read John 13:17 to learn what will make us happy:

   "If ye know these things, happy are ye if ye do them."

♪ *About the Song*

Judith Parker was the music chairman for the Primary General Board when *Sing with Me* was prepared. She wrote "My Heavenly Father Wants Me to Be Happy" for the 1968 reverence program. For this songbook, the title was changed to the first line. Sister Parker is a music research scholar and believes that "music opens doors to other lands and cultures." (*Friend*, Oct. 1986, p. 45.)

HEAVENLY FATHER, NOW I PRAY

MESSAGE: As I pray, I ask Heavenly Father to watch over me and help me feel his love.

ENRICHMENT IDEAS:

1. Display on a chalkboard a picture of a child praying (62217 or 62310). Write the rhyming words *pray, day, me,* and *thee* around the picture. With each repetition, invite a child to erase one of the words.

2. Encourage the children to sing in a prayerful, but full tone.

3. Relate the story of Alvin Beesley, the composer of this song, who used to lead the singing in his ward. During practice time, he would sing in a vibrant tone and walk up and down the aisles to encourage everyone to sing. You may want to try using his method.

ATTENTION-GETTER:

- *When we pray, we thank our Heavenly Father for the many blessings he gives us. What else do we do? (We ask him for things we need.)*

- *I know a song that asks for Heavenly Father's help. As I sing, listen to discover what I ask Heavenly Father to help me feel. [His love]*

LISTENING AND SINGING EXPERIENCES:

Sing the song several more times, asking one question each time you sing.

- *What else do I ask Heavenly Father to do for me? [Guide and guard me.]*
- *When do we want him to guide and guard us? [Every day]*

Explain that Heavenly Father guides and guards us by helping us know what is right and what is wrong.

Explain to the children that in one part of the song the melody steps down the scale and then back. Sing the last two measures on "la" with pitch leading.

- *Listen as I sing the song again and tell me which words occur on that melody. [This I humbly ask of thee.]*

Discuss the meaning of the word "humbly."

A SONG OF THANKS

MESSAGE: We thank Heavenly Father for everything.

MATERIALS:

Letter cards: T-H-A-N-K T-H-E-E. (Number them on the back in order 1 through 9.)

Pictures: child praying, the world, an apple, a bird

ATTENTION-GETTER:

Pass out the letter cards to nine children. Ask each child to come forward in order, to tell something he is thankful for, and to post his letter on the board, spelling "Thank thee."

- *This is how we thank Heavenly Father. We use the word "thee" instead of "you" because it is more respectful.*

- *Listen as I sing to discover what we say "thank thee" for in this song.*

As responses are given, have the children post pictures of the world, food, and birds under the words "thank thee."

LISTENING AND SINGING EXPERIENCES:

Sing again and let the children arrange the pictures in order.

Repeat the song again, omitting the words "world," "food," and "birds." As you point to the pictures, ask the children to sing the missing words and the last phrase. Make sure that the interval from "thee" to "God" is sung correctly.

Read I Thessalonians 5:18: *"In every thing give thanks: for this is the will of God . . . ."* Explain that as they sing this song, they can say "Thank thee, God, for everything," just as the scripture says we should.

Sing the entire song with the children. Read the scripture again and remind the children to thank Heavenly Father for all their blessings.

ENRICHMENT IDEAS:

1. Use echoing to teach the song: Sing one phrase at a time; then, without breaking the rhythm, have the children echo the phrase back to you.

2. Divide the children into three groups, having each group sing one phrase. Invite the whole group to sing the last phrase.

3. Let children come to the chalkboard and draw pictures of the blessings they hear mentioned in this song.

4. Make a mobile with cutouts of the world, an apple, a bird, a child praying.

THANKS TO OUR FATHER

MESSAGE: We thank our Heavenly Father because he gives us everything.

ENRICHMENT IDEAS:

1. As the children sing the song, post pictures of each blessing on a drawing of a cornucopia.

2. Have the children pantomime the words along with you.

3. Pitch lead to teach the melody line. When the song is well learned, have the children pitch lead with you. Then use a two-beat pattern to convey a reverent feeling.

4. Have the children name blessings that they are thankful for that begin with the letters T-H-A-N-K-S.

5. Have an older child read Psalm 92:1: "It is a good thing to give thanks unto the Lord . . . ."

MATERIALS:

Verse One, Letter cards: T-H-A-N-K-S

Verse Two, Pictures: eyes, ears, hands, feet, clothes, food

Verse Three, Pictures: father, mother, baby

ATTENTION-GETTER:

Can you solve this riddle? I am an important word. I have six letters. You love to hear me spoken when you do something nice for someone. What word am I? Post the letters T-H-A-N-K-S.

LISTENING AND SINGING EXPERIENCES:

- *Our Heavenly Father has given us many blessings. Listen as I sing and tell me why we should thank our Heavenly Father.* Sing the first verse to the children. *[He gives us everything.]*

Sing the last line for the children one more time, and invite them to sing it with you.

- *Listen to compare the first line to the second.* Sing and pitch lead the first line. Have the children sing the second line with you. *Are the melodies the same or different? [Different in the last two measures]*

- *Now sing all of verse one with me.*

With the accompaniment, sing verse two, doing actions for but not singing the words "eyes," "ears," "hands," "feet," "clothes," and "food." Sing only the words "and," "to wear," and "to eat."

Use this same activity for verse three, using pictures or hand gestures showing height for "father," "mother," and "baby small."

- *What do you notice about verse one and verse four? [They are the same.]* Sing verse four.

- *I hope we will remember to thank our Heavenly Father daily for our blessings.*

FOR HEALTH AND STRENGTH

MESSAGE: We praise our Heavenly Father for giving us our health and strength and daily food.

MATERIALS:

Melody picture

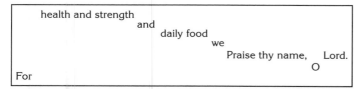

```
        health and strength
                    and
                        daily food
                               we
                                   Praise thy name,   Lord.
                                                 O
        For
```

ENRICHMENT IDEAS:

1. Post the word cards HEALTH, STRENGTH, FOOD, PRAISE, and LORD on colored paper. Place them in a circle to indicate round singing.

2. Invite two children to read these scriptures:

   "Therefore will I give thanks unto thee, O Lord, among the heaven and sing praises unto thy name" (Ps. 18:49).

   "And they did sing praises unto the Lord, . . . and he did thank and praise the Lord all the day long and when night came they did not cease to praise the Lord" (Ether 6:9).

ATTENTION-GETTER:

Post the melody picture and ask the children to follow it as you sing this song of thanks.

Point out how the melody moves step-by-step down the scale.

LISTENING AND SINGING EXPERIENCES:

Invite the children to refer to the chart and pitch lead with you as you sing —it again.

• *For what are we thanking or praising the Lord? [Health and strength, daily food]*

Invite the children to sing with you. Encourage them to listen to their singing on the large skip between "For" and "health" so they will sing it accurately.

When the song is well learned, divide the children into groups and sing the song as a round as indicated on the music.

Express your gratitude to Heavenly Father for your health and strength and daily food.

• *Let's sing the song one more time as a prayer of thanks to our Heavenly Father.*

FOR THY BOUNTEOUS BLESSINGS

MESSAGE: We give thanks to the Lord for his blessings, his word, and his kindness.

ENRICHMENT IDEAS:

1. When this song is well learned, have the older children sing it as a two- or four-part round without accompaniment. You could have a leader for each group.

2. Point out the words in the first line that begin with the same letter, encouraging the children to articulate as they sing. *[Bounteous/Blessing and Wondrous/Word.]*

3. Illustrate the word "bounteous" with objects or pictures of various blessings. Show the scriptures to represent the "wondrous word." Explain that all of these show the "loving kindness" of the Lord.

4. This is the only prayer song in a minor key. Be sure to try it as a round.

MATERIALS:

Pictures: "bounteous blessings" (Family Fun 62384), "wondrous word" (Both Books of Scripture Testify of Christ 62373), "loving kindness" (Children Looking at Spring Flowers 62270), "we give thanks" (Family Prayer 62275)

ATTENTION-GETTER:

* *I have so many blessings, and I want to give thanks for them. Listen as I sing for the name of someone you and I could thank. [The Lord.]*

Have the children sing the last two measures together several times. Affirm that the Lord is pleased when we thank him.

LISTENING AND SINGING EXPERIENCES:

Sing the song several times, encouraging the children to listen by using questions and statements listed below. Ask the children to sing the last two measures with you each time.

* *Name three things for which we give thanks. [Bounteous blessings, wondrous word, loving kindness]* Post pictures.

* *This song has four short phrases. Three of them begin with the same word. What is that word? [For]*

* *Which one of the three "for"s sounds higher than the other two? [The third]*

Invite the children to sing the song as you pitch lead.

Tell the children that you really enjoy singing when you have a thankful feeling inside, like David, who said, "I will sing unto the Lord, because he hath dealt bountifully with me" (Ps.13:6).

* *What words in this song tell us that this is a prayer song? [We give thanks, O Lord.]*

* *Sometimes we sing heartily and sometimes quietly to express our thanks. How should we sing to express thanks in this song? [Calmly and quietly.]*

Add the accompaniment so that the children feel the calmness of the minor key.

A PRAYER SONG

MESSAGE: We reverently prepare to talk to Heavenly Father

MATERIALS:

Prayer boy as illustrated

ATTENTION-GETTER:

• *Watch me as I sing to see how we prepare for prayer.*

Demonstrate with prayer boy cutout or with actions.

LISTENING AND SINGING EXPERIENCES:

• *What three things do we do to get ready pray?* [Bow our heads, fold our arms, close our eyes.]

• *Listen and you will know to whom we talk when we pray.* [Heavenly Father] Sing that phrase only. Then invite the children to sing it with you as you pitch lead.

Sing the melody to "We bow our heads in prayer today" on "loo" as you pitch lead. Have the children discover which words are sung on the descending scale as you sing the entire song. [Bow our heads in prayer today.]

Invite the children to sing the entire song with you, challenging them to sing the large intervals on the words "we bow" and "together" accurately.

Bear testimony that we feel more reverent and closer to our Heavenly Father if we prepare for prayer in the ways this song teaches.

ENRICHMENT IDEAS:

1. Invite the children to do the three actions as they hear them sung: Bow head, fold arms, and close eyes.

2. Invite a child to demonstrate the actions on the prayer boy cutout.

3. Use the picture (Classroom Prayer 62200).

4. See also "Preparation for Prayer" in the *Sharing Time Resource Manual*, p. 140.

♪ About the Song

In simplifying his song, Robert Manookin changed it from the key of B-flat to G major and said, "I have taken out the dissonant spots and made it flow, I think, a bit better. Thank you for the privilege of adding my little bit to the children's worship and learning through music." Then he left for a temple mission to Manilla.

Prayer Boy Instructions:

Cut out eye blanks on prayer boy face. Cut out eye square and blank face carefully on dotted lines to form a slot. Thread the eye square through the slot so the eyes are in the center of the slot. With the eyes facing you, run a tiny amount of glue around the edge of the blank face and glue to the back of the prayer boy's head so that the eyes align properly. Attach the arms and head with brads The dot should be on top. You should be able to make the eyes appear to open and close by sliding the eye square up and down through the slot.

A PRAYER

MESSAGE: If we ask Heavenly Father for help in trying to be happy, kind, honest, fair, and willing to share, we will have a lovely day.

ENRICHMENT IDEAS:

1. Post the word cards DAY and FAIR. Challenge the children to find a rhyming word for each of these. Then post DAY, PLAY, FAIR, and SHARE as answers are given.

2. Use the pictures in random order, challenging a child to put them in the correct order.

MATERIALS:

Pictures to illustrate the following qualities: happiness—girl smiling (My Daddy Loves Me 62552), kindness—one child helping another (Sharing the Tricycle 62317), honesty—talking to the Lord (An Eleven-Year-Old Kneeling in Prayer 62218), fairness—taking turns (Waiting Our Turn 62316), sharing—child sharing toys (Jumping Rope 62523)

ATTENTION-GETTER:

- *What makes a day lovely? Is the day lovely only when the sun shines? We can make a day lovely for ourselves and for those around us when we are happy, kind, and fair.*

- *Father in Heaven will help us if we ask him. As I sing this song, listen to tell me how many times I ask Father in Heaven to "help me." [Three times]*

LISTENING AND SINGING EXPERIENCES:

Sing the song several times to receive the answers to questions similar to the following:

- *There are five things I want Heavenly Father to help me to be or do. Listen to find the answers. [Happy, kind, honest, fair, share blessings with others]* As you sing, post the pictures listed.

- *When should we be honest and fair? [Always] The melody moves to a high tone to emphasize the importance of being honest and fair always, not just most of the time.*

Invite the children to sing the song with you, adding the accompaniment.

- *If we ask for Heavenly Father's help in trying to be happy, kind, honest, fair, and willing to share, we will have a lovely day.*

FATHER UP ABOVE

MESSAGE: We ask our Heavenly Father to look upon us and bless us today with his love.

MATERIALS:

Word cards (or use chalkboard): TODAY, PRAY, LOVE, ABOVE
Bible

ATTENTION-GETTER:

- *I want to read a scripture that tells us that Heavenly Father can see us and he cares about us. "The Lord looked down from heaven upon the children of men, to see if there were any that did understand, and seek God (Ps. 14:2)."*

LISTENING AND SINGING EXPERIENCES:

- *As I sing a beautiful little prayer song, listen for two things that we ask Heavenly Father to do for us. [Look on us today, and bless us with his love.]*

- *In whose name do we pray? [Jesus']*

Sing again, having one side of the group find the word card that rhymes with today *[PRAY]* and the other side to find the word that rhymes with love*[ABOVE]*

Ask the children to sing the rhyming words as you come to them in the song. Help the children to understand that the Lord will indeed look on us, just as the scripture says, and he knows just how to bless us. Sing the whole song with the children.

ENRICHMENT IDEAS:

1. Suggest that this song is a prayer, and invite the children to fold their arms reverently as they sing.

2. Divide the children into three groups. Have each group sing one of the notes on "humbly pray" (G, E, C). Have them sustain their notes long enough to hear the C major chord.

HEAVENLY FATHER, WHILE I PRAY

MESSAGE: On this Sabbath day, I pray that I may worship reverently and think of Heavenly Father.

ENRICHMENT IDEAS:

1. Show the picture (Class Prayer 62200). Emphasize that we are worshiping reverently as we listen to the words of a prayer and think of Heavenly Father.

2. Explain that because this song is a prayer to our Heavenly Father, we should fold our arms while singing it.

MATERIALS:

Word cards or pictures: SABBATH DAY, PRAY, WORSHIP, THINK OF THEE

ATTENTION-GETTER:

Ask a child to prepare this song and sing it for the children. Ask the children to listen for the mention of a special day as the song is sung.

LISTENING AND SINGING EXPERIENCES:

- *What special day is mentioned? [This holy Sabbath day.]* Post the word card SABBATH DAY as a heading.

- *Listen carefully for three things we may do on the Sabbath day. [PRAY, WORSHIP, THINK OF THEE (Heavenly Father)]*

As answers are given, post the words PRAY, WORSHIP, and THINK OF THEE under the heading SABBATH DAY. Point out that these are three things we can do to keep the Sabbath day holy.

- *To worship means to show love and honor to Heavenly Father.*

- *There are four melodic phrases. Each phrase begins on the same tone as the last note of the preceding phrase.* Have the children watch your hand as you smoothly conduct pitch levels.

Invite the children to sing the song with you in a prayerful, reverent manner.

THANK THEE, FATHER

MESSAGE: We thank the Lord for his love and for the blessings of each day. We pray that we will do his will and be led by his holy light.

MATERIALS:

Bible

Word cards or pictures: DAY, WORK AND PLAY, SUN, LOVE

ATTENTION-GETTER:

- In Psalms 50:14 we read, "Offer unto God thanksgiving . . ." Every day can be a day of thanksgiving for the many blessings God gives us. Our thanks can be expressed in our daily prayers or in songs that sound like prayers.

LISTENING AND SINGING EXPERIENCES:

- As I sing, listen for the blessings for which we are thankful. [This day, work and play, shining sun, Heavenly Father's great and tender love] As children respond, post pictures or word cards in order given.

Invite the children to place the word cards or pictures in the correct order as you sing the song again. Sing again, asking the children to find the blessing that is sung on the highest note. [Sun]

Point out the parallel between the high tone and the sun high above. Have the children sing that phrase with you.

Sing once more, leaving off the rhyming word of each phrase and having the children sing the word you leave out. Point to word cards or pictures as needed.

Invite the children to join you in singing the first verse. Add accompaniment.

ENRICHMENT IDEAS:

1. Divide the children into four sections. Have each group sing a phrase in turn as if they were making a list of blessings. Trade phrases.

2. Play a recording of an arrangement of "The Lord's Prayer."

♪ *About the Song*

Originally the title of this song was "Lord, We Thank Thee" and verse two said "Help us Lord. . ." In the Old Testament and in the world at large, "Lord" and "God" are used interchangeably. In the LDS Church today, "God" usually refers to Heavenly Father and "Lord" to the Savior. So the title and words were revised to more clearly address Heavenly Father.

WE BOW OUR HEADS

MESSAGE: We bow our heads and close our eyes and thank our Father for our many blessings. We ask him to keep us safe.

ENRICHMENT IDEAS:

1. Make a prayer boy cutout using brad fasteners to make it movable. (See page 62.) Use this visual aid to demonstrate how we get ready for prayer.

2. This song reminds us to first thank Heavenly Father for our blessings before we ask him for help.

3. Explain that a great prophet named Alma has given us suggestions about what we might say when we pray to God. Read Alma 7:23. Alma says we should always thank Heavenly Father for our blessings. Alma also teaches us to ask for whatever we need.

4. Prepare flannel board cutouts (33239). Put in place as you sing the song.

♪ *About the Song*

Anna Johnson was a special feature writer for the *Deseret News* and the author of "Hopscotch Valley," a children's column. Many books of her poetry were published, and Dr. Alexander Schreiner, tabernacle organist, wrote tunes for over a hundred of them. His tune for "We Bow Our Heads" was also used for the words, "An Angel Came to Joseph Smith." Brother Schreiner was born in Germany and began playing the piano at the age of five. At age eight, he became a church organist. He came to Salt Lake City at the age of eleven and played his first recital in the Tabernacle while in his teens. For fifty-three years, he was Tabernacle organist and millions of people have heard his organ broadcasts. (*Friend*, Oct. 1986, p. 45.)

ATTENTION-GETTER:

Invite two children to come forward. Have one child bow his head and the other child close his eyes.

Ask the children to listen as you sing to find what two things we do to prepare for prayer. As the accompaniment is played, sing only the words "we" and "and" as you point to your assistants. Then sing to the end of the song.

LISTENING AND SINGING EXPERIENCES:

Verse One:

- *What two things can we do to get ready to say a little prayer? [Bow our heads and close our eyes.]*

- *Listen as I sing again to tell me how we thank our Father? [Graciously]* Explain that "graciously" means politely or kindly.

- *What can we thank our Father for? [For blessings we all share]*

Verse Two:

Point out that this verse begins with the same words as the first verse.

- *What do we ask the Lord to do for us through the day? [Keep us safe from harm.]*

- *Where are three places Heavenly Father might keep us safe from harm? [At home, at school, or play]*

I LOVE TO PRAY

MESSAGE: I love to kneel and pray in the morning and at night to thank Heavenly Father for my blessings.

ATTENTION-GETTER:

- *When should we pray? Let children respond. There are many times when we should pray. I love to pray.*
- *As I sing, listen to discover two of the times when I love to pray. [In the morning when I wake, and when I go to bed at night]* Sing both verses.

LISTENING AND SINGING EXPERIENCES:

Sing the song several times for the children, asking a question with each repetition.

Verse One:

- *In the morning, what do I always remember to do? [To kneel and softly pray]*
- *In the morning, I pray before I do what? [Work or play]*

Verse Two:

- *When I go to bed at night, what do I thank my Heavenly Father for? [Blessings of the day]*
- *This time as I sing verse two, raise your hand when you hear me use a prayer language word that means "you." [Thee] Using the word "thee" instead of "you" shows respect to Heavenly Father.*

ENRICHMENT IDEAS:

1. Sing the last two measures more slowly as indicated in the music.

2. Use pictures to review this song. First put them in random order, then challenge a child to put them in the correct order as you sing the song.

3. Invite the children to name as many blessings as they can in thirty seconds. Encourage them to remember to thank Heavenly Father for their blessings when they pray.

4. Bear your testimony that we should pray in the morning to ask our Heavenly Father to watch over us and help us to do what is right. We pray to him at night to report back how we did during the day and how well we kept his commandments. We also thank him for his help and blessings.

REVERENTLY, QUIETLY

MESSAGE: Reverently and quietly we ask our Heavenly Father for his Holy Spirit to be with us.

ENRICHMENT IDEAS:

1. Ask older children how many words in the song end in "ly." *[Ten]* Sing the song again to check. Point out that all the words ending in "ly" will help them prepare themselves to be worthy to receive the Holy Spirit.

♪ *About the Song*

While serving on the Primary General Board, Clara McMaster was asked to write a song for the first reverence program. She worked hard and prayed that she would be prompted to write what would be best for the children. One day as she was looking out the window and pondering her assignment, an idea came to her. She went to the piano and quickly wrote it down. The new song was "Reverently, Quietly." "I felt very humble," she said. "If you prepare and do all that you can do, then Heavenly Father will help you."

Sister McMaster was the eleventh child in her family, and she learned to love music at an early age. She sang and accompanied others on the piano as she grew up in Brigham City, Utah. For twenty-two years she was a member of the Tabernacle Choir. Sister McMaster feels that "Music is a rich gift of God, and it is in the world to make the lives of His children happier and better." (*Friend*, Oct.

MATERIALS:

Word cards: LOVINGLY, SOFTLY, and HUMBLY

ATTENTION-GETTER:

- *I have a question for you. What two words describe how we think about Heavenly Father, how we sing about Heavenly Father, and how we pray to him?* Sing the song. *[Reverently, quietly]*

LISTENING AND SINGING EXPERIENCES:

- *Listen as I sing again and tell me how many times I sing the words "reverently, quietly." [Three]*
- *Being reverent doesn't mean just being quiet. It means having an attitude of worship and being ready to learn more about our Father in Heaven.*
- *As I sing the song, please join me singing just the words "reverently" and "quietly."*

Ask questions using word cards.

- *What do we do lovingly? [Think of thee]*
- *What do we do softly? [Sing our melody]*
- *What do we do humbly? [Pray]*

Explain that to humbly pray is to be ready to repent and obey Heavenly Father.

Post the word cards and ask the children to put them in the correct order as you sing.

Invite the children to sing the entire song with you.

REVERENCE

MESSAGE: Being quiet will help me feel gratitude to the Lord today.

MATERIALS:

Picture: reverent children (Class Prayer 62200)

ATTENTION-GETTER:

Show a picture of reverent children.

• *These children are being quiet in order to do something for the Lord. As I sing the song, listen to hear what it is. [To thank Heavenly Father for the many things he has given me]*

LISTENING AND SINGING EXPERIENCES:

Ask the children to listen as you sing the song for answers to questions such as:

• *What words do I use to call upon Heavenly Father? [Dear Father]*

• *What two respectful prayer language words mean "you" and "your"? Listen to find them. [Thee and thou]*

• *What other prayer language word means "has"?* Invite the children to sing with you once more to find the answer. Enunciate very clearly. *[Hast]*

Invite the children to sit as quietly as they can as they sing with you.

ENRICHMENT IDEAS:

1. Ask the children to name or draw some of the many things that the Lord has given them. Have them show their pictures as the last line is sung.

2. Help the children understand that being quiet is one way they can show their thankfulness. What are some other ways?

3. Ask the children to see if they can remember to be quiet for the rest of the time in Primary today. Tell them that they could be a good example to help each child remember.

WE ARE REVERENT

MESSAGE: Being quiet is only part of being reverent. Being truly reverent also means doing what is right—in learning, singing, and praying.

ENRICHMENT IDEAS:

1. Post word cards: DO, RIGHT, and REVER-ENT in random order. Ask the children to put them in correct order. Children may enjoy discovering which of the three words is sung on a tone higher than the other two. *[Learn] Which is lower? [Reverent]* Repeat the process using word cards LEARN, SING, and PRAY for the second verse.

2. Divide the children into two groups—one to sing the first phrase and one to sing the second phrase—then join together on the last line.

♪ *About the Song*

Sister Mabel Jones Gabbott, the author, said: "Deep waters do run quietly, but they are not stagnant or inactive. Deep within, the water is moving and fulfilling its purpose. Meadows, likewise, look quiet and still in the summer sun, but a growing and a buzzing are going on within. So children, though they are quiet, to be truly reverent must be doing what is right . . . not a blank loss of action, but a quiet growing, learning reverence within, and learning the gospel."

MATERIALS:

Feather

Pictures: deep waters (62481), sunny meadows (Children Looking at Spring Flowers 62270), reverent children (Class Prayer 62200), doing right (Passing the Sacrament 62021)

Melody picture:

ATTENTION-GETTER:

- *As the music is playing, I want you to close your eyes and think of something that is very quiet.* Have the accompanist play the song with quiet simplicity.
- *What quiet things did you think about as you listened?*

Ask the children to listen as you drop a feather and describe the sound.

LISTENING AND SINGING EXPERIENCES:

- *I know three other things that are quiet. Listen as I sing about them.*

Sing, then post the pictures in random order.

- *What three quiet things did I sing about? [Deep waters, meadows, and reverent children]*

Sing again, asking the children to put the pictures in correct order.

Show the melody picture. Hum the first four tones of the song, then ask the children to hum, the tones as you point to the melody chart. Sing the song again. Ask what words go with that melodic phrase? *[Quiet as deep, still as meadows.]*

Invite them to sing those words with you, listening carefully to the low tone so they will sing it accurately.

Point out that though the waters and meadows appear to be quiet, they are moving and growing within to fulfill their purpose. Likewise, being quiet is only part of being reverent.

Continue teaching the second verse in the same way to discover that we should be ready to learn, sing, and pray to be truly reverent.

I WANT TO BE REVERENT

MESSAGE: I want to show my love for my Heavenly Father by being reverent.

MATERIALS:

Pictures: as described in attention-getter.

ATTENTION-GETTER:

Show five pictures to illustrate the following:

- *This is David (#1). He is very quiet, but is he being reverent? If we could see into David's mind, do you know what we would see? He is thinking about the bicycle (#2) he just got for his birthday.*

- *This is Debbie (#3). She looks like she's all ready for prayer. Her eyes are closed; her arms are folded. She looks like she is being very reverent. But if we could look into Debbie's mind, what would we find? She is thinking about her favorite doll (#4).*

- *This is Darlene (#5). Her eyes are closed; her head is bowed. I wonder if she's being just quiet or being reverent. If we could see into Darlene's mind, we could hear her saying . . . Sing the song.*

LISTENING AND SINGING EXPERIENCES:

Sing the song several times, encouraging the children to listen by using questions and statements similar to those listed below. As children discover answers, invite them to sing that part of the song with you. Add one phrase at a time to the ones already learned.

- *Where does reverence begin?* [With me]

Pitch lead, helping children to notice the repeated notes in the descending scale.

- *What will I do quietly?* [Listen] Sister Watkins, the composer, created a quiet, reverent feeling in the way she wrote the melody in this phrase. Notice how it is sung on only one tone. Sing this phrase several times.

- *What do I want to be?* [Reverent]

- *Why do I want to be reverent?* [To show my love for Heavenly Father]

Explain that reverence is more than just being quiet. It is having your mind clear of worldly things and being ready to learn about Heavenly Father and Jesus.

ENRICHMENT IDEAS:

1. Sing the melody on "loo" one time before singing the words.

2. Make sure that the children are singing "rev-rent," not "rev-runt."

3. Prepare three children to do a demonstration. Have them come to the front, forming a line. Have the first child fold his arms and portray a reverent child. Instruct the second child to watch and follow, then the third child to watch and follow. Ask which child was a good example. Explain that reverence can begin with each of us.

I WILL TRY TO BE REVERENT

MESSAGE: Because I love my Heavenly Father, I will try to be reverent in his house. Then he'll be near to me.

ENRICHMENT IDEAS:

1. You may wish to have an older child read D&C 88:63, "Draw near unto me and I will draw near unto you . . ."

2. Challenge the children to sing this song softly, sitting as still and quietly as they can.

MATERIALS:

A melody picture drawn on posterboard or a chalkboard to illustrate the descending/ascending note pattern on second line

ATTENTION-GETTER:

- *I love my Heavenly Father. Because I love him, how will I try to be when I'm in his house? [Reverent]* Sing the song for the children.
- *Being reverent is an important way to show our love for our Heavenly Father.*

LISTENING AND SINGING EXPERIENCES:

Direct the children's listening by asking questions like the following with each repetition.

- *If I try to be reverent, what blessing will I receive? [He'll be near to me.]*
- *What word do I sing on the highest tone of the song? [Reverent]* As you sing, pitch lead to emphasize the high note on the first syllable of "reverent."

Using the melody picture, point out how the phrase "Reverent when I'm in his house" goes down and then right back up again

- *Sing the song with me, but be sure to take a deep breath before you sing.*

Express your love for your Heavenly Father. Challenge the children to show their love for him by being reverent in his house.

FATHER, I WILL REVERENT BE

MESSAGE: I will be reverent in my Heavenly Father's house by walking quietly, being ready for prayer, listening to my teachers, and keeping my thoughts and words reverent.

MATERIALS:

Picture: a chapel

Small pictures to be placed around the chapel picture: shoes, folded arms, bowed head, closed eyes, ears, mouth, child thinking

ATTENTION-GETTER:

Ask the children to close their eyes. Have the pianist softly play the song. Express the reverent feeling that you like to experience in Heavenly Father's house.

Explain that each child can have that same warm, reverent feeling by doing just a few specific things. Ask them to listen to find out what they can do to feel reverent.

LISTENING AND SINGING EXPERIENCES:

Repeat the song several times, directing the children's listening by asking questions. Post the small pictures around the picture of the chapel as the questions are answered.

- *How should we walk in our Heavenly Father's house?* [Quietly] Post picture of shoes.
- *How do I prepare for prayer?* [Fold my arms, bow my head, close my eyes.] Post pictures of folded arms, bowed head, closed eyes.
- *What do I listen to?* [The words I hear] Post picture of ears.
- *How should we speak?* [More reverently] Post picture of mouth.

Have the children sing the entire song.

- *How many times did you sing the prayer word "thy"?* [Three]
- *How do we act when we are guests in someone's house?* [our best] We are guests in the Lord's house. We come here to learn about him and need to show respect for him here.

Explain that we use prayer language to show respect for our Heavenly Father.

ENRICHMENT IDEAS:

1. Have children hold the small pictures out of sequence. As they listen to the song, put pictures in correct order. Sing the song several times if necessary. When children can sing each part correctly, remove the corresponding picture.

2. Sing the octave intervals in lines four and five accurately. Have the children find the octaves. Explain that an octave is two pitches eight tones apart. Have half the children hold the lower tone while the others hold the higher tone.

3. Make a prayer boy with arms that fold, head that bows, eyes that close. Show prayer boy doing actions as song is sung. Refer to lesson plan for the song "A Prayer Song," on page 62, for complete prayer boy instructions.

4. Younger children will enjoy doing actions to this song.

5. Use the Primary Visual Aids Cutouts. Set One: 33239, eyes, ears. Set Two: 33242, shoes, reverent girl.

THIS IS GOD'S HOUSE

MESSAGE: The chapel is God's house, and he is here listening to our songs and prayers.

ENRICHMENT IDEAS:

1. Divide the children into four groups. Give each group one phrase (1/2 line) to sing. Then rotate the assignments.

2. Indicate the repeated notes and the step-by-step melody by pitch leading. Have the children pitch lead with you.

MATERIALS:

Picture of a chapel (Primary Visual Aids Cutouts—Set 10 33250) or enlarged drawings from this page.

ATTENTION-GETTER:

Without comment or introduction, sing this song while showing the children a picture of a chapel.

- *When a chapel is completed, the members of the ward come to a special meeting called a "dedication." A church leader says a special prayer, and by the power of the priesthood, he dedicates the meetinghouse to the Lord. This makes it His house, a sacred place, a place where we worship our Heavenly Father.*

LISTENING AND SINGING EXPERIENCES:

- *Whose house is this? [God's]* Acknowledge the answer, then sing "This is God's house, and he is here today."

Ask again: *Whose house is this?* Request the children to sing the answer—line 1—with you as you pitch lead. Ask the accompanist to play the melody only.

- *What does Heavenly Father do when we sing and pray?* Ask the children to sing the answer with you—line 2.

Invite the children to sing the entire song. Add the accompaniment.

Bear your testimony that God's Spirit will be with us in church and that Heavenly Father will hear us sing and pray if we come with an attitude of worship and reverence.

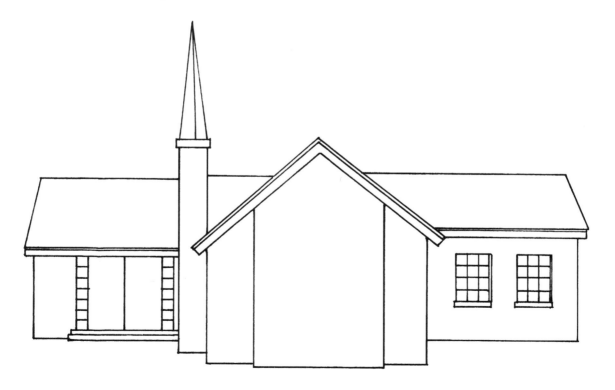

OUR CHAPEL IS A SACRED PLACE

MESSAGE: Our chapel is a sacred place. As we sing and pray here, we will think of our Heavenly Father.

MATERIALS:

Prepare three melody pictures on posters or chalkboard:

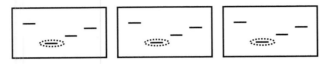

ATTENTION-GETTER:

By name, compliment specific children who entered the chapel quietly.

- *The chapel is a holy place where we can worship Heavenly Father and Jesus Christ.*
- *Listen as I sing a song. See if you can find another word that means "holy" and that describes our chapel. [Sacred]*

LISTENING AND SINGING EXPERIENCES:

- *Now listen for two things we do as we think of our Heavenly Father. [Sing and pray]*

Sing the song again.

Invite the children to sing with you on the last line. As you sing, show a melody picture of each phrase in the last line, pointing to each pitch to discover what word comes on the lowest tone in each chart. *[Fa-"ther," and, will]*

Sing the last line again, stopping on the lowest pitch of each chart to check for accuracy.

Compliment the children on following you.

Invite them to sit tall on the front of their chairs and sing in their most beautiful voices.

ENRICHMENT IDEAS:

1. Sing the song to the children, leaving out the last word or words in each phrase. Invite the children to sing the missing parts: "sacred place," "quietly," "sing and pray," "thee."

2. Display a picture of a chapel from (Primary Visual Aids Cutouts—Set 10 33250). Discuss briefly with the children the way to behave in a sacred place. You may wish to read D&C 132:8, "Behold, mine house is a house of order, saith the Lord God, and not a house of confusion."

REVERENCE IS LOVE

MESSAGE: Reverence is more than just being quiet. It is thinking of Heavenly Father and all the blessings he has given me. I show my love for Heavenly Father and Jesus in my words and actions. When I am reverent, I feel that Heavenly Father and Jesus are near me.

ENRICHMENT IDEAS:

1. Elder Vaughn J. Featherstone said, "One of the most Christlike qualities we ought to develop is reverence, an attitude that shows how we feel about Heavenly Father and the things He has asked us to do." (*Friend*, Sept. 1976, p. 8.) Have the children sing this song once more to show Heavenly Father and Jesus how much we love them.

2. Sing the last phrase of the song, pointing out the up-and-down flow of the melody pattern. Then invite the children to draw this flowing pattern in the air with you.

MATERIALS:

Word cards written on eight red hearts: QUIETLY SITTING, THINKING, FEELING, LOVE, SHOWS, FOLLOW, KNOW, NEAR, REVERENCE IS

ATTENTION-GETTER:

- *Today we are going to learn a song that teaches us about reverence. As I sing it, I want you to listen for my favorite four-letter word that tells us what reverence is. Sing the entire song.* [Love]

- *What is my favorite four-letter word?* [Love]

- *Reverence is love. By being reverent, we are showing Heavenly Father and Jesus how much we love them.*

LISTENING AND SINGING EXPERIENCES:

- *Listen as I sing this beautiful song. Count how many times I sing the word "reverent" or "reverence."* [Five]

- *As I sing again, I want you to listen very closely. I'm going to leave out the most important key words, and you will have to fill in the blanks. Sing the song again, leaving out the key words.*

Pass out the hearts to eight children. Invite all the children to join you as you sing to help the eight children arrange themselves in the correct order, according to the key words they are holding. Sing the song as many times as needed until the children have arranged themselves in the correct order.

Invite a child to take away key words as you and the children sing—until all are removed.

- *I'm grateful for the message of this song. It helps me remember that reverence is more than just being quiet. It's thinking of Heavenly Father and all the blessings he has given me. Let's try our best through our words and actions to be reverent and show our love for Heavenly Father and Jesus.*

77

The Savior

The songs about the Savior are in chronological order—the prophecy of the savior's birth, the Christmas songs, Jesus' childhood and ministry, songs of Easter, resurrection and the sacrament, why we want to be like him, and songs of His second coming.

HE SENT HIS SON

MESSAGE: Our Heavenly Father sent his Son, Jesus Christ, to show us how we should live. He asks us to live like his Son.

MATERIALS:

Prepare wordstrips cut from two colors of paper. Write the five questions in the song on one color and the five answers on the other color. You could also use the following pictures to help depict the answers: his birth (62495), his life (62494), his sacrifice and death (62505), live like his Son—(Boy Being Baptized 62018), (Jesus the Christ 62572)

ATTENTION-GETTER:

- *Can you remember when you were a spirit living with Heavenly Father before you were born? None of us can remember our life in the spirit world, because that is the way Heavenly Father planned it. But we all lived there together before we came to earth.*

- *When we lived with him, our Heavenly Father held an important meeting. He announced that an earth was going to be created and that we could come here to receive a physical body and to learn to choose the right. If we did our best, we would live with Heavenly Father forever.*

- *Because we can't remember our life with Heavenly Father, he sent us someone to show us the right way to live.*

- *Who did Heavenly Father send to show us how to live? [Jesus Christ]*

- *In this beautiful song, two other words are used instead of the name of Jesus Christ. Listen to discover which words refer to Jesus.* **Sing the song.** *[His Son]*

LISTENING AND SINGING EXPERIENCES:

- *This song is a series of questions and answers. The questions are about what Heavenly Father wants us to learn. The answers tell us what he did to teach us these important principles.*

Show the children the wordstrips you have prepared, with the questions in proper sequence and the answers out of sequence. As you sing again, challenge the children to match the correct answer with each question. Sing the song again to check the order of the wordstrips.

Point out that the song is written in four important sections: (1) His birth; (2) His life; (3) His sacrifice and death; 4) What he asks of us. Help them see that the logical sequence of this song will help them remember the words.

Invite the children to sing the song with you, referring to the wordstrips. As they become more confident with the words, begin removing the wordstrips.

Express your deep love for your Heavenly Father and for his Son, Jesus Christ. Close by reading Moroni 7:48.

ENRICHMENT IDEAS:

1. Invite children to hold pictures depicting the birth, life, and sacrifice of Jesus Christ, and a picture depicting a child doing right. Ask them to arrange the pictures in the correct order as the song is sung.

2. Divide the children into two groups. Group 1 sings the questions, and group 2 sings the answers. Then switch parts.

3. Observe the written dynamic markings. Encourage the children to emphasize the words "live like his Son" at the end of the song.

♪ *About the Song*

Sections I and II of the *Children's Songbook* are linked by this song because it tells about the mission of the Savior. Mabel Jones Gabbott said she wrote this poem when she was wondering about our Father in Heaven sending his spirit children to earth to be tested. How would he teach them the way to return to him? (See *Friend*, Oct. 1985, p. 15)

Sister Gabbott has written for the Church for many years. Sixteen of her poems are used in this book. (See p. 305 of the *Songbook*, "How to Use the Songbook," for a list of authors and composers.) Each year, she and her Bountiful, Utah, neighbor, Michael Moody, write a Christmas song to serve as a greeting to their family and friends. "He Sent His Son" was their 1981 greeting.

Brother Moody says, "Music is a tool for building families. It can bring a sweet spirit into the home. My family sings before scripture reading, before meals, and when we're traveling in our car." Brother Moody has wonderful talent for both writing music and bringing out the best in everyone he works with. He is chairman of the General Church Music Committee, was executive chairman of the Hymnbook project, and supervised every step of the *Children's Songbook.*

SAMUEL TELLS OF THE BABY JESUS

MESSAGE: Samuel the Lamanite prophesied that Jesus would be born in Bethlehem. The prophecy was fulfilled, and angels sang at his birth. We are so blessed that our Lord was born. Let us gladly sing and rejoice.

ENRICHMENT IDEAS:

1. Divide the children into two groups. Ask each group to sing a line of each verse and to join together for the chorus.

2. Hold up the picture (Samuel the Lamanite on the Wall 62370). Ask the children to retell the story that they have learned from singing the song.

3. Ask a man to sing the verse as a solo and invite the children to join him on the chorus. Notice that the tempo of the chorus is faster and the mood is more joyous.

MATERIALS:

Book of Mormon

ATTENTION-GETTER:

Ask an older boy to portray Samuel the Lamanite by wearing a simple costume and reading Helaman 13:5 and 14:2-4 or by telling it in his own words.

Introduce "Samuel" by reading Helaman 13:2-4. The boy then stands on a table or chair and recites or reads:

"Behold, I, Samuel, a Lamanite, do speak the words of the Lord which he doth put into my heart. . ." (Hel. 13:5).

". . . Behold, I give unto you a sign; for five years more cometh, and behold, then cometh the Son of God to redeem all those who shall believe on his name.

And behold, this will I give unto you for a sign at the time of his coming; for behold, there shall be great lights in heaven, insomuch that in the night before he cometh there shall be no darkness. . . .

. . .There shall be one day and a night and a day, as if it were one day and there were no night" (Hel. 14:2-4).

Samuel then jumps off the wall and runs out. Explain to the children that Samuel had to run from wicked Nephites who wanted to kill him.

- *Samuel made a very important announcement. As I sing, listen to hear again Samuel's important prophecy.* Sing the first verse and chorus.

LISTENING AND SINGING EXPERIENCES:

Teach the chorus first by pitch leading. Have the children echo back each phrase to you as they discover the answer to your question.

- *As we sing the chorus, find a word that is a joyful expression of praise to our Heavenly Father. [Hosanna]*
- *How many times do we sing "Hosanna?" [Two]*
- *Can you hear how the melody goes up and then down on the words "How blessed that our Lord was born?" Sing that with me.*
- *The words "Let earth receive her king" mean "Let all people accept the Lord as our God and King." Now sing the entire chorus with me.*

Verse One:

Sing the verse several times, asking questions similar to the following:

- *How many years after Samuel's prophecy would Jesus be born? [Five years]*
- *What was the sign that told of Jesus' birth? [A night will be as day]*
- *Where would Jesus be born? [In a land far, far away]*

Verse Two:

- *Where did Jesus come to earth? [Across the sea, in Bethlehem]*
- *Samuel told of something that would happen in the future. What word means that he told about something before it happened? [Prophesied]*
- *Who sang at Jesus' birth? [Angels] Since we had not yet been born, we might have been among the hosts of angels who sang for joy at Jesus' birth.*

STARS WERE GLEAMING

MESSAGE: Stars were gleaming as the angels announced the birth of Christ to the shepherds on the hill. The Wise Men were guided through the desert by the Christmas star.

MATERIALS:

Verse One: Bell-shaped flip-chart as illustrated

One complete bell with "ing" printed on the clapper; four bell tops with one word on each: sing, ring, wing, bring. Bells will be hooked together with a ribbon or a metal ring through a hole at the top.

Verse Two: Star-shaped flip chart

Seven stars with the following key words printed on them: SHOWING, SHINING, GROWING, GOING, GLEAMING, GLOWING, LEADING.

ATTENTION-GETTER:

Ask the children to close their eyes.

- *Let's use our imagination. Pretend you are actually there on that sacred night when Christ was born. Think of how dark the night is—yet the stars are gleaming. There, over the stable, is one great golden star that marks the sacred spot.*
- *We can hear in the distance the angels telling about the birth of Christ and singing "Glory to God in the highest."*
- *In the stable, we can smell the fresh hay that has become the bed for the Christ Child. We can hear the mooing of the cow and the baaing of the sheep.*
- *This is where the miracle takes place. The Son of God is born here in the stable. It is such a sacred night.*
- *Keep your eyes closed and listen as I sing about the night this miracle took place.*

LISTENING AND SINGING EXPERIENCES:

Verse One:

Challenge one side of the room to listen to discover what the stars were doing. *[Gleaming]* Ask the other side to listen to discover what the shepherds were doing. *[Dreaming]* Point out that these two words rhyme.

- *Listen to these two phrases again to discover if the rhythm is the same or different. [Same]* Point out that this rhythm is the same throughout the entire song. Sing again, asking the children to finger tap as you sing.
- *What two words describe that sacred night. [Dark and chill]*
- *Where were the shepherds when they heard the angels? [On the hill]* Point out that the melody is identical on lines one and two.
- *As I sing the next phrases count the words that end in an "ing" sound. [Four]* To help teach the order of the "ing" words, use the bell-shaped flip chart as indicated above.
- *The song says "Listen! We can hear it still," but the word "listen" isn't used. What is another word for "listen"? [Hearken]*
- *The last line brings the whole song together by emphasizing that even today, we can hear the story of our Savior's birth.* Sing the last line again, then sing the entire verse.

Verse Two:

- *Where was the star leading and guiding the Wise Men? [Through the desert dark and far]*

As you sing the next phrases, challenge the children to find the many "ing words. Display the cutout stars as answers are given. Sing verse two again, challenging the children to put the stars in the correct order.

- *What is still leading us? [Our Christmas star]* The star has become one of the important symbols of Christmas. When you see a star on top of a Christmas tree, remember the Christmas star of long ago.

ENRICHMENT IDEAS:

1. Display cutouts of the Nativity figures as the children sing the song: stars, shepherds, angels, hill, Wise Men, desert. See Primary Visual Aids Cutouts—Set 8: Christmas Figures (33248).

2. Define difficult words: "gleaming" (sending out rays of light, shining); "earthward winging" (bringing to earth); "hearken" (to listen closely or pay attention); "blessed" (holy); "glowing" (giving off light, shining brightly).

3. Challenge the children to follow your dynamics as you lead the phrase "Ah, that singing. . ." very softly and increase the volume with each measure to the end.

♪ *About the Song*

At the suggestion of the correlation committee, a significant word change was made in the first verse. The text had been "Stars were gleaming, shepherds dreaming; winter night was dark and chill." Inasmuch as we believe that it was in the spring of the year when the Savior was born, "winter" was changed to "and the." The notation was returned to the form in the *Children Sing*, beginning on beat 3 (pickup) rather than beat 1 (downbeat) as in *Sing With Me*. Try it both ways and you will feel why it was changed.

WHEN JOSEPH WENT TO BETHLEHEM

MESSAGE: Joseph was kind and good, and he loved Jesus.

ENRICHMENT IDEAS:

1. Make a melody picture as shown below. Have the children discover what words go with each melody line. Tell the children that the melody goes up and down the staff, like the hills of Bethlehem.

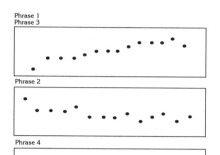

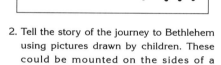

2. Tell the story of the journey to Bethlehem using pictures drawn by children. These could be mounted on the sides of a square box and turned as you sing.

3. Use the following library pictures: shop (62124), Joseph leading donkey (62119), busy inn (62115), (The Birth of Jesus 62116).

MATERIALS:

A small linen sack with a drawstring at the top, containing a wheel of cheese and a loaf of homemade bread

Wood shavings

A doll wrapped in strips of cloth, or a picture showing baby Jesus in swaddling clothes (The Nativity 62495)

ATTENTION-GETTER:

- *Inside my sack are some things that Joseph and Mary might have eaten as they journeyed to Bethlehem.*
- *As I sing a song about Joseph, listen to discover what might have been in his sack.*

LISTENING AND SINGING EXPERIENCES:

As you sing the song, direct the children's listening by asking questions such as:

Verse One:

- *What two things did Joseph carry in his little linen sack? [Bread and goat cheese]* Invite the children to sing the answers with you. Continue in the same way.

Take the cheese and bread from the sack. Discuss why they had to prepare food ahead of time and carry it in a strong sack.

- *Joseph wanted the donkey to move along. What word tells us that he encouraged the donkey? [Urged]*
- *When Joseph went to Bethlehem, I think he took great care to make other preparations, too. He had to close his carpentry shop. Listen for two things he had to do to close his shop. [Place his tools (put them away), and leave no shavings there (sweep them up)]* Let the children smell the fresh wood shavings.

Verse Two:

- *What two words describe Joseph at the busy inn? [Meek and mild]* Define "meek" and "mild": [humble, patient, and kind].
- *Joseph felt honored to be the guardian of Mary's sacred child. Listen for another word that means "honored." [Awed]*
- *A guardian is a person chosen to care for a child. Heavenly Father chose Joseph to be the guardian of His Son. Listen to see if the notes on the word "guardian" move up or down or stay on the same note. [Same]*
- *What did Joseph do all through the chilly hours? [He smoothed the swaddling bands.]* Show a doll wrapped in swaddling cloth or the Nativity picture. Explain that it was the custom to wrap babies tightly to help them feel secure.
- *What did Jesus feel? [The quiet strength of Joseph's gentle hands]*

Verse Three:

- *And close beside the manger bed, what did Joseph dim? [The lantern's light]*
- *How did Joseph hold little Jesus upon that holy night? [Close]*
- *Joseph was kind and good to be the guardian of Jesus. He loved Jesus very much.*

LITTLE JESUS

MESSAGE: Jesus came to earth to show us the way to live. We sing praises to him on Christmas Day.

ATTENTION-GETTER:

- *I love the Christmas season! I love the decorations, the smells, the happiness, and the music. One of my very favorite things to do at Christmas time is to sing Christmas songs. When we sing these beautiful songs, we are singing praise to our Heavenly Father and his Son.*

- *Listen as I sing a Christmas song for you, and tell me when we sing praise. [On Christmas Day]*

LISTENING AND SINGING EXPERIENCES:

Verse One:

- *What do we sing on Christmas Day? [Praise]* Invite the children to sing the last phrase with you, and join you on that phrase each time you repeat the song.

- *At one place in the song we sing five notes all on the same tone. What words do we sing on the five repeated notes? [Little Jesus Child]*

- *What two words tell us what Jesus was like when he came to earth? [Meek and mild]*

- *What did he come to earth to do? [Show the way]*

Invite the children to sing verse one with you.

Verse Two:

- *Who smiled from the heavens? [Angels]*

- *What do we lay before the baby Jesus? [A gift]*

ENRICHMENT IDEAS:

1. Ask the children to find the rhyming words.

2. Make four melody pictures to represent each of the four phrases. Invite a child to match each picture with the correct phrase.

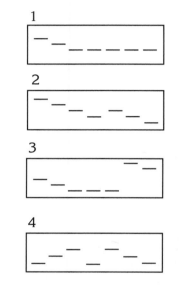

♪ *About the Song*

Mark Newell was Primary age when he wrote the tune for this song—just ten years old!

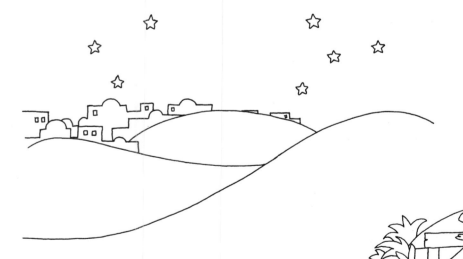

THERE WAS STARLIGHT ON THE HILLSIDE

MESSAGE: When Jesus was born, there was starlight and music. Heavenly hosts sang, and the shepherds came to worship him.

ENRICHMENT IDEAS:

1. Let the children put the figures onto the flannel board.

2. Use the flannel board and the figures as a "choosing chart" for reviewing other Christmas songs. Print the song titles on the back. These figures can be used with other Christmas songs, such as "Stars Were Gleaming" (p. 37), "Picture a Christmas" (pp. 50-51), and "Nativity Song," (pp. 52-53).

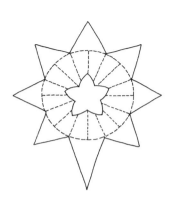

MATERIALS:

A flannel board scene with a dark blue background: a hillside, star, stable, music notes, angels, shepherds, Jesus, manger, and a Bethlehem scene. (See Primary Visual Aids Cutouts—Set 8: Christmas Figures 33248.)

ATTENTION-GETTER:

Have the flannel board pieces in order as you begin this presentation. As you ask each question, place the corresponding piece on the board.

LISTENING AND SINGING EXPERIENCES:

Teach the song to the children by asking questions similar to those below. Invite the children to sing each phrase back to you as they discover the answers to the questions.

Verse One:

- *As I sing for you, listen to discover where the starlight was. [On the hillside]*
- *Where did one star bend? [Very low]*
- *Where did it pass? [Above the stable]*

Sing verse one with the children.

Verse Two:

- *As I sing the next verse, see if you can find out where the shepherds were? [On the hillside]*
- *What two words mean "angels"? [Heavenly hosts]*
- *What were the heavenly hosts proclaiming? [Joyous tidings unto them]*

Verse Three:

- *Listen to see where Jesus was. [In the manger]*
- *Why did the shepherds leave the hillside? [To worship him]* Move the flannel board figures of the shepherds to the Bethlehem scene.

Sing verse three with the children.

Remove all of the pieces from the flannel board and place them there again as the children sing the entire song with you.

- *We can read about these events in our scriptures. I have a testimony that these things did happen just the way this beautiful song teaches.*

THE SHEPHERD'S CAROL

MESSAGE: Jesus is our King and Savior. We will sing his praises.

MATERIALS:

Word cards: MARY, JOSEPH, JESUS, SAVIOR

ENRICHMENT IDEAS:

1. For younger children, use pictures instead of word cards.

ATTENTION-GETTER:

Display the word cards.

- *Two of these words are sung two times and two are sung only once. Listen as I sing to discover which words are sung only once. [Jesus and Savior]*

LISTENING AND SINGING EXPERIENCES:

Divide the singers into four groups. Teach each group one of the four parts in this round by rote.

Sing the song with each group singing their phrase in succession. Repeat the song this way several times. Trade parts and sing again.

Invite the children to sing the whole song together. Then divide into parts for two- or four-round singing, as marked on the music.

ONCE WITHIN A LOWLY STABLE

MESSAGE: In a lowly stable, Mary cared for her baby—the Christ child—in a manger filled with hay. Our Father in Heaven sent this loving baby to show all people how to help and love each other.

ENRICHMENT IDEAS:

1. Show pictures that portray the Christmas story. The children could draw these previously on separate sheets of paper or on a large roll of butcher paper.

2. Divide the children into two groups. Group one sings the first, third and fifth phrases, and group two echos back, singing the second, fourth and sixth phrases.

3. Have the children play a harmony line on the tone bells or pipe chimes using G, A, and B tones in this order:

   G G G G G G A A G G G G G G B B A G A
   G G G A G (two beats each)

4. Let the children create their own bell harmony using G, A, B tone bells. Invite them to experiment by listening and then selecting which tone bell should be played. Write the chosen response on the chalkboard.

5. Dramatize Mary laying her baby in the manger.

6. Use flannel board figures as you sing: stable, sheep, oxen, Mary, baby, and manger. (See Primary Visual Aids Cutouts—Set 8: Christmas figures 33248.)

7. For a review, make a poster similar to the illustration on this page in the *Children's Songbook*.

♪ *About the Song*

The selection committee for the *Children's Songbook* had not been able to find any information about Patty Hill, the author of this song. However, they knew she had also written "Happy Birthday, to You." An article in a newspaper had the headline "'Happy Birthday'" Not Expected to Go for a Song." The article told about the sale of the copyright and gave Patty's complete name, birth date, and the fact that she had been a kindergarten teacher in Louisville, Kentucky, around the turn of the century. The copyright holder was contacted for verification and credit given to Patty and Mildred, her sister, rather than to "words anon." The committee feels sure they did not "find" this information, but were led to it.

ATTENTION-GETTER:

- *Jesus was born in a stable where animals were kept. In the stable, there was a trough or feedbox filled with hay. What do you think the hay was for? [To feed to the animals]*
- *Listen carefully as I sing to find another name for this trough or feedbox. [Manger]*

Sing verse one to the children.

LISTENING AND SINGING EXPERIENCES:

Verse One:

Teach this song, using questions and instructions such as the following.

- *Listen as I sing to find out who is the mother in this song and who is the baby. [Mary and the Christ]*

Sing the last phrase for the children once more; then have them sing that phrase with you as you pitch lead.

- *Where did Mary lay her baby? [In a manger filled with hay]*

Pitch lead that phrase as you sing it again, and have the children join you.

- *What animals were in the stable with Mary and the baby Jesus? [Sheep and oxen]* Invite the children to sing this phrase with you and continue to the end.

Hum the first two measures; then ask the children what two phrases we sing on that melody. [*Once within a lowly stable, and loving mother laid her baby*]

Invite the children to sing verse one with you.

Verse Two:

- *Who sent us this loving baby? [God]*
- *What did Jesus come to earth to show all people? [How to help and how to love]*
- *Who sang for joy that Christmas night? [Angels]*

Hum the first two measures; then ask what two phrases we sing on that melody in verse two. [*God sent us this loving baby, and He came down to show all people*]

- *As we sing about this beautiful event, I remember a special scripture. Read Luke 2:7, and 12.*

AWAY IN A MANGER

MESSAGE: The little Lord Jesus lay asleep in a manger filled with hay. I love him and ask him to be near me forever and to bless all the children in his care.

MATERIALS:

Nativity pictures: manger, baby Jesus, stars, cattle

New Testament

ATTENTION-GETTER:

Post Nativity pictures to set a peaceful mood. As the accompanist softly plays the song, have an older child read Luke 2:1, 3-7.

- *When the Lord of us all was born, he had no crib for his bed. He slept in a manger, which was a feedbox for the animals in the stable. Listen as I sing to hear what Jesus was sleeping on. [The hay]*

LISTENING AND SINGING EXPERIENCES:

Sing the song several times, encouraging the children to listen by using questions and statements similar to those listed below. As children discover answers, invite them to sing that part of the song with you. Add one phrase at a time to the ones already learned.

Verse One:

- *What was Jesus sleeping on? [The hay]* Tap the rhythm to make certain the children are singing "sleep on the hay" correctly.
- *What looked down where he lay? [The stars in the heavens]*
- *Jesus is called a very special name in this song. What is it? [The little Lord Jesus]*
- *What was it that Jesus didn't have? [A crib for his bed]*

Sing the first line again and ask the children to find the other phrase we sing on that same melody. *[The stars in the heaven looked down where he lay.]*

Invite the children to sing verse one; add the accompaniment.

Chorus:

After the children have heard the chorus several times, invite them to sing the word "asleep" every time until they have learned the chorus well. Then have one group sustain the melody note on the word "asleep," while the other group sings the echo.

- *How many times did I sing asleep? [Ten]*
- *Where did our Savior sleep? [In a stall]*
- *Listen for a word that rhymes with stall. [All]*
- *The little Lord Jesus born in that stall so long ago is indeed the Lord of us all. We love him, and he loves each of us very much.*

Teach the other verses in this same manner, directing the children's listening through questions. You might define "cattle are lowing" (cattle are mooing) and "nigh" (near).

ENRICHMENT IDEAS:

1. Let the children post flannel board pictures as you sing. (See Primary Visual Aids Cutouts—Set 8: Christmas Figures 33248.)
2. Use tone bells or chimes on the chorus.
3. Young children may enjoy humming and pretending to rock a baby in their arms.
4. Teach the older children and teachers the harmony to this lullaby.

MARY'S LULLABY

MESSAGE: Mary sings a lullaby to her newborn child.

ENRICHMENT IDEAS:

1. Teach a group of older children or teachers the beautiful descant or invite a guest to play the descant on the flute or on another instrument.

2. Add dynamics. Encourage the children to follow you as your leading pattern gets larger (louder) or smaller (softer).

3. Smaller children might enjoy pretending to rock a baby as they sing.

4. On a poster, draw a baby with its eyes open. Also draw and cut out a pair of closed eyes. When the children are able to sing the entire song, attach the closed eyes, making it look like the baby has fallen asleep.

5. Challenge one class to sing only the word "lullaby" (six times) and the rest of the children to sing all other lyrics.

♪ *About the Song*

Originally, the words to this song were a German translation of the poem "Mary's Lullaby to the Infant King." The copyright holders were asking $2,000 royalty for the use of the song, payable every ten years rather than for the life of the book. That seemed extremely high when most other commercial copyrights were available at $40 or so. However, it was the melody that made the song wonderful. The music was in public domain, meaning that it could be used without a fee. So why not write a new text that could be copyrighted by the Church? Jan Pinborough was asked to read the original German, and then write two verses that would teach about the divinity of the Savior. Darwin Wolford masterfully wove the melody into the accompaniment and supported the descant with the left hand.

ATTENTION-GETTER:

- *Sometimes I have a hard time falling asleep. It usually happens on the night before something important or exciting is going to happen. When do you have a hard time falling asleep? [The night before birthdays or before the first day of school, vacations, Christmas Eve, etc.]*

- *When you were very small and you couldn't get to sleep, your mother may have sung you a lullaby to help you relax and get sleepy. Listen as I sing this lullaby, and see if you can discover who is singing it. [Mary]*

LISTENING AND SINGING EXPERIENCES:

- *Mary called her son "my little one." Listen as I sing again to discover another loving name she called her baby. [My child so dear]*

Point out that the words of the last line are exactly like the words of the first line. Sing the last "Lullaby, lullaby" to the end once more and invite the children to sing it with you each time you come to that part in the song.

- *What did Mary say had just begun? [Thy precious life]*
- *Who watches through the night? [Joseph]*
- *What does the star reflect? [Thy light]*

Invite the children to sing the entire lullaby with you, listening to find a word that rhymes with dear [near] and night [light].

- *Mary loved her newborn infant king. She may have sung him to sleep with a lullaby very much like this one. Let's sing it again in our very sweetest voices.*

Bear your testimony that this sweet baby grew up to be the Savior of the world.

WHO IS THE CHILD?

MESSAGE: The baby Jesus is the Son of God.

ATTENTION-GETTER:

• *Most of the people who were in Bethlehem on that special night when Jesus was born did not know what was taking place. If they had been aware of baby Jesus' birth, they might have asked some questions. Listen for the last question as I sing the first verse of this song.*

LISTENING AND SINGING EXPERIENCES:

Each time you sing the first verse, ask one of the following questions. Have the children listen for the answer and then sing that line with you.

Verse One:

• *What question did you hear last? [Who is this little stranger?]*

Demonstrate with pitch leading how the melody line of the last phrase goes right down the scale. Have the children sing that phrase with you each time you come to it in the song.

• *Who is watching nearby? [Mary and Joseph]*

• *Where is the child? [Lying asleep in the manger]*

• *What is the first question? [Who is the child in the swaddling clothes, lying asleep in the manger?]*

Invite the children to sing verse one and add the accompaniment.

Verse Two:

• *We have learned verse one very well, but we haven't answered the question, "Who is this little stranger?" As I sing, listen for the answer. [The Son of God]*

• *What is Jesus doing? [Jesus is quietly sleeping.]*

• *Who have come to worship him? [Shepherds]*

• *What are the angels doing? [Their watch are keeping]*

Have the children sing verse two and then the entire song. Bear testimony that Jesus is truly the Son of God, born that sacred night so long ago.

ENRICHMENT IDEAS:

1. Use flannel board pictures of the Nativity. Build the scene as you sing the song. (See Primary Visual Aids Cutouts—Set 8: Christmas Figures 33248.)

2. Have the children wear costumes or hold pictures and stand in a tableau, forming a life-size Nativity scene.

3. Call attention to the repetition of notes beginning phrases 1, 2, and 3 by pitch leading this song.

4. Bring a doll wrapped in swaddling clothes. Explain that swaddling clothes are narrow strips of material that bind the child and make him feel secure. Also explain that a manger is a trough or open box in which feed for animals is placed.

5. Invite children to play the melody on bells or conduit pipe chimes.

SLEEP, LITTLE JESUS

MESSAGE: I can sing a lullaby about the birth of Jesus.

ENRICHMENT IDEAS:

1. There are three one-syllable words in each verse that are sung on two tones. Challenge the children to find them. [V.1, "love," "bright," "star"; V.2, "hosts," "peace," "men"]

2. Pitch lead to point out the octave climb up the scale from "come" to "bright" on the third line of verse one.

3. Add dynamics, especially to the message of the angels on the second verse: "Alleluia, Peace to all men, Alleluia."

4. Small children might enjoy pretending to rock a baby as they sing.

5. Place cutouts on the flannel board as you sing the first verse. (See Primary Visual Aids Cutouts—Set 8: Christmas Figures 33248.) Or use Nativity picture (62116 or 62495).

6. Divide the children into five groups. Have each group sing and hold a note on the last "Alleluia." Practice on the syllable "ah" first.

MATERIALS:

Newspaper

ATTENTION-GETTER:

Display the newspaper.

- *When something very important happens in the world, how does the news get to us? [Newspaper, radio, or television]*

- *In the days when Jesus was born, there were no televisions or newspapers or radios. Listen as I sing to find out who told the good news of Jesus' birth.* Sing the first verse to the children.

LISTENING AND SINGING EXPERIENCES:

Sing the song several times, encouraging the children to listen by using questions and statements similar to those listed below. As children discover answers, invite them to sing that part of the song with you.

Verse One:

- *Who is telling the news of His birth? [The angels]*

- *As I sing the song again, see if you can discover who is Lord of the earth. [Jesus]*

- *What will the shepherds bring? [Love]*

- *What is shining in the heaven above? [A star]*

- *As we sing the entire song together, listen for two prayer language words. [Thy and Thee]* Explain that these are respectful words meaning "your" and "you."

- *As we sing the song again, listen for the word that we sing on the highest note. [Bright] The star was so high in the sky and so glorious that the composer put that word on the highest note.*

- *As we sing this verse again, let's sit up straight and tall so that we can sing this beautiful melody just like the angels.*

Verse Two:

- *As I sing the second verse for you, listen to discover who the earth has waited for. [Her Savior and King]*

- *As I sing the song again listen carefully to find out another name for angels. [Heavenly hosts]*

- *What great message do the heavenly hosts sing? [Alleluia, Peace to all men, Alleluia]*

- *"Alleluia" is an expression of joyful praise and thanksgiving.*

Pitch lead to point out the ascending notes of the second ending.

- *It was a glorious time when little Jesus was born. You and I might have been among the heavenly hosts that sang alleluia on that special night.*

OH, HUSH THEE, MY BABY

MESSAGE: I feel a parent's love as I sing a lullaby to my baby about the birth of Jesus.

ATTENTION-GETTER:

In advance, arrange for a father or mother with a new baby or a child with a doll to come to Primary and sing this lullaby to the children.

LISTENING AND SINGING EXPERIENCES:

Thank your guest for singing the lullaby.

- *What is a lullaby, children?* [A gentle, loving, reassuring song to quiet a baby]

- *"Lullaby" is a fun word to sing in this song, because it has an interesting rhythm. Please tap the rhythm with me.* Demonstrate long, short, long pattern:

- *Listen as I sing the chorus to discover how many times we sing "Lullaby."* [Four]

- *Tap the rhythm to the chorus with me as I sing it.* Repeat until the children seem comfortable with the rhythm.

- *Let's sing the chorus together.* Have the children join you in singing the chorus.

- *Listen as I sing the verse. Try to find an ending word that rhymes with sea.* [Thee] *"Thee" is one of our prayer language words. It means "you."*

- *Now listen to find out where Jesus was born.* Sing the entire verse. *[In a far country, way over the sea] Let's sing that line together.*

- *Now listen to find a word that rhymes with "tell."* [Dwell] Explain that "to dwell" means "to live."

- *Let's start from "Oh, hush thee, my baby" and sing the song all the way to the end, tapping the rhythm as we go.*

When the children are comfortable with the song, then add the accompaniment and encourage the children to sing this beautiful lullaby in their sweetest voices.

In subsequent weeks, teach the children the other verses, using same method.

ENRICHMENT IDEAS:

1. Teach the older children the harmony line or the ostinato as printed on the music.

2. Invite a child or guest to play the harmony line on a flute or stringed instrument.

3. Develop a tableau portraying the Christmas scene. Have the children wear simple costumes.

4. Use Nativity picture (62495 or 62116).

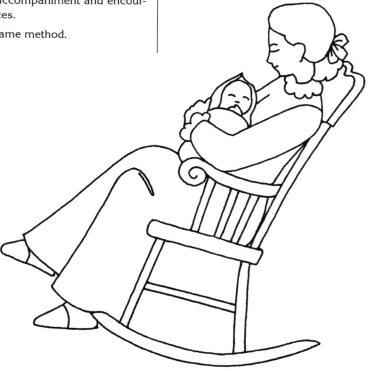

PICTURE A CHRISTMAS

MESSAGE: As you picture Christmas in your mind, think of the birth of baby Jesus and his life and words so dear.

ENRICHMENT IDEAS:

1. Show the children a hold sign ⌒ and challenge them to find one in this song. Overemphasize the fermata over "Remember him" so that the children can find it. Point out that holding this word a little longer helps us remember how important it is to remember Jesus. It also gives us a few extra seconds to remember him as we sing.

2. Children could dress in costumes or hold Nativity pictures.

3. Make a large picture frame and place a flannel board behind it. As you sing, place pictures on the flannel board to make a nativity scene—or use a wooden nativity set. (See Primary Visual Aids Cutouts—Set 8: Christmas Figures 33248.)

4. Invite each class to stand and sing one of the phrases.

♪ *About the Song*

In 1977, Pat Graham, the composer, was asked to write the Christmas program for her ward. In order to make it personal, she asked several people to share their own true Christmas experiences—a picture of Christmas that they treasured in their memory. While each story was told, a scene was posed in a wood panel frame with an oval cutout. A song relating to each story was selected, and Pat wrote "Picture a Christmas" to tie it all together. Later, the words were revised to focus on the Savior's birth.

ATTENTION-GETTER:

- *What do you see in your mind when you think of Christmas? A brightly decorated tree? Candy and tasty foods? Greeting cards and pretty packages? Family celebrations?*

- *There are many wonderful ways to picture Christmas, but the true picture of Christmas is the birth of Jesus.*

LISTENING AND SINGING EXPERIENCES:

Sing the song several times, encouraging the children to listen by using questions and statements similar to those listed below. As children discover answers, invite them to sing that part of the song with you and add that phrase to phrases already learned.

Chorus:

- *Listen as I sing to hear what we should do as we picture Christmas this year. [Sing praise to him, remember him].*

- *This time as I sing, listen for the answer to this question: When we picture the little baby Jesus, what should we think of? [His life and words so dear]*

Sing this phrase again and invite the children to join you and to continue to the end of the song.

Verse One:

Divide the children into two groups. Ask one side to discover *"What can you hear?"* [The angels near] and the other group to listen for *"What can you see?"* [The star so bright] as you sing the song again.

- *As I sing the song once more, listen for two words that describe the kind of night it was. [Sacred and silent]*

- *And now listen and picture where the stable was. [In Judea]*

Tap the rhythm to "Picture a" ♫♫ and challenge the children to count the number of times they hear this triplet as they sing the entire song with you, with the accompaniment. *[Four]* You might ask them to find the words in one triplet that are unlike the others. [*Think of his*]

- *This year as you celebrate this holiday season, remember to picture Jesus and the wonderful Christmas story. As you picture Jesus, you will want to be more like him. That is the greatest gift that you could give to him.*

Verse Two:

- *What are two words that describe Joseph? [Kind and gentle]*

- *What word describes the mother Mary? [Fair]*

- *What can you see so reverently? [The shepherds kneeling there]*

HAVE A VERY MERRY CHRISTMAS!

MESSAGE: There are many activities we can participate in to help us have a very Merry Christmas.

MATERIALS:

A box wrapped in Christmas paper and ribbon with a removable lid. Inside the box put pictures or items depicting the items named in each verse.

Verse One: A picture of a happy family at Christmas, a picture of a child or a group singing carols, and someone doing something kind for a neighbor

Verse Two: A bell, a tree ornament, a Christmas stocking, and a twig of holly

Verse Three: A picture of a family gathering, a picture of the baby Jesus, a heart with a bow around it

ENRICHMENT IDEAS:

1. Have the children pitch lead this song with their bodies—stand on tiptoe for the highest notes, squat for the lowest notes, etc.

2. Divide the children into four groups. Invite each group to sing one of the four phrases in this song. Then trade parts.

3. Invite everyone wearing red or green to stand and sing.

ATTENTION-GETTER:

- *Christmas is a merry time! I know three ways to make sure that you have a very, merry Christmas. Listen as I sing to find the three ways.* Sing the song for the children. As you sing, pull the pictures for verse one out of the Christmas package and show them to the children.

LISTENING AND SINGING EXPERIENCES:

Verse One:

- *What three things can we do to have a very, merry Christmas? [Scatter gladness everywhere, sing the carols of the Christ child, let your neighbor know you care.]* Sing the verse until the children get all answers.

- *Find the word over which a fermata ⌒ has been placed. [Christ child]* The hold sign is placed over "Christ child" to emphasize the most important words in this Christmas song.

Sing the verse again, playing "stop and go." Point to yourself as you begin singing. Then point to the children when you want them to sing. Trade back and forth several times.

Verse Two:

Pass out the items from your Christmas package in random order to four children. Challenge them to stand in order as they listen for the four things we can do to have an exciting Christmas. *[Ring a bell, trim a tree, stuff a stocking for a loved one, hang the holly joyously]*

Sing the verse again with the children to check the order of the items.

Verse Three:

Proceed as on verse two. This time, give the pictures and items to three children and have them stand in the correct order as you ask them to listen for the three things we can do to help us have a happy family Christmas. *[Gather all your loved ones near, talk about the baby Jesus, wrap your hearts in love this year]*

THE NATIVITY SONG

MESSAGE: Christmas is a time to tell the true story of Jesus' birth—when, as a baby, Christ came to earth.

ENRICHMENT IDEAS:

1. Post flannel board pictures in random order. Invite the children to put them in the correct order as they sing. (See Primary Visual Aids Cutouts—Set 8: Christmas figures 33248.)

2. Alternate the singing of verses by different groups as you indicate: teachers, boys, girls, left, right.

   (Repeat)

3. Let a few children arrange a wooden Nativity scene as everyone sings the song.

4. Challenge the children to find the rhyming words. These could be printed on stars.

MATERIALS:

Enlarge pictures to posterboard size. Make each figure out of one sheet of brightly colored posterboard. For the face and arms, use a flesh-colored file folder. Use black marker for simple outlining—no coloring is necessary.

ATTENTION-GETTER:

As you sing the song, have several children hold the pictures and come forward to form a live Nativity scene. You may wish to practice ahead of time to help the children know where to stand.

After introducing the song, invite the children to be seated.

LISTENING AND SINGING EXPERIENCES:

Teach each verse, referring to the pictures and directing the children's listening by asking a question with each repetition.

- *What words describe this season? [Beloved of the year]*

Sing this phrase once more for the children and then have them join you. Encourage them to sing the whole phrase in one breath.

- *What will soon be here? [Christmas time]*

Sing this phrase again, asking the children to listen for two words that rhyme. *[Rhyme and time]* Have them sing it with you and add it to the first phrase.

- *What true story will we tell? [Of Jesus' birth, when, as a baby, He came to the earth]*

Sing the phrase again and then have the children sing it with you.

Invite the children to sing all of verse one and ask them to find the word that is sung on the highest tone. *[Came]*

Teach the other verses in a similar way, asking a question for each phrase.

CHRISTMAS BELLS

MESSAGE: Christmas bells proclaim the birth of Jesus in Bethlehem.

ATTENTION-GETTER:

Invite a guest to play the melody line on tone bells. Join with him, singing the melody as he plays it a second time.

LISTENING AND SINGING EXPERIENCES:

- *These beautiful Christmas bells have a happy message for you. What do they say to you? [That Jesus is born in Bethlehem]* Sing the song again to the children.

- *Did I sing the word "Bethlehem" more than once? Listen to check.* Sing the song once more. *[Yes, two times]*

Divide the children into two singing groups. Teach group one to sing, "Christmas bells are ringing. Hear what they say to you." Teach group two the answer, "Jesus is born in Bethlehem, in Bethlehem." After several times, alternate the groups.

Teach the optional descant to a group of older children. Combine the two parts only after the children have thoroughly learned each part. You might ask someone to play the descant on tone bells, a flute, or a violin.

The rhythm for both parts must be accurate to blend the two melodic harmonies. Note the syncopation when the two voices are sung together.

ENRICHMENT IDEAS:

1. Have the children sing softly to achieve the delicate yet joyous quality of the bells.

2. Have the children listen for the bell-like quality of the accompaniment. The accompaniment could be played an octave higher.

3. Divide into two groups. Have one group sing the first phrase, the other group the second phrase. All sing phrase three together. Trade parts.

4. Cut two bells as illustrated out of posterboard. Use a brad or ribbon to hook one on top of the other. Choose a child who is singing especially well to hold and turn the bells.

JESUS ONCE WAS A LITTLE CHILD

MESSAGE: Jesus was once a little child like me. I will try to be like him.

ENRICHMENT IDEAS:

1. Display the pictures of Jesus as a child (62124, 62500). In your own words briefly tell the scripture story of Jesus as a child in the temple. (See Luke 2:41-52.) End by quoting, "And the child waxed strong in spirit, filled with wisdom and the grace of God was upon him" (Luke 2:40).

2. Teachers and older children might enjoy singing the harmony (alto part).

3. Younger children will enjoy either swaying or gently finger tapping to the rhythm as they sing.

MATERIALS:

Pictures: Jesus as a child (62124, 62500)

ATTENTION-GETTER:

In advance, ask a child to learn the words of the first verse as a poem. Ask another child to learn the words of the second verse. Have the children recite the words, and you sing the chorus after each verse.

LISTENING AND SINGING EXPERIENCES:

Chorus:

Sing the chorus several times, encouraging the children to listen and to answer a question with each repetition.

· *How many times did I sing the word "try"? [Four]*

· *Who should we try to be like? [Him—Jesus]*

· *What word is sung on the highest note? [Try]*

· *We sing the word "try" on the highest note to emphasize how important it is for you and me to "try" to be like Jesus.*

Invite the children to sing the chorus with you.

Verse One:

· *How was Jesus once like you and me? [He was once a little child.]*

· *What three words describe Jesus and show us how a little child should be? [Pure and meek and mild]* Sing as many times as necessary to obtain the answers.

Sing the entire verse and chorus with the children.

Define the words "pure" (true and fair), "meek" (humble and modest), and "mild" (gentle and patient).

These words describe how Jesus was when he was a child. We should always try to be like him. Sing the song again.

Verse Two:

· *What did he always speak? [The truth]*

· *The song tells us that Jesus never got angry when the game went wrong. What word in the song means "angry"? [Vexed]*

· *What did he play? [Pleasant games of youth]*

I THINK WHEN I READ THAT SWEET STORY

MESSAGE: When I read in the scriptures how Jesus loved being with the children, I wish I had been with him then.

MATERIALS:

Pictures: Christ with the children in Jerusalem (62467) and with the Nephite children (62541 or 62542)

Standard works

ATTENTION-GETTER:

Show the pictures.

- *When Jesus lived on the earth in Palestine and when he came to America after his resurrection, he loved being with children.*
- *Look closely at these pictures and see how happy the children were to be with Jesus. I have read this sweet story of old in the scriptures, and I know a song that describes just how we might feel about living when Jesus lived.*

LISTENING AND SINGING EXPERIENCES:

Sing the song several times, encouraging the children to listen by using questions and statements similar to those listed below. As children discover answers, invite them to sing that part of the song with you.

Verse One:

- *As I sing, listen for where I should like to have been. [With him then]*
- *The song compares little children to a precious little animal. What animal is it? [A lamb]*
- *Another name for Jesus is the "Good Shepherd." Shepherds care for and love their lambs. Jesus loves and cares for little children.*
- *Who did Jesus live among? [Men (meaning all people)]*
- *How does this song describe the scripture story about Jesus? [That sweet story of old]*

Show the standard works. *This is where we can read that beautiful story of old.*

Invite the children to sing verse one as you add the accompaniment.

Verse Two:

- *Listen as I sing. Tell me three things that I wish. Sing the entire verse, then sing again to check all three answers. [That his hands had been placed on my head, that his arms had been thrown around me, that I might have seen his kind look]*
- *What are the words that Jesus said? ["Let the little ones come unto me."]*

Read Luke 18:16: "*. . .Suffer (let) little children to come unto me, and forbid them not: for of such is the kingdom of God.*" Sing the second verse again.

Conclude by bearing your testimony that you know Jesus loves each of his children, just as he did the children of his day.

ENRICHMENT IDEAS:

1. With young children, you may want to use the following actions:

Verse One:

I think—point to head.

Story of old—hands pretend to hold book.

Jesus was here among men—out-stretched hands.

Called little children—motion to come.

I should like to—fold arms.

Verse Two:

hands—hands on head.

Arms—wrap arms around shoulders.

I might have seen—point to eyes.

Let the little ones come—motion to come.

Unto me—point to yourself.

2. Share with the children the beautiful account of Jesus blessing the Nephite children: 3 Ne: 17:21-24.

3. Make a book with relevant pictures of this sweet story of old. Use rings so the pages turn.

TELL ME THE STORIES OF JESUS

MESSAGE: I love to hear the stories of Jesus!

ENRICHMENT IDEAS:

1. Children could relate stories of Jesus and show appropriate pictures: Mark 10:13-16—(Christ and the Children 62467); Luke 8:22-27—(Stilling the storm 62139).

2. Teach the older children the two-part harmony.

3. Divide the children into two groups. Have each group sing two measures of each line as you indicate, trade parts, and repeat.

4. Challenge the children to sing each line in one breath.

ATTENTION-GETTER:

- *I love to hear all kinds of stories. Listen as I sing to discover what stories I love to hear the very most.*

LISTENING AND SINGING EXPERIENCES:

Direct the children's listening by asking questions like the following with each repetition.

Verse One:

- *What do I love to hear? [The stories of Jesus]*

Sing the last phrase again, asking what word is sung on the highest note. [*Stories*] Invite the children to sing the last phrase with you.

Show the children a hold sign ⌢. *When this sign is placed over a note in the music, the singers can hold that note a little longer. See if you can find the fermata as we sing the song again.* Overemphasize the word "Je-sus" on the last line.

- *If Jesus were here, what two stories would I ask him to tell me? [Scenes by the wayside, tales of the sea]*

Explain that wayside means "off the main road" or "countryside." "Tales" are stories.

- *Do you know of a scene in the scriptures when Jesus was in the countryside? Or do you know a story about Jesus at the sea?*

Be prepared to briefly share a story of Jesus teaching or healing in the countryside, for example, the Sermon on the Mount (Matt. 5:1-2), and of calming the seas (Matt. 8:23-27), or calling the fishermen (Luke 5:4-11).

Invite the children to sing verse one with you.

Verse Two:

- *What is the word that means Jesus' face had a special glow? [Lovelight]*
- *What words describe Jesus' words and deeds? [Words full of kindness, deeds full of grace acts of love]*
- *What shall I imagine? [His blessings resting on me]*
- *What do I want to hear first? [How the children stood round his knee]*

Verse Three:

- *What did Jesus do to the wind? [Hushed the wind]*
- *What did Jesus do to the billows? [Chided (scolded)]*
- *What two words describe the Master? [Ready and kind]*
- *Where was the boat tossing? [In a tempest on Galilee]*
- *What do I want to be told in accents of wonder? [How rolled the sea]* Explain that accents of wonder means "words of amazement."

LITTLE LAMBS SO WHITE AND FAIR

MESSAGE: We should try to be as obedient to Heavenly Father as the little lambs who
follow and obey their shepherd.

MATERIALS:

Flannel board figures: a shepherd holding a lamp, several lambs, a green pasture, a picture
of the Good Shepherd

ATTENTION-GETTER:

- *What is a shepherd?*
- *A shepherd guides his sheep so they won't get lost. Each little lamb is very important to him. The sheep know the sound of the shepherd's voice, and they follow him wherever he leads them.*
- *Listen as I sing to discover where this shepherd is leading his little lambs.* As you sing, post the flannel board figures.

LISTENING AND SINGING EXPERIENCES:

Direct the children's listening by asking questions and then inviting them to sing the answers
with you.

Verse One:

- *Where does the shepherd lead the lambs' tender feet?* [Into pastures green and sweet]
- *What words tell us that he is always watching, never turning away?* [Constant care]
- *What two words describe the little lambs?* [White and fair]
- *We've heard the melody of that phrase before. What other phrase has that same melody?* [Now he leads their tender feet.]

Invite the children to sing this verse with you, adding accompaniment.

Verse Two:

- *What three things do the little lambs do?* [Listen, obey, follow]
- *Where are they following?* [Where he leads the way]
- *What do we ask Heavenly Father?* [May we be thus obedient unto Thee.]
- *There is one prayer language word in that phrase. What is it?* [Thee]

Hold up a picture of a shepherd.

- *Jesus is our shepherd. He knows us and cares for us. If we follow him as the lambs follow their shepherd, we can return to Heavenly Father.*

ENRICHMENT IDEAS:

1. *Sometimes a shepherd calls his sheep, sometimes he whistles, and sometimes he uses a little instrument that sounds like this. Using a recorder or flute-like instrument, play the melody of the song.*

2. Invite the children to softly toe tap the rhythm of this flowing song with their "tender feet."

JESUS IS OUR LOVING FRIEND

MESSAGE: Jesus is our loving friend and is always near to guide us.

ENRICHMENT IDEAS:

1. Make a melody picture by putting a small heart on each tone of the melody, pointing out the two repeated descending scales. Point to the hearts while the children sing; then let a child point to them a second time through.

♡ Last Phrases

♡ First Phrases

2. Divide the children into four groups. Teach each group a phrase of the song. Have each group sing their phrase in sequence.

MATERIALS:

A sack or box with the words "Jesus is our loving friend because . . ." printed on the outside.

Three wordstrips (for younger children, use pictures): *He is always near. He will guide us when we pray. Every child is dear.*

ATTENTION-GETTER:

Have three children come to the front and choose a wordstrip from the sack or box. Then say, *"Jesus is our loving friend because. . ."* and invite one child to read his wordstrip. Repeat the statement again before each wordstrip is read. Have the children hold the wordstrips for the other children to see. They may be out of order.

LISTENING AND SINGING EXPERIENCES:

Verse One:

• *Listen as I sing to see if these statements are in the right order.*

Invite a child to arrange the wordstrips in the right order.

Conduct pitch levels, pointing out that the melody of the first and second lines is the same—with the exception of the last note.

Sing the first verse several times, referring to the wordstrips. Then, as the children become more confident, let them remove the wordstrips one at a time.

Verse Two:

• *What do we do reverently and sweetly? [Our voices raise]*

• *Because Jesus is our loving friend, what do we do? [Sing his praise]*

• *When Jesus was on earth, he loved the children very much. The scriptures say, "And he took them up in his arms, put his hands upon them, and blessed them" (Mark 10:16).*

• *Jesus loves each one of us, just as he loved the children of his day. He can be near to us as we pray.*

JESUS LOVED THE LITTLE CHILDREN

MESSAGE: Jesus loved the little children. He blessed, helped, and taught them.

MATERIALS:

Picture: Verse One, (Christ and the Children 62467)

Verse Two, (Jesus Healing the Nephites 62541)

ATTENTION-GETTER:

Introduce the song by singing it for the children and showing the pictures as you sing.

LISTENING AND SINGING EXPERIENCES:

Verse One:

Discuss the love that is evident in the picture.

• *Jesus loved the little children, little ones like all of you.*

Sing the first line, then pitch lead and invite the children to sing it back to you. Repeat until learned.

Sing the phrase "He would bless and help them." Invite the children to sing it back to you until learned.

Sing the last phrase, "and take them on his knee." Sing this phrase with the children.

• *We can see from this picture and this song how much Jesus loved the little children. It would have been wonderful to live back then and have him look in your face with such love. Jesus loves you with that same love. He loves you just as much as he loved the children of his day.*

Sing the song again with the children.

Verse Two:

• *Jesus taught the children many lovely things—things we all should do. Listen to discover four things that Jesus taught the children. [To love and help each other and be honest, kind, and true] Sing again to get all the answers.*

• *We can feel close to Jesus when we try to be honest, kind, and true.*

Invite the children to sing verse two.

ENRICHMENT IDEAS:

1. Show the picture (Jesus Healing the Nephites 62541) and read 3 Nephi 17:21–24.

2. Consider teaching verse two with word cards: LOVE, HELP, HONEST, KIND, TRUE.

3. For review, invite the children to sing only the ending word, of each phrase ("children," "me," "them," "knee") as you and the teachers sing the rest. Trade parts.

JESUS WANTS ME FOR A SUNBEAM

MESSAGE: Jesus wants me to be his sunbeam to shine for him and to please him wherever I am. I'll be a sunbeam for him.

ENRICHMENT IDEAS:

1. Using yellow posterboard, cut out a large circle to represent the sun. Attach a picture of Jesus to the front. Punch six holes with a paper punch and tie six ribbon streamers onto the sun. Let one taller child hold the sun and six others hold the streamers, or sunbeams, as you sing.

2. The older children will enjoy this song that is traditionally for the younger children by adding a simple ostinato.

A   sun-beam a . . .

ATTENTION-GETTER:

- *Have you ever been outside on a dark, cloudy day, when all of a sudden the clouds part and a ray of sunshine peeks through? It feels so good as it warms your back, and it brightens everything around you. We can be like this sunbeam. When we try to please Jesus, we make others feel warm and good. When we spread his goodness and love, we are his sunbeams.*

- *Listen as I sing verse one and the chorus. Count how many times I sing the word "sunbeam." [Seven]*

LISTENING AND SINGING EXPERIENCES:

Chorus:

Teach the children "a sunbeam, a sunbeam" on the first part of the chorus; then sing the second phrase. Bring them in again on "a sunbeam, a sunbeam," and sing to the end.

- *Jesus wants me for a sunbeam, so what will I be? [A sunbeam for him]* Sing the chorus again to discover the answer.

Invite the children to sing the chorus with you.

Verse One:

- *Name three places where we can please Jesus. [At home, at school, at play] To please Jesus means to live as he has taught us and to love everyone.*

- *For whom does Jesus want us to shine? [For Jesus] Who do we shine for each day?*

Sing the first phrase, "Jesus wants me for a sunbeam," and ask the children what other words we sing on that same melody. *[In every way try to please him]*

Encourage the children to sing "sunbeam" very sweetly to avoid overemphasizing "beam." ("Sun" is the important syllable.) They could stand on "sun" and sit on "beam."

Remind the children that sunbeams are quiet.

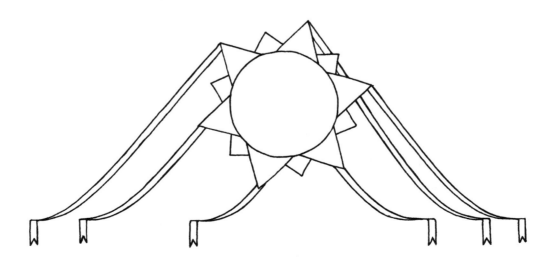

JESUS SAID LOVE EVERYONE

MESSAGE: Jesus said love everyone. When you are loving and kind, others will love you, too.

MATERIALS:

Picture: (Christ and the Children 62467)

ATTENTION-GETTER:

Show the picture Christ and the Children.

- *When Jesus lived on earth, he taught the children something very important. Listen to what he said.* Sing the song to the children.

LISTENING AND SINGING EXPERIENCES:

- *Who did Jesus say we should love? [Everyone]*
- *How did Jesus say we should treat everyone. [Kindly]* Sing the song again.
- *When your heart is filled with love, what will others do? [Love you]* Sing the song once again.

Have the children join in singing the entire song as you add the accompaniment.

ENRICHMENT IDEAS:

1. Prepare four individual cardboard or paper hearts. On each heart, put a picture representing each phrase of the song: Jesus with the children, children being kind to one another, a heart with "love" written on it, happy children.

   Arrange the hearts out of sequence and invite four children to put them in the correct order as you and the other children sing the song.

2. Challenge the children to show love and kindness to someone who needs a friend or who has been unkind to them. Refer to Matthew 5:44.

3. Have children suggest ways they can love and show kindness to others.

4. Sing related songs, such as "Love One Another" (p. 136) or "Kindness Begins with Me" (p. 145).

5. Give each child a sealed envelope with a heart on it and a few candy hearts inside. Tell them that as soon as they help someone or do something kind for someone, they can open the envelope and eat the candy.

BEAUTIFUL SAVIOR

MESSAGE: Jesus shines brighter than all of God's creations. He brings love to all the world and comforts those who are sad. I will praise and honor him forever.

ENRICHMENT IDEAS:

1. Teach the descant to a small group of older children, or use it as an instrumental obbligato.

2. When singing the words ending in "er," teach the children to emphasize the first syllable and to soften the second: bright-er, fair-er, pur-er.

3. Challenge the children to watch you carefully as you lead the marked dynamics.

♪ *About the Song*

The words to this tune date back to the 12th century—proof of the appeal of the song.

MATERIALS:

Pictures: V.1, sun, moon, stars, and Jesus, (Primary Visual Aids Cutouts—Sets 1, 3 and 6) and a heart; V.2, meadows, woodlands, Jesus, and a sad person

Wordstrips: *Beautiful Savior, Lord of the nations, Son of God, Son of Man, glory, honor, praise, adoration*

ATTENTION-GETTER:

- *What did Heavenly Father put in the sky to shine and give us light during the day and night? [Sun, moon, stars] He loves us very much to give us the warm bright sun to light our days and the moon and stars to light the night.*
- *Listen as I sing to discover who shines brighter than all of these.*

LISTENING AND SINGING EXPERIENCES:

Verse One:

- *Who shines brighter and purer than the sun, moon, and stars? [Jesus]* Display the picture of Jesus. Point out that the melody pattern and rhythm are the same on "Jesus shines brighter" and "Jesus shines purer," but the second phrase starts one step lower. Sing these phrases.
- *What does Jesus bring to all the world? [His love]* Display the heart picture.
- *There is a descending scale in this phrase. Listen to discover the five words that we sing when the melody goes down the scale. [All the world his love]*
- *What three things are fair in heaven above? [Sunshine, moonlight, and all the stars]* Display the cutouts by the picture of Jesus in order. Invite the children to sing the phrases they know, then the entire verse, referring to the pictures.

Verse Two:

Post a picture with each question that follows.

- *What two creations are fair? [Meadows, woodlands]*
- *In what are the meadows and woodlands robed? [Flowers of blooming spring]*
- *Who is fairer and purer than the meadows and woodlands? [Jesus]*
- *A beautiful meadow or woodland can bring a very peaceful feeling to our spirits. Jesus can bring even more peace and happiness to our spirits than can nature. He can make our unhappy spirits sing. Listen for other words that mean "unhappy spirit." [Sorrowing spirit.]*

Verse Three:

- *In this verse, we reverently give Jesus four titles of honor. What are they? [Beautiful Savior, Lord of the nations, Son of God, Son of Man]* Display the wordstrips as the correct responses are given. Sing again to check the order.
- *Christ is known as the "Son of Man," because he is the Son of our Heavenly Father, a holy man.* (See Bruce R. McConkie, *Mormon Doctrine*.)
- *Name four feelings of reverence that we give our Savior. [Glory, honor, praise, adoration]* Display wordstrips as the correct responses are given. Sing again to check the *order.*
- *How long will we give praise and adoration to Jesus? [Evermore]*
- *Find the prayer language word meaning "yours." [Thee]*

Bear testimony of the importance of honoring and giving glory to the Savior by doing what he asks of us.

DID JESUS REALLY LIVE AGAIN?

MESSAGE: Because Jesus was resurrected, I will be resurrected and live forever, too.

MATERIALS:

Pictures: (Burial of Jesus 62180) and (Mary and the Resurrected Lord 62186)

ATTENTION-GETTER:

Show the picture Burial of Jesus.

- *After Jesus was crucified, his friends took his body into a tomb. Then they rolled a large stone in front of the opening. Jesus had told the disciples that he would rise from the dead on the third day after he died. Early on the third day, Mary came to the tomb and discovered that Jesus' body was not there. Then Christ appeared to Mary and called her by name.* Show picture Mary and the Resurrected Lord.

- *Imagine how Mary felt. She had seen Jesus crucified and had seen his body placed in the tomb three days earlier. Now he was alive and standing before her. Later, the Apostles and others were in a room discussing how this could be possible. The question must have been asked, "Does Jesus really live again?"*

- *As I sing this beautiful story for you, listen to discover the answer to this question.*

LISTENING AND SINGING EXPERIENCES:

Sing the song several times, directing the children's listening by asking questions similar to those listed below with each repetition.

Verse One:

- *Did Jesus really live again when the third day came?* [Yes]
- *What did he do when he wakened?* [He left the tomb.]
- *Whose name did he call?* [Mary's]

Invite the children to sing verse one.

Verse Two:

- *Who did Jesus come to?* [Those he loved]
- *What did the people touch?* [His feet] Explain that they touched his feet to feel the nail prints. They also touched the wounds in his hands and his side.
- *What two things did he truly eat?* [Fish and honeycomb]

Sing verse two with the children.

Verse Three:

- *Where were the nail prints?* [In his hands] Explain that they were also in his feet.
- *What kind of wound was in his side?* [A spear wound]
- *Because Jesus really lives again, what great blessing is mine?* [I shall also live again.]

Sing verse three with the children. Always teach all three verses of this song. The story is not complete if a verse is left out.

Bear your testimony that the resurrection of Jesus Christ was a glorious event. Because of the sacrifice and resurrection of Jesus Christ, we will all be resurrected and live forever.

ENRICHMENT IDEAS:

1. Invite part of the group to sing the lines that ask a question. Have the others join in on the answers, then everyone sing together on the last line: "Oh yes. . . ." Explain that as the children sing this line, they are bearing their testimony of the resurrection of Jesus Christ.

2. Show and pass around some honeycomb for the children to see and taste. (Available at health food stores.) Explain that Jesus ate fish and honeycomb after his resurrection to show the disciples that he had a body of flesh and bones. Read Luke 24:42–43.

3. In a book form, make a "sing-a-story" using one picture for each phrase:

Verse One: (The Resurrected Jesus Christ 62187), (Mary and the Resurrected Lord 62186).

Verse Two: Jesus appearing to the Apostles (62494), fish and honeycomb (draw).

Verse Three: (Jesus Shows His Wounds 62503), (The Second Coming 62562).

♪ *About the Song*

The *Children's Songbook* committee received the following letter from Diane Cahoon which said in part:

"Did Jesus Really Live Again?" was truly a blessing to our family after the passing of my grandmother. My three-year-old daughter was very troubled by the death and could not be comforted. She would plead every night with her Father in Heaven that He would bring her grandma back to her. It broke my heart to see her that way.

"Finally, one day as we talked about the Savior together, she and I sang Sister Gabbott's beautiful song and the Spirit touched her heart. She truly received a testimony of the resurrection when she was barely four. Never again has she been troubled by death. Now her prayers contain a request that Heavenly Father will watch over Grandma until she can see her again."

HE DIED THAT WE MIGHT LIVE AGAIN

MESSAGE: We rejoice because Jesus gave his life that we might live again.

ENRICHMENT IDEAS:

1. Divide the children into four groups. Have the groups hold the D, F, A, and C notes on the words "rejoice, rejoice," forming a chord.

2. Introduce the song another week by showing a pretty package. Discuss the difference between a gift we get for our birthday and the gift Jesus gave. Sing the song, asking what Jesus' gift was.

3. Choose one or two key words from each phrase. Write them on the chalkboard in order. With each repetition, have a child erase one or two.

4. Challenge the children to find four names in this song for our Heavenly Father's Son. *[Lord Jesus, Redeemer, Savior, King]*

5. Teach the children how to pitch lead the melody of "rejoice, rejoice" with their hands and then with their bodies (squatting to standing). You could also play that part on tone bells.

MATERIALS:

Pictures: (The Crucifixion 62505) and (Mary and the Resurrected Lord 62186)

Scriptures

ATTENTION-GETTER:

Have the children listen to the following true story.

• *On January 20, 1982, an airplane crashed into a bridge in Washington, D.C., and then plunged into the icy Potomac River. Many people were killed, but six people hung onto the plane's tail while a helicopter threw them a life-preserver ring. The water was icy cold, and it was hard to hang onto the plane's tail. These people were afraid they might die before their turn came to grab the life preserver and be carried to safety. But every time the rescuers lowered the life preserver to one man, he passed it on to someone else so that they could be rescued. He did this until everyone around him had been rescued, and then he could not hold on any longer. When the helicopter came back to get him, he had slipped under the water. He died before anyone could save him. (Adapted from "The Man in the Water," Time, 25 Jan. 1982, p. 86.)*

• *Why do you think he kept passing the life preserver?* Express your feelings about the courage and love it would take to be able to give your life for others as this man did.

• *There is someone who has given his life for you. Listen to see who this is.* Sing the song for the children.

• *Who died for us? [Jesus]*

LISTENING AND SINGING EXPERIENCES:

• *We are so thankful for his great love that we sing a word of great gladness. Listen as I sing again to find what is it? [Rejoice]*

• *Notice that the ascending melody on the words "rejoice, rejoice" helps us express our gladness.* Pitch lead the ascending notes. Repeat for emphasis.

• *We rejoice and sing, sing, sing.* Pitch lead the entire phrase as the children join you. Have the children sing this part with each repetition.

• *Why did Jesus die for us? [That we might live again]* Explain that this means we will live again after we die.

• *What is another name for Lord Jesus? [Our Redeemer]* "Redeemer" is another name for the Savior.

• *Where did he die? [On Calvary's lonely hill]* Show the picture The Crucifixion.

• *Who did he give his life for? [Me and you]*

• *What happened on that Easter morn? [He rose from the grave.]* Show the picture Mary and the Resurrected Lord.

• *What are two other names for Christ? [Our Savior and our King]*

• *For whom did he show his love? [All mankind]*

Read the scripture John 15:13, "Greater love hath no man than this, that a man lay down his life for his friends."

• *Jesus loved all of us so much that he was willing to die for us. He knew it was worth all his suffering to make it possible for us to be resurrected and live forever. I am so grateful that our Savior was willing to do this for me and you.*

HOSANNA

MESSAGE: Hosanna! Let our voices ring with praises to our Heavenly King.

MATERIALS:

Word cards: HOSANNA, RING, KING, SING, BRING

ATTENTION-GETTER:

- *Hosanna! Will you say that word with me? [Hosanna]*
- *Hosanna is a joyous expression of praise.* Display the "hosanna" word card. *Can you think of a hymn where we sing the word hosanna? ["The Spirit of God" (*Hymns, *no. 2)]*
- *Today we are going to learn a song called "Hosanna." As I sing, count the number of times I sing the word "hosanna."*

LISTENING AND SINGING EXPERIENCES:

- *How many times did I sing hosanna? [Three]*

Sing just the word "hosanna" and ask the children to echo it back to you. Then sing the entire song, inviting the children to sing "hosanna" as you indicate.

Challenge the children to find the four rhyming "-ing" words. *[RING, KING, SING, BRING]* Display the word cards as the children give responses. Then sing to check the order, bringing the children in on the hosannas.

- *Jesus is called our "Heavenly King." Listen for a word near the end of the song that describes this King. [Triumphant]* Explain that "All hail, triumphant King" is another expression of praise.

Help the children sing in a rejoicing, majestic manner as you refer to the posted word cards.

Let the children sing the echo. Trade parts with the children singing the melody and you singing the echo.

ENRICHMENT IDEAS:

1. Invite an older child to read D&C 19:37. See if the children can guess what song you are going to sing next from a clue given in this scripture. *[Hosanna]*

2. Older children may enjoy singing the descant or playing it on chimes or bells. Younger children could play triangles as you indicate.

3. Ask the children other questions about the song: *To whom do our voices ring with praise? [To our heavenly King] To whom does every living creature sing? [To him who life did bring]*

4. Use the four "-ing" word cards for review.

5. Show the picture (Triumphal Entry 62173).

6. Invite two children to play "ding, dong, ding" on tone bells.

EASTER HOSANNA

MESSAGE: The prophecies were fulfilled, and Jesus Christ appeared to the Nephites as a resurrected being. The righteous people rejoiced and sang: "Hosanna! Blessed be the name of the Most High God!"

ENRICHMENT IDEAS:

1. Teach older children the three-part harmony on "Hosanna!" Tone bells could be used.

2. Invite an older child to read 3 Nephi 11:17. Emphasize how much the people must have loved Jesus to say these beautiful words and to fall down at his feet and worship him.

3. To introduce the second verse or as a testimony after teaching the first verse, read the account of Jesus appearing to the Nephites (3 Ne. 11:8–17).

4. Use key word or rhyming word cards for review.

MATERIALS:

Pictures: (The Crucifixion 62505), (Jesus Teaching in the Western Hemisphere 62380), (Jesus Shows His Wounds 62503)

ATTENTION-GETTER:

Show picture The Crucifixion.

- *When the Savior of the world was crucified, darkness, earthquakes, and destruction shook the earth. Jesus' body was placed in a tomb for three days. Then he arose from the dead as he promised he would. Jesus was alive again!*
- *Listen as I sing this Easter song to see who Jesus visited. [The Nephites]* Sing the song to the children.
- *To whom did Jesus reveal himself? [The Nephites in the promised land] That's right.* Show the picture Jesus Teaching in the Western Hemisphere.

LISTENING AND SINGING EXPERIENCES:

Chorus:

- *What words did the Nephites cry as they rejoiced? [Hosanna! Blessed be the name of the Most High God!]*

Sing the first repetition of that phrase. Invite the children to sing it as you pitch lead.

- *Notice as you sing the second half of the chorus that it is the same as the first half, except for one word. Which word is it? [High]* Sing the entire chorus.

Verse One:

- *As I sing the first phrase, find a word that means that the prophecies came to pass or happened. [Fulfilled]* Invite the children to sing this phrase.
- *As I sing the next phrase, see if the melody is the same or different. [Same]* Have the children sing this phrase and then add it to the first phrase.
- *Now find two words that describe how Jesus looked. [White-robed and glorified]* Point out the analogy of the descending scale: "As he came down from heaven. . . ."

Sing the melody of the first phrase and challenge the children to find the words that are sung on different notes. *[Received their Lord and cried]* Have the children join you on this phrase.

Bear testimony to the children that you know that Jesus Christ did appear to the Nephites after his crucifixion. Sing verse one and the chorus together.

Verse Two:

- *Jesus Christ appeared to the Nephites on the American continent. What is another name in this song for the American continent? [Promised Land]*
- *What did the righteous people see? [His wounds]* Show picture Jesus Shows His Wounds.
- *What did they come to understand? [That he (Jesus) was risen]*
- *What are three other names for Jesus Christ? [Savior, Lord, and King]*
- *The Nephites rejoiced. Now who else rejoices? [We rejoice.]*

Bear your testimony that you rejoice every time you read of Jesus appearing to the Nephites.

JESUS HAS RISEN

MESSAGE: As we sing praises to our friend Jesus this Easter, our hearts fill with joy because he has risen and lives again.

MATERIALS:

Pictures: (Burial of Jesus 62180) and (Mary and the Resurrected Lord 62186)
Bible

ATTENTION-GETTER:

- *Imagine that we are with the friends of Jesus after his death. I am sure we would feel very sad because our good friend Jesus had been crucified and placed in a tomb.* Show picture of the burial of Jesus.
- *I think we would cry with Mary and the disciples, and we wouldn't be able to understand how anyone could hurt Jesus. Our hearts would be heavy, and we would be longing to see him again.*
- *Imagine our great joy when one of his followers brought the happiest message the world has ever known. Listen as I sing that message.* Sing the song with conviction.

LISTENING AND SINGING EXPERIENCES:

Sing the song several times, encouraging the children to listen by asking questions about the message. Invite the children to sing each phrase with you as they learn it—and add that phrase to those they have already learned.

- *The most important message of the song is repeated three times. What is it? [Jesus has risen.]*

Explain that "Jesus has risen" means that Jesus died, arose from the dead, and lives again. Display the picture Mary and the Resurrected Lord.

- *This message is so important that the composer placed a fermata or hold sign above the word "risen" on one of the repetitions. Listen as I sing again, and tell me which repetition has the fermata. [Third]*

Point out that the melody on the last repetition of "Jesus has risen" rises, symbolizing the Resurrection. Then have the children sing the last four measures.

- *The song uses another beautiful name for Jesus. We sing it two times. What is it? [Savior Divine]* Sing the song again, inviting the children to sing the last four measures.
- *Savior divine is a very holy name for Jesus.* Pitch lead the last eight measures; then have the children sing that part with you.
- *When do we sing praises to Jesus? [This Easter time] To sing praises is to worship Jesus.* Sing this phrase again; then have the children join you and sing to the end.
- *Why does joy fill our hearts? [He lives again.]* Pitch lead this phrase as you sing; then have children add it to those learned.
- *Jesus is our Savior. What else do we call him in this song? [Our friend]*

Invite the children to sing the entire song with you.

Read Matthew 28:6–7 as a conclusion and bear your testimony about the reality of the Resurrection.

ENRICHMENT IDEAS:

1. Use chimes or bells with the introduction and with the descant on the last two measures.
2. Invite part of the group to sing the descant on the last two measures.
3. Divide the children into two groups. Alternate singing each two-measure phrase; then join together for the last four measures ("Jesus has risen, Savior divine!"). Trade parts.

♪ About the Song

The composer, Thelma J. Ryser, a former member of the Primary General Board says, "My desire in composing this Easter song was to impress the children that Jesus, though he lives in heaven, is our friend, loves us, and hears and answers our prayers."

TO THINK ABOUT JESUS

MESSAGE: Even though I am small, I can sit still and think of Jesus and all that he did for me.

ENRICHMENT IDEAS:

1. For older children, you might want to adapt the words "even though I am small" to "even though I've grown tall."

2. Point out to the children the identical sounds of the phrase endings (G G G F)—the exception being the last phrase (E E D C). Consider using tone bells for the phrase endings.

3. Make a melody picture for each of the six phrases. Challenge the children to put them in the correct order as you sing. These can be used to point out the similarities of the phrases.

4. Have the children listen for rhyming words.

5. Make a flip-chart with the suggested pictures. Or you might make a poster, copying the illustration of the child on p. 71 of the *Children's Songbook* and adding a "think" bubble above the child. Add smaller pictures on rings at the top of your poster and turn them to match each phrase in the song.

MATERIALS:

Pictures: A child sitting quietly thinking about Christ during the sacrament (Passing The Sacrament 62021), (The Crucifixion 62505), (Gethsemane 62175), (Jesus the Christ 62572), (Jesus with His Disciples 62494), (Christ and the Children 62467)

ATTENTION-GETTER:

Bring a child to the front and ask him to sit very tall in a chair without moving a muscle. Keep silent and time him for thirty seconds to see if he can keep perfectly still.

- *It is hard to sit perfectly still when you don't have something to think about. Listen as I sing, and tell me who we can think about as we sit very still. [Jesus]* Sing the song for the children.

LISTENING AND SINGING EXPERIENCES:

Direct the children's listening by asking questions as you sing.

Verse One:

- *How many times do we sing the words, "It shouldn't be hard"? [Three]* Invite the children to join you on those words each time you sing.

- *Listen as I sing the first phrase again.* Sing the first three measures.

- *Now listen to the next phrase and tell me if it has the same melody or if it is different. [Same, except for the first note]*

- *That melody is repeated one more time. Listen as I sing the whole song and find the other words that we sing on that melody. [It shouldn't be hard, even though I am small].*

- *The song mentions two things that we can think about as we think of Jesus. Listen to discover what they are. [His cross on the hill, all that he suffered and did for me]*

Show the pictures of the Crucifixion and Gethsemane.

- *Jesus suffered and paid for our sins—not only on the cross, but also in Gethsemane.*

Sing the phrase "And all that he suffered and did for me." Ask the children to find other words that we sing on the same melody. *[It shouldn't be hard to sit quietly.]* Observe the markings in this measure. (Slower, fermata.)

Invite the children to sing the song with you, adding the accompaniment.

- *When we think of Jesus it's . . .* (Sing the final measure: "not hard at all.")

Display a picture of Jesus and a picture of a child sitting quietly during the sacrament. Challenge the children to sit very still and think only of Jesus the next time the sacrament is passed.

Verse Two:

- *Jesus didn't walk miles on paved roads. Where did he walk? [In the dust]* Show picture of Jesus with disciples.

- *What did Jesus help the children to do? [To love and to trust]* Show picture of Jesus with the children.

- *What three things shouldn't it be hard to do? [Sit tall in my seat, listen politely, and quiet my feet]* Refer to picture of a reverent child.

THE SACRAMENT

MESSAGE: As I take the sacrament, I think of Jesus and remember that he gave his life for me.
I want to serve him thankfully.

MATERIALS:

Picture: (The Last Supper 62174)

Scriptures

ATTENTION-GETTER:

- *When someone you love lives far away from you, what kinds of things would you want to have to help you remember him or her? [Pictures, tapes, videos, journals]*

- *When Jesus died, he didn't leave pictures of himself for us. But he wanted us to remember him. Before he died, he gathered his Apostles around him and blessed and passed the bread and water. This was the first sacrament. The sacrament helps us think of Jesus and remember that he gave his life for us.*

- *Listen as I sing to discover what words Jesus said. [This do in remembrance of me.] Hold up picture The Last Supper as you sing.*

LISTENING AND SINGING EXPERIENCES:

Sing the song several times, each time asking the children to respond to statements or questions such as the following. After their responses, invite them to sing that phrase with you.

Verse One:

- *The words Jesus said were so important that we sing them more than once in this song. How many times do you hear Jesus' words "This do in remembrance of me"? [Two times]*

- *What happens the second time I sing the words "this do"? [There is a pause in the singing, but the accompaniment keeps going.]*

- *This pause gives us time to fill our minds with memories of Jesus. It is a short pause, but it is long enough to imagine Jesus giving his Apostles the sacrament* (show the picture The Last Supper) *or to imagine him caring for children, healing the sick, helping the needy, teaching the people, or remembering other good and kind things he did.*

- *In this song, we use a different name for Jesus. What is the name we sing? [Savior]* When the correct answer is given, sing that line again.

- *Which important word comes on the highest note? [Savior]* Encourage the children to sit tall so that when they sing the important word on a high note, they will sing it correctly.

- *As we take the sacrament, which do we partake of first—the water or the bread? [Bread] In this song we sing about the water first so that the word "bread" can rhyme with what word? [Said]*

- *Notice how the melody moves up to the important words "bread" and "water."* Invite the children to pitch lead as they sing.

Invite a child to read Luke 22:19. Bear your testimony that the sacrament is a great blessing to help us remember the Savior and his sacrifice for us. Explain that it is as important today as it was on the night when Jesus Christ first gave it to his Apostles.

Invite the children to sing the entire first verse with you.

Verse Two:

- *Who will I remember? [Him (Jesus)]*
- *How do we want to serve him? [Thankfully]*
- *What did Jesus give for me? [His life]*

ENRICHMENT IDEAS:

1. Display a chart of a musical slur and explain what it means.

As,   take,   said,   me

Tell the children that several words in this song are sung with two tones. Challenge them to raise their hands each time they hear a slur in verse one: *[As, take, said, me.]*

2. Explain that the Savior also gave the sacrament to the people on the American continent after he had been resurrected. Invite a child to read 3 Nephi 18:11.

3. Refer to the sacrament prayers in D&C 20:75–79. Point out that we eat the bread and drink the water in remembrance of Jesus Christ. Each time we take the sacrament, we promise again to keep his commandments.

4. Create a poster for review, using pictures: (Passing the Sacrament 62021), (The Crucifixion 62505), (Boy Being Baptized 62018), (Jesus Shows His Wounds 62503)

BEFORE I TAKE THE SACRAMENT

MESSAGE: Before I take the sacrament, I remember that Jesus came to earth and died for me. I think of the children who lived when he lived—and as I take the sacrament, I am reminded to try to be that kind of child.

ENRICHMENT IDEAS:

1. Discuss the importance of reverence during the sacrament.

2. Invite a child to post flannel board figures as the song is sung. V.1, Child sitting quietly in church; Jesus' crucifixion. V.2, Children in Jesus' day; Jesus walking. V.3, Sacrament water and bread; happy child.

MATERIALS:

Piece of bread

Sacrament cup filled with water

Pictures: (The Crucifixion 62505), (Christ and the Children 62467), (Passing the Sacrament 62021)

ATTENTION-GETTER:

Hold up a piece of broken bread and a sacrament cup filled with water.

• *I am holding a piece of bread and a cup of water. When these are blessed during the sacrament prayer by those having the authority, these two simple things represent something very important.*

Ask the children to listen very carefully for the answer as you invite an older child to read Matthew 26:26–28:

"And as they were eating, Jesus took bread, and blessed it, and brake it, and gave it to the disciples, and said, Take, eat; this is my body.

"And he took the cup, and gave thanks, and gave it to them, saying, Drink ye all of it;

"For this is my blood of the new testament, which is shed for many for the remission of sins."

• *What do the bread and water represent? [The body and blood of Jesus Christ]*

• *Each time we take the sacrament, we should think of what the bread and water represent.*

• *As I sing this song about the sacrament, listen for some other things we can think*

LISTENING AND SINGING EXPERIENCES:

Verse One:

• *How do we sit before we take the sacrament? [So quietly]*

Pitch lead this phrase, pointing out the repeated notes. Have the children pitch lead with you and then join you in singing this phrase.

Sing the song again.

• *What do I know about Jesus? [That Jesus came to earth and died for me]*

Sing this phrase again and point out that the descending scale on the first two measures of the second line helps us visualize Jesus coming from heaven down to earth.

Invite the children to pitch lead with you and then sing this phrase. Then sing verse one with the accompaniment.

Verse Two:

• *Whom did Jesus know? [All the boys and girls]*

• *When did he walk upon the earth? [So long ago]*

Verse Three:

• *What do I try so hard to be? [The kind of child that Jesus loved]*

• *Where did he live when he loved those children? [In Galilee]*

Bear testimony that Jesus loves us as he loved the children in Galilee. Encourage them to think of Jesus as they take the sacrament.

HELP US, O GOD, TO UNDERSTAND

MESSAGE: Heavenly Father, help us to understand our Savior's love and his great sacrifice for us. His teachings will help us to love him and return to thee.

MATERIALS:

Picture: (Jesus the Christ 62572)

ATTENTION-GETTER:

- *I'm thinking of a very important person. Raise your hand when you think you know who it is.*
- *This person loves you and cares about what happens to you.*
- *This person has a special concern about the choices you make each day.*
- *This person is a wonderful example. And if you follow that example, you will be happy.*
- *This person lived on earth many years ago and was willing to give you a priceless gift.*
- *Who am I thinking of? [Jesus]* Post the picture Jesus the Christ.
- *That's right. Jesus loves you so much. Listen as I sing a song about his great love, and find another name for Jesus. [Our Savior]* Sing verse one to the children.

LISTENING AND SINGING EXPERIENCES:

Verse One:

- *Now listen as I sing again to discover what we want God to help us understand. [Our Savior's love for us]*

Sing the first line again and then invite the children to sing that phrase as you pitch lead.

- *For what did he pay the price? [All our sins]*
- *Jesus loved us so much, he was willing to die for us.*

Sing this phrase again, challenging the children to find the one-syllable word that is sung on two notes. *[All]* Then invite them to sing this phrase with you.

- *Where did our Savior die? [On the cross]*

Invite the children to sing this last phrase with you.

Invite the children to join you as you sing the first verse.

Verse Two:

Teach in the same manner, asking questions such as the following:

- *Even though we cannot see our Savior, what do we want help to do? [To love him more each day]*
- *What two things will lead us back to Heavenly Father? [His teachings and his loving heart]*
- *What word is sung on the highest note? [Loving]*

Bear your testimony that our Savior died for us because he loves us. We love him, too, and are grateful for his sacrifice for us.

ENRICHMENT IDEAS:

1. Make a melody picture for each of the four phrases as shown. Put the cards out of order. As you sing the song, have the children put them in the correct order.

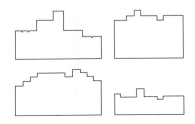

2. Post the following pictures as you sing:

V.1, (Christ and the Children 62467), (The Crucifixion 62505); V.2, (Bedside Prayer 62217), scriptures (62373), (Christ and the Children 62467)

I FEEL MY SAVIOR'S LOVE

MESSAGE: I feel the love that my Savior freely gives me. I will follow him and give all my life to him.

ENRICHMENT IDEAS:

1. Let the children feel the rhythm change from even to uneven by tapping the rhythm of the chorus.

2. Point out that every phrase begins with the same interval (major 6th). Sing the song, pitch leading at the beginning of each phrase. Invite the children to pitch lead as they sing.

3. Display and discuss pictures that depict various times a child might feel the Savior's love: (Boy Being Baptized 62018), (Girl Being Confirmed 62020), (Passing the Sacrament 62021), prayer (62218), (Family Home Evening 62521).

4. Divide the children into groups, have each group sing one phrase or verse, then sing the chorus together.

5. Post word cards to review: SAVIOR'S LOVE, WORLD, SPIRIT WARMS, EVERY-THING, FOLLOW, GIVE, FREELY.

♪ *About the Song*

Some songs that appear to be "new" to the 1989 *Children's Songbook* were printed in previous Children's Sacrament Meeting Presentations. One favorite is "I Feel My Savior's Love," a tender, sensitive song originally written for the pageant *Third Nephi*. Verse four was written specifically for the sacrament meeting program.

MATERIALS:

Picture: (Christ and the Children 62467)

ATTENTION-GETTER:

Show the picture Christ and the Children.

- *What do you see in this picture?* Let children respond.
- *Were any of you there to feel the Savior's arms around you?*
- *We weren't there with him, but the Savior loves us just as much as he loved the children of his day.*
- *As I sing this beautiful song, listen to find out how I know that the Savior loves me.* Sing the song and ask questions similar to the following.

LISTENING AND SINGING EXPERIENCES:

Verse One:

- *How do I know that the Savior loves me?* [I feel it.]
- *Listen as I sing again, and tell me how many times you hear me sing the words "I feel my Savior's love."* [Two times]
- *Where do I feel my Savior's love?* [In all the world around me]
- *What does his Spirit warm?* [My soul] This means his Spirit gives me a good feeling. Our souls feel warm when we look around and see all that the Savior has given us.

Pitch lead this phrase, pointing out that the melody begins the same as the first phrase.

Chorus:

- *What does the Savior know?* [I will follow him.]
- *What will I give to him?* [All my life] We want to serve him all our lives.
- *How does he give his love to me?* [Freely] Let the children know that you personally feel the Savior's love when you follow him and give your life in service as he asks.

Verse Two:

- *The gentleness of the Savior's love is all around me. What word in the song means it is all around me?* [Enfolds]
- *What happens when I kneel to pray?* [My heart is filled with peace.]

Verse Three:

- *What do I know that he will do for me?* [Bless me]
- *What do I offer him?* [My heart]
- *As I offer him my heart, what will he be?* [My shepherd] A shepherd is one who watches over his flock.

Verse Four:

- *What will I do with my Savior's love?* [Share it]
- *How can I share my Savior's love?* [By serving others freely]
- *What happens when I'm serving?* [I am blessed.]
- *What happens when I'm giving?* [I receive] We receive a good feeling when we give to others.

THIS IS MY BELOVED SON

Songbook
76

MESSAGE: "This is my Beloved Son. Hear Him!" These are the words Heavenly Father spoke when Jesus was baptized, when the Savior appeared to the Nephites, and when Joseph Smith saw two glorious beings. I, too, can hear these words in my heart as I read the scriptures.

MATERIALS:

Pictures: (The Baptism of Jesus 62133), (Christ Appears to the Nephites 62047)

ATTENTION-GETTER:

- *What is happening in this picture?* Show picture The Baptism of Jesus.
- *On that glorious day when Jesus was baptized, something wonderful happened— Heavenly Father spoke from heaven.*
- *Listen as I sing, and tell me what words Heavenly Father said. ["This is my Beloved Son. Hear Him!"]* Sing verse one to the children.

LISTENING AND SINGING EXPERIENCES:

Verse One:

- *As I sing these beautiful words again, find a one-syllable word that is sung on three notes. [Hear]* Sing "Hear Him" with the children.
- *Heavenly Father didn't just say "This is my Son." He used a word that described his great love for his Son. [Beloved]* Sing this phrase to the children again.

Help the children learn the interval between "my" and "Beloved." Ask them to sit up tall and sing this reverent message in their sweetest voices.

- *The song doesn't say "Heavenly Father" spoke from heaven. Another of his names is used. What is it? [God, the Father]* Sing verse one, bringing the children in on the last line.

As you sing the song again, ask half of the group to listen for the answer to the question, "When was Jesus baptized?" [When His work had just begun]

Ask the other half to discover the answer to the question, *"Where was Jesus baptized?" [In Jordan's waters]* Have the children join you on the last line.

- *What a glorious experience it must have been to hear Heavenly Father's voice as he spoke from heaven! Let's sing this verse reverently with accompaniment.*

Verse Two:

- *After Jesus was resurrected, he told his apostles he had other people to visit who lived far away. These people were the Nephites.* Show the picture Christ Appears to the Nephites.
- *After the great destruction that followed the crucifixion of Christ, the Nephites gathered together at the temple. As they looked heavenward, they heard Heavenly Father speak. Listen to his words. ["This is My Beloved Son. Hear Him!"]*
- *The Nephites heard the Father testify that this was his Beloved Son. The song uses another word for "testify." What is it? [Witness]*
- *What words describe how the Savior looked as the Nephites gazed into heaven? [White-robed]*

Verse Three and Four:

Continue asking questions the children can answer by listening to the song.

ENRICHMENT IDEAS:

1. In the fourth verse, on the words "In my heart I'll hear" have groups of children hold each of the five tones to form a chord. You might also try this on the words "Hear Him!" on the last ending.

2. Using the pictures suggested, present a "sing-a-story" by connecting the verses with appropriate scriptures or dialogue.

3. For verses three and four use pictures (The First Vision 62470), (A Family Reading the Scriptures 62521).

♪ *About the Song*

The scripture references on the song mark three places where Heavenly Father presented his Son. If ever you were asked to give an impromptu talk, you could discuss the scriptures, sing the song and bear your testimony.

THE CHURCH OF JESUS CHRIST

MESSAGE: I belong to The Church of Jesus Christ of Latter-day Saints and I will follow Jesus.

ENRICHMENT IDEAS:

1. Scramble the word "belong." Ask the children to unscramble this word as you lead a discussion about the importance of belonging to family, school, and Church.

2. Make word cards with letters missing, and let the children discover the words.

3. Invite the children to finger tap the rhythm of this song with you.

4. Ask the children to count the number of times we sing either "I" or "I'll." [Ten]

5. Create a poster using the following pictures: baptism (62018), Jesus (62572), sacrament (62021), prayer (62217), reverent class (62200).

6. Have the children look for the name of the church on their meetinghouse.

B_l_ng (belong)

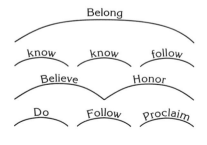

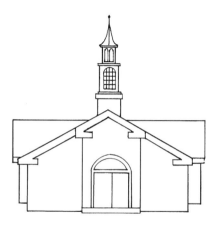

MATERIALS:

Baptismal certificate

Doctrine and Covenants

Pictures: (Jesus the Christ 62572) or (The Resurrected Jesus Christ 62187)

Masking tape

Phrase chart

Word cards: BELONG, KNOW, KNOW, FOLLOW, BELIEVE, HONOR, DO, FOLLOW, PROCLAIM

ATTENTION-GETTER:

Show the children a baptismal certificate.

• *This is a very important piece of paper.*

• *After I was baptized, I received this special certificate that means that I belong to The Church of Jesus Christ of Latter-day Saints.*

Display a picture of Jesus Christ and ask a child to read D&C 115:4, ". . . For thus shall my church be called in the last days, even The Church of Jesus Christ of Latter-day Saints."

• *The last days are also called latter-days.*

Sing the first line and invite the children to sing it with you.

LISTENING AND SINGING EXPERIENCES:

• *Listen to find out what two things I know because I am a member of The Church of Jesus Christ of Latter-day Saints? [I know who I am. I know God's plan.]*

Post word cards KNOW and KNOW and invite the children to sing the answer.

• *Listen as I sing to find what six things we do because we belong to the Church of Jesus Christ of Latter-day Saints. [Follow him in faith; believe in the Savior; honor his name; do what is right; follow his light; truth I will proclaim]* Post word card BELONG.

Post the remaining word cards as the children give the correct answers. Sing again as needed to obtain all answers and then invite the children to sing these answers with you.

To help the children remember the order of the things we do as members of The Church of Jesus Christ of Latter-day Saints, use the phrase chart or draw it on the chalkboard.

Invite the children to imitate your arm actions as you sing the song and trace the phrase lines.

Take the word cards off of the board and pass out in random order to nine children. Challenge them to correctly place them on the chalkboard or phrase chart. Invite all to sing only the key words while you sing the complete verse.

Invite the children to sing the entire verse with you to see if the key words are correctly placed.

Bear testimony that it is a privilege to belong to the true Church of Jesus Christ and that we have a responsibility to do the things we have been singing about in this song.

• *As we learn to do these things, we will be following Jesus Christ, whose church this is.*

I'M TRYING TO BE LIKE JESUS

MESSAGE: I'm trying to be like Jesus—to love as he did and to listen as the still, small voice whispers the things Jesus taught.

MATERIALS:

Pictures: (Christ and the Children 62467) and children showing kindness (62316, 62313, 62317, 62365)

Word cards: LOVE, KINDNESS, GENTLE, LOVING

ATTENTION-GETTER:

Display the suggested pictures of children showing love and kindness.

- *These children are all trying to be like someone. This person taught us all to love one another as he loves us. Who are they trying to be like? [Jesus]* Display the picture Christ and the Children.

- *It is so important for us to try to be like Jesus and follow in his ways. I'm trying to be like Jesus, too. Listen so you can tell me how many times I sing the words "try" or "trying." [Four]* Sing the first verse and chorus.

LISTENING AND SINGING EXPERIENCES:

Verse One:

- *Listen as I tap the catchy rhythm of the first phrase.* Tap the phrase with your fingers and then invite the children to do it with you.

- *Let's see if this same rhythm continues. Tap with me as I sing.* Sing from the beginning through "all that I do and say."

- *Listen as I sing that much again, and find the two rhyming words. [Ways, say]* Now sing that much of the song with me.

- *At times I am tempted to make a wrong choice, but who do I try to listen to? [The still small voice]* Sing first verse and chorus, then have children sing the first three lines with you.

Chorus:

- *This song mentions three important things that the still, small voice—the Holy Ghost—will whisper. What is the first message?* Sing from "at times I am tempted . . ." *[Love one another as Jesus loves you.]*

Display the word card LOVE. As you ask the following questions, place word cards around the picture of Jesus.

- *What is the second message he whispers? [Try to show kindness in all that you do.]* Sing just the chorus and post KINDNESS.

- *What is the third message he whispers? [Be gentle and loving in deed and in thought.]* Sing the chorus only and post GENTLE and LOVING.

- *He whispers for us to be gentle and loving in our actions and thoughts. What is the word in the song that means "action"? [Deed]* Sing verse one and chorus.

Verse Two:

- *Who am I trying to love? [My neighbor]* Our neighbors are not just the people who live next door. They are all of Heavenly Father's children.

- *Who am I learning to serve? [My friends]* We should help our friends all we can.

- *What is the day of gladness? [When Jesus will come again]*

- *What do I try to remember? [The lessons he taught]*

- *Then who enters into my thoughts? [The Holy Spirit]* The Holy Spirit is another name for the Holy Ghost.

ENRICHMENT IDEAS:

1. Divide the children into two groups. Invite each to sing alternate phrases as you indicate.

2. Explain that all people are tempted to make wrong choices and to be unkind at times. Challenge each child to try to be like Jesus and to ask themselves "What would Jesus do?" whenever these situations arise.

3. Make a tape recording of the children singing. Have them sing along with the tape as you play it back. Or have them alternate singing phrases and listening to phrases as you indicate.

4. Use one picture for each phrase in the order given to review the song.

Verse One:

(Jesus Praying with the Nephites 62542), (Family Home Evening 62521), (Jesus Healing the Nephite children 62541), (Waiting Our Turn 62316), (Bedside Prayer 62217), a picture of happy children

Chorus:

(Children Looking at Spring Flowers 62270), (Sharing the Tricycles 62317), (Family with a Baby 62307), Jesus blessing the Nephite children (62541)

Verse Two:

(Helping Grandmother Bake Cookies 62365), (A Family Working Together 62313), (My Daddy Loves Me 62552), (The Second Coming 62562), (Christ and the Children 62467), girl praying (Morning Prayer 62310)

HAD I BEEN A CHILD

MESSAGE: Had I been a child when Jesus came to the Nephite children, he might have held me in his arms, forgiven me, and blessed me. When my Savior comes again, I hope my heart will be as pure as were the hearts of those Nephite children.

ENRICHMENT IDEAS:

1. Discuss the great love that is portrayed by Jesus to the children and by the children to Jesus. Show pictures 62541 and 62380.

2. Teach the children how to conduct 3/4 time as they sing this song. Then invite a child to conduct the song as the children sing again.

3. Make a Nephite sing-a-story by singing "Samuel Tells of the Baby Jesus" (p. 36), "Book of Mormon Stories" (p. 118), "Easter Hosanna" (p. 68), and "I Think When I Read That Sweet Story" (p. 56).

4. Invite the children to hum the song as an expressive reader reads 3 Nephi 17:11-12, 21-25.

♪ *About the Song*

The composer Darwin Wolford is a music professor at Ricks College who had served on the 1985 Hymnbook committee before being asked to implement changes needed for the *Children's Songbook*. The job required a monumental time commitment, with no recognition. The musical standard of the book is due to his careful scrutiny and advice. All who enjoy the songbook are very much in his debt.

MATERIALS:

Pictures:

Verse One: (Jesus Praying with the Nephites 62542), (Jesus Shows His Wounds 62503), (Jesus Teaching in the Western Hemisphere 62380)

Verse Two: (Jesus Healing the Nephites 62541)

Verse Three: (Christ and the Children 62467)

ATTENTION-GETTER:

To introduce this song, invite a child to sing it as a solo. The child might hold the picture Christ and the Children.

- *What would it have been like to be a child when Jesus came to the Nephites that day?* (Let the children respond.)

LISTENING AND SINGING EXPERIENCES:

Sing (or have your soloist sing) the song several times, directing the children's listening by asking questions with each repetition. Have the children sing each phrase with you; then add it to those they have already learned.

Verse One:

- *Why did Jesus kneel with them?* [To pray] Show the picture Jesus Praying with the Nephites.

- *What did he show them?* [The wounds in his hands and his feet] Show the picture Jesus Shows His Wounds.

- *What word describes the day when Jesus came?* [Blessed] It was a blessed day. The people had waited for hundreds of years for Jesus to come. Show the picture Jesus Teaching in the Western Hemisphere.

Invite the children to sing verse one, adding the accompaniment.

Verse Two:

- *Where might he have placed his hands?* [Upon my head] Show the picture Jesus Healing the Nephites.

- *What words might he have spoken to me?* [A word of forgiveness, of blessing, of love]

- *Where might he have looked?* [In my eyes]

- *Where might he have held me?* [Safe in his arms]

Verse Three:

- *Where did they gather?* [Around his knee] Show the picture Christ and the Children.

- *What do I hope?* [My heart will be as pure as the hearts of the children that day.]

- *Who will come again?* [My Savior]

Bear your testimony that Jesus will come again. We look forward to that blessed day, and we pray that our hearts will be pure so that we will be ready and eager to receive him, as were the Nephites of old.

WHEN HE COMES AGAIN

MESSAGE: I wonder what it will be like when Jesus comes again and if I will be ready to meet him.

MATERIALS:

Camera

Picture: (The Second Coming 62562)

Doctrine and Covenants

ATTENTION-GETTER:

Show a camera.

- *Could you take a picture of something that hasn't happened yet? It would be impossible, wouldn't it? However, an artist can paint a picture of something that will happen in the future. I have one to show you.* Show the picture The Second Coming.

- *Can you guess what this picture is about? [The Second Coming] We know Jesus Christ will come again because the scriptures say, "I, the Lord God have spoken it; but the hour and the day no man knoweth, neither the angels in heaven, nor shall they know until he comes" (D&C 49:7).*

- *We don't know when he'll come, but we can wonder what it will be like.* Sing the song for the children.

LISTENING AND SINGING EXPERIENCES:

Verse One:

- *As I sing this song again, listen and see if you can tell me the words Jesus said about the children in days gone by? ["Suffer them to come to me."]* Sing that phrase for the children and then have them join you. Explain that "suffer" means to "allow" or "let."

- *Where does the song say Jesus will call the children to sit? [Round his knee]*

Divide the room in half, asking one group to listen for what might happen to the daylight and the other group to listen for what the songbirds might do. *[Will daylight stay the whole night through? Will songbirds leave their nests?]*

- *What might happen to one star? [It might shine far brighter than the rest.]*

- *When Jesus comes again, the world might know spring—or it might be white with what? [Drifted snow]*

- *Who might sing when Jesus comes again? [Herald angels]*

- *It won't matter what season it is. When Jesus comes again it will be a most glorious time.* Invite the children to sing verse one with you.

Verse Two:

Teach the second verse, asking thoughtful questions such as the following:

- *Jesus loves us so much. When he comes again, what do you hope he'll say to you? ["You've served me well, my little child; Come unto my arms to stay."]*

- *The song says that I hope others seeing me may seek for something. Can you discover what that is? [Greater light divine] This means that when we follow Jesus and try to be like him, others will want to follow Jesus as well.*

- *What two things will I try to do each day? [Each day I'll try to do his will and let my light so shine.]*

- *What two things will I be ready to do when he comes again? [To look upon his loving face and join with him in prayer]*

ENRICHMENT IDEAS:

1. Invite each class to stand and sing one of the "questions" from the song as you indicate.

2. Show the children a ⌒ hold sign. Challenge them to find the three words in verse one over which a fermata has been placed. Exaggerate the "hold time" so the children can find them.

3. Sing the first line; then challenge the children to find other words sung on that melody. *[I'm sure he'll call his little ones together round his knee.]*

4. You could use simple line drawings to help with the order of the phrases: angels sing; winter scene; spring; one star; daylight; songbirds leaving their nests.

5. To review, show the picture The Second Coming (62562) and read Matthew 16:27. See if the children can guess what song they will be singing.

♪ *About the Song*

On this particular song a copyrights agreement was made which now allows it to be copied.

The Gospel

This is the largest section of the book and contains 81 songs. They are grouped according to the following topics:

1. Restoration
2. Temples and Family History
3. First Principles of the Gospel
4. Scriptures
5. Church Leaders
6. The Commandments
(songs about being kind and choosing the right)
7. Missionary Work
8. Songs Appropriate for Leaders

The two basic topics of the gospel are love and service.

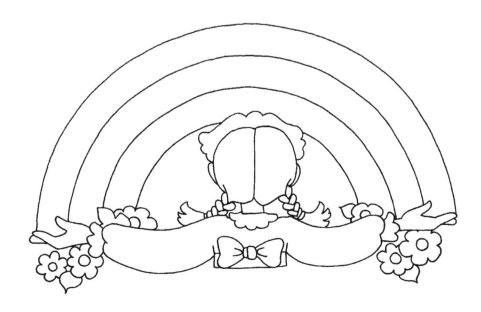

AN ANGEL CAME TO JOSEPH SMITH

MESSAGE: An angel came to Joseph Smith and gave him a sacred record. This record—the Book of Mormon—tells of people who were led to a favored land and had peace when they obeyed the Lord. As I read the book, I understand why Heavenly Father loves us all in every land.

MATERIALS:

Word cards: WHO? WHAT? WHERE? WHY? WHEN? WHICH?

Pictures: V.1, (Joseph Receives the Gold Plates 62012); V.2, (Lehi and His People Arrive in the Promised Land 62045), (Jesus Teaching in the Western Hemisphere 62380)

Note: Before teaching this song, practice conducting the meter change (3/4 to 2/4) with your accompanist.

ATTENTION-GETTER:

Sing "The Golden Plates" (p. 86), asking the children to listen for the message.

- *What is this song about? [The Book of Mormon] I know another song about the Book of Mormon. As I sing it for you, listen to find out the answers to the following mystery words. Post: WHO? WHAT? WHERE? WHAT?*

LISTENING AND SINGING EXPERIENCES:

Verse One:

- *WHO came to Joseph Smith? [An angel]* Demonstrate the "slow-quick-quick-slow" pattern and sing it together. ♩♫♩ pattern.
- *WHAT did he take from the ground? [A sacred record]* A record is a written history.
- *WHERE was it hidden? [There—in the ground]*
- *WHAT two words describe the book? [Precious and holy]*

Invite a child to hold picture 62012 as the children sing the verse.

Testify that the sacred record was the Book of Mormon and that the angel was Moroni.

Verse Two:

Post picture 62045 and word cards WHEN? WHO? WHAT? WHY?

- *The second verse tells of Lehi's family as they journeyed across the sea. Discover the answers to the mystery words: WHEN? WHOSE? WHAT? and WHY?*
- *WHEN did the people live? [Long ago]*
- *WHOSE hand led them? [The Lord's]*
- *WHAT two things did these people do? [Left their homes and crossed the sea]*
- *WHY did they leave their homes and cross the sea? [To reach a favored land] This land is favored because the Lord chose it as a place where the gospel would be restored.* End by reading 1 Nephi 18:23.

Verse Three:

- Introduce by showing the picture: 62380. Describe the tremendous love and peace that the righteous people felt. Post word cards: WHICH? WHAT? WHERE?
- *WHICH two groups of people came to dwell? [The Nephites and the Lamanites]*
- *WHAT did they have when they obeyed the Lord? [Peace]*
- *WHERE does it tell this story? [In the sacred records—the Book of Mormon]* Hold up a copy of the Book of Mormon.

Verse Four:

Continue asking questions which the children can answer by listening to this verse.

Bear your testimony of the truthfulness of the Book of Mormon and how important it is for each of us to read it every day.

ENRICHMENT IDEAS:

1. Make a replica of the Book of Mormon with a black posterboard cover and the title in gold lettering. The pages might contain one or two pictures for each verse, as suggested:

   V.1: (Joseph Receives the Gold Plates 62012); (Moroni Hides the Plates 62462)

   V.2: (The Liahona 62041); (Lehi and His People Arrive in the Promised Land 62045)

   V.3: (The Stripling Warriors 62050); (Jesus Teaching in the Western Hemisphere 62380)

   V.4 (Reading the Scriptures 62344); (Family Prayer 62275)

2. Write the mystery words on question mark-shaped word cards.

3. How to conduct this song:

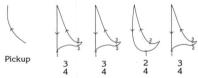

Pickup / 3/4 / 3/4 / 2/4 / 3/4

The rhythm of both lines is the same. Be sure to keep the same speed through the change, and to practice with your accompanist before you teach.

♪ About the Song

A melody by Alexander Schreiner was originally used for two poems by Anna Johnson—"An Angel Came to Joseph Smith" and "We Bow Our Heads." "We Bow Our Heads" has become one of the most often used prayer songs. It seemed that the other poem deserved its own music. Laurence Lyon was asked to write new music. When he sent his ideas, he explained that the natural feel of the words seemed to suggest a change of meter in the song. He had not meant to make it "difficult" and tried the 2/4 measure with 3 beats (as in the first measure) but felt it worked best with the meter change. There is a definite charm to the change. The real difficulty is convincing music leaders that it is possible for them to lead it correctly! If you can comfortably sing the meter change in "Come, Come Ye Saints," you will be able to do this song as well.

THE GOLDEN PLATES

MESSAGE: Nephi's golden plates were buried in a mountainside until Heavenly Father brought them forth through the Prophet Joseph Smith. Now we can read the stories found in the golden plates in the Book of Mormon.

ENRICHMENT IDEAS:

1. Define golden plates: a book of metal pages of gold, not to be confused with dinner plates.

2. Hold up a paper or a "golden plate" upon which you have drawn symbols similar to the ones on this page. Ask the children if they can read the writing. What would they need in order to be able to understand or translate these symbols without any schooling in the language? [Heavenly Father's help]

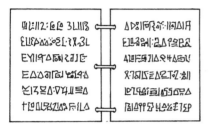

3. Prepare a visual aid as shown, with a pocket behind the rock which holds a replica of the gold plates. Put plates in the hillside as you sing.

4. For variety, use the accompaniment for this song found in Sing With Me, p. B-57 (the orange Primary songbook).

5. Sing related songs, such as, "Book of Mormon Stories" (p. 118), "The Books in the Book of Mormon" (p. 119), and "An Angel Came to Joseph Smith" (p. 86).

♪ About the Song

When Sing With Me was being compiled, there was a need for songs with specific Mormon themes. The compilers contacted Rose Thomas Graham, a poet, for possible texts. "The Golden Plates" was selected from a collection of her poems, and J. Spencer Cornwall was asked to write music for her words.

When Brother Cornwall was only four years old, he learned to play music on a pump organ. Because his legs were too short to reach the pedals, his brother pumped them for him. Spencer was so eager to learn that he would have a lesson in the morning, practice in the afternoon, and then go running back the next morning for another lesson. He directed the Tabernacle Choir for twenty-three years. When he was ninety-five years old, he was still composing.

MATERIALS:

Picture: (Moroni Hides the Plates in the Hill Cumorah 62462)

Book of Mormon

ATTENTION-GETTER:

Show the picture Moroni hides the plates in the Hill Cumorah.

- *After the Book of Mormon prophets finished writing on the gold plates, there was war upon the land. They wanted their writings to be safe. What did they do with them? [They buried the plates.]*

- *Listen as I sing this song. Tell me where the plates were hidden.*

LISTENING AND SINGING EXPERIENCES:

Verse One:

- *Where did the golden plates lay hidden? [Deep in the mountainside]*

- *The low notes remind us that the plates were buried in the ground. Pitch lead line one with me as we sing it together.*

- *God found one faithful in whom he could trust. The song doesn't use the word "trust." Listen as I sing again to see what word you hear. [Confide]*

- *Who was this important man? [Joseph Smith] Sing the last line with me.*

Verse Two:

Teach in the same manner as verse one, asking:

- *Who was the record made by? [Nephi] Explain that a record is a written history.*

- *When was the record written? [In days of old]*

- *Where are the stories from the golden plates retold? [In the Book of Mormon]*

- *Let's sing the entire song with the accompaniment.*

Bear testimony that Joseph Smith was led to the gold plates which contain a record of the Nephites and Lamanites. Because he was, we have the Book of Mormon today.

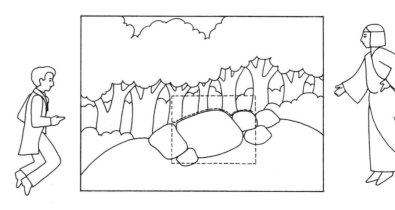

THE SACRED GROVE

MESSAGE: The Sacred Grove was beautiful as Joseph knelt in fervent prayer. The Father and the Son appeared and spoke to him. Their words answered his important question and made his heart rejoice.

MATERIALS:

Picture: (The First Vision 62470)

ATTENTION-GETTER:

Ask the children to close their eyes as you describe what it was like on that special morning when Joseph entered the Sacred Grove.

- *It was a beautiful clear morning. The sun was shining through the tall trees. Everything was green and fresh. Bees were humming and birds were singing, and it was peaceful when Joseph knelt to pray.*

While their eyes are closed, sing or have a guest sing the song for the children. You might consider playing a tape recording of birds chirping as the song is sung.

LISTENING AND SINGING EXPERIENCES:

Sing or have the guest sing the song several times. Direct the children's listening by asking questions similar to those listed below with each repetition:

Verse One:

- *What two words describe the sacred grove? [Green, fresh]*
- *As I sing this song for you, tell me how the morning sun shone. [Bright around]*
- *Sing the first two phrases with me.*
- *As I sing the song again, listen for what Joseph did. [Knelt in fervent prayer]* Explain that "fervent" means "with all his heart."
- *The descending notes on "Joseph knelt" remind us that Joseph humbly knelt down to pray.*
- *Where did he kneel? [Upon that sacred ground]*

Invite the children to join you as you sing those phrases. Sing the entire first verse.

Verse Two:

- *Who appeared to Joseph? [The Father and the Son]* Show the picture The First Vision.
- *How did they speak to him? [As with one voice]* Heavenly Father and Jesus were united in the important message they gave to Joseph Smith.
- *What two things did their message do? [It answered all his fears and made his heart rejoice.]*

Close with your testimony of the appearance of the Father and his Son Jesus Christ to Joseph Smith in the Sacred Grove.

ENRICHMENT IDEAS:

1. Sing related songs, such as "Search, Ponder, and Pray" (p. 109), "Faith" (p. 96), "I Pray in Faith" (p. 14), and "Joseph Smith's First Prayer" (*Hymns*, no. 26).

2. Read Joseph Smith—History 1:14–17.

3. Ask an older child to look up "sacred" in the dictionary and read the meaning. Ask the children to name other sacred places.

4. Invite a guest who has visited the Sacred Grove to tell the children about the experience.

5. Use simple pictures of trees, the sun, Joseph kneeling, and the Father and the Son to form a scene on a flannel board, magnetic board, or overhead transparency. To make a flip-chart use four pieces of laminating film and draw pictures with markers. Attach all to a piece of posterboard. Begin with the posterboard and overlay pictures to form the complete scene as you sing.

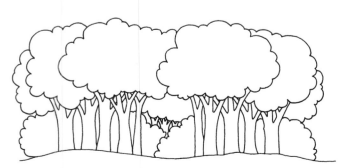

ON A GOLDEN SPRINGTIME

MESSAGE: Spring is the season when seedlings push up toward the light. Christ rose from the tomb in the springtime so that all men could live and look upward to Heavenly Father's light. It was also a beautiful spring morning when the Father and the Son appeared to Joseph Smith so that all people could receive the gospel's light.

ENRICHMENT IDEAS:

1. Review the three springtime miracles taught in this song—

    The miracle of the seed pushing up toward the warm sunlight.

    The great miracle of the Resurrection: Jesus Christ awoke and left the tomb.

    The miracle of the Restoration: The Father and the Son appeared to Joseph Smith.

2. Small children may enjoy imitating a small seed pushing upward to the light. They can do this by pitch leading with their bodies on the last line of verse one.

3. Print rhyming words on cards and challenge the children to put them in the correct order as you sing.

4. Teach verse one alone as a spring song for the younger children. You could make a simple string picture and raise the flower and sun as you sing.

5. Additional pictures and an Easter program are found in the *Friend*, March 1986, p. 38.

♪ *About the Song*

Children easily identify with the miracles of spring, and hopefully will transfer that same faith to the Resurrection and the Restoration. Virginia Kammeyer was asked to write the lyrics for this song making a parallel between the awakening of springtime, the Resurrection, and the Restoration. Crawford Gates was asked to provide melody and accompaniment. The song was composed on the way to a rehearsal of the Beloit Symphony Orchestra, which he conducts. Among his most revered compositions are The Hill Cumorah Pageant music and *Promised Valley*.

MATERIALS:

V.1: a seed and a plant

Pictures: V.2, (Burial of Jesus 62180), (Mary and the Resurrected Lord 62186); V.3, (The First Vision 62470)

ATTENTION-GETTER:

- *I love the springtime. The sun is warm and bright, the blossoms are fragrant, and the breeze is cool and fresh. It is a season of miracles. Tiny seeds asleep in the ground feel the warmth of the spring sunlight and begin to do something. As I sing this song, listen to discover what the seeds do with all their might when the day is warm and bright. [Push upward to the light]* Sing verse one.

Sing the last phrase, "The day is bright. With all your might, push upward to the light." Pitch lead the ascending scale of the last two measures and ask the children to visualize a tiny seed pushing through the soil. Invite them to sing the last line with you.

LISTENING AND SINGING EXPERIENCES:

Verse One:

- *Listen as I sing the song. Find a word that describes the springtime. [Golden]*
- *What lay asleep until the sun shone down? [A tiny seedling]*
- *What will the seed do when it awakes? [Push upward to the light]* Show seed and plant.
- *Let's put all the phrases together as we sing the first verse with the accompaniment.*

Verse Two:

- *After Christ's death, his body was taken from the cross, wrapped in burial clothes, and placed in the tomb of a friend.* Show the picture (62180). *As I sing the second verse, discover two things that happened after Jesus Christ awoke on that golden springtime morning. [He left the tomb where he had lain, the bands of death he broke.]*
- *Jesus was the first person to be resurrected. He broke the bands of death and arose from the tomb. This means Jesus lived again.* Show picture (62186).
- *Where should the sleeping world look after it awakes? [Look upward to the light]*
- *Challenge the children to find the word on the highest note. [Awake]* Sing this phrase again from "awake, awake."
- *Now listen carefully to one more question. Because Christ awoke and arose from the tomb, what two things may all men do? [Live again and look upward to the light.]*

Invite the children to sing verse two with you.

Verse Three:

- *When Joseph Smith was fourteen years old, he wanted to know which church was right. He read in the Bible that if he had an important question, he should ask Heavenly Father for the answer. Listen as I sing the first line to discover where this event took place. [In a forest glade]*
- *As I sing the rest of the song, see if you can hear who appeared as Joseph knelt and prayed. [The Father and the Son]* Show the picture The First Vision.
- *This time, listen for why all nations should awake. [To receive the gospel light]*
- *If we truly accept the gospel, what will we also receive? [Its glorious light]*

Bear testimony that the Father and the Son did appear to Joseph Smith in a forest glade on a beautiful spring morning. Now we can each look toward the light of the gospel that has been restored.

THE PRIESTHOOD IS RESTORED

MESSAGE: Heavenly Father has restored the priesthood to the earth.

MATERIALS:

Pictures: (John the Baptist Conferring the Aaronic Priesthood 62013), (The Restoration of the Melchizedek Priesthood 62371)

ATTENTION-GETTER:

- *If you wanted to announce something very important, how would you do it? [Newspaper, television, radio]*

- *Long ago, when something important was announced, trumpets would sound, and someone would read a proclamation (an important message) from a scroll.*

As the pianist plays the accompaniment, ask the children to close their eyes and imagine that they are hearing trumpets.

- *This song makes a very important proclamation. As I sing it, listen and discover what that proclamation is. [The priesthood is restored]*

LISTENING AND SINGING EXPERIENCES:

Sing the song several times, encouraging the children to listen by using questions and statements similar to those listed below. As children discover answers, invite them to sing that part of the song with you. Add one phrase at a time to the ones already learned. Add the accompaniment when the children have learned the song.

- *The priesthood was brought back to the earth. The song doesn't use those words. Listen to find the word that means "brought back." [Restored]*

Show the pictures of the restoration of the Aaronic and Melchizedek Priesthoods.

- *The priesthood was on the earth when Jesus was here, but then it was taken away. In 1829 the priesthood was restored to Joseph Smith by John the Baptist and Peter, James, and John.*

Sing "The priesthood is restored" and invite the children to sing this phrase with you.

- *What was made known to man? [The truth (the fullness of the gospel)]* Point out that the rising melody fits the message that the truth lifts our spirits and blesses our lives.

- *To whom has God spoken? [To the earth (to people living on the earth)]*

Through pitch leading, show that the descending melody on this phrase is like God coming down to earth to restore this great power and to talk to his prophets.

- *What is here again? [Power]* Explain that the word "power" is sung on one syllable.

- *What does the word "power" mean in this song? [The priesthood which is the power or authority to act in God's name]*

- *What three words are held the longest? [Restored, man, again]* Encourage the children to take a deep breath before each phrase so they can hold the ending notes for the full note value.

Add the accompaniment as the children sing the entire song.

Briefly tell the children about a time when the priesthood blessed your own life.

- *The priesthood is one of the greatest gifts we have on earth because it gives men and boys the authority to do what Heavenly Father or Jesus would do if they were here. We always want to live worthy to receive the blessings of the priesthood.*

ENRICHMENT:

1. Ask one of the older boys to read D&C 13:1 and tell how the priesthood was restored.

2. Show the following library pictures and briefly discuss ways the priesthood is used today: (Boy Being Baptized 62018), (Girl Being Confirmed 62020), (Passing the Sacrament 62021), (Blessing the Sacrament 62343), (Ordination to the Priesthood 62341), (Administering to the Sick 62342).

3. Invite the children to pitch lead with you.

4. Use tone bells on the melody line.

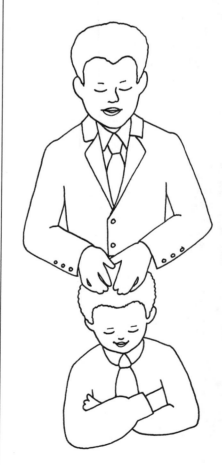

TRUTH FROM ELIJAH

MESSAGE: The hearts of the children have turned to their fathers. We can preserve the names and memories of our loved ones by striving to be worthy to go to the temple and having our loved ones sealed to us for eternity.

ENRICHMENT IDEAS:

1. Invite older children to read D&C 2:1–3 and Malachi 4:5–6.

2. Softly clap the rhythm of the quarter notes and eighth notes.

3. Briefly tell the children about Elijah, the prophet. See Bible Dictionary.

4. Sing other related songs such as "Genealogy—I Am Doing It" (p. 94), "The Hearts of the Children" (p. 92), and "Families Can Be Together Forever" (p. 188). For choosing time, put the titles of these songs on the back of a few pictures illustrative of ancestors.

MATERIALS:

Pictures: Your ancestors or people who lived many years ago, and a temple picture to illustrate the Spirit of Elijah.

ATTENTION-GETTER:

Show the pictures.

- *What is an ancestor? [Our relatives who lived on earth before we were born]*

- *Do any of you know something about your ancestors? Let the children respond.*

- *It is interesting to think about our ancestors and what their lives were like so long ago. Many of our ancestors died without hearing the gospel. They are waiting for us to find their names and do their temple work so they can be sealed to us for eternity.*

- *Elijah, a prophet of old, taught us this truth. The song we are learning today, "Truth from Elijah," tells of our hearts turning to our fathers, or ancestors.*

- *As I sing, hold up a finger every time you hear me sing the word "turned." [Eight times] Sing again to check the answer given.*

LISTENING AND SINGING EXPERIENCES:

Sing the first and second phrases (first five measures) again and have the children sing them back to you.

- *Listen as I sing the third and fourth phrases to see if the melody is the same or different. [Same]*

Invite the children to sing these phrases with you, and then add them to the first and second phrases.

- *Just like the children, who can we seek out? [Our loved ones]*

- *What can we preserve? [Their names and their memory] Have the children sing this phrase with you: "And we as his children . . . memory."*

- *The melody of the next phrase is the same as the last, except for a few notes. Listen to find the words that are sung on a different melody. [For eternity]*

- *Eternity means "forever." It is such an important word that it is sung on the highest note in the song. The composer also put a fermata or hold sign over it. Add this phrase to the ones already learned.*

- *Sing the last line with me and watch carefully as I pitch lead to help with the change in melody on the last phrase.*

THE HEARTS OF THE CHILDREN

MESSAGE: As prophesied, the hearts of the children have turned to their ancestors, and families can be sealed for eternity.

MATERIALS:

Cutout: A large heart with a picture of children on one side and pictures of grandparents on the opposite side.

ATTENTION-GETTER:

Show the children a large heart framing the picture of children.

- *There is a picture of some important people on the other side of this heart. Can you guess who the people are?*

Turn the heart around to reveal picture of grandparents.

- *This little boy has never met his great-grandfather and great-grandmother. But these people love him. Wouldn't it be nice if this boy could get to know his great-grandparents? Thinking and caring about our families of long ago is the way we turn our hearts to our fathers.*

LISTENING AND SINGING EXPERIENCES:

Sing the song several times, encouraging the children to listen by using questions and statements similar to those listed below. As the children discover answers, invite them to sing that part of the song with you. Add one phrase at a time to the ones already learned.

- *As I sing, listen to discover how long our families are sealed. [For eternity]*
- *Eternity means "forever." And being sealed means that we can all be together as a family when we go back to live with Heavenly Father.*
- *Eternity is such an important word in the music that it is held for a long time. Join me in singing that phrase.*
- *As I sing the song again, listen to discover to whom the hearts of the children are turning? [To their fathers] "Fathers" refers to ancestors or relatives who lived long ago. Sing that phrase with me.*
- *As I sing the song again, listen to find out who prophesied that the hearts shall turn. [Malachi] To "prophesy" means to tell of something that is going to happen at a later time. A prophet needs Heavenly Father's help to prophesy. Malachi was a prophet who lived 420 B.C. He prophesied that someone would come and bring the sealing power to the earth so we can be families forever.*
- *Join me as I sing the song again. Tell me who fulfilled the prophecy. [Elijah]*
- *"Fulfill" means to make it come true or to bring it to pass. Elijah made the prophecy come true by giving the sealing power to Joseph Smith.* Conduct pitch levels on the word "prophecy," pointing out the small intervals.

Have an older child read D&C 2:2: *"And he shall plant in the hearts of the children the promises made to the fathers, and the hearts of the children shall turn to their fathers."*

- *This means that we will have a growing desire to find out who our fathers, or ancestors, are, and we will want to have them sealed to us forever.*

Invite the children to sing the song again, adding the accompaniment.

ENRICHMENT IDEAS:

1. Have the children take a big breath after "sealed" so they can sing "eternity" without breathing.

2. Sing other songs to reinforce the message of this song: "Genealogy—I Am Doing It" (p. 94), "Families Can Be Together Forever" (p. 188), "I Love to See the Temple" (p. 95), and "Truth from Elijah" (p. 90).

3. Add flute, violin, or voice for the obbligato.

4. For a Sharing Time idea, refer to the Bible Dictionary for background on Elijah and Malachi. Also see the *Friend*, Feb. 1983, p. 27.

5. Make a heart-shaped poster, cutting two hearts out of one posterboard. Join these hearts with rings so the pages will turn like a book.

GENEALOGY—I AM DOING IT

MESSAGE: My genealogy is a record of my family. What joy I will feel when I meet my ancestors, knowing that we can be together through all eternity!

ENRICHMENT IDEAS:

1. Challenge the children to sing all the words except "genealogy."

2. The children will enjoy marking time by standing and bending their knees on the first beat of each measure.

3. Invite the children to slap their laps, clap and snap—over and over to the rhythm of the song.

4. Bring a Book of Remembrance. Show the children the pedigree charts, family group sheets, personal histories, and old photographs.

♪ About the Song

Jeanne Lawler, the composer of this song, practices what she preaches. She has served several missions for the Church, the last one being a temple mission in Sweden. Originally, the words to verse two said, "People living now and the ones who've died *are on my pedigree.*" Now it says what should be done—"*can all be sealed to me.*" Sister Lawler loves to write musical theater and oratories for children.

MATERIALS:

Word cards: YEGGELONA, GENEALOGY

ATTENTION-GETTER:

Show the word card with the letters YEGGELONA on it, and ask the children if they know what this word means.

* *This is a mixed-up word. If we rearrange the letters, they form an important word.*

* *Listen for the word as I sing the song. You will hear the word several times.*

Sing the song and have them discover that the word is "genealogy." Display the word card showing the correct spelling of the word.

ATTENTION-GETTER FOR YOUNGER CHILDREN:

* *It's fun to learn a big new word. I like big words. Sometimes it's fun to just say them. Try saying this one with me: genealogy.* Have the children repeat the word until all can pronounce it correctly.

* *Listen as I sing and count how many times I sing the word "genealogy." [Three]*

LISTENING AND SINGING EXPERIENCES:

Verse One:

* *As I sing this song again, listen to find out what genealogy is. [It's a record of my family.] A "record" is a written history, not a record played on a stereo.*

Have the children tap the rhythm of the last line as you sing it again; then have the children join you in singing this part with each repetition.

* *The song mentions something I will keep and something I will write as I do my genealogy. As I sing, listen for what these are. [My Book of Remembrance, my history]*

* *A Book of Remembrance is the book in which I keep my family records.* Have the children practice singing "re-mem-brance" with three, not four, syllables.

* *As I do genealogy, what is very clear to me? Listen to the song to find out the answer to this question. [The reasons why I am doing it]*

* *We do genealogy because it is a commandment and so that we can have the eternal blessing of being families forever.*

* *Are any of you writing your history or making a family tree chart? If you are, this line will have special meaning to you.* Sing the first line.

Verse Two:

* *If I do my genealogy, what great blessing can come to me and my loved ones? [They can all be sealed to me]*

* *"Sealed" means we can all be together when we go to live with Heavenly Father.*

* *Of what am I sure as I can be? [That someday I'll meet every one of them]*

* *We'll be happy when they say what to me? [We're all a family. I am yours and you are mine now, Through all eternity] What a wonderful thing that will be—to be together forever.*

I LOVE TO SEE THE TEMPLE

MESSAGE: I love to see the temple. It is a holy place. I will prepare myself to go there someday.

MATERIALS:

Picture: temple nearest your home

ATTENTION-GETTER:

Show a picture of the temple nearest to your home.

- *What is this building? Where is it? Have you ever been inside it? Would you like to someday?*

LISTENING AND SINGING EXPERIENCES:

Sing the song several times, encouraging the children to listen by using questions and statements similar to the following:

Verse One:

- *When will I prepare to go to the temple? [While I am young]*

- *Why is it so important that we prepare ourselves? [This is my sacred duty]*

Invite the children to sing the last line with you. Then have one group of children listen to discover what kind of place the temple is *[a place of love and beauty]*, and have the other group listen to find out what is another name for the temple. *[A house of God]*

- *What two things will I do there? [Listen and pray]*

- *When I go to the temple someday, what will I feel? [The Holy Spirit]*

Invite the children to sing verse one. Add the accompaniment.

Verse Two:

Teach the second verse in a similar manner by asking the following questions.

- *Because I love to see the temple, where will I go someday? [Inside]*
- *What two things will I do there? [I'll covenant with my Father; I'll promise to obey.]*
- *In the first verse, the composer called the temple "a house of God." What does she call it in this verse? [A holy place]*
- *What special blessing will we receive when we go there? [We will be sealed together.] Being "sealed" means that we can all be together as a family when we go back to live with Heavenly Father.*
- *As a child of God, I've learned an important truth. What is it? [A family is forever.]*
- *The scriptures tell us: "Whatsoever thou shalt bind on earth shall be bound in heaven" (Matt. 16:19). If we can learn this truth and prepare ourselves while we're young, we can go to the temple to become a family forever.*

ENRICHMENT IDEAS:

1. Have the children share experiences they have had in visiting the temple or the temple grounds. Or share a personal experience.

2. Display a ⌢ card and hold it up when a fermata appears in the song. Explain that this sign means the music director can decide how long to hold a certain note.

3. For choosing time, write the names of songs having to do with temple work on the back of temple pictures: "Genealogy—I Am Doing It" (p. 94), "I Have a Family Tree" (p.199), "The Hearts of the Children" (p. 92), "Truth from Elijah" (p. 90), "I Love to See the Temple" (p. 95), "Families Can Be Together Forever" (p. 188).

4. See also posters to enhance the meaning: (Eternal Marriage 67075), (Sacred Ordinances 67074), (Life Eternal 67076), (Temples Worldwide 67073), (Why Do Mormons Build Temples? 67070)

♪ *About the Song*

As a child, Janice Kapp Perry loved to travel to the Idaho Falls Temple to do baptisms for the dead. Now she lives in Provo and can see the temple from her home. After her tiny baby died, she was especially grateful that their family had been sealed. She is reminded of that blessing every time she sees the spire of the temple.

MESSAGE: Through faith, I can know and feel many wonderful things. My faith is strengthened whenever I obey.

ENRICHMENT IDEAS:

1. Invite a child to lead the children in the actions as they sing the first verse. Raise your arms to form the sun; Fold your arms to pray; Plant a seed in your hand and raise your arms to indicate its growth; Hold your hands on your heart.

2. Make a poster as illustrated.

3. Help the children enunciate the ending consonants of words such as heart, seed, and right, and to soften the "r" on birth and earth.

4. Encourage the children to follow you as you add dynamics, such as: increase volume on "The sun will rise" and decrease on "knees to pray," increase as the melody moves up the scale as the plant grows, and continuing in full volume to the end. (The Holy Ghost often confirms truth to us as beautiful music is sung. Ask the children if they feel warm inside as they sing.)

MATERIALS:

Word cards or simple pictures: SUN, CHILD PRAYING, SEEDS, HEART

Wordstrip: *Faith is . . .*

ATTENTION-GETTER:

Ask the children the following questions:

- *Do you have a heart? How do you know you have a heart? Have you seen it?*

To have faith is to know something exists, even though we haven't seen it.

LISTENING AND SINGING EXPERIENCES:

Verse One:

Each time you sing the song, ask one of the following questions and have the children listen for the answer.

- *Listen as I sing a song about faith, and count the number of times I sing the word "faith." [Four]*

- *What words do I sing at the beginning of each phrase? [Faith is]*

- *Faith is like something that is very small. Listen and discover what it is. [Faith is like a little seed.]*

- *Tap the rhythm and sing the seven notes all on the same pitch.*

- *Faith is also something within my heart that seems to grow larger and larger. Can you find a word that means growing larger and larger? [Swelling]*

- *I feel that swelling in my heart when I do what? [When I do right, I know]*

- *The first part of our song tells us that faith is knowing two things. Listen and discover these two things. [The sun will rise, lighting each new day, and the Lord will hear my prayers each time I pray.]*

- *The melody in the first phrase moves in an upward direction, indicating the rising of the sun. Sing that phrase with the children and then invite them to put together the phrases they know.*

- *If we have faith, we can be just as sure that God will hear our prayers as we are sure that the sun will rise.*

Verse Two:

Post the wordstrip: *Faith is. . .*

- *Faith is knowing I lived with God. When did I live with him? [Before my mortal birth] Our mortal birth is our birth into earth life.*

- *Faith is knowing I can return to Heavenly Father. When will I return to him? [When my life ends on earth]*

- *Faith is believing in God above and in Christ, who showed the way. What is another word that means "believing in?" [Trust]*

- *Faith is strengthened and I feel it grow whenever I do what? [Obey]*

Sing the complete second verse with the children.

Bear testimony of the beautiful plan of salvation referred to in this verse.

GOD'S LOVE

MESSAGE: We can feel God's love and know that he watches over us, even though we cannot see him.

MATERIALS:

Objects: Small fan and a scarf, feather, leafy plant, or pinwheel

ATTENTION-GETTER:

Ask your accompanist to play this song. While the children listen to the music, use a small fan or some other means to blow a light scarf, a feather, leaves of a plant, or a pinwheel.

• *What does the wind look like? How do you know it is there? Can you hear it or feel it? Although we cannot see the wind, we can see what it does by the motion of the scarf (or other object).*

LISTENING AND SINGING EXPERIENCES:

Verse One:

• *Listen for something else the wind moves whenever it goes by. [The grasses].* Sing the song.

• *What does the wind make the grasses do? [Bend]* Sing the song again. Invite the children to sing the last line with you.

• *The song says that we do not see the wind, but we can hear it do something. Listen as I sing to find the answer. [Sigh]* Bring the children in on the last line.

Invite the children to sing the first verse with you.

Verse Two:

• *There is something else we cannot see that is even more important to us than the wind. Listen as I sing to find out what it is. [God's love]*

• *Where do we feel God's love? [In our hearts]*

Have the children sing line one with you, and sing it again each time they answer the questions you ask them.

• *How does he show us that he loves us? [He watches over us.]*

• *Where does he watch over us? [Wherever we may go]*

Verse Three:

• *There are some words in this verse that are repeated. Listen and tell which words they are. [We do not have to see]* Let the children chant the words "We do not have to see" to learn the differing rhythms of these words on line one and line two.

• *There are two things that we can know without seeing. What are they? [The wind is here; God's love is near.]*

Bear testimony that we can feel Heavenly Father's love and know that he watches over us, even though we cannot see him.

ENRICHMENT IDEAS:

1. Young children may enjoy moving their arms and hands like bending grasses as they sing.

2. Sing the song to the children, leaving off the ending word of each phrase: wind, sigh, bend, by. Have the children "fill in the blanks" by singing these words.

3. Invite the children to pitch lead with you.

4. Divide the group into three sections. Let each group sing a verse; then trade verses several times so each group sings the entire song.

5. Sing related songs, such as "Faith" (p. 96), and "God's Daily Care" (*Hymns*, no. 306).

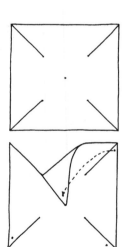

MESSAGE: "I am sorry" is not always easy to say when I've done something wrong. I'll try to repent, to do better, and to pray so that Heavenly Father will help me be strong.

ENRICHMENT IDEAS:

1. Invite a child to read Psalms 38:18. "I will be sorry for my sin." Have the children recite it back.

2. Sing the song leaving out the last word of each phrase. Challenge the children to fill in the missing words.

3. Post the words "say" and "wrong." Ask the children to raise their hands when they hear the words that rhyme with "say" and "wrong." *["Pray" and "strong"]*

MATERIALS:

Word cards: REPENT, DO BETTER, PRAY

ATTENTION-GETTER:

• *I know some words that are not always easy to say. But they are words I should say when I've been thoughtless or done something wrong. What are they? [I am sorry]. That's right.* Begin singing the song.

LISTENING EXPERIENCES:

• *What is not always easy to say when you know you've been thoughtless and done something wrong? [I am sorry]*

Sing the first two lines again and then invite the children to sing with you.

• *Listen as I sing and discover what three things I will try to do if I've done something wrong. [To repent, to do better, to pray]* Sing again if necessary to get all the answers.

Invite the children to sing the third line with you as you post the word cards.

• *If I do these things, what will Heavenly Father do? [Help me to be strong.]*

Tap the dotted rhythm on "Heavenly Father will help me be strong." Add the accompaniment and invite the children to join you in singing the complete song. Challenge them to find the word sung on the highest note. *[Father]*

Bear testimony that when we try to repent, to do better, and to pray, Heavenly Father does bless us to be stronger—not in our muscles, but in our ability to resist temptation the next time we feel it.

HELP ME, DEAR FATHER

MESSAGE: Heavenly Father, help me to live nearer to thee by forgiving others and truly repenting.

MATERIALS:

Word card: FORGIVE

Picture: (The Crucifixion 62505)

ATTENTION-GETTER:

Post the word card: FORGIVE.

• *Jesus taught us what it means to truly forgive.*

Post the picture: The Crucifixion.

• *Near the time when Jesus would be crucified, the soldiers did unkind things to him. They hit him, whipped him, spat on him, put a crown of thorns on his head, and called him names. Then the soldiers led Jesus to a hillside called Calvary and nailed him to a cross. Jesus wasn't angry with the soldiers for what they did to him. He said, "Father, forgive them; for they know not what they do. . ." (Luke 23:34).*

• *Jesus was the greatest example of forgiveness. He taught us to pray and ask "Help me dear Father."* Sing the first verse for the children.

LISTENING AND SINGING EXPERIENCES:

Verse One:

• *The words of this song are a prayer asking Heavenly Father for help. In this song what is another name for Heavenly Father? [Dear Father]*

• *What is the first thing we are asking our Father in Heaven to help us do? [To freely forgive] What does it means to "forgive?"* Let the children respond.

• *To "forgive" means to change angry feelings toward others to kind feelings. If we forgive others, we don't try to hurt them or get even. We treat them with kindness.*

• *Listen carefully to find out whom we should forgive. [All who may seem unkind to me]*

Divide the group into two parts. Ask one section to listen for how often we pray for our Father's help. [Each day] Ask the other half to listen for what we are praying for each day. [To live nearer, nearer to thee] To live nearer to Heavenly Father means that we feel close to him. Learning to forgive others is one way we can feel nearer to him.

Invite the children to sing the first verse with you.

Verse Two:

Invite the children to sing the last two lines of this verse with each repetition.

• *What am I asking Heavenly Father to help me do? [To truly repent]*

• *I can begin to repent by doing what? [Making things right, and changing my ways]* Give the children some examples of "making things right," and tell them that "changing their ways" means they will try to do better.

Invite the children to sing the second verse. Point out that repenting will also help us feel nearer to Heavenly Father.

Ask the children to think of their own actions and how they can be more forgiving to those who are unkind to them. Challenge them to try to truly repent of things they do wrong.

ENRICHMENT IDEAS:

1. As an attention-getter for verse two show a bottle of clear water. Add several drops of food coloring to the water. Now pour bleach in the bottle, turning the water clear again. Explain that through repentance we can become clean again and be forgiven of our sins.

2. Read and explain a supporting scripture on forgiveness and repentance, such as Matthew 6:14-15, D&C 58:42–43, or D&C 19:13. Or use one of these scriptures as a clue to help the children guess which song they will be singing.

3. Teach the children how to conduct 3/4 time. Then invite a child to lead the song.

4. Ask a class to sing only the words, "help me" as they occur in the song and all other children to sing the remaining lyrics.

MESSAGE: Jesus was obedient to Heavenly Father's commandments and was baptized by immersion. We can show our obedience by following the example of Jesus.

ENRICHMENT IDEAS:

1. Compare the children's baptisms with the baptism of Jesus. How are they alike and how are they different?

2. Have the children listen to the accompaniment for the rippling sound of the gentle River Jordan.

3. Sing the song, leaving out the key words. Have the children sing the missing words.

4. Have a recently baptized child briefly tell of the experience.

5. Explain any difficult words: Judea, immersion, fulfill, witness.

6. Read John 3:5 or Matthew 3:13–17.

♪ *About the Song*

The original beautiful accompaniment was referred to as "the hardest song for pianists to play in *Sing With Me*." A simplification had been given in the 1981 CTR A manual p. 198, and it was further simplified, and fingering was added for the 1989 *Children's Songbook*.

MATERIALS:

Chalk

Picture: (John the Baptist Baptizing Jesus 62133)

Word cards: WHO? WHERE? WHEN? HOW? WHERE?

ATTENTION-GETTER:

Ask an older child to recite the Fourth Article of Faith.

- *What are the four principles and ordinances of the gospel mentioned?* Write each one on a poster or chalkboard: (1) faith (2) repentance (3) baptism by immersion (4) laying on of hands for the gift of the Holy Ghost.

Ask the children to listen as you sing Verse One for the ordinance this song is about. *[Baptism by immersion]*

Display picture 62133.

LISTENING AND SINGING EXPERIENCES:

Verse One:

- *This is a story about baptism—and stories have characters in them. As I sing the song again, listen to discover who the characters are in this story. [Jesus, John]* Have a child post WHO? by the picture. Explain why John was known as "the Baptist." Invite the children to sing that phrase with you.

- *Now tell me where Jesus found John. [In Judea]* Sing the first two lines again. Have a child post WHERE? by the picture.

- *When did it happen?* Sing the first two lines again. *[Long ago]* Have a child post WHEN? by the picture. Ask the children to sing those two lines with you.

- *How was Jesus baptized? [Jesus was baptized by immersion]* Sing the last two lines. Have a child post HOW? *Immersion means being covered over with water. Notice that the music goes down on the word "immersion," just like you go down into the water to be baptized.* Have the children sing that word several times.

- *Where was Jesus baptized?* Sing the last two lines again. *[In the River Jordan's flow]* Have a child post WHERE? Ask the children to sing the last two lines with you. Sing the entire song again, referring to the word cards, and adding the accompaniment.

Share your own baptism story, or read from Matthew 3:13–17 or Mark 1:9–11.

Teach the second and third verses in a similar manner, using mystery words and questions.

Verse Two:

- *Why was Jesus baptized? [To fulfill the law]*
- *Who questioned Jesus? [John the Baptist]*
- *Why else was Jesus baptized? [To enter with (my) father into (his) kingdom]*
- *Where is Heavenly Father's kingdom? [Up on high]*

Verse Three:

- *What must we witness? [Faith in Jesus' word]*
- *Why should we be baptized? [To show obedience]*
- *Who was baptized to show us the way? [Jesus Christ, our Lord]*

WHEN JESUS CHRIST WAS BAPTIZED

MESSAGE: When Jesus Christ was baptized, three members of the Godhead were present. I will follow the example of Jesus and be baptized by immersion to become a member of Heavenly Father's kingdom.

MATERIALS:

Book of Mormon

Pictures: V.1, (John the Baptist Baptizing Jesus 62133), (Boy Being Baptized 62018)

Word cards: V.1, GODHEAD, RIVER JORDAN, SPOKE, DESCENDED

Word cards: V.2, BAPTIZED, IMMERSION, PRIESTHOOD POWER, KINGDOM, HOLY SPIRIT

ATTENTION-GETTER:

- *How many of you have ever heard the word Godhead? The Godhead is made of three heavenly beings. Who are those beings? [Heavenly Father, Jesus Christ, and the Holy Ghost]*

Show the picture of Jesus being baptized. *As I sing this song about when Jesus Christ was baptized, listen for how many members of the Godhead were present there that day.*

LISTENING AND SINGING EXPERIENCES:

Verse One:

- *How many members of the Godhead were present that day? [Three] Who were they? [Heavenly Father, Jesus Christ, and the Holy Ghost]* Post the word card GODHEAD. Invite the children to join you on "Three members of the Godhead were present there in love."

- *As I sing again, listen to discover where Jesus Christ was baptized. [Down in the River Jordan]* Post RIVER JORDAN above GODHEAD. Invite the children to sing the first line. Then sing both the first and second lines together.

Invite one group of children to listen to find out what the Father did, and the other group of children to discover what the Holy Ghost did. *[The Father spoke from heaven; The Holy Ghost descended as gently as a dove]*

Post the words SPOKE and DESCENDED and invite the children to join you on the last two lines. Explain that descended means "came down."

- *This song has a rhythm pattern that repeats over and over again. It goes like this:* Sing and tap.

When Jes- us Christ was bap- tized

Tap this rhythm with me as we sing the song together.

Add the accompaniment as the children sing the first verse again.

Verse Two:

- *The scriptures tell us the importance of following the example of Jesus Christ in all things. As I sing the second verse listen for something we can do to follow Christ's example. [Be baptized]* Post BAPTIZED and invite the children to join you as you sing the song to that point.

- *As I sing again, see if you can hear the words that describe how Jesus was baptized. [By immersion through sacred priesthood power]* Post IMMERSION and PRIESTHOOD POWER and sing those two phrases with the children. Add them to those already learned.

- *Now listen for what we will be a member of. [Heavenly Father's kingdom]* Post KINGDOM and sing that phrase with the children, along with those already learned.

- *This time, listen to discover who will guide us every hour. [The Holy Spirit]* Post HOLY SPIRIT and sing the last line with the children.

- *Let's sing the complete second verse with the accompaniment.*

Bear testimony of how happy you were to be baptized.

ENRICHMENT IDEAS:

1. Using the pictures listed to compare the baptism of Jesus to our baptisms. Point out the similarities and differences.

2. Challenge the children to discover which word comes on the highest note of the song. *[Father]*

3. As an alternate Attention-Getter, have an older child read Matthew 3:13–17.

4. Pass word cards in random order to several children. Invite the children to come and stand in the correct order as the song is sung. As the song is reviewed, some of the word cards could be taken away. Repeat until all are removed.

5. For younger children, teach verse one using simple visuals such as—a picture of Jesus and a river, the number 3, ♡ , simple drawings of Heavenly Father, Jesus, and a dove.

WHEN I AM BAPTIZED

MESSAGE: The rainbow reminds me that I want my life to always be as clean as it is when I am baptized. I know I can be forgiven and improve myself so that I can live with God again.

ENRICHMENT IDEAS:

1. Draw a rainbow and place key words on the various colors. Put key words for the second verse on the reverse side.

2. When teaching the chorus, have the children follow the melody by pitch leading with their bodies—stooping and standing as the melody goes up and down.

3. Challenge the children to find the word in verse one that has a ⌒ or hold sign over it. [Can]

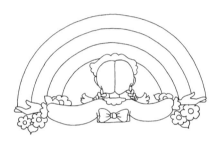

MATERIALS:

Colored chalk

Pictures: V.1, (Boy Being Baptized 62018); V. 2, rainbow

ATTENTION-GETTER:

Tell a personal experience about seeing a rainbow, such as the following:

- *One day when it was raining, I looked out my window just as the clouds parted. Beautiful rays of sun burst through the clouds lighting up the wet earth below. Suddenly, a glorious rainbow arched across the sky. How many of you have seen a rainbow? Show me the shape of a rainbow. [Arch]*

- *Listen as I sing, and see if you can "hear a rainbow" in the melody of this song.*

As you sing the first verse, draw an arch with the flat side of a piece of colored chalk for the first line, change colors for the second line, and then continue to sing the chorus.

Invite two children to come forward as you sing the first verse again and have them repeat what you did with two other colors of chalk—forming a rainbow.

LISTENING AND SINGING EXPERIENCES:

Verse One:

- *As I sing this song again, listen for what I think about or ponder on when I see a rainbow. [The beauty of an earth made clean again]*

Invite the children to sing the first two lines with you, drawing their own imaginary rainbow in the air.

- *The earth is so clean and fresh after it has rained. I would like my life to be as clean as something mentioned in this song. What is it? [Earth right after rain]*

Through pitch leading, point out the interval jumps and repeated notes on "I want my life to be as clean as earth right after rain." Invite the children to pitch lead this part as they carefully sing these intervals.

- *If I live the best I can, with whom will I be able to live again? [God (Heavenly Father)]*

- *This last phrase starts like the phrase we pitch led together, but there is one note that goes just a little higher than any others. As we sing the song together, listen to see what word we sing on this high note? [Best] Invite the children to sing verse one with the accompaniment.*

Verse Two:

Hold up the picture Boy Being Baptized.

- *As I sing the second verse, listen to discover what is washed away when I am baptized. [My wrongs (my sins)]*

- *We do have a fresh, clean start when we are baptized. And later when we do make wrong choices, we can renew our baptismal covenants by taking the sacrament, repenting and be forgiven. Then we are clean and fresh once again. As I sing, listen for something I must do as part of being forgiven. [Improve myself each day]*

Show a picture of a rainbow or refer to the one drawn on the chalk board. Challenge the children to look for a rainbow whenever there is rain and to think about how they can make their lives as clean as earth right after rain.

I LIKE MY BIRTHDAYS

MESSAGE: I can't wait until my eighth birthday, because I'll be baptized and confirmed as Jesus was.

MATERIALS:

Birthday cake with eight candles (or a picture of one)

Pictures: (Boy Being Baptized 62018), a smiling child, the number 8

ATTENTION-GETTER:

Show a birthday cake with eight candles on it.

- *Birthdays are wonderful. I still get excited when mine is almost here. There's one birthday for members of the Church that is the best of all. There is something on this cake to give you a big clue which birthday this is. [Eight candles]*

LISTENING AND SINGING EXPERIENCES:

Sing the song several times, encouraging the children to listen by using questions and statements similar to those listed below. As children discover answers, invite them to sing that part of the song with you. Add one phrase at a time to the ones already learned.

Verse One:

- *As I sing this song for you, tell me what I like. [My birthdays]* Show the birthday cake or display the picture.
- *What does each birthday bring to me? [Greater joy]* Post the picture of a smiling child.
- *As I sing again, see if you can discover two things: First, I can't wait until what? [I'm eight] Second, what will happen when I'm eight? [I'll be baptized] You'll have to listen very carefully to find both of them.* Post the number 8 and the picture Boy Being Baptized as the children discover those answers.

Invite the children to sing verse one, referring to the pictures.

Verse Two:

Teach the second verse in a similar manner, asking questions such as:

- *I will be baptized like whom? [Jesus]*
- *By whom will I be baptized? [One who holds the priesthood true]*
- *What will I be obeying? [God's holy laws]*

Verse Three:

- *What will I receive when hands are laid upon my head? [The Holy Ghost]*
- *What will I have if I listen carefully? [The blessings I want most]*
- *Two of our greatest blessings are our membership in The Church of Jesus Christ of Latter-day Saints, and the Holy Ghost, who is our constant companion to help us each day. Both of these blessings come when we are baptized and confirmed.*

Challenge the children to prepare for these great blessings.

ENRICHMENT IDEAS:

1. Have a child express his feelings about the day he or she was baptized and confirmed.

2. Show the picture (John the Baptist Baptizing Jesus 62133). Jesus set the example for us to follow. He was baptized by immersion, which means that he was totally covered with water. We are baptized just as he was.

3. Invite the children to tap the short—long rhythm of this song with you.

4. Display pictures to represent the message of each verse: boy with birthday cake, Jesus' baptism (62133), (Boy Being Baptized 62018), (Girl Being Confirmed 62020).

5. Read John 3:5 or Matthew 3:13–17.

6. Sing other songs relating to the subject, such as "Baptism" (p. 100), "The Holy Ghost" (p. 105), "Listen, Listen" (p. 107), and "The Still Small Voice" (p. 106).

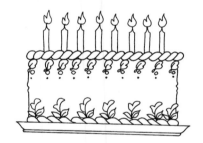

THE HOLY GHOST

MESSAGE: Christ promised he would send the Holy Ghost to comfort us. The Holy Ghost whispers with a quiet voice and testifies of God and Christ. If we will listen, he will guide us and help us make right choices.

ENRICHMENT IDEAS:

1. Post key word cards: CHRIST PROMISED, HOLY GHOST, COMFORT, FRIEND, HOLY SPIRIT, TESTIFIES, HEART. Invite the children to sing the first verse referring to the key words. With each repetition, have a child remove key words.

2. Post the word cards in random order. As the children sing, have one child arrange the words in the correct order.

3. Explain that the Holy Ghost is an important member of the Godhead. He is a real personage of spirit, and though we can't see him with our eyes, he can speak to our minds and hearts.

4. Help the children pitch lead the melody line. Notice the many repeated notes in this song.

5. As an alternate attention-getter say in a very quiet voice, *"Everyone who can hear my voice, put your finger on your nose. Everyone who can hear my quiet voice, put your hand on your head."* Explain that even though you were speaking very quietly, when they listened, they could hear and obey your instructions. Tell them that you are going to sing a song about someone who has a still small voice and who tells our hearts and minds important things.

MATERIALS:

Well-used baby blanket

New Testament

ATTENTION-GETTER:

Show the baby blanket.

- *How many of you had a special blanket when you were younger that you really needed when it was time for bed? Your blanket was wonderful to snuggle with because it comforted you. It made you feel comfortable inside so that you could go to sleep.*

- *When we are baptized and confirmed a member of the Church, we are given a true, eternal friend. Jesus called him the Comforter because he comforts us and helps us to be happy. As I sing this song, listen for two other names for the Comforter. [The Holy Ghost, the Holy Spirit]*

LISTENING AND SINGING EXPERIENCES:

Before inviting the children to sing with you, sing the song several times, directing the children's listening by asking questions.

Verse One:

- *Jesus promised he would send us the Holy Ghost. What two words describe the kind of friend the Holy Ghost is? [True, eternal] This means the Holy Ghost will always tell you the truth, and he will be your friend forever.* Sing the first two lines with the children.

- *As the Holy Ghost whispers with a still small voice, he testifies of two very important beings. Listen as I sing to see of whom the Holy Ghost testifies. [God and Christ]*

- *When we hear these great things, what does it make our hearts do? [Rejoice] This means we feel good inside as the Holy Ghost whispers these great truths to us.*

Invite the children to sing verse one with the accompaniment. Have an older child read John 14:26. Bear your testimony that the Holy Ghost helps us to know that Heavenly Father and Jesus Christ live, and that he can teach us all the things that are good for us.

Verse Two:

Teach the second verse in the same manner as the first, asking the following questions:

- *By what power are we confirmed? [Sacred priesthood power]*
- *Why is the Holy Ghost given to us? [To guide us every hour]*
- *To what may I always listen? [To the still small voice]*
- *What will I do each time I make a choice? [With his light, I'll do what's right]*
- *I know that the Holy Ghost will be with us to help us make good choices.*

Briefly relate a personal experience.

THE STILL SMALL VOICE

MESSAGE: The Holy Ghost will guide and protect me if I listen to his still small voice.

MATERIALS:

Picture: Harold B. Lee

Word cards: GUIDE ME, SAVE ME, DIRECT ME, PROTECT ME

Doctrine and Covenants

ATTENTION-GETTER:

Show a picture of Harold B. Lee and tell the following story:

- *When President Harold B. Lee was a young boy, his grandmother, his mother, and two or three of the younger children in his family, were seated before an open door. They were watching a severe thunderstorm raging over the mountain near their home. A flash of lightning, followed by an immediate loud clap of thunder, indicated that the lightning had struck very close.*

Harold was standing in the doorway, and his mother gave him a vigorous push that sent him sprawling on his back out of the doorway. At that instant, a bolt of lightning came down the chimney of the kitchen stove and through the open doorway. It split a large tree from top to bottom immediately in front of the house. If Harold had remained in the open door, he would have been struck by lightning.

His mother felt she was guided by the still small voice as she made this split-second decision.

LISTENING AND SINGING EXPERIENCES:

- *As I sing, listen for another name for the still small voice. [The Spirit]*
- *As I sing the last two lines again, count how many times you hear the word "listen." [Four] It must be important to listen if it is repeated four times in the song.*

As you sing again, invite the children to sing the word "listen" with you each time and to notice that the melody and the words are the same each time.

- *Now as I sing the whole song, listen to find other words that have the same melody as the word "listen."* Pitch lead just these words to help the children notice they are the same. *[Voice, me, right, night]* Invite them to sing those words only, as you sing the whole song again, bringing them in on the last two lines each time.
- *What will the Holy Ghost give me that helps when things get dark? [Give my soul his light]* Soul means your body and spirit; light represents truth and love.
- *If I try to do what's right, where will the still small voice lead me? [Through the night]* Night represents evil or difficulty.
- *This time, listen to discover what the still small voice will save me from. [The evil I may see]*
- *Listen for ways the still small voice can help you and me.* Post the responses as the answers are given. *[GUIDE ME, SAVE ME, DIRECT ME, PROTECT ME]*

Help the children find the answers by noticing that the melody of these word phrases is the same. Then sing the entire song and challenge the children to put the word cards in the correct order.

- *The still small voice may speak through your mind or your heart. It can speak with feelings that warn us not to do wrong, or that cause us to feel good when we do right.*

Have an older child read D&C 8:2. Bear your testimony of this principle.

ENRICHMENT IDEAS:

1. As you sing, do not put your hand to your ear on the words "listen, listen," because the Holy Ghost often whispers in other ways, rather than with an audible sound.
2. Show pictures of a girl or boy being confirmed (62020, 62341). Explain that when a person is confirmed, he is told to receive the Holy Ghost. Each of us should prepare ourselves every day to be worthy to receive this wonderful gift.
3. Enhance the words by gradually singing with more volume until the word "listen." Then sing the ending softly to emphasize the still small voice.
4. Help the children to listen and respond to the quiet, peaceful mood of this song by having them listen to a violin, flute, or organ solo as they hum the melody.
5. Sing the phrases "through a still small voice" and "try to do what's right." Point out that the repeated notes stress the importance of these words.

♪ About the Song

With the exception of this song, all other songs in the *Children's Songbook* have chord symbols (C, F, G7, etc.) above the melody line. These can be used when playing chord casios and organs, guitar, or autoharp. See pages 302 and 303 in "Using the Songbook" section, for a chord chart and explanation. This song is modal (it has no key). The committee tried adding simplified chording, but finally decided to drop the chords rather than lose the unique sound of the accompaniment.

LISTEN, LISTEN

MESSAGE: If you listen carefully to the still small voice, he will guide you when you have to make a choice.

ENRICHMENT IDEAS:

1. To reinforce the importance of listening, sing this song as a round. Refer to *Children's Songbook*, page 107 or page 304, for detailed instructions on rounds.

2. Have the children sing "The Still Small Voice" (p. 106) or "The Holy Ghost" (p. 105) to help support the message of this song.

3. Have children read Moroni 10:5 and D&C 8:2.

4. Make a fermata sign ⌒. As the children sing the song, challenge them to hold the word as long as you hold up the sign. They will have to watch closely to know when to sing the word "*always*." Tell the children that they can take a breath whenever they need to, but to keep singing until you put the sign down.

5. Show the melody picture as illustrated. Sing the direction of the melody by replacing the words with: down, down, down, down, down, up, up. Ask the children what words are sung to this melody. *[Listen to the still small voice]*

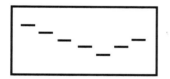

MATERIALS:

Picture: Harold B. Lee

ATTENTION-GETTER:

Show a picture of Harold B. Lee.

• *When Harold B. Lee was ten years of age, he was about to enter an old dilapidated shed out in a field where he was walking. Suddenly, he heard a voice distinctly say, "Harold, don't go in there!" He looked around and could not see anyone, so again he began to enter. But the voice repeated the warning. This time he listened and obeyed, because he knew that it was the still small voice that he heard quietly within his mind and heart. It was the Holy Ghost guiding his steps to prevent harm from coming to him.*

LISTENING AND SINGING EXPERIENCES:

Quietly sing the song, then ask in a whisper what the children should "listen" to. *[The still small voice]* Remind them that the still small voice is the Holy Ghost, a member of the Godhead.

Sing the song again, asking how many times they hear the word "listen." [Three]

Invite the children to join you in singing the second and third repetitions of the word "listen" as you sing the song again.

• *What will the Holy Ghost do for you? [He will guide you always.]* Have the children sing the answer. Point out that the word "you" is held so long before singing "always" because there is a ⌒ over the note.

• *If we listen to the still small voice when we have choices to make, he will guide us and help us know the truth of all things.*

SEEK THE LORD EARLY

MESSAGE: I'll seek the Lord and his truth by reading the scriptures, praying, and obeying the prophets and Heavenly Father's commandments.

MATERIALS:

A novel

Pictures: scriptures (Both Books of Scripture Testify of Christ 62373), (Bedside Prayer 62217), (Latter-day Prophets 62575), obeying commandments (Sharing a Tricycle 62317)

ATTENTION-GETTER:

Flip through the novel and then act as if you are reading the last page.

- *Oh, so that's how it ends! Have you ever read the last page of a book first because you couldn't wait to see how the story ended? Some endings are just too good to wait for!*

- *I know a song that offers us a great reward at the very end. The reward does require work that we can't skip over, but it is worth it! Listen as I sing, and discover what this wonderful reward is. [He (the Lord) will be found.]*

LISTENING AND SINGING EXPERIENCES:

Sing the song several times and direct the children's listening by asking questions such as the following:

- *As I sing the song again, listen for (1) Which words on the last line have the two fastest notes? [I will] (2) Which words are sung on the two longest notes? [He, found]*

Have the children clap these rhythms as they sing the last line with you.

Sing the last line again and help the children sing the interval from "He" to "will" correctly.

Help the children understand that Heavenly Father isn't "lost" so we aren't seeking him physically. We are trying to feel close to him, and we find him when we feel his love.

- *To seek the Lord is so important that we sing that phrase more than once. As I sing the song again, count how many times I sing "I'll seek the Lord." [Three]*

Bring the children in on the last line of each repetition. Point out that two times we sing "I'll" and the last time we sing "I will."

- *When we sing "I'll seek the Lord early" the first two times, is the melody the same or different? [Same] Sing the song again if necessary to obtain the answer.*

- *If I seek him, what will he help me to know? [The truth]*

- *As I sing again, discover four ways we can seek the Lord.* As the children name the ways, post pictures listed below to represent each answer.

    1. Search the scriptures (62373).

    2. Go to our Father in fervent prayer (62217). (*Notice that the melody suggests kneeling down and staying on our knees.*)

    3. Obey the living prophets in all they say (62575).

    4. Keep the commandments (Sharing a Tricycle 62317).

- *Sing the song with me and listen for a word that means the Lord's love is everywhere. [His love will abound] This means there will be so much love that it will surround you.*

- *We can develop a deep understanding and love for Heavenly Father and Jesus Christ as we seek them through scripture study, prayer, and obedience. If we seek the Lord while we are young, we will find him.*

ENRICHMENT IDEAS:

1. Define important words: "Seek," "Early," and "Fervent prayer."

2. To introduce the song another week, have one child be "it" and ask him to quickly find another child who is hiding in the room. *What is the name of this game?* [Hide and seek.] *What does the word "seek" mean?* [To look for, to try to find] Post the word "seek." Again, help the children understand that we aren't seeking Heavenly Father physically. We find him when we feel his love.

3. Draw eight phrase lines on the chalkboard as shown. Write the ending word of phrases one, three, five, seven (*youth, there, obey, abound*) at the end of the line. Sing the song and have the children discover and write the rhyming words at the end of phrases two, four, six, and eight (*truth, prayer, say, found*).

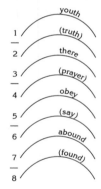

4. Prepare a simple poster as shown to review the song.

SEARCH, PONDER AND PRAY

MESSAGE: If I search, ponder, and pray, Heavenly Father will bless me with a testimony to know that the scriptures are true. I'll prayerfully read the scriptures every day and come to understand and keep the Lord's commandments.

ENRICHMENT IDEAS:

1. Make phrase charts as illustrated. Pass out the word cards: READ, SEARCH, PONDER, PRAY on yellow cards: START, GROW, GUIDE on blue cards; and TESTIMONY, TRUE, KNOW, TRUE, on green cards. As you sing the song have them put their word card on the phrase chart where it belongs. Follow the phrase lines with your finger as you sing. Sing again to see if they are placed correctly.

Verse   Chorus

2. Sing the chorus, using sign language.

3. Tell the story of Joseph Smith searching James 1:5 that led to his vision. Read and emphasize that the scriptures can guide us in all we do.

4. President Howard W. Hunter has said, "Families are greatly blessed when wise fathers and mothers bring their children about them, read from the pages of the scriptural library together, and then discuss freely the beautiful stories and thoughts." (*Ensign*, Nov. 1979, p. 64)

5. Hum the melody picture and challenge the children to find the words that match the melody on the last phrase.

♪ *About the Song*

In 1986, this song was a winner in the Church Music Contest and was printed in the Children's Sacrament Meeting Presentation. The words from the preface to the songbook apply to this song: "As you sing, you may feel good inside. The Holy Ghost gives you warm feelings to help you understand that the words and messages of the songs are true."

MATERIALS:

Scriptures

Word cards: TESTIMONY, SEARCH, PONDER, PRAY, READ, EACH DAY, UNDERSTAND HEED, DO

Rhythm card:

ATTENTION-GETTER:

Hold up the scriptures with word card TESTIMONY inside.

• *Inside my scriptures is a word that describes what you can have if you study the scriptures. There are clues in the song that will help you know what this word is.* Sing the song to the children. Open your scriptures and show the word card: TESTIMONY. *The word "testimony" means that you know the scriptures are true.*

LISTENING AND SINGING EXPERIENCES:

• *Listen as I sing again, and tell me what three things I must do to know for myself that the scriptures are true.* Sing the first verse and chorus. As the children respond display the words SEARCH, PONDER, and PRAY.

• *When we sing the words "search, ponder, and pray," we are saying that we need to "study, think about and pray about" the scriptures to know that they are true.*

• *As I sing the first line of the chorus again, listen for which of the three words is sung on the highest note. [Ponder]*

Invite the children to sing "search, ponder, and pray are the things that I must do."

• *What will the spirit help me know deep inside? [The scriptures are true.]*

• *Listen as I sing the last line again, to find two rhyming words. [Guide, inside]*

Verse One:

• *I love to read the holy scriptures, and, every time I do, I feel the Spirit start to grow within my heart. What is this feeling? [A testimony that it's true]*

• *Does the melody on the word "testimony" go up or down? [Up] Pitch lead this verse with me and find the one-syllable word that is sung on two notes. [True]* Invite the children to sing the complete verse and chorus.

Show the rhythm card and challenge the children to listen as you clap it and to count the number of times they hear this rhythm. *[Three]* Then invite the children to sing and tap.

• *What are the words that are sung on that rhythm?* Sing the entire song.

• *As we search, ponder, and pray about the scriptures, we will learn to love them. Heavenly Father will bless us to know that the scriptures are true.*

Verse Two:

• *What will I prayerfully do? [Read the scriptures]* Post: READ.

• *How often will I read the scriptures? [Each day my whole life through]* Post: EACH DAY.

• *What will I come to do? [Understand]* Post: UNDERSTAND.

• *What is another word meaning to "obey" the Lord's command? [Heed]* Post: HEED

• *What word is sung on two notes? (Hint: We sing this word twice.) [Do.]* Post: DO.

• *This verse has taught us four things we can do to gain a testimony that the scriptures are true. (Refer to the key words.) If we prayerfully read the scriptures each day, we will come to understand them. We can heed the commandments and do as the Lord would have us do.* Sing the second verse and chorus.

FOLLOW THE PROPHET

MESSAGE: If I follow the prophet, I will not go astray.

MATERIALS:

Pictures: (Adam and Eve 62461), (Building the Ark 62053), (Abraham Taking Isaac to be Sacrificed 62054), (The Crossing of the Red Sea 62100), (Boy Samuel Called by the Lord 62498), (Daniel in the Lion's Den 62096)

ATTENTION-GETTER:

- *In thirty seconds, name as many Old Testament prophets as you can. Ready, get set, go!*
- *Who was our very first prophet? [Adam]*

LISTENING AND SINGING EXPERIENCES:

Chorus:

- *Listen as I sing this song about the prophet Adam. Tell me how many times I sing the words "Follow the Prophet." [Six]*
- *As I sing and tap the rhythm to the chorus, listen for two reasons why we should follow the prophet. [So we "don't go astray," because "he knows the way"] Now tap the rhythm as I sing the chorus again.*

Verse One: Adam (See Moses 5:4–12, 58–59.)

- *Adam was the first prophet that we know. Listen and tell me where he lived and helped things to grow. [Eden]* Sing entire song, bringing children in on the chorus.
- *Listen as I sing the first two lines again, and tell me what one-syllable word is sung on two tones. [Grow]* Invite the children to sing this much with you.
- *How did Adam serve the Lord? [By following his ways]*
- *What words mean we are part of Adam's family in the latter days? [We are his descendants]* Have the children pitch lead the descending scale on "in the latter days." Invite the children to stand and sing the first verse with you.
- *Heavenly Father's servants, the prophets, speak his will and teach what Heavenly Father would teach if he were here.* Have a child read D&C 1:38.

To introduce verses 2-7 use the library pictures or illustrations below and ask the children what they know about that prophet. Refer to the scriptures for each verse.

ENRICHMENT IDEAS:

1. Dress a child to resemble the prophet you are singing about. Use props such as— The number 1 (Adam); halo (Enoch); ark or boat (Noah); the number 12 (Abraham); stone tablets (Moses); Word card HERE I AM (Samuel); whale (Jonah); lion (Daniel).

2. Begin singing the chorus softly and increase the volume to "don't go astray." Repeat again from soft to loud to the words "he knows the way" to give emphasis to the important words. You might try reversing the dynamics and letting the children decide which dynamics match the words of the song.

♪ *About the Song*

Since the Children's Sacrament Meeting Program of 1988, boys and girls have been enjoying the additional verses to "Book of Mormon Stories." The Songbook Committee thought children would enjoy a song about the Old Testament stories—with, of course, a Jewish flavor. A memorable chorus could contain the main message of the song. Duane Hiatt, who performed musical comedy professionally with the "Three D's," was asked to try the idea. He played his guitar and made nine verses with a catchy melody. As a father of fifteen children, he knew what children would enjoy singing. The "hook of the song," or the part you remember, is the chorus. Scripture story references are included on this page.

THE COMMANDMENTS

MESSAGE: There are ten commandments, but the greatest commandments are to love God with all thy heart and thy neighbor as thyself.

ENRICHMENT IDEAS:

1. As the children sing about each commandment, lead a brief discussion on its meaning.

2. Have an older child or twelve children read the commandments from the scriptures. (See Exodus 20:3–17 and Matthew 22:36–39.)

3. Make tablets as illustrated. Pass out the tablets to twelve children in random order. As you sing the song, invite the children to come to the front and stand in the correct order. Sing again to check the order.

MATERIALS:

Pictures: (The Crossing of the Red Sea 62100), or (Moses and the Burning Bush 62239)

Cutouts: Twelve "tablets" on which you have written the commandments as they appear in the song.

ATTENTION-GETTER:

To play "Who Am I?" hold the picture of Moses so the children can't see it and say:

• *I was a prophet of God called to free the Israelites who had been slaves to the Egyptians for four hundred years. I led them out of Egypt into the wilderness. The people soon became wicked because they had no laws or commandments to live by. I went up on Mt. Sinai to ask the Lord for help, and the Lord wrote the Ten Commandments on tablets of stone. Who am I? [Moses]*

Show the picture and sing "The Commandments" for the children. Display the twelve individual "tablets." (The last two commandments were not part of the Ten Commandments given to Moses.)

LISTENING AND SINGING EXPERIENCES:

Teach through repetition, referring to your tablets.

• *When Jesus lived on the earth, he was asked which of the commandments is greatest of all. Jesus answered: (Have an older child read Matthew 22:36–39.)*

• *How many prayer language words do you hear? [Ten: thou (1), shalt (1), thy (7), thyself (1)]*

• *Challenge the children to find the commandments with similar melodies.*

• *When the children are very familiar with the song, begin removing the tablets. This may not happen the first week.*

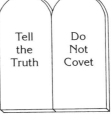

THE BOOKS IN THE OLD TESTAMENT

MESSAGE: I know the names and order of the books in the Old Testament.

MATERIALS:

Poster: Make a book by folding a black poster board in half or cut it in two and attach it together with rings. On the cover, write The Old Testament. On the inside, place removable white wordstrips, one for the name of each book in the Old Testament.

ATTENTION-GETTER:

Show the children the book-like poster you have prepared with the removable names of the books of the Old Testament attached (see illustration.) Explain that these are the names of the books of the Old Testament.

• *Count the number of books as I point to them and sing their names. [Thirty-nine]*

LISTENING AND SINGING EXPERIENCES:

Learning this song will require many repetitions. Make sure that you are confident with the rhythm, as it has been slightly changed from "Do What Is Right" (*Hymns*, no. 237) to accommodate the words. Practice pronouncing the books before you begin.

Teach this song by rote, a few books at a time. Have the children sing back to you as many times as necessary until they are secure. Teach only as much as the children can handle in one week.

When the children are very familiar with all the books, invite a child to remove several word strips with each repetition of the song. Sing until all are removed.

ENRICHMENT IDEAS:

1. Let the children open their Bibles and sing from the contents page.

2. Divide the children into smaller groups and teach each group four measures of the song. Invite each group to stand and sing the part they've practiced.

3. Show a wordstrip for each book in the Old Testament and sing the song. Using a timer, ask the children to decide how many books of the Old Testament they think they can learn in five minutes. Set the timer and begin teaching the song. As the children learn the name of a book, remove it from the list. When time is up, see how many books they can sing without your help. Any books missed must be put back on the chart.

4. This song can also be taught as a rap. Speak a phrase of the song in rhythm, pointing to the children when you want them to "rap the phrase back to you. Teach additional phrases each week.

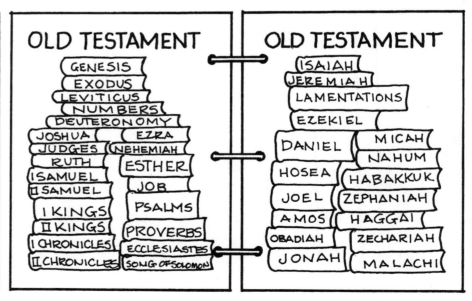

THE BOOKS IN THE NEW TESTAMENT

MESSAGE: I know the names and order of the books in the New Testament.

ENRICHMENT IDEAS:

1. Challenge the children to count the number of books in the New Testament. *[Twenty-eight]*

2. Display the names of the books of the New Testament on individual wordstrips. These could be displayed on a clothesline. With each repetition of the song, have a child remove two of the wordstrips.

3. Refer to the Enrichment Ideas for "The Books in the Book of Mormon," p. 149.

4. Older children may enjoy singing the list of books from the contents page in their Bibles.

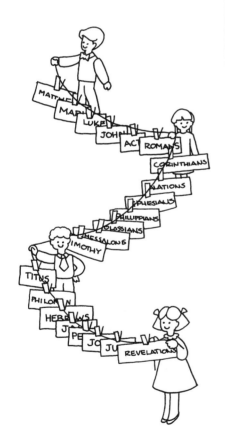

MATERIALS:

Fermata Card: ⌒

Melody picture:

ATTENTION-GETTER:

- *Today we are going to begin learning the names of all the books in the New Testament in order!*

Divide the children into four groups. Sing and teach the words of the first line as follows: To group 1: Matthew, Mark. To group 2: Luke, John. To group 3: The Acts. To group 4: and Romans. Make sure each group is secure in their part. Then have each group sing their part and sustain the last note to form the C major chord. Trade parts several times; then sing the first line together.

LISTENING AND SINGING EXPERIENCES:

- *Listen as I sing the entire song, and find how many times the melody of the first line repeats. [Two]* Check the answer and repeat as necessary.

Second line:

- *The first phrase names six books, but the second phrase lists only two. What are these last two? [First and Second Corinthians]* Sing and tap the second line.

Sing the first two lines.

Third line:

- *The next phrase is similar to the first melody we learned. How many books are named in this phrase? [Four]* Sing until the children can repeat all the names back to you. Sing the first three lines together.

Fourth line:

- *The melody of the fourth phrase is similar to which line you have already sung? [Second line] What is similar about the words? [The words "first" and "second"] Notice how the melody drops at the end of the word "second" on the fourth line.* (This may be enough to teach the first week.)

Fifth line:

- *What other books are sung to the same tune as "Timothy, Timothy"? [Titus, Philemon] Notice that although the word "Timothy" repeats, the rhythm does not.* Invite the children to tap the rhythm.

Sixth line:

Show and explain a fermata. *On what word does it occur? [Hebrews]*

Show the melody picture *On which book do we sing a descending scale? [James]* Let children pitch lead it with you as they sing.

- *The book of James is not called a book; it is called something else. What is it? [Epistle] In New Testament times, letters were sent from one branch of the Church to another. They were very important letters, because they taught the members of the Church the gospel. Twenty-one of the twenty-seven books of the New Testament are these "teaching letters," or "epistles."*

Seventh line:

- *How many times do we sing "Peter" and "John." [Peter (two), John (three)] What are the last two books in the New Testament? [Jude and Revelation]*

BOOK OF MORMON STORIES

MESSAGE: Book of Mormon stories tell about the Lamanites and the Nephites, who were given this land by Heavenly Father if they lived righteously.

ATTENTION-GETTER:

Tap a steady beat, accenting the first of every four beats. Then begin softly chanting "Book of Mormon" to the beat. Invite the children to join you. As they continue to softly chant, start singing the words to the verses.

LISTENING AND SINGING EXPERIENCES:

Repeat the song several times, directing the children's listening by asking questions.

- *As I sing, listen to discover which people of the Book of Mormon are mentioned in verse one. [Lamanites] The Lamanites are some of the people of the Book of Mormon who were descendants of Lehi. We call them Native Americans.*
- *Who tells me Book of Mormon stories? [My teacher]* Sing the first two phrases with the children.
- *From where did the Lamanites' fathers come? [Far across the sea]*
- *What were the Lamanites given if they lived righteously? [The land]*

Invite the children to sing the last line as they answer this last question. Then ask them to sing the entire first verse as you pitch lead.

Define other words: "ancient" (of times past), "history" (an account of what happened), "the land" (America), "liberty" (freedom).

ENRICHMENT IDEAS:

1. The words of the song may be illustrated with Native American sign language. Or the children could make up their own simple actions, such as forming a book with their hands, two fingers behind their heads for feathers, rolling of hands like waves, pointing to land, folding arms, etc.

2. Sing "The Golden Plates" (p. 86) and "The Books in the Book of Mormon" (p. 119).

3. Teach the additional verses. Using the pictures, list key words:

   V 1-2: *Lehi* (62045)

   V 3: *Alma* (62332) See Mosiah 27:8-37.

   V 4: *Abinadi* (62042) See Mosiah 11:20; 12:9, 17; 15:1; 16:13; 17:5, 13:20.

   V 5: *Ammon* (62535) See Alma 17:30-39.

   V 6: *Army of Helaman* (62050) See Alma 53:18-22.

   V 7: *Samuel* (62370) See Helaman 16:1-8.

   V 8: *Christ* (62541) See 3 Nephi 17:11-25.

♪ *About the Song*

Elizabeth Bates, the composer, is a piano teacher and the mother of six children. She became totally blind in 1951. She accepted her blindness as a challenge and decided that she would learn to do everything that she could. In 1969, she wrote "Book of Mormon Stories" because she loves the Book of Mormon and is grateful for America. She said, "Any enjoyment of this song is due to the fact that the Book of Mormon is true."

THE BOOKS IN THE BOOK OF MORMON

MESSAGE: I know the names and the order of the books in the Book of Mormon.

ENRICHMENT IDEAS:

1. On stiff paper prepare fifteen pages with the name of one of the books in the Book of Mormon written on each page. (File folders work well and can be punched and assembled with rings when the song is learned.) Pass clothespins and these pages in random order to fifteen children. Invite two children to hold a clothesline or rope in front of the group. Challenge the children to arrange the pages on the clothesline in the correct order while the group is singing the song. (Or the pages could be placed upright in the chalkboard tray.)

2. Pass out copies of the Book of Mormon and sing the song from the list of books on the contents page.

3. Have the children pitch lead this song with their bodies rising and stooping as they follow the melody line.

4. Use tone bells to accompany this song.

5. Ask if anyone knows other words to this melody. [Ten Little Indians]

♪ About the Song

For the *Children's Songbook*, the last phrase was changed from "singing this is so fun" to "In the Book of Mormon" which emphasized the message of the song, and also avoided the unimportant word "so" on an important musical accent.

MATERIALS:

Book of Mormon

Key words: Verse One: BOOKS, J E J O, WORDS & M, B OF M

Verse Two: A H, 3-4 N, M E M

Melody Picture:

ATTENTION-GETTER:

Hold up a Book of Mormon.

- *Can anyone tell me the names of the books in the Book of Mormon in the correct order? By the end of singing time today, you will all be able to!*

LISTENING AND SINGING EXPERIENCES:

Verse One:

Divide the children into four groups. Sing two measures to the first group and have them sing that phrase back to you; then sing the next two measures to the second group, and so on.

Switch parts and repeat the process. Use key words to help the children learn the names of the books: BOOKS, J E J O (for Jacob, Enos, Jarom, Omni), WORDS & M, and B OF M. Write the key words on the blackboard or make word cards.

Sing verse one again and ask if anyone noticed a place where the melody came down in steps. *[In last two measures]* Show the melody picture. Invite everyone to sing "in the Book of Mormon." Sing the entire first verse, using the key words.

Verse Two:

- *As I sing the second verse, listen to find out what we learn in the Book of Mormon. [The teachings of the prophets]* Invite the children to sing the last four measures with you.

Now divide into two groups and teach the remaining two lines of verse two as you did with verse one, using key words: A H (for Alma and Helaman), 3-4 N (for 3 and 4 Nephi), and M E M (for Mormon, Ether, and Moroni).

NEPHI'S COURAGE

MESSAGE: Nephi was willing to do whatever the Lord asked of him because he knew that the Lord would provide a way for him to do it. I, too, will be courageous and do what the Lord commands.

MATERIALS:

Book of Mormon

ATTENTION-GETTER:

Hold up a Book of Mormon.

- *Who is the first person mentioned in the Book of Mormon? [Nephi]* Have an older child read 1 Nephi 1:1.

LISTENING AND SINGING EXPERIENCES:

Sing the song several times and direct the children's listening by asking questions such as the following:

Verse One:

- *The Lord commanded Nephi to go and get something. What was it? [The plates]* Sing this phrase, and invite the children to sing it back to you.
- *Who had the plates and wouldn't give them to Nephi? [Laban]*
- *Where was the wicked Laban waiting? [Inside the city gates]*
- *Who were the two brothers who were afraid to try? [Laman and Lemuel]*
- *Was Nephi afraid? [No]* Sing "Nephi was courageous. This was his reply." Then open the scriptures and sing his reply as if you were reading it from the scriptures.
- *As I sing the chorus again, listen for the reason why Nephi had enough courage to go and do what the Lord commanded him. [Because he knew that the Lord provides a way]* Pitch lead and invite the children to sing the chorus with you. Then sing the song from the beginning.

Verse Two:

Teach this verse in the same manner using thought questions and inviting the children to sing each phrase.

- *After Nephi and his family had crossed the wilderness to the ocean, what did the Lord command Nephi to build? [A boat]*
- *Who believed the boat would not float? [Laman and Lemuel—Nephi's older brothers]*
- *Did Laman and Lemuel say he should try to build the boat? [No] As they laughed and mocked, what did they tell Nephi? [They said he should not try]*
- *Again, Nephi was courageous. This was his reply.* Invite the children to sing the chorus with you, and then verse two from the beginning.

Verse Three:

Sing the verse to obtain the answers to these questions.

- *The Lord gives us commandments, and what does he ask of us? [To obey]*
- *What are we sometimes tempted to choose? [Another way]*
- *When we're discouraged and think we cannot try, what will we be? [Courageous]*
- *And what will we reply?* Invite the children to sing the chorus.

ENRICHMENT IDEAS:

1. Ask the children to notice how the music sounds very sad or dark when we sing about those who doubted what the Lord commanded. It sounds positive and happy when we sing about Nephi's courage to obey the Lord's command.

2. Sing "I will go, I will do," and ask the children to listen for the phrase which has the biggest jump. Make harmony by asking half the children to sing "I will go," and hold their note while the other half sings, "I will do." You could also challenge the children to sing "I will go, I will do, the thing the Lord commands" in one breath.

3. Use pictures: (Nephi Subdues His Rebellious brothers 62044), and (Lehi and His People Arrive in The Promised Land 62045).

4. Invite a child to read 1 Nephi 3:7.

5. You could make pictures of the events in the song as illustrated. Mount on butcher paper and unroll as you sing, or use in a roller-box.

♪ *About the Song*

In 1986, the focus of Primary was the Book of Mormon and this song was published in the *Friend* Magazine. It was written by the Hansens, a husband and wife who like children to have fun when they are singing. A third verse was added that applied Nephi's message to the child.

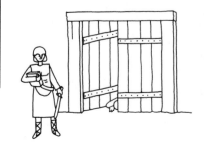

THE FIRST ARTICLE OF FAITH

ENRICHMENT IDEAS:

1. To help with recall, teach the key word GODHEAD (see the *Friend*, Aug. 1987, p. 12). You could use the illustration on that page.

2. Use the picture and wording of the First Article of Faith (the *Friend*, May 1985, p. 24) or the library word chart (65001).

3. Write the First Article of Faith on the chalkboard and have a child erase several words with each repetition.

♪ About the Song

Most children's songs have strong rhymes and repeated musical patterns that make them memorable. The words in the Articles of Faith are difficult and do not rhyme, so they are set to music in the approximate rhythm you would speak them. The melody will help you remember the words, and when you memorize these songs, you are memorizing scripture. Vanja Watkins, the composer, has given the music for each of the Articles of Faith an appropriate mood, and once you have learned the song, you'll never forget the words again! Sister Watkins was a television music teacher. She has written music for twenty-seven songs in the *Children's Songbook* and has served on the Primary General Board and the General Music Committee of the Church. Notice the author of the Article of Faith songs.

MATERIALS:

Word card: GODHEAD

Picture: (The First Vision 62470)

Three melody pictures: Prepare without words. The melody is represented by lines.

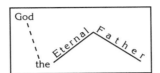 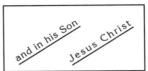 

ATTENTION-GETTER:

- *How many Articles of Faith do we have? [Thirteen] That's right, we have thirteen Articles of Faith and the first one is about the Godhead.*

Display word card GODHEAD. *Listen as I sing, and tell me who the three members of the Godhead are.* Sing the entire First Article of Faith.

LISTENING AND SINGING EXPERIENCES:

- *Who are the three members of the Godhead? [God (the Eternal Father), Jesus Christ (his Son), and the Holy Ghost]*

Hold up the picture The First Vision. *Because of Joseph Smith's vision, we know there are three members of the Godhead. But we don't have a picture of one member. Who can't we see? [The Holy Ghost]*

- *Why don't we have a picture of the Holy Ghost? [Because he has a body of spirit—not of flesh and bones]* Read D&C 130:22.

- *The first member of the Godhead is God. Listen as I sing the First Article of Faith to find another name for God. [The Eternal Father]*

Post the three melody pictures out of order (omitting words) and challenge the children to find the melody picture for "God, the Eternal Father" as you sing the song again.

Once again sing and challenge the children to find the melody picture that matches the words "and in His Son, Jesus Christ, and in the Holy Ghost."

Invite the children to sing this Article of Faith as you refer to the melody pictures.

MATERIALS:

Four melody pictures:

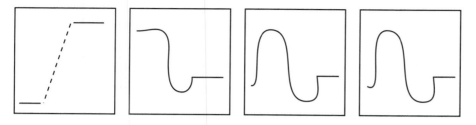

Word cards: TRANSGRESSION, TRANSGRESSION, OWN SINS

Picture: (Adam and Eve 62461)

ATTENTION-GETTER:

Show the four melody pictures in mixed order. Ask children to listen to the song and determine which one they think comes first. If they have trouble determining which is first, give them a clue by singing the first two words of the song, emphasizing the melody by holding your hand very low on the first two notes and raising it high on the third.

LISTENING AND SINGING EXPERIENCES:

Sing the song several more times, helping the children get all the cards in the correct order. Help them notice which two cards are the same, and try to identify the words that go with those cards. *[And not for Adam's transgression]*

- *The last word on each of these cards means "to sin." What is that word?* *[Transgression]* As you sing, point to the last two word cards. As the correct answer is given, place the TRANSGRESSION word cards on the last two melody pictures.

Show the picture of Adam and Eve.

- *The Lord commanded Adam and Eve not to eat the fruit from the tree of knowledge of good and evil. When they ate of the fruit, they disobeyed God. This was their transgression. Their punishment was that they could no longer live in the Garden of Eden.*

- *What two words occur at the end of the second chart?* *[Own sins]* Place the word card OWN SINS on the second melody picture when the answer is given. Discuss the importance of being accountable for our own behavior in the eyes of the Lord.

Invite the children to sing the melody on the first chart as they reach low with their hands ("We Be— . . .") on the low tones, and raise their hands over their heads on the high tone ("—lieve"). The physical movement will help them to sing the large jump accurately.

Add the accompaniment as you invite the children to sing the Second Article of Faith.

ENRICHMENT IDEAS:

1. To help with recall, teach the key word MEN (see the *Friend*, Aug. 1987, p. 12). You could also use the illustration on that page.

2. Use the picture and wording of the Second Article of Faith (the *Friend*, June 1985, p. 24) or the library word chart (65002).

Own Sins

Transgression

THE THIRD ARTICLE OF FAITH

ENRICHMENT IDEAS:

1. To help with recall, teach the key word ATONEMENT (see the *Friend*, Aug. 1987, p. 12). You could use the illustration on that page.

2. Use the picture and wording of the Third Article of Faith (the *Friend*, July 1985, p. 24) or the library word chart (65003).

3. Sing the song from the Article of Faith chart, or each child could sing the words using their own scriptures. (See the Articles of Faith at the end of the Pearl of Great Price.)

4. Ask the children who wrote the words of this song? [Joseph Smith]

5. Ask a child to read one of these scriptures: Hebrews 5:9, D&C 93:38, or Helaman 5:9.

MATERIALS:

Melody pictures (prepare without words):

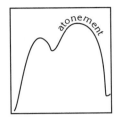 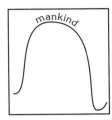 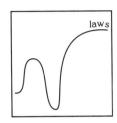 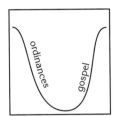

Word cards: ATONEMENT, MANKIND, LAWS, ORDINANCES, GOSPEL

Picture: (Jesus Praying in Gethsemane 62175)

ATTENTION-GETTER:

Place the melody pictures before the children. Have the word cards ready to place on the charts as the children discover the answers.

LISTENING AND SINGING EXPERIENCES:

Sing the song.

• *What word occurs at the top of the highest hill on the first melody picture?* [Atonement]

Show the picture of Jesus in Gethsemane. Discuss the Atonement, explaining that because Jesus loved us so much, he was willing to suffer the punishment for all of our sins. Because of Jesus we don't have to suffer for our sins if we ask Heavenly Father to forgive us and try to live like Jesus. Invite the children to sing the first phrase.

Invite a child to trace the lines so the children can determine what word occurs at the top of the second hill (picture two). [Mankind] Invite the children to sing the first two phrases.

• *What must we obey in addition to ordinances? Hint: The word occurs on the highest step of the third phrase.* [Laws] *Sit tall for the last half of the song in order to sing the high tone on "laws" accurately.*

Refer to melody picture four and help the children discover which word goes down and which word goes up in the last phrase. [Ordinances, gospel] Ask them to rehearse the melody down and up correctly.

Discuss ordinances of the gospel. (Include baptism, confirmation, priesthood ordination, and blessing the sick.) You could show pictures to help the discussion.

THE FOURTH ARTICLE OF FAITH

MATERIALS:

Word cards: F_ _ _ _, R_ _ _ _ _ _ _ _ _, B_ _ _ _ _ _, L_ _ _ _ _ O_ O_ H_ _ _ _.
     PRINCIPLES, O_ _ _ _ _ _ _ _ _.

Melody picture (See Enrichment at right)

Pictures: (Family Home Evening 62521), (Bedside Prayer 62217), (Boy Being Baptized 62018), (Girl Being Confirmed 62020)

ATTENTION-GETTER:

Invite a newly baptized child to come to the front.

- *As you prepared to be baptized, you developed a belief in Jesus Christ. What is another word for this belief and trust?*

Post the word card F_ _ _ _. When the correct response is given, fill in the missing letters on the word card. FAITH

- *You asked Heavenly Father to forgive you for your mistakes. What is this called?* Post the word card R_ _ _ _ _ _ _ _ _. Fill in the word. REPENTANCE

- *When your special day came, you were immersed in water, and your sins were forgiven. What is this called?*

Post the word card B_ _ _ _ _ _. Add letters for to fill in the word. BAPTISM

- *You were also given the gift of the Holy Ghost. How was this done?*

Post the word card L_ _ _ _ _ O_ O_ H_ _ _ _. Fill in the words. LAYING ON OF HANDS

- *Two of these four items are gospel principles.*

Post word card PRINCIPLES.

- *The other two are called something that begins with an "O."*

Display O_ _ _ _ _ _ _ _ _ and challenge them to discover what that word is as they listen to the song. When the children answer correctly, fill in the word card ORDINANCES.

LISTENING AND SINGING EXPERIENCES:

Ask the children to listen to the song and post the wordstrips under the correct headings.

PRINCIPLES	ORDINANCES
1st faith	3rd baptism
2nd repentance	4th laying on of hands

Part of the rhythm in this song bounces in a long-short pattern. Clap "principles and ordinances of the gospel" to demonstrate. *What important words come on that rhythm?* Sing and clap the first phrase.

- *After the number of each principle and ordinance in this song, the composer has placed a rest or break to emphasize the principle or ordinance.* Challenge the children to tap the beat but not sing on the rest after each number.

- *After one of the numbers, there is a large leap downward, followed by an upward scale.* Show the melody picture as you sing "loo" in place of the last phrase. *Listen to the song again and find which number has the melody with the large leap [Fourth]* Pitch lead entire song.

- *What is the fourth principle or ordinance? [Laying on of hands]* Invite the children to sing the last phrase of the song with you. Help them by pitch leading.

- *What words fall on the tune that is the same as the first line? [Third, baptism by immersion for the remission of sins]* Notice that although the melody is the same, the rhythm is very even when singing about baptism. Invite the children to sing the entire song, continuing to clap short-long pattern and rests.

ENRICHMENT IDEAS:

1. To help with recall, teach the key word FIRST PRINCIPLES (see the *Friend,* Aug. 1987, p. 12). You could use the illustration on that page.

2. Use the picture and wording of the Fourth Article of Faith (the *Friend,* Aug. 1985, p. 24) or the library word chart (65004).

3. For younger children, use the pictures listed above in place of wordstrips.

4. Tell stories about faith, repentance, baptism, or the Holy Ghost.

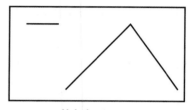

Melody picture

ENRICHMENT IDEAS

1. To help with recall, teach the key word HANDS (see the *Friend*, Aug. 1987, p. 12). You could use the illustration on that page.

2. Use the picture and wording of the Fifth Article of Faith (the *Friend*, Oct. 1985, p. 24) or the library word chart (65005).

3. Use the following pictures to review the song: Called of God by prophecy (Administering to the Sick 62342), the laying on of hands (Ordination to the Priesthood 62341), authority to preach (Missionaries Tracting 62611), administer ordinances (Blessing the Sacrament 62343)

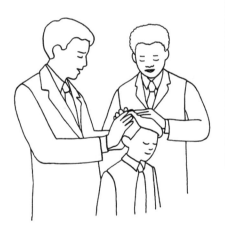

MATERIALS:

Melody picture:

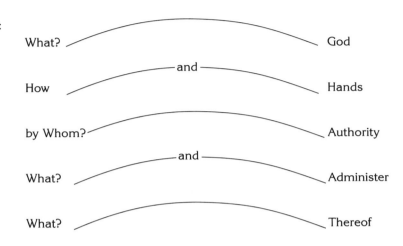

What?	God
How —and—	Hands
by Whom?	Authority
What? —and—	Administer
What?	Thereof

ATTENTION-GETTER:

Post the melody picture. *Today we are going to learn the Fifth Article of Faith by discovering the answers to these mystery words. Notice that five clue words have been given. Each clue word comes at the end of a musical phrase. Each phrase will answer one of our mystery words.*

LISTENING AND SINGING EXPERIENCES:

- *As I sing the entire song, listen to discover what we believe. [That a man must be called of God]* As you sing, follow the first phrase line with your finger to the clue word "God."

As you sing that phrase again, draw attention to the words that fall on the repeated notes. [Be-"lieve that a man"] Invite the children to sing the first phrase.

- *How is a man called of God? [By prophecy, and by the laying on of hands]* Follow the phrase line as above.

Next, "loo" the melody to "laying on of hands" and challenge the children to find the words that occur on this descending scale. Invite the children to sing the first two phrases.

- *By whom are men called? [By those who are in authority]* Invite the children to sing this phrase. *Which of the other two phrases we have learned sounds exactly like this one? [The first one]* Sing all three phrases.

Sing the last two phrases and challenge the children to discover the answers to the next two mystery words.

- *What two things do these men have the authority to do? [Preach the gospel and administer in the ordinances thereof]*

THE SIXTH ARTICLE OF FAITH

MATERIALS:

Word cards: APOSTLES, PROPHETS, PASTORS, TEACHERS, EVANGELISTS

ATTENTION-GETTER:

- As I sing this song, listen for a word that describes the church when Jesus was alive. This word means the "first" church. [Primitive]

LISTENING AND SINGING EXPERIENCES:

Display the word cards in mixed order. Explain that these terms are names of leaders in the primitive church, or the church at Jesus' time. Point out that our church is organized like that primitive church.

- As I sing this Article of Faith for you, listen to the names of the priesthood leaders, and help me place the cards in the correct order. Ask five children to arrange the word cards correctly.

Point out that when the words on the cards are sung, the rhythm is usually long-short, long-short, etc. ♩ ♪ ♩ ♪ ♩ but one word has a rhythm that is short-long. ♪ ♩

- Which priesthood leader has the short-long rhythm. [Teacher]

Invite children to sing the names of all the priesthood leaders, being careful to sing the rhythm accurately. Repeat as necessary to secure the rhythm of the words.

Sing the entire song with the children. Each class could sing a different leader's title. Challenge the children to sing all the words in their heads so they won't lose the rhythmic flow as they listen to each other singing the names.

ENRICHMENT IDEAS:

1. To help with recall, teach the key word ORGANIZATION (see the *Friend*, Aug. 1987, p. 12). You could use the illustration on that page.

2. Use the picture and wording of the Sixth Article of Faith (the *Friend*, Nov. 1985, p. 24) or the library word chart (65006).

3. In simple words, explain the meaning of the names of the priesthood leaders. After the discussion, consider letting the children match the following words and definitions.

   APOSTLES (Twelve special witnesses for Christ)

   PROPHETS (Those who speak the will of Heavenly Father)

   PASTORS (Bishop—the person in charge of your ward or branch)

   TEACHERS (Those who teach the gospel of Jesus Christ)

   EVANGELISTS (Patriarchs)

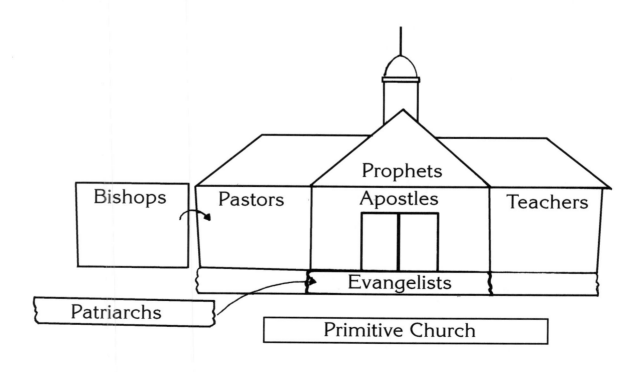

THE SEVENTH ARTICLE OF FAITH

ENRICHMENT IDEAS:

1. To help with recall, teach the key word GIFTS (see the *Friend*, Aug. 1987, p. 12). You could use the illustration on that page.

2. Use the picture and wording of the Seventh Article of Faith (the *Friend*, Jan. 1986, p. 24) or the library word chart (65007).

3. Ask the children the meaning of each word card, giving help when necessary. (Refer to Bruce R. McConkie, *Mormon Doctrine*, 2nd ed. [Salt Lake City: Bookcraft, 1966].)

4. Share personal stories that relate to these gifts.

5. In teaching this song, refrain from using a wrapped gift to represent these spiritual gifts.

6. Ask the children to find the two words that are sung on the longest notes. *[Tongues, so]*

7. Draw a melody picture on the chalkboard, as shown, and challenge the children to find which words are sung on this octave scale. *[In the gift of tongues, prophecy]*

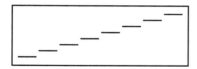

8. Invite the children to tap the catchy rhythm as they sing.

9. You may wish to read one of the following scriptures as reinforcement for this Article of Faith: Mormon 9:7–8; I Corinthians 12:7-10.

10. Use these pictures to help explain the meaning of words: prophecy (Samuel the Lamanite on the Wall 62370), revelations (Isaiah Writes of Christ's Birth 62339), visions (The First Vision 62470), healings (Healing the Blind 62145)

MATERIALS:

Word cards: GIFT OF TONGUES, PROPHECY, REVELATION, VISIONS, HEALINGS, INTERPRETATION OF TONGUES

ATTENTION-GETTER:

Display the word cards in mixed order. Ask the children to put them in the correct order as they listen to the song. Sing as many times as necessary to get the order right.

LISTENING AND SINGING EXPERIENCES:

Sing the song several times, removing one card each time you sing and asking children to sing just the missing word. Have only one card missing each time you sing.

Try removing two cards at a time until no cards are left.

After singing several times, invite the children to sing the whole song with you.

To feel the beat of this song, invite the children to tap their laps on the strong beat of each measure and to tap two fingers of one hand in the palm of the other as they sing.

```
          palm palm        palm palm
    lap                lap
```

Challenge the children to sing the entire song in one breath as you add the accompaniment.

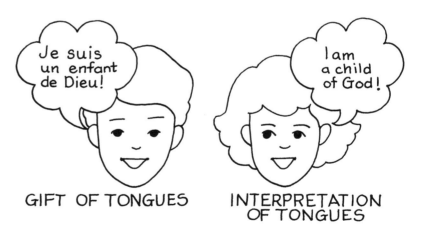

GIFT OF TONGUES   INTERPRETATION OF TONGUES

MATERIALS:

Bible and Book of Mormon

One of these melody pictures:

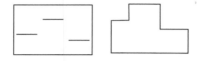

ATTENTION-GETTER:

- *I'm sure each of you have read many books. But how many of you have read a book that is the word of God? There are four books of scripture. They are called the standard works. Can you name them?* Let children respond.

- *Listen as I sing the Eighth Article of Faith, and see which of these scriptures is mentioned.*

Hold up your Bible and Book of Mormon and bear testimony that these two books are indeed the word of God.

LISTENING AND SINGING EXPERIENCES:

- *"The Eighth Article of Faith" is written in what is called a minor key. It helps give a feeling of reverence to these sacred books. Close your eyes and listen to the special mood of the music.*

Have the accompanist play the entire song. Sing the first six tones of the song on "loo," while following the melody chart with your finger. Explain that this is the shape of the melody pattern you sang and that this little melody pattern occurs on several important words in the song.

"Loo" the melody pattern again and then sing the entire song.

- *What words occur on that melody pattern? (Clue: There are four.)* [We believe the Bible, be the word of God, also believe, Book of Mormon] You may need to sing the song several times to allow the children to discover all the answers.

Sing the song again, inviting the children to join you on the parts of the song that come after the melody pattern.

Tap the rhythm of the second line, pointing out the triplet. ♩♪♩ Tap the rhythm for the children, and then invite them to tap it as they sing the second line.

Invite the children to sing the last line of the song, encouraging them to hold the last tone of the word "God" until they hear the accompaniment play the last chord.

- *Because the Bible has been translated so many times through the years, there may be parts of it that are unclear. However, we know that the Book of Mormon is translated correctly, because the Prophet Joseph Smith translated it by the power of God.*

ENRICHMENT IDEAS:

1. To help with recall, teach the key word TRANSLATE (see the *Friend,* Aug. 1987, p. 12). You could use the illustration on that page.

2. Use the picture and wording of the Eighth Article of Faith (the *Friend,* Feb. 1986, p. 24) or the library word chart (65008).

3. Challenge the children to pitch lead the main melody picture on the first and third lines, and to tap the rhythm on the second and fourth lines as they sing the entire song.

4. If tone bells are available, a child could play the melody pattern each time it occurs. (Three pitches: F A E)

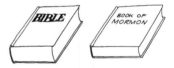

WORD OF GOD

Translated Correctly

ENRICHMENT IDEAS:

1. To help with recall, teach the key word REVELATION (see the *Friend*, Aug. 1987, p. 12). You could use the illustration on that page.

2. Use the picture and wording of the Ninth Article of Faith (the *Friend*, Mar. 1986, p. 24) or the library word chart (65009).

3. Invite a child to read Amos 3:7.

4. Invite the children to lead the 4/4 meter as they sing.

5. Challenge the children to pitch lead the last line with their bodies.

6. Use these pictures to help explain the meaning of the song: "has revealed" (Isaiah Writes of Christ's Birth 62339), "does now reveal" (Morning Prayer 62310), "yet reveal" (Search the Scriptures 62521), "pertaining to the kingdom of God" (Salt Lake Temple 62433)

MATERIALS:

Word cards: GOD HAS, YET, NOW, REVEALED, REVEAL, REVEAL, PERTAINING

Melody pictures:

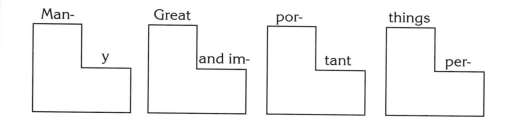

ATTENTION-GETTER:

Show the children the following three word cards in mixed order. *[GOD HAS, NOW, YET]* Ask the children to listen to the song to discover the correct order of the words. Sing as many times as necessary for the children to discover the correct answer.

LISTENING AND SINGING EXPERIENCES:

Sing again and ask how many times the word "reveal" is sung. *[Three times, including "revealed."]* When the correct answer has been given, post the three words.

REVEALED   REVEAL   REVEAL

• *When Heavenly Father wants us to know important things about his kingdom or church, he tells, or reveals, these things to his prophet and other Church leaders.*

Sing the song again and ask the children to match the three reveal words with the first three word cards. *[God has revealed, now reveal, yet reveal]*

• *The Lord continues to reveal important things about his kingdom. In the song we don't say the word "about." Listen as I sing the song, and discover what word means "about."* When the correct answer is given, post PERTAINING and ask the children to sing the last line with you.

Make four melody pictures, as shown, but without words. Display the charts and tell the children the shapes represent the melody in part of the song. "Loo" the third line, while pointing to the steps of the shape. Sing the entire song, asking the children to discover the words that occur on this downward moving tune. *[Many great and important things per-]*

When the children have discovered the answer, invite them to sing that line as you point to the shapes. Ask them what word is not completed with the shapes. *[Pertaining]*

The children should be able to sing the song all the way through, following the word cards and the melody shapes. Consider removing one or two word cards each time the children repeat the song.

MATERIALS:

Draw the following phrase lines on a chalkboard, without the key words:

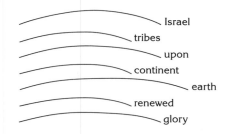

Israel
tribes
upon
continent
earth
renewed
glory

Word cards: ISRAEL, TRIBES, UPON, CONTINENT, EARTH, RENEWED, GLORY

ATTENTION-GETTER:

- *Jacob had twelve sons. Each of these sons became the leader of a tribe, or large family. Two of the tribes, Judah and Joseph, are among us today, but the other ten are lost. We don't know where they are. When Christ comes again, these ten tribes will be brought back.*

- *Today we are going to learn the Tenth Article of Faith, which teaches us about the gathering of the tribes of Israel. It also tells of other events that will happen when Christ comes to earth again.*

LISTENING AND SINGING EXPERIENCES:

Show the children the melody curves and explain that these are phrase lines. Sing the song, following the phrase lines with your hand, and challenge the children to discover the word that comes at the end of each phrase line. Have them choose the appropriate word card to place at the end of each phrase.

Sing the song several times to allow the children to find the correct answer for each phrase.

- *What kind of gathering do we believe in? [Literal] This means that many people throughout the earth will actually be gathered with the members of the Church in the last days.*

Sing and tap the rhythm of the first phrase, and invite the children to sing and tap with you.

- *The song also says that the ten tribes will be brought back. What is the word used in the song that means "brought back"? [Restoration]*

Invite the children to sing the first line; then ask them to listen to the song again and tell you which other phrase has the same tune and similar rhythm. *[That Zion (the New Jerusalem) will be built upon]*

- *What is another name for Zion? [The New Jerusalem] Help the children sing that line; then, as you sing the whole song, invite the children to sing the phrases they have learned.*

- *As I sing again, discover where Zion will be built. [Upon the American continent]*

- *As I sing the song again, listen to discover who will reign personally upon the earth. [Christ] Explain that "reign" means to rule.*

- *What will happen to the earth? [It will be "renewed" (made like new again) and receive its paradisiacal glory]*

Teach the children to pronounce the word "paradisiacal" correctly as they listen to you sing. Invite children to sing the last line with you.

Add the accompaniment and sing the entire song.

ENRICHMENT IDEAS:

1. To help with recall, teach the key words TEN TRIBES (see the *Friend*, Aug. 1987, p. 12). You could use the illustration on that page.

2. Use the picture and wording of the Tenth Article of Faith (the *Friend*, April 1986, p. 24) or the library word chart (65010).

3. Challenge the children to name five things that will happen in the last days that are mentioned in the Tenth Article of Faith. List these on the board or put them on wordstrips. Have the children arrange them in the correct order as the song is sung.

   a) Gathering of Israel

   b) Restoration of the ten tribes

   c) Zion will be built on the American continent

   d) Christ will reign personally upon the earth

   e) The earth will be renewed and receive its paradisiacal glory

4. Challenge the children to sit tall and get plenty of air to sing the longest line in one breath.

5. Show a map of the United States and pinpoint where Zion—the New Jerusalem—will be built when Christ comes to reign (Missouri).

6. Briefly discuss the meaning of "the Ten Tribes," "Zion," "paradisiacal glory." (See "Zion," Bible Dictionary.)

THE ELEVENTH ARTICLE OF FAITH

ENRICHMENT IDEAS:

1. To help with recall, teach the key word WE CLAIM (see the *Friend*, Aug. 1987, p. 12). You could use the illustration on that page.

2. Use the picture and wording of the Eleventh Article of Faith (the *Friend*, May 1986, p. 24) or the library word chart (65011).

3. Display the following word cards, in mixed order: PRIVILEGE, ALMIGHTY, DICTATES, CONSCIENCE, ALLOW, PRIVILEGE, WORSHIP. Ask the children to determine the correct order of these words by listening as you sing. Sing the song more than once, if necessary, to allow children to get all the words in the correct order.

4. Challenge the children to refer to the word cards and find the words that mean "supremely powerful" *[Almighty]*, "guidance" *[Dictates]*, etc. Define other words if necessary.

5. Invite the children to watch you very closely to make sure the word "privilege," on the third line, receives its full three counts.

6. Challenge the children to find a one-syllable word that is sung on two long notes. *[Same]*

7. Have the children pitch lead the last line with their bodies, beginning in a stooping position.

MATERIALS:

Word cards: HOW? WHERE? WHAT?

ATTENTION-GETTER:

Discuss how religious freedom was sought and obtained in America by the Pilgrims and how blessed we are to live in a country where we can go to any church we want.

LISTENING AND SINGING EXPERIENCES:

- *We are very privileged to be able to come to our church, and we believe that all people should be able to worship where they want, what they want, and how they want.* Post word cards out of order.

- *Joseph Smith thought this idea was so important that he expressed it in our Eleventh Article of Faith. Listen as I sing to determine in which order Joseph said these three words.* (HOW, WHERE, WHAT)

- *All three of these words are sung on different pitches. As I sing the song again, listen carefully and arrange these words according to their pitch level.* [HOW, WHERE, WHAT, *on an ascending scale*] Invite the children to sing this last phrase with you.

- *Who do we claim the privilege of worshiping?* [Almighty God]

- *How should we worship Almighty God?* [According to the dictates of our own conscience] This means that we should be able to worship as we want.

- *What do we allow all people?* [The same privilege to worship how, where, or what they may] This means that all people should be able to worship as they want.

- *This is the only one of the Articles of Faith that does not begin with the words "We believe." Listen to discover how this article of faith begins.* [We claim] Invite the children to sing the whole song.

THE TWELFTH ARTICLE OF FAITH

MATERIALS:

The flag of your country

Word cards: OBEY, HONOR, SUSTAIN, KINGS, PRESIDENTS, RULERS, MAGISTRATES

Melody pictures: (prepare without words)

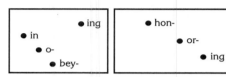
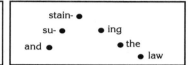

ATTENTION-GETTER:

Display your country's flag.

• *This flag represents our country and its laws or rules. Did you know that God has told us that the laws of our country are very important? As I sing the Twelfth Article of Faith, listen for three things that we must do concerning the laws of our land.*

As answers are given, post OBEY, HONOR, and SUSTAIN. Sing as many times as needed to get the three answers.

• *When we obey a law, we do what the law tells us to do. When we honor a law, we feel respect for it. When we sustain a law, we do all we can to support the law.*

LISTENING AND SINGING EXPERIENCES:

Post the three melody pictures (without the words) and challenge the children to find which chart goes with each of the three words as you sing.

Invite the children to sing and pitch lead these phrases with you, paying close attention to see that they sing the interval on *obeying* correctly.

• *Listen as I sing again, and tell me the four kinds of leaders that we believe in obeying, or being subject to. [Kings, presidents, rulers, magistrates]*

Post word cards as the answers are given. Sing again to check the order.

• *"Kings" are men who rule countries all by themselves. "Presidents" rule countries with the help of other people. "Rulers" are leaders, too. They might be mayors, who lead cities—or governors, who lead states. "Magistrates" are people who make laws and help people keep them. They might be judges or policemen or others who help with laws.*

Sing the song together.

• *As members of the Church, we are expected to obey, honor, and sustain our leaders and the laws of the land.*

ENRICHMENT IDEAS:

1. To help with recall, teach the key word LAW (see the *Friend*, Aug. 1987, p. 12). You could use the illustration on that page.

2. Use the picture and wording of the Twelfth Article of Faith (the *Friend*, June 1986, p. 24) or the library word chart (65012).

3. *Which of the four leaders do we sing about on the highest notes? [Rulers]*

4. Invite the children to tap the rhythm with you as you sing the song from the beginning.

5. Show the children how to conduct the 3/4 beat pattern as they sing.

6. Display your flag and a picture of the ruler of your country. Invite the children to stand and discuss the meaning of allegiance to your country. Also discuss ways to obey specific laws of the land.

ENRICHMENT IDEAS:

1. To help with recall, teach the key word ADMONITION (see the *Friend*, Aug. 1987, p. 12). You could use the illustration on that page.

2. Use the picture and wording of the Thirteenth Article of Faith (the *Friend*, July 1986, p. 24) or the library word chart (65013).

3. Invite a child to read Philippians 4:8 and 1 Corinthians 13:4, 7.

Scale Strips: Melody Hills:

Phrase Chart A: showing six phrases with breath marks.

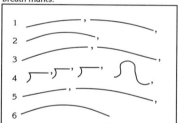

Phrase Chart B: showing completed chart.

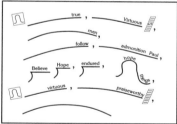

MATERIALS:

Phrase charts, Scale strips, Melody hills

Chart A showing six phrases with breath marks, Chart B showing completed chart

Word cards: (Set 1) TRUE, VIRTUOUS, MEN, FOLLOW, PAUL, THINGS, VIRTUOUS, PRAISEWORTHY; (Set 2) BELIEVE, HOPE, ENDURED; (Set 3) HOPE, ADMONITION

ATTENTION-GETTER:

Show phrase chart A with breath marks (commas) and ask the children what they notice. *[Several lines, three are the same, some are short and flat, one large hill, commas]*

- *Listen as I sing to determine the purpose of the commas.* Sing the song, follow the phrase marks with your finger, and take a big breath at each comma.

LISTENING AND SINGING EXPERIENCES:

As children make discoveries about the music, place the words and melody shapes on the chart as illustrated. Continue singing and following the phrase lines with your finger as you ask the following questions:

- *What word comes before each breath mark?* [TRUE, VIRTUOUS, MEN, FOLLOW, THINGS, VIRTUOUS, PRAISEWORTHY] Post word cards (Set 1) on the phrase chart, placing THINGS at the end of the fourth phrase.

- *What words occur on each of the flat parts (or repeated notes) of the fourth phrase?* *[BELIEVE, HOPE, ENDURED]* Place word cards (Set 2) on the flat lines as they answer, in mixed order.

- *Listen to determine if the words are in the right order, and tell me what important word comes at the top of the hill.* [Hope] Post word card HOPE (Set 3) and invite the children to sing that line, sitting tall so they can sing the high note "hope" in tune.

Show picture of scale strip; ask what they notice. *[Lines going up, one has "S" on its side.]*

- *These are scale strips. They indicate when the melody goes right up the scale.* "Loo" the tune to the phrase "lovely or of good report or praiseworthy" as your finger follows the lines up the chart without the turn.

- *The scale strip with the "S" turn sounds a little different.* "Loo" the tune to the words "honest, true, chaste, benevolent, virtuous." *As I sing the song listen to determine what words occur on each scale pattern.* Post them on the phrase chart, as shown.

- *What long word occurs on the "S" turn in the music that means "kind."* [Benevolent]

Invite children to sing the first, fourth and fifth phrases with you.

Show the children the melody hills that occur in the first and fifth phrases and "loo" the melody to "We believe" as your finger follows the line. Ask the children to determine what words go with that melody in phrases one and five. *[We believe, anything]*

- *What long word occurs in the 3rd phrase that means "counsel," "suggestion," or "direction"?* [Admonition] Post the key word and sing the third phrase. Have the children sing the song with the accompaniment. The children may enjoy taking turns following the chart with their fingers. Continue asking questions the children can answer by listening to the song.

LATTER-DAY PROPHETS

MESSAGE: I know the names and order of all the latter-day prophets.

MATERIALS:

Pictures: all latter-day prophets (Latter-day Prophets 62575), the current prophet

ATTENTION-GETTER:

Show the children a picture of our prophet today.

- *When the Lord chooses a prophet from the Council of the Twelve Apostles, he is sustained as a prophet of God during the general conference of the Church.*
- *All members of the Church are asked to raise their hands to sustain the new prophet of God. It is an honor and a privilege.*
- *There have been many prophets since the Church was restored to the earth. In just a few minutes you will be able to name every latter-day prophet in the correct order!*

LISTENING AND SINGING EXPERIENCES:

Teach by displaying the picture of each of the latter-day prophets in the order they appear in the song.

As you sing, refer to each picture, including one for President Howard W. Hunter, using the new words. Change "we honor him" on next to last line to "we honor <u>them</u>." Change final words from "We hear and follow their words today," to "<u>It's Howard W. Hunter today</u>**."**

The children will learn the song quickly through repetition.

ENRICHMENT IDEAS:

1. Point to the picture of each prophet and ask who he is. Ask the children to tell something they know about each one. Be prepared to give information if the children don't respond. (Examples: Our first prophet was Joseph Smith. He translated the Book of Mormon. Brigham Young led the pioneers across the plains to the Salt Lake Valley.)

2. Divide the children into five groups. Teach each group one line of the song in succession. Then have all five groups sing together on the last line (about our prophet today).

3. Pass out name cards of the prophets and challenge the children to come forward and stand in the correct order as you sing.

4. Coloring Songbook, *Latter-day Prophets*, ©1991 Aspen Books. The last picture and paragraph in this book could be used for a matching activity.

MESSAGE: Even though our bishop is very busy, he always finds time to be friendly and kind to the children. Let us try to help him, too.

ENRICHMENT IDEAS:

1. Divide the children into two groups. Have one group sing parts of the "riddle" and the other group sing, "he's our bishop." Then trade parts.

2. Invite your bishop to Primary to hear the children sing to him. Let him respond.

3. Discuss ways the children could "help him in every way."

4. Have the children listen for rhyming words.

   Verse One: be—me, pay—day—way

   Verse Two: Lord—ward, right—sight—might

5. Challenge the children to listen carefully and raise their hands when they know over what word a ⌒ or hold sign has been placed. [Day]

6. Invite several children to play the melody of the words "he's our bishop" on the tone bells each time it occurs.

7. Display a picture of your bishop.

ATTENTION-GETTER:

Sing the entire song as a riddle, leaving out the words "he's our bishop."

- *Who is this song about? [Our bishop]*

Teach the last "he's our bishop" by pitch leading and have the children join you in singing that phrase each time you sing the song. Ask questions to direct the children's listening.

Add the accompaniment when the children have learned the song well.

LISTENING AND SINGING EXPERIENCES:

Verse One:

- *Listen to find how many times you sing "he's our bishop." [Three]*
- *Though he's a busy man, what does he find time to do? [Talk to me]*
- *To whom does he always speak kindly words? [To the children every day]*
- *Because he's so kind to us, what do we want to do for him? [Help him in every way]*
- *This time as I sing the parts of the riddle, would you sing the phrase "he's our bishop?"*

Sing the phrase "busy as a man can be." *This melody is sung two more times. Listen for other words that are sung on this melody. [He finds time to talk to me. Let us help him every way.]*

Express your feelings of love and appreciation for your bishop and invite the children to sing verse one.

Verse Two:

- *Who does our bishop cheerfully serve? [The Lord]*
- *What is another way to say he is the bishop of our ward? [The father of our ward]*
- *He helps us to do right in whose sight? [In Heavenly Father's sight]*
- *How much do we love him? [With all our might]*

LOVE ONE ANOTHER

MESSAGE: Jesus said, "Love one another; as I have loved you."

MATERIALS:

Picture: (The Last Supper 62174)

ATTENTION-GETTER:

Show the picture The Last Supper.

- *The night before Jesus gave his life for us, he gathered his Apostles to him. They met in an upper room for the very last time. It must have been a sad time for Jesus, for he knew this would be their last night together. He looked into his disciples' faces and, with great love, spoke to them saying . . . (Sing the song for the children.)*

LISTENING AND SINGING EXPERIENCES:

Sing the song several times, encouraging the children to listen by using questions and statements similar to those listed below.

- *How many times do I sing the words "love one another?"* [Three]
- Ask an older child to read John 13:34–35. *Listen to discover from his own words how many times Jesus said "Love one another."* [Three]
- *As Jesus loved you, whom should you love?* [One another]
- *What was this new commandment that Jesus gave?* [Love one another]
- *What word means to be a follower of Jesus?* [Disciple] *As we show love to one another, other people will know that we are disciples, or followers, of Jesus.*

Refer to the picture The Last Supper again.

- *Jesus loved these disciples very much. And he loves you with that same love. He asks you to love one another as he loves you.*

Add the accompaniment and invite the children to sing the song with you.

[Note: For a program it can be effective to have the children sing this song as written. Then while the melody is played on a violin have the children "sign" the words. The final time through, add a violin obbligato while the children both sing and sign the words. Be aware that the arrangement in *Hymns*, no. 301, is written in a different key.]

ENRICHMENT IDEAS:

1. Sing this song directly from the words of Jesus. Display the words of the scripture (John 13:34–35) on a poster and sing the song, pointing to the words as they are found in the scripture. Or you could print the scripture inside a large heart.

2. Add the violin obbligato when singing this song for a special program number.

3. Sing related songs to reinforce the message, such as: "Where Love Is" (p. 138), "Kindness Begins with Me" (p. 145), "Home" (p. 192), "A Happy Family" (p. 198), "Jesus Said Love Everyone" (p. 61), and "Love at Home" (*Hymns*, no. 294).

4. Record the children's voices as they sing this song and then have them sing along with the tape recording to "double" the beautiful sound.

5. Display pictures of Jesus showing love to those around him (62145, 62169, 62380, 62467, 62541, 62542, 62550, 62557). Or show pictures of children demonstrating love (62270, 62307, 62313, 62316, 62317, 62340, 62365, 62523, 62552).

6. This song is beautifully done with sign language. Invite a guest to teach the actions, or refer to the *Children's Songbook* (p. 137).

7. Additional references on the songs and the composer: the *Friend*, Oct. 1985, p. 15; Karen Lynn Davidson, *Our Latter-Day Hymns*, (Salt Lake City: Deseret Book Co., 1988), p. 308.

♪ *About the Song*

This song is part of an Easter Cantata written by Luacine Fox. The dialogue and background music surrounding "Love One Another" tell the events of the Easter story. Sister Fox is the daughter of J. Reuben Clark. She feels that music is the most heavenly of all the arts and says, "When we sing to Heavenly Father, it is like praying."

WHERE LOVE IS

MESSAGE: Where love is, there God is also. Show me the way so that I can dwell with Heavenly Father eternally. Where God is, I want to be.

ENRICHMENT IDEAS:

1. To review, sing the song, leaving off the ending word of each phrase. Challenge the children to sing the missing words.

2. Review this song, using the important key words to aid the children's learning: GOD, GUIDE, TRUTHS, HELP, OBEY, etc. With each repetition, remove a few key words.

3. When the children have learned the song well, add dynamics, such as increasing the volume as the melody rises, and decreasing it as the melody falls. Challenge the children to watch carefully.

♪ About the Song

In 1969, Joanne Doxey was asked to write a song for a Primary conference. "After praying for help," she said, "a pure flow of inspiration came with both words and music." Her melody and words were then arranged by Marjorie Kjar. Since then, Sister Doxey has served with her husband as mission president in Spain, as a member of the Primary General Board, and as a counselor in the General Relief Society Presidency.

The song, "Where Love Is" became a favorite of both adults and children and has been sung on every occasion imaginable! There have been many versions of the song published. Sister Doxey and Sister Kjar prepared this as the official "short" version. Sister Kjar believes that music can bring happiness to the soul, and she teaches piano "to help children prepare to serve in the Church as musicians." (*Friend*, Oct. 1986, p. 45).

MATERIALS:

A cutout or picture of a heart with LOVE written on the back.

ATTENTION-GETTER:

Hold up the heart.

- *What does this represent? [Love]* Turn the heart over to see the word LOVE. *Love is such a wonderful, warm, happy feeling. Where love is, there God is also. Listen as I sing to see where we want to be. [Where love is]* Sing verse one to the children.

Sing that phrase again and invite the children to join you as you pitch lead.

LISTENING AND SINGING EXPERIENCES:

Teach one or two parts a week by singing them to the children and directing their listening through questions. Invite them to sing the phrases as you teach them.

Part One:

- *If we want to be where God is, what do we need to follow? [His truths]*
- *Who do you think we are asking to guide us? [Parents and teachers]* Heavenly Father planned for us to come to earth to loving parents who love us and guide us.
- *What else do we want our parents and teachers to help us do? [Obey him faithfully]* Pitch lead the descending/ascending melody pattern.

Part Two:

- *What words in this next part do you already know? [Where love is, there God is also]*
- *How do we think of him? [Reverently]*
- *What two things do we want our parents to teach us? [To pray, to talk with him above]*
- *We know that Heavenly Father will guide us with what? [His love]*

Part Three:

- *What gives us comfort? [Loving arms around us]* Challenge the children to count on their fingers the number of repeated notes. *[Nine]*
- *The melody on the next phrase goes up and down like this:* (Demonstrate with your hand). *What word do we sing at the highest point?*

  [Makes] Invite the children to pitch lead this phrase with you.
- *What do we feel when love has found us? [Happiness]*
- *What do we get when we give love? [Love]*

Part Four:

- *With whom do we want to be? [God (Heavenly Father)]*
- *How do we want our parents and teachers to guide us? [Tenderly]*
- *What word means being with Heavenly Father forever and ever? [Eternally]*
- *If we obey Heavenly Father faithfully, it will be our reward and blessing to live with Heavenly Father and to feel his love forever and ever.*

I'LL WALK WITH YOU

MESSAGE: I will show my love to Heavenly Father's children who have special needs. I will be their friend.

MATERIALS:

Before you teach this song, select a boy for a demonstration who will understand the important message of this song. Use tape to attach a stick, ruler, or dowel to the front and back of one of the boy's legs, making his knee immobile.

Wordstrips: *Jesus walked away from none; He gave his love to everyone; Jesus blessed all he could see.*

ATTENTION-GETTER

- Invite the "handicapped" child forward. Draw attention to his "handicapped" walk by saying, *"(child's name), you don't walk the way most people do. Do some people walk away from you?"* [The child responds "Yes."] *"Some people might walk away from you, (child's name), but I won't! I won't!"*
- *"Will you?"* (Direct this question to the Primary children, and let them respond.)
- *(Child's name) really can run and play. But you may know a child who really can't walk or talk as you do.* Be sensitive to any children with disabilities.

LISTENING AND SINGING EXPERIENCES:

- *Listen as I sing, and tell me how I can show my love to these special children of Heavenly Father.* Sing the entire song. [*I'll walk with you. I'll talk with you*]

Sing the response one more time ("I'll walk with you. I'll talk with you. That's how I'll show my love for you."). How many times is this phrase sung? [*Two*]

Sing the song again, inviting the children to sing the response with you as you pitch lead.

Divide the children into two groups. Sing the first half of the song as follows:

Group 1: "If you don't walk as most people do," Group 2: "Some people walk away from you," Together: "But I won't! I won't!" Group 2: "If you don't talk as most people do," Group 1: "Some people talk and laugh at you," Together: "But I won't! I Won't! I'll walk with you. I'll talk with you. That's how I'll show my love for you."

- *Jesus taught us by example the way we should treat everyone. What three ways does the song mention?* [*Jesus walked away from none. He gave his love to everyone. Jesus blessed all he could see.*] Sing from "Jesus walked away from none" to the end. Post wordstrips as answers are given. Sing again to check the order.
- *Jesus has set the example. What has he said to us?* [*Come, follow me*]
- *The composer emphasized our promise to follow Jesus by repeating the words "I will" four times. Let's sit up tall and promise Jesus that we will follow him by singing the four "I will's" again. Notice that the last two "I will's" are sung a little higher. This emphasizes our desire to follow Jesus.*
- *We keep our promise to follow Jesus by walking with, talking to, and showing love to all of Heavenly Father's children. Let's sing the entire song, renewing our promise to follow Jesus.*

ENRICHMENT IDEAS:

1. Sing related songs, such as pp. 60, 136 and 145.
2. For a review, use the Coloring Songbook *I'll Walk with You,* ©1991, Aspen Books.
3. Use the picture of Jesus healing the Nephites (62541) to point out the love and compassion Jesus had for all.
4. Teach some of the children to sing the optional ending harmonic notes.

♪ *About the Song*

Evaluating the songs from the survey, the *Songbook* Committee realized that there were no songs on special needs. They brainstormed about the content of such a song. Carmen Pingree on the Primary Board said it should teach how to treat people with problems—handicaps as well as things that make people feel uncomfortable. It should show the Savior's example and cause a feeling of commitment. They wrote a sample message in free verse and then contacted Carol Lynn Pearson in Walnut Creek, California. She was willing to help and the ideas were mailed to her. While Sister Pearson was flying to Salt Lake for a rehearsal, she worked on the poem and dropped it off at the Church Offices with the comment, "Feel free to revise or fix this in any way to fit your purpose." After one slight revision and approval from correlation, her poem was ready to have music added.

Reid Nibley, the composer who wrote "I Know My Father Lives," has a daughter with special needs and the committee felt he would have a sensitivity for the topic. When he returned his music, he said he wanted it to sound like "walking" in the left hand accompaniment. The original accompaniment was simplified—remember, he is a concert pianist!

EVERY STAR IS DIFFERENT

MESSAGE: Every star is different and so is every child. Each one is needed for just what he can do.
I can let my light shine as I follow the commandments and love and help others.

ENRICHMENT IDEAS:

1. Use word cards to review Verse Two. (SHE, LOVE, FOLLOW, GOD, HELP, CHOOSE, FAITH AND COURAGE, STAR, SHINE)

2. Show the melody of "Ev'ry star is different" with star stickers. Ask the children how many times they hear that melody picture.

3. Refer to obbligato suggestions at the beginning of the song. Try singing with only the piano obbligato as your accompaniment.

4. Make several poster-size stars. Cut a circle out of the middle for children to peek through, showing that every star and child is different, but every child can let his light shine.

5. Invite a child to read "Let your light so shine . . . (Matt. 5:16).

6. Sing related songs, such as "Kindness Begins with Me" (p. 145), "Jesus Said Love Everyone" (p. 61), and "Love One Another" (p.136).

7. Invite half of the children to sing the optional harmonic notes on the last two words.

MATERIALS:

Large star cut out of yellow posterboard with a mirror glued in the middle.

Star-shaped word cards: BRIGHT, HAPPY, MEEK, MILD, NEEDED, DO

ATTENTION-GETTER

Hold the large star with the mirror in the middle in your hands. As you walk around the room ask several children to look into the star (mirror) and ask various questions, for example:

· *What color eyes does this star have? What color hair? Do you see a happy star?*

· *Every star is different and so is every child but you're the only person that ever can be you.* (Sing just the last line "You're the only person that ever can be you.") Invite the children to sing just that line with you as you ask a question and sing the song.

· *What are some things that can shine?* (Let the children respond.) *Do you realize that you, too, can shine? You have a light within you.*

LISTENING AND SINGING EXPERIENCES:

(You may wish to teach this song in three weeks: verse one, chorus, and verse two.)

Verse One:

· *Listen as I sing and find four words that describe different children.* Post word cards BRIGHT, HAPPY, MEEK, MILD, NEEDED, and DO. Draw attention to differences in melody on "Every one is needed."

Sing the song, referring to star word cards. With each repetition remove one of the stars.

Chorus:

· *Listen for how many times you hear the words "shine" or shining."* [6]

· *Now find all the words that rhyme with "star."*

· *How many times do you hear the word "brightly" or "bright?"* [5]

Invite the children to sing the chorus.

Verse Two:

Sing this verse and ask the children to listen for the answers to the following questions:

· *As I shine for others what can I let them feel?* [my love] Sing the first line with the children.

· *What can I help another to learn?* [to choose the right]

Invite the children to join you on the first three lines.

· *What do I need to have to let my star shine bright?* [faith and courage]

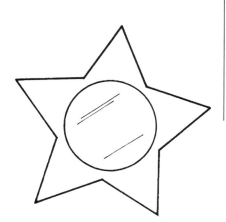

SHINE ON

MESSAGE: Each of us has a light within that comes from God and shines for all to see.

ATTENTION-GETTER:

- *I know a song about one of our scriptures.* Have a child read Matthew 5:16.
- *Each of us has a light within that comes from God. When we live the gospel, we are like a light shining—or an example—for all to see.*

Have two children who have prepared ahead of time, sing the song as a duet.

LISTENING AND SINGING EXPERIENCES:

Teach this song using questions and statements similar to the following. Have the children listen to find the answers as you sing the song or parts of the song; then invite the children to sing that part with you. You may want to have the two guest singers sing each repetition.

Verse One:

- *Listen again to discover how big my light is.* [A little one]
- *What other words do you hear on that same melody?* [But lo! it glows like God's great sun] Explain that "but lo" is an exclamation.

Invite the children to join you on these two phrases.

- *What kind of light are we singing about?* [My light of faith and prayer] When we have faith and pray, we are good examples, and we seem to shine.
- *Why does such a little light glow like God's great sun?* [For it was lighted there.] God put the light in the sun, and he gave us our light, too.
- *Notice that the rhythm ♪♪♩ occurs on three of the answers above.* Clap the rhythm with the children and ask them which words occur on that rhythm. [Little one, God's great sun, faith and prayer] Sing the song as many times as necessary for the children to discover the answers.

Chorus:

- *Find some words in the chorus with that same rhythm.* [Bright and clear]
- *Count how many times we sing "shine on."* [Five]
- *Notice each time we sing "shine on" the words are sung on repeated tones except the last time. What happens to the melody on the last "shine on"?* [The melody starts higher, then steps down.]
- *"The day is here" means that we should shine and be a good example today.*

Add the accompaniment as the children sing verse one and chorus with you.

Verse Two:

Teach verse two in the same manner as verse one.

- *What are you told not to do with your little light?* [I may not hide it]
- *Why are we told not to hide it?* [Because the Lord told me so]
- *Why are we told to keep it in sight?* [That all may see it glow] "Tis" is a contraction for "it is."

Challenge the children to do something during the following week so that their lights will shine. Follow up next week by asking what they did and how it made them feel.

ENRICHMENT IDEAS:

1. Jesus is the "Light of the world." Have a child read John 8:12. How can we be "lights" with our friends and families?

2. Show pictures of children helping, sharing, etc., to depict obedience and example. Correlate with other songs about being a good example, being kind, etc., such as "Kindness Begins with Me" (p. 145), "I Pledge Myself to Love the Right" (p. 161), "Stand for the Right" (p. 159), and "I Am Like a Star" (p. 163).

3. Teachers and older children may learn the alto part and join with those singing the melody.

4. Prepare three large cut-out stars for word cards. Cut a circle in the middle for a child's face. Add the words: FAITH AND PRAYER, SUN-LIGHTED, SHINE-ON. Invite three children to put their faces through the sun and represent the light shining from within.

A SPECIAL GIFT IS KINDNESS

MESSAGE: I am happy, and my heart sings when I bring happiness to others by being kind.

ENRICHMENT IDEAS:

1. Ask teachers or parents to write examples of kind deeds performed by children. Place the written notes in the gift box and read them in coming weeks. Be sure to explain that happiness is the result of these kind deeds.

2. Add to the sides of the gift box the following: a smile or happy face, a kindness picture, a singing heart. Sing and turn the box for each phrase. The same pictures could be attached to craft sticks as visual aids.

3. Play "pass the box" game. In a gift box, place the names of songs related to kindness, such as "Kindness Begins with Me" (p. 145), "Jesus Said Love Everyone" (p. 61), "A Happy Helper" (p. 197), "When We're Helping" (p. 198), "Love Is Spoken Here" (p. 190), and "Go the Second Mile" (p. 167). Begin singing "A Special Gift Is Kindness" as children pass a box around the room. Instruct the children to stop singing and passing the box when the pianist stops playing. Have the child holding the box select and read a title from the box. Then have the children begin singing the new song until the pianist stops again, and the game continues.

MATERIALS:

A beautifully wrapped package, with the word card KINDNESS inside.

ATTENTION-GETTER:

Show the package to the children.

• *A very special gift is inside. Listen as I sing the song to see what the gift is.*

Have a child open the lid on the package and find the word card KINDNESS inside. Explain that kindness is a special gift.

LISTENING AND SINGING EXPERIENCES:

• *Listen to the song and discover what happens "when I am kind to others." [My heart sings]* Sing again, inviting the children to sing the last phrase with you.

Repeat the song, asking the children to notice the high note on "heart." Invite the children to sing that part as you repeat the whole song.

• *As I sing the song again, listen to discover what kindness brings. [Happiness]* Have the children sing the first line.

Sing the first phrase, asking the children to listen for other words that have the same melody. *[I am kind to others.]* Invite children to join you in singing the entire song.

KINDNESS BEGINS WITH ME

MESSAGE: Kindness begins with me.

MATERIALS:

A box with a mirror inside

ATTENTION-GETTER:

Invite several children to peek inside the box. As they are looking ask, *With whom does kindness begin? [Me]* Look in the box yourself and say, *You're right.* Sing the phrase "kindness begins with me."

Ask the children to sing that phrase with you.

LISTENING AND SINGING EXPERIENCES:

Direct the children's listening by asking questions as you sing.

• *To whom do I want to be kind? [To everyone]*

• *Why do I want to be kind to everyone? [For that is right, you see]* Invite the children to sing the first line with you.

• *What do I say to myself? [Remember this: kindness begins with me]*

Add the accompaniment and invite the children to sing the entire song with you.

After singing the song, lead a brief discussion on how we can be kind to our mothers, fathers, brothers, sisters, neighbors, friends, teachers.

ENRICHMENT IDEAS:

1. Have a child read Luke 6:31. Discuss the "Golden Rule."

2. On the day you plan to teach this song, have someone present the story of the Good Samaritan. (See Luke 10:30–37.)

3. Use pictures of being kind, sharing, helping others, etc. Discuss each picture.

4. For review use the poster idea as shown.

KEEP THE COMMANDMENTS

MESSAGE: Safety, peace, and other blessings are in store for us if we listen to our prophet and keep the commandments.

ENRICHMENT IDEAS:

1. Challenge the children to find the word over which a fermata or hold sign has been placed. [Commandments] For fun, let a child hold up a fermata sign over any three places he or she wishes.

2. Teach this song with mystery word cards:

   •WHAT should we do? [Keep the commandments]

   •WHY should we keep the commandments? [In this there is safety and peace, and He will send blessings]

   •WHO said we should keep the commandments? [A prophet]

3. Show a melody picture of the first line. Tell the children that this melody is repeated somewhere in the song. Challenge the children to discover the words where the melody repeats. [He will send blessings]

4. Tell the children that there are four repeated notes in the song. Ask them what words occur on the repeated notes. ["Words of a proph"-et]

5. Make a visual aid by placing pictures on "tablets of stone" cut from heavy cardboard or posterboard. Join tablets together with rings into a book form.

♪ About the Song

When Harold B. Lee became the President of the Church, he was asked if he had a message for the world. "Keep the commandments," was his reply. Barbara McConochie used those words for the message of this song. Because it was included in the 1989 hymnbook, another version was needed for this book. Sister McConochie said that since she first wrote the song she has had many difficulties in her life. Now she knows that keeping the commandments doesn't mean we won't have problems, but rather that we can be strong enough to meet our tests. She was suffering with tendonitis and as she tossed and turned in her bed she thought of Abraham 3:24–25, "and we shall prove them herewith." She wrote the new second verse expressing that idea. An obbligato for voice or instrument was added.

MATERIALS:

Picture: President Harold B. Lee

ATTENTION-GETTER:

Show a picture of President Harold B. Lee.

• The day President Harold B. Lee was ordained as President of the Church, a newspaper reporter asked, "What is the greatest Message that you could give to the membership of the Church?" President Lee said that the most important message he could give would be: "Keep the commandments." Sing the song for the children.

LISTENING AND SINGING EXPERIENCES:

Sing the song several times for the children, directing their listening by asking the following questions:

• How many times do we sing the phrase "Keep the commandments" in the first verse? [Three] These words are so important that we sing them three times.

• The first two times we sing that phrase, the melody pattern is the same; the second time, the melody moves up.

• What are two blessings we receive from keeping the commandments? [Safety and peace]

• What will He send to us if we keep the commandments? [Blessings]

• Who said the words, "keep the commandments"? [A prophet]

Invite the children to sing the song with you.

• I want to encourage you to keep every commandment of God with exactness and honor so you can feel peace and safety in your lives.

I WANT TO LIVE THE GOSPEL

MESSAGE: I will try in all I do and say to live the gospel more each day.

MATERIALS:

Word card: SLOPEG on one side and GOSPEL on the reverse side

Picture of Jesus

Scriptures

Melody pictures:

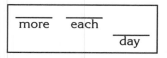 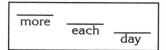

ATTENTION-GETTER

- *Boys and girls, do you know what "SLOPEG" means?* Hold up word card SLOPEG. *You don't? If you were to rearrange the letters of this word, you could spell a word that is important to each of us. As I sing the song, you will hear this important word three times. Listen to discover what that word is. [Gospel]* Display the word card GOSPEL.

LISTENING AND SINGING EXPERIENCES:

Sing the song several times, encouraging the children to listen by using questions and statements similar to those listed below. As children discover answers, invite them to sing that part of the song with you. Add one phrase at a time to the ones already learned.

Chorus:

- *What do I want to live more each day? [The gospel]*
- *How will I try to live the gospel? [In all I do and say]*
- *These words are so important that we sing them more than once. Count how many times I sing them. [Two times]*

The melody on these two phrases is the same, except for the words "more each day." As you sing the chorus again, show the children the two melody pictures and have them decide which one is sung first.

Invite the children to sing the chorus with you as you add the accompaniment.

Verse One:

- *How will I live? [As he wants me to do]*
- *Whose plan will I follow? [My Savior's]*

Have a child hold up a picture of Jesus.

- *The Savior's plan is the gospel. He has given us teachings and commandments so we can be happy and return to him.*
- *Where do we find his teachings?* Hold up the scriptures.
- *What do I want to live? [The gospel]*

Bear testimony of the blessings you have received because you want to live the gospel.

Verse Two:

Teach in a similar manner, asking questions such as these:

- *I know that I will be happy because I've learned to do something. What have I learned? [To obey]* (Note the two-note slur on "know.")
- *When am I heard? [When I pray]*

ENRICHMENT IDEAS:

1. Ask the children, "Is it enough to know the gospel?" Sing the chorus, stressing that we must live the gospel.

2. Discuss ways that children can live the gospel, using pictures listed: be kind (62317), be helpful (62365), obey (62018), learn the gospel (62200), honor parents (62206), take turns (62316), pray (62218), be baptized (62018), be confirmed (62020), help with baby (62307)

3. Draw a picture of the word phrases on the board and invite the children to post the key words (listed below) on the proper phrase lines. Point out that the word "live" is sung four times in the first verse. Sing softer and slower on the last four measures where the words are repeated.

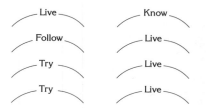

4. Divide the children into two groups. Have the first group sing the first part of each phrase: "I want . . ." "To know . . ." The second group could finish each phrase: ". . . to live the gospel," ". . . that its teachings are true," etc.

5. Teach the older children the simple harmony in the chorus.

♪ About the Song

Naomi Randall served as first counselor to General Primary President LaVern Parmley. She said: "It is my hope that the children will make a personal commitment to live the principles of the gospel more today than they did yesterday and that they may experience the joy and happiness that come from living the gospel." Sister Randall is also the author of "I Am a Child of God."

Roy Darley, a former tabernacle organist, wrote the music for this song. Among his many contributions, he used to give a series of ten organ lessons in the Assembly Hall to people who were called to be ward organists.

I BELIEVE IN BEING HONEST

MESSAGE: I believe in being honest, so I will form good habits that will help me be honest in all I say and do.

ENRICHMENT IDEAS:

1. Have the children close their eyes for a few seconds. Then ask them to open their eyes. Ask them if they thought about the breaths they took while their eyes were closed. We don't think about breathing all the time; we just do it automatically. We should practice being honest until it becomes as automatic as breathing. We should be able to do it without thinking about it. It should be a habit.

2. Sing the song and leave off the last word of each phrase. Invite the children to sing the ending words.

3. Challenge the children to find the three sets of rhyming words: true—do, youth—truth, right—bright.

4. Change the dynamics as you sing from "soft" to "full volume." (Never say "loud"!) Challenge the children to watch you as you indicate "soft" or "full volume" with your conducting pattern.

5. Show the pictures and have a "What would you do if . . ." discussion. You could also make a poster to review.

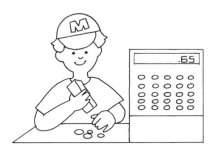

MATERIALS:

Word cards: KEEP, TELL, SPEAK, UP, KEEP, letters H-O-N-E-S-T

ATTENTION-GETTER:

Display the letter cards spelling T-H-O-N-E-S.

• *I am sure that you have not heard about "thones" before. But if you rearrange the letters, you will discover something that you believe in. Listen to discover the word as I sing.*

LISTENING AND SINGING EXPERIENCES:

Each time you sing, use one of the following questions or activities and have the children listen for the answer; then have the children sing that phrase several times. (You may wish to teach only lines one and two the first week, three and four the following week.)

Lines One and Two:

• *By rearranging T-H-O-N-E-S, what word did you discover? [Honest] President Benson said, "The Lord expects us to be honest." (1987 Children's Sacrament Meeting Presentation.)*

Have the children reverently tap the rhythm of the first phrase as you sing it. Then have the children tap and sing the phrase.

• *Listen for another phrase that has almost the same rhythm and that tells something else I believe in being. [I believe in being true]*

• *Do these phrases remind you of an article of faith?* Ask a child to volunteer to repeat the first part of the Thirteenth Article of Faith.

• *The Article of Faith started with "we," but our song starts with "I."*

Invite the children to sing the first two phrases they have learned.

• *Now listen for a word that is similar to the word honest as you sing the second line of the song. [Honesty] Sing the phrase again.*

• *Now listen for the word that rhymes with honesty. [Me]*

• *When should it start with me? [In all I say, in all I do]*

Lines Three and Four:

(The first enrichment idea makes a good Attention-Getter as you begin teaching these lines.)

• *Listen for four habits that will help us to be honest. Sing until all responses are given, and display the word cards as the children answer. [KEEP my word, TELL the truth, SPEAK UP in defending right, KEEP my name and honor bright]*

Divide the children into four groups. Invite each group to sing one of the above phrases. Then rotate the assignments.

• *When should I form good habits? [In my youth]*

Challenge the children to sing about all four habits. (Lines three and four.)

• *Does it sound like we're at the end of the song? [No] That's right. The part about habits is the middle part of the song. The end of the song is the same as the beginning, and we've already learned that part!*

Invite children to sing the entire song and to listen for the last word of the song. [Do] Emphasize the importance of doing what we believe. Ask a child to read the words of King Benjamin in Mosiah 4:10, *"And now, if you believe all these things see that ye do them."*

I'M GLAD TO PAY A TITHING

MESSAGE: When I think of all Heavenly Father gives me, I'm glad to pay my tithing.

MATERIALS:

Chalk and chalkboard

Beautifully wrapped present

ATTENTION-GETTER:

Show the children the present.

- *How many of you like presents or gifts? I do, too! But you know, the greatest presents we receive do not come wrapped in paper with bows on the top. They are gifts from our Heavenly Father, and they are around us all the time.*

LISTENING AND SINGING EXPERIENCES:

Sing the song several times, encouraging the children to listen by using questions similar to those listed below. As children discover answers, invite them to sing that part of the song with you.

Verse One:

- *Find three gifts that Heavenly Father has given us. [The sun that shines, the rain that falls, the meadowlark that sings]* As each answer is given, draw a simple shape on the chalkboard while you sing the answer. Then invite the children to sing the answers.

Drawing the melody pictures descending, as illustrated below (without note names), will help the children to notice that the melody descends in a similar fashion.

```
  B
      G       A                   G
          F       F       E
            E       E       D       D
                      D       C       D
                        C
```

Sing the last line of the song again, helping the children notice that the rhythm on "sun" and "meadowlark" is uneven, but the rhythm on "rain" is even. Demonstrate by clapping as the children sing the last line with you again.

- *What two words describe these beautiful gifts. [Good and lovely]*
- *Who gives us these good and lovely things? [Heavenly Father]*
- *Look around you each day and notice all the good and lovely things Heavenly Father has given you.*

Verse Two:

- *We have sung about many good and lovely things our Heavenly Father has given us. As I sing the second verse of the song, listen to see what I'm glad to do. [Pay my tithing]*
- *How much should I pay? [One-tenth of all I earn]*
- *Does the song say it's a big or little thing to pay tithing? [Little]*
- *What do I think of? [All God gives me in return]*
- *During this coming week, think of all God has given you and just how little one-tenth is to give God in return.*

ENRICHMENT IDEAS:

1. Invite ten children to come forward and hold ten large cardboard or paper pennies. Count the pennies together. Post the word TEN. Separate from the group one of the children holding a penny. Explain and post the words ONE-TENTH and TITHING.

2. Use simple actions for the very small children.

3. You could use cutouts from the flannel board kit for review.

I WANT TO GIVE THE LORD MY TENTH

MESSAGE: I want to pay my tithing. When I think of all the gifts Heavenly Father gives me, my tenth seems very small. But it shows my gratitude to him.

ENRICHMENT IDEAS:

1. Pass out the ten coins to ten children in random order. As the group sings, challenge the children to stand in the correct order.

2. Encourage the children to make a tithing bank and to pay tithing regularly.

3. Try singing one phrase out loud and the next in "inner hearing" (continuing to sing the song silently in their minds). Open your hand to indicate when the children sing, and close your fist to indicate inner hearing.

MATERIALS:

Prepare ten large coins out of paper or poster board. Write one of the following key words or phrases on each coin: GIVE THE LORD, TENTH (emphasize this word by using a different color paper or ink), THINK, GIFTS, GIVES TO ME; LIFE, WORLD, SMALL, GRATITUDE, LORD.

ATTENTION-GETTER:

- *Our Heavenly Father has given us so many blessings and gifts. What are some of your gifts?* Lead a brief discussion.

- *He has given us everything. There is something I can give him to show my gratitude.*

- *Listen as I sing, and see what I can give.* [My tenth, or tithing] As you sing, post the large coins in random order.

LISTENING AND SINGING EXPERIENCES:

Verse One:

- *How much do I give the Lord to show my gratitude?* [My tenth] Post the TENTH key-word coin above the others. Explain that a tenth is a very small amount—only one out of ten.

- *Why do I want to give the Lord my tenth?* [It makes me think of all the gifts he gives to me and you]

Sing the first verse again asking the children to post the first verse key word coins in the correct order. Repeat as necessary.

Sing the first verse, referring to the key words.

Verse Two:

- *What two things does he give us?* [Life and this lovely world]

- *How does my tenth seem?* [Small]

- *To whom does it show my faith and gratitude?* [To Him, the Lord of all]

Sing again, asking the children to put the coins for the second verse in the correct order. Repeat as needed. Ask the children to turn over or remove one or two key word coins with each repetition of the song.

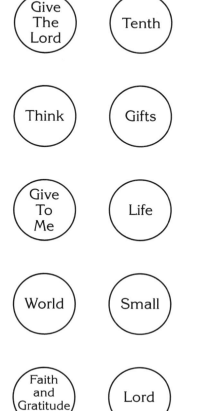

I AM GLAD FOR MANY THINGS

MESSAGE: I am happy and thankful for the many things Heavenly Father has given me.

ATTENTION-GETTER:

- *I am glad for many things. What are you thankful for?* Let the children respond.
- *You are thankful for many things, too!*

LISTENING AND SINGING EXPERIENCES:

Verse One:

- *I know a song about being thankful for many things. As I sing it listen to find out how many times I sing many things. [Four]* Sing again to check the answer, having the children hold up fingers as they count.
- *The song doesn't use the word "thankful" for many things. It uses a word that means happy. Listen to hear what that word is. [Glad]*

Invite the children to sing the song with you.

- *We sing the words "I am glad for many things" two times. Watch as I pitch lead those two phrases, and discover if the melody is the same or different. [Same]*

Have the children sing the entire song, but pitch lead only the first and third phrases. The skips in the melody of the last measure may be difficult for the children to sing accurately. Ask the children to listen as you sing the last measure several times. Then have the children join in as you pitch lead.

Verse Two:

- *We have talked about many things Heavenly Father has given us. What should we say to him? [Thank you]*
- *When I am thanking Heavenly Father, what does my heart do? [It sings]*
- *"My heart sings" means I feel very happy and thankful inside. And when we sing with our hearts, Heavenly Father hears our songs of thanks.*

Invite the children to thank Heavenly Father with all their hearts by singing the second verse.

(Sing the third phrase "Thank you for the many things" confidently. In verse two, the words of the third phrase do not match the first phrase—like they do in verse one.

ENRICHMENT IDEAS:

1. Ask the children what they are thankful for, and sing the song using their responses. Example: I am glad for mother dear, family, my good food, etc.

2. Have the older children sing the song as a round. The second group begins after the second measure. Repeat several times without accompaniment.

3. Have the accompaniment played an octave higher for a music box effect.

4. Use the Visual Aids Cutouts (08456) or library pictures as the children name blessings for which they are thankful.

   Teacher, class, friends, prayer (62200)

   Family, food (62384)

   Beautiful world, friends (62270)

   Animals (62483)

   Latter-day Prophets (64324)

   Salt Lake Temple (62433)

   Scriptures (62373)

   Parents (62552)

   Jesus (62572)

HUM YOUR FAVORITE HYMN

MESSAGE: Before you say or think something you shouldn't, clear your mind by humming your favorite hymn.

ENRICHMENT IDEAS:

1. Challenge the children to find the rhyming words.

2. Ask the children to stand up and sing with vigor and vim.

3. Invite a child to hum the first line of a favorite hymn for the others to guess. This could be used as Attention-Getter for coming weeks.

4. Invite six children to play the chorus on tone bells.

5. Play "stop and go" (see p. 30) by dividing the children into two groups (right and left sides, girls and boys, or teachers and children). Indicate which group is to sing as you "stop and go" each phrase. Sing the chorus all together.

♪ *About the Song*

This song was first published in the Young Women collection, *Songs of the Heart*, p. 89. The text was difficult for children, and so was simplified to be age-appropriate.

ATTENTION-GETTER:

- *What is your favorite hymn?* Accept titles of hymns and Primary songs.

- *I have a favorite hymn, too. I like to hum it while I'm doing the dishes, while I'm driving in the car, and even when I'm in the shower. It lifts my spirit and makes me happy.*

- *As I sing, listen to find out what you can do to clear your mind?* Sing entire song.

LISTENING AND SINGING EXPERIENCES:

Chorus:

- *What will you find clears your mind? [To hum your favorite hymn]* Have the children join you in singing this phrase each time you repeat the chorus.

- *When you hum your favorite hymn, how should you sing out? [With vigor and vim. (With enthusiasm and energy)]*

Tap the rhythm pattern of the first phrase. ♩♩ ♩♩♩ ♩. Challenge the children to tap the rhythm with you; then count the number of times they hear that rhythm pattern. *[Three times]*

Invite the children to sing the chorus.

Verse One:

- *On occasion, you might be tempted to say words that you know you shouldn't say. These are times when your language is in question.* Sing the first line then invite the children to sing it with you.

- *At those times, what kinds of thoughts might come to your mind? [Ugly thoughts]*

- *What word rhymes with "question"? [Suggestion] Is the melody the same on "suggestion" as it is on "in question?" [No]* Point out that "in question" moves up the scale. "Suggestion" moves down the scale.

Verse Two:

- *Before you say an angry word, what should you remember? [You'll regret it]*

- *What happens once an angry word is said? [The harm is done, because some folks won't forget it.]*

- *When you say something ugly or mean, you may be sorry you said it, but then it's too late. Maybe you didn't mean to say these words, but you let your anger out. Next time remember to . . .* (Sing chorus "Just hum your favorite hymn . . ." etc.)

THE LORD GAVE ME A TEMPLE

MESSAGE: The Lord gave me a body to be the temple of my spirit. If I keep my body clean and pure, I can claim celestial blessings promised me.

MATERIALS:

Mystery word cards: WHAT? HOW? WHAT? WHERE? WHEN? WHO?

ATTENTION-GETTER:

- *Elder Boyd K. Packer of the Quorum of the Twelve said: "Pretend that my hand represents your spirit. It is alive. It can move by itself. Suppose that this glove represents your physical body. It cannot move. When the spirit enters into your physical body, then it can move and act and live. Now you are a person—a spirit with a physical body, living on earth." (Teach Ye Diligently, p. 231–32.)*
- *Our bodies are sacred because the Lord gave them to us to house our spirits. As I sing a beautiful song for you, listen to discover another name for this body that our Father gave to us. [A temple]*

LISTENING AND SINGING EXPERIENCES:

Continue teaching the song by singing it several times, directing the children's listening by posting the mystery words. Ask the children to discover answers to the mystery questions and to sing the corresponding phrase with you.

Verse One:

- *WHAT is another name for my body? [A temple]*
- *HOW will I keep my spirit? [Free]* Explain that our spirits can be kept free when our lives are free from sin.
- *WHAT will I make my temple become? [Brighter]* We keep our temple brighter by keeping our bodies clean and pure.
- *WHERE was I a spirit? [In heaven]*
- *WHEN did I leave my home? [At birth]*
- *WHO gave me this temple to live within on earth? [The Lord]*

Verse Two:

- *WHAT may I claim if I keep my body clean and pure and habit-free? [Blessings promised me]*
- *WHERE may I claim blessings promised me? [In Father's temple]*
- *WHEN will I take my body bright? [On resurrection morning]* Our spirits and bodies will be reunited one day. That is called resurrection.
- *WHERE will I live forever when I receive my celestial glory? [In light]* Living in the light of Heavenly Father and Jesus Christ forever is a wonderful reward for keeping our temples clean and pure.

Bear testimony of the Resurrection, and challenge the children to live for the promised blessings.

ENRICHMENT IDEAS:

1. Discuss how to keep our temple bright. (No smoking, get plenty of rest, eat good food, exercise, etc.)
2. Display two melody pictures, pointing out the descending scales. Show that the scale on chart one sounds a little higher than the pattern on chart two. Challenge the children to find the words that match each scale.

I'll make my temple brighter.

I'll keep my spirit free.

3. Challenge the children to listen carefully and find two words with two syllables that are sung on three notes. [Temple (line 1) and spirit (line 2)]
4. *What word is sung on the very highest note? [Make]*

♪ About the Song

Darwin Wolford, the composer, revised the beginning pitch, changed the key and simplified his accompaniment in this version of his song. He suggested the original second verse, which had not been used previously, seemed vital for this generation and ought to be included to provide an opportunity to strengthen children against substance abuse.

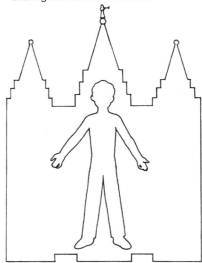

THE WORD OF WISDOM

MESSAGE: If we obey the Word of Wisdom, the Lord has promised us a clean body, a clear mind, and a spirit in tune with the Lord.

ENRICHMENT IDEAS:

1. Invite the children to sway to the two-beat meter.

2. Coordinate the teaching of this song with a presentation of the story of Daniel and his belief in eating healthy foods. (See Daniel 1.)

3. Briefly discuss the things that the Word of Wisdom counsels us not to eat, and emphasize the good foods mentioned that we should eat.

4. Ask the children to turn to D&C 89 in their own scriptures. Have one child read verses 18–21.

MATERIALS:

Objects: V.1, Basket of fruits, vegetables, bread, cheese, nuts, eggs

Melody pictures:

Wordstrips: V.2, *a clean body, a clear mind, a spirit in tune with the Lord.*

ATTENTION-GETTER:

- *When a car runs out of gas, what happens to it? [It stops working.] What do we give it to make it work again? [Gas] Will a car run on water? [No, it needs the right fuel to make it work properly]*

- *Our Heavenly Father has given us wonderful fuel for our bodies to make them work properly.* Show the children the basket of healthy foods.

- *Our fuel is healthy food. Heavenly Father has given us such a variety of good things to eat. He tells us in the scriptures how important it is for us to eat only the foods that are good for us. We call his counsel the Word of Wisdom. Listen as I sing, and discover what we are promised if we obey the Word of Wisdom.* Sing the first verse.

LISTENING AND SINGING EXPERIENCES:

Verse One:

- *If we obey the Word of Wisdom, what are we promised? [Beautiful blessings]* Point out the descending scale and have the children sing and pitch lead it with you.

- *If we want these beautiful blessings, we need to do two things. What are they? [Obey and follow in faith]* When we follow the Lord's commandments in faith we are obeying.

Post the two melody pictures and challenge the children to find the words that match the ascending and descending melody patterns. *[And follow in faith and beautiful blessings are]*

- *To whom did the Lord reveal the Word of Wisdom? [Joseph Smith, the Prophet]*

- *There is an octave jump between two words in the first phrase. Listen and tell me what words we sing on this eight-note interval. [The word]* Ask the children to sit up tall to sing this correctly.

Verse Two:

- *What are the three beautiful blessings that are promised to those who obey the Word of Wisdom? [A clean body, a clear mind, a spirit in tune with the Lord]* Display the wordstrips as the responses are given, and then sing again to check the order.

- *When we are in tune with the Lord, the Holy Ghost helps us know what is good for us. Several words in this phrase are sung on long notes to give them emphasis. Which important word is sung on the longest note? [Lord]* Let's make sure we sing this word for its full time value.

- *To whom are these promises given? [To all who follow the word and will of God]*

- *This phrase is made up of long and short notes. Listen as I sing and tap the rhythm.* Invite the children to sing and tap with you. Sing again. *The will of God is his desire for us to obey his word or commandments.*

When the children have learned both verses well, sing verses 1 and 2 together.

Share a personal experience about obeying the Word of Wisdom.

REMEMBER THE SABBATH DAY

MESSAGE: Remember to keep the Sabbath day holy. It was blessed by the Lord as the day for us to worship him.

ATTENTION-GETTER:

- *Have any of you children ever been asked by a friend to go swimming, to a movie or to a party on Sunday? It was probably difficult to say "no." But it can be easy to do what is right if you listen to the Holy Ghost. He will whisper to your mind, "Remember the Sabbath Day . . ."* Sing the entire song.

LISTENING AND SINGING EXPERIENCES:

Sing the song several times, directing the children's listening by asking questions similar to those listed below. Invite the children to sing each phrase as the answers are discovered. Continue until all are learned.

- *The song uses another word for "Sunday." What is it?* [The Sabbath day]
- *How should we keep the Sabbath day?* [Holy]
- *What did the Lord do to the Sabbath day?* [He blessed and hallowed it] This means that the Lord made Sunday a sacred day—different from the other six days in the week.
- *This time, listen for why the Lord blessed and hallowed the Sabbath day.* [That we might worship him]

Invite the children to sing with you as you pitch lead. Add the accompaniment.

Share a personal experience about the importance of keeping the Sabbath day holy.

ENRICHMENT IDEAS:

1. Invite a child to read Exodus 20:8, "Remember the sabbath day, to keep it holy."
2. Sing "Saturday" (p. 196) as a related song.
3. Discuss appropriate Sunday activities that are meaningful and fun.
4. Divide the children into four groups. Have each group sing one of the phrases. Trade parts.
5. Listen for two words that are sung on the highest notes. [Holy and Lord]

THE CHAPEL DOORS

MESSAGE: The chapel doors remind me to be still. The chapel is a reverent place where we learn of Jesus, sing, and pray.

ENRICHMENT IDEAS:

1. Invite the youngest children to sing the "Sh, be still" phrases as the rest of the children sing the song.

2. Sing the song, leaving out the phrase "Sh, be still" and putting finger to lips in place of the words. You may wish to hum this phrase.

3. Make a chart of a fermata ⌢. Have fun by holding up the sign for an exaggerated length of time on pray and doors.

4. Invite a child to read Leviticus 26:2, "Ye shall keep my sabbaths, and reverence my sanctuary: I am the Lord."

5. Very young children could role-play entering the room quietly, while others are singing.

♪ *About the Song*

Generally, only one verse of a prayer song is sung. Combining the first half of the first verse with the second half of the second verse put the emphasis on the positive "We gather here on the Sabbath day to learn of Jesus, to sing and pray".

MATERIALS:

Picture: meetinghouse, as illustrated, with doors that can be opened. Write "Sh" on the inside of the doors, and attach a picture of reverent children to the "inside" of the church.

Word cards: LEARN OF JESUS, SING, PRAY

ATTENTION-GETTER:

Show the picture of the meetinghouse.

• *Our church is a sacred place because it was dedicated, or blessed, as a place to worship Heavenly Father and Jesus.*

• *When we enter the chapel doors, they seem to say something to me. What do they seem to say? ["Sh, be still."] Sing the song for the children, opening the doors each time you sing, "Sh, be still."*

LISTENING AND SINGING EXPERIENCES:

Sing the song several times, encouraging the children to listen by asking questions about the message. Invite the children to then sing each phrase with you.

• *As I sing the song again, listen for how many times we sing "Sh, be still"? [Three]*

Invite the children to join you on "Sh, be still" as you sing the whole song.

• *Now listen to discover what kind of place this is. [Reverent]*

• *When do we gather here? [On the Sabbath day]*

• *Now as I sing for you, see if you can hear what three things we gather together to do? [Learn of Jesus, sing, and pray] Post the word cards as answers are given.*

• *Let's sing the song together and add the accompaniment.*

• *I want to encourage each of you to show by your actions that you have reverence for our sacred meetinghouse. Each time you come through the chapel doors, I hope you think of the words "Sh, be still."*

WHEN I GO TO CHURCH

MESSAGE: I always have a happy feeling when I go to church and reverently participate.

MATERIALS:

Melody pictures.

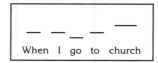

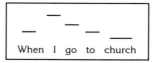

Pictures: flower, tree, home, friends, and family. (Visual Aids Cutouts 08456.)

ATTENTION-GETTER:

- *I always have a happy feeling when I go to a certain place. Listen for a clue as our accompanist plays the introduction to our song.* Have the accompanist play the chime-like introduction.
- *Where do I always have a happy feeling?* Let children respond.
- *Let's see if you're right!* Sing the first verse.

LISTENING AND SINGING EXPERIENCES:

Sing the song for the children, directing their listening by asking questions and inviting them to join you as you sing phrase by phrase.

Verse One:

- *When do I always have a happy feeling? [When I go to church]* Post the melody line charts and sing both phrases "When I go to church" while referring to the charts. Point out the differences in the melody, and invite the children to sing those phrases each time you come to them during the presentation.
- *As I sing the song again, listen to discover how the organ plays. [So soft and sweet]*
- *How do I get to my seat? [I tiptoe softly.]*
- *This time, see if you can hear whom I greet? [My teachers and my friends]*

Verse Two:

- *What do I like to raise in singing? [My voice]*
- *What do I do while prayer is said? [Fold my arms, bow my head, and listen]*
- *I do not talk, but what do I do instead? [Think]*

Verse Three:

- *Who do I learn about in church? [My Heavenly Father]*
- *There are six things I thank him for. What are they? [Each flower and tree, home, and friends and family, and all the lovely things I see]* Display pictures as responses are given. Sing again, challenging a child to put the pictures in the correct order.

ENRICHMENT IDEAS:

1. Listen for three rhyming words in each verse:

Verse One: *sweet, seat, greet*

Verse Two: *head, said, instead*

Verse Three: *tree, family, see*

2. Divide the children into groups, each singing a different phrase as you indicate. Have everyone join in on "When I go to church."

3. Sing the song for the children, omitting one word of each line or phrase, and challenge them to fill in the missing word.

4. Have the children draw pictures to represent a phrase of the song. Use these pictures to teach proper sequence.

5. Use chime or melody bells on the introduction to give a feeling of being in church.

To simplify the *Children's Songbook*, any phrase repeated in all verses was printed only once—for example, "When I go to church". This was done throughout the book.

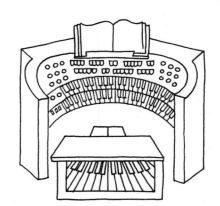

MESSAGE: Dare to do those things that you know are right, regardless of what others might want you to do.

ENRICHMENT IDEAS:

1. Post the word DARE. Attach other word cards to children's clothing. Have them stand in the correct order as the song is sung. Word cards might include: RIGHT, TRUE, WORK, BRAVELY, KINDLY, WELL, ANGELS, HASTEN, and STORY.

2. Define words or phrases that need to be explained:

   "Other men's failures can never save you": Don't excuse your mistakes because of the mistakes others make.

   "Stand like a hero and battle till death": (Life can be a battle and we are admonished to endure to the end). (See D&C 6:13, 63:47, 14:7.)

   "Hasten": (hurry).

3. Sing related songs, such as "Stand for the Right" (p. 159), and "Do What Is Right" (Hymns, no. 237).

4. The harmonization in 3rds and 6ths frequently lends itself to part singing.

MATERIALS:

Melody pictures:

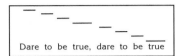

Dare to be true, dare to be true

You have a work that no oth - er can do

ATTENTION-GETTER:

- *I have a letter for you from Elder Rex D. Pinegar, which says:*

"*My dear friends,*

I dare you! are words boys and girls often hear from friends who want you to prove to them that you are brave or strong or daring. They may ask you to do something that your parents or teachers have told you not to. . . . I have learned that when we do something we know is wrong, we show weakness rather than strength. A person shows true bravery and strength only when he has the courage to do right.

Once, when I was about seven years old, I had a pal whom I liked very much. We often walked home from school together. . . . Sometimes we would dare each other to jump across a ditch or to climb a tree just to prove that we were brave. As we came to my home one day we stood out by the road and talked about who was the fastest runner in the school. . . . When I strongly insisted that I could run faster than my friend, he turned to me and said, 'If you're so fast, I dare you to run across the road before that car gets here!' I looked up the road and saw a car a short distance away. Without another word I dashed into the road to prove that I was fast and brave. A moment later the car's brakes squealed! Its bumper hit me, and I landed in an unconscious heap. When I opened my eyes, my aching body, a hurt pride, and my mother's anxious face made me realize that I had been neither fast nor brave. I had only been foolish. I had brought sadness to myself and to others. The lesson I learned . . . has been valuable to me throughout my life. I learned that the only dare a person should ever accept is the . . . Sing the chorus, 'Dare, dare, dare to do right, etc.'" *(Friend Oct. 1979.)*

LISTENING AND SINGING EXPERIENCES:

Sing the chorus one more time, asking the children to listen for how many times you sing the word "dare." [Eight] Sing again to check their answer.

- *When we dare to do right, we also dare to be something else. Listen for what it is, and count how many times I sing it. [True, three times]*

- *Listen for the words I am singing when my voice goes right down the scale. [Dare to be true]* Have the children pitch lead that phrase it with you. Post melody picture 1.

Sing the verse, asking the children to listen for another phrase that goes right down the scale, almost like the last one. [*You have a work that no other can do*]

Post melody picture 2 and ask the children what is different about the second phrase. [*The melody goes up at the end*]

- *Listen for three words that describe how we should do our work. [Bravely, kindly, well]* These will be easy to remember because they are in alphabetical order.

- *Who will hasten (hurry) the story to tell? [Angels]*

Let's all follow Elder Pinegar's advice and dare to do right every day. Invite the children to sing the entire song again with you.

STAND FOR THE RIGHT

MESSAGE: Our prophet tells us that no matter where we are, we should be true and stand for the right.

MATERIALS:

Pictures: President Spencer W. Kimball, and our current prophet.

ATTENTION-GETTER:

- *How many of you children feel that you are old enough to make an important decision?* Show a picture of President Kimball.

- *President Spencer W. Kimball decided when he was a young child to never break the Word of Wisdom. He said: "Occasionally some respected speaker said he had never tasted the forbidden things . . . and then I made up my mind. Never would I use these forbidden things the prophets preached against. That decision was firm and unalterable. . . . Now is the time to set your life's goals. Now is the time to set your standards firmly and then hold to them throughout your life." ("Decide Now," Friend, May, 1985, p. IFC.)*

- *You can make important decisions now that will affect your whole life.* Show a picture of the current prophet.

- *Who is this? He is our prophet. A prophet is a man who speaks for the Lord on the earth. Listen as I sing, and discover the words the prophet has for us.*

LISTENING AND SINGING EXPERIENCES:

- *What words does the prophet have for you?* ["Be true, be true and stand for the right."] Sing the answer again, pointing out the way the melody comes down in steps.

Invite the children to pitch lead the descending scale.

- *To "be true and stand for the right" is more than standing physically. It means to have the courage to be obedient to gospel teachings.*

- *Listen as I sing again. Count the number of times I sing the words "Be true."* [Four] Have the children join you on the last line.

- *Where should we be true?* [At work or at play]

- *When should we be true?* [In darkness or light] *That means twenty-four hours a day, or in other words, all the time.*

- *All the prophets have taught us to "be true and stand for the right."* President Ezra Taft Benson said, "May God bless us all to be true and faithful to the commandments of the Lord." (Ensign, July 1986, p. 3.)

- *Let's sing the song together, knowing it's a true message from a modern day prophet.*

Challenge the children to stand for the right at all times.

ENRICHMENT IDEAS:

1. Review by asking children to sing "Be true" while you sing the rest of the song. Then switch parts.

2. Have the children stand up on the words "stand for the right."

3. Slow slightly on the last phrase: "stand for the right."

4. Share a personal experience when it took courage for you to be true. Teach the principle that it's not always easy to stand for the right, but it will always be easier once the decision to do it has been made.

5. Show a picture of Moses (62100), and have a child read Deuteronomy 6:18: "And thou shalt do that which is right and good in the sight of the Lord: that it may be well with thee. . . ." Ancient prophets as well as latter-day prophets have urged us to be true to gospel teachings and stand for the right.

6. Tell a short example of children who have been true and stood for the right, such as Joseph Smith, or the sons of Helaman (see Alma 53:10-23).

7. Display the mystery word cards WHO, WHAT, WHERE, WHEN.

Ask the following questions:

- *WHO has some words for us?* [Our prophet]

- *WHAT are the words?* [Be true]

- *WHERE shall we be true?* [At work or at play]

- *WHEN?* [In darkness or light]

8. You could make a flip-chart of plastic protectors held together with rings. Pictures and word cards could be easily inserted: PROPHET, WORDS, "BE TRUE," WORK, PLAY, "DARKNESS" (black paper), "LIGHT" (white paper), "Be true," right.

 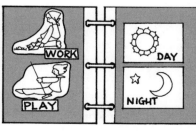 

MESSAGE: If I choose to live as Jesus taught, I will be happy.

ENRICHMENT IDEAS:

1. Invite the CTR class to sing this song—their class song—for the other children. Ask what choosing the right means to them.

2. Post the CTR symbol and ask the children to relate experiences of when they chose the right.

3. Alternate boys and girls singing: Boys sing phrases 1, 3, and 5. Girls sing phrases 2, 4, and 6. All sing "I must always choose the right."

4. Let the children join you in conducting the 3/4 time signature.

5. Make a "Super Singer" badge for a child to wear. As the song is sung, choose a "Super Singer" to come in front of the group. As the song is repeated, the "Super Singer" chooses another "Super Singer."

MATERIALS:

Pictures: (Jesus the Christ 62572), happy boy, happy girl

V.1, *Ten footprints on which you have written "choice" questions, such as choosing to (1) say your morning prayers, (2) pay your tithing, (3) sleep in and miss church, (4) be friendly to a new boy at school, (5) obey your mother when she asked you to be home by 5:00 p.m., (6) cheat on a test, (7) swear when you were angry, (8) let your brother play with your toys, (9) be baptized, (10) come quickly when your mother called you.*

Word cards: V.2, PRAYERFUL, FAITH, REPENT, OBEY.

ATTENTION-GETTER:

Put the picture of Jesus the Christ at the top of the chalkboard, with a happy girl and boy on either side.

Read the "choice" questions; let the children decide if the choice leads them to Jesus and the happy children or away from them. Place footprints on the board accordingly.

* *There's a right way to live and be happy. As I sing this song, listen for what I must do to be happy. [Choose the right way] Sing the first verse and chorus for the children.*

LISTENING AND SINGING EXPERIENCES:

Sing the song several times, encouraging the children to listen by using questions and statements similar to those listed below. As the children discover the answers, invite them to sing that part of the song with you. Add one phrase at a time to the ones already learned.

Chorus:

* *What must I always do? [Choose the right way] Pitch lead the last phrase, showing how the words are sung in steps moving up the scale. Sometimes a composer will make a melody go up the scale to emphasize an important idea or word.*

* *What important word comes at the top of the scale in this song? [Right]*

* *When we choose the right way, how will we feel? [Happy]*

Help the children notice that the melody and rhythm are the same by singing and tapping the phrases "choose the right way" and "and be happy."

Verse One:

* *What is the right way to live and be happy? [Choosing the right every day]*

* *When should we choose the right? [Every day]*

* *What am I learning? [The teachings of Jesus]*

* *Name the two things the teachings of Jesus will do? [He will help me and show me the way]*

Verse Two:

Through the gospel, I learn four things. What are they? *[To be prayerful, to have faith, to repent, to obey].* With each answer, post that word leading to the picture of Jesus.

I know that if I live by his teachings, What will I truly be? [Happy each day.]

I PLEDGE MYSELF TO LOVE THE RIGHT

MESSAGE: I pledge myself to be honest and true and to love the right.

MATERIALS:

Prepare and display the following chart:

```
I Pledge Myself
     to Love _____ ,    _____ ,
             _____ and _____
     to Keep _____ and _____
```

Word cards: Set A, THE RIGHT, THE GOOD, THE FAIR, AND TRUE; Set B, MY FAITH, HONOR, BRIGHT, EVERYTHING I DO.

One-syllable word chart:

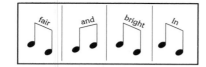

ATTENTION-GETTER:

- *A promise is very important. A past Church leader, Karl G. Maesar, once said that if he drew a circle on the ground around him and promised that he would never cross that line, he would die in that spot before he would break his promise.*

- *As I sing this song, listen to hear another word for "promise." [Pledge]*

LISTENING AND SINGING EXPERIENCES:

- *I promise, or pledge, myself to love four things. What are they? [The right, the good, the fair, and true]* Sing again if necessary to secure answers. As children answer, post the set A word cards on the chart.

- *I pledge to keep two things bright. What are they? [My faith and honor] To "keep my faith and honor bright" means I will do what I promise to do.* Post set B word cards on the chart.

- *The majestic sound of the music of this song reinforces the importance of the message. As I sing, join me in tapping the beat, noticing the march-like quality.*

- *As we sing the song again, find the four one-syllable words that are each sung on two notes. [Fair, and, bright, in]* Post the one-syllable word chart. Encourage children to sing those words clearly.

ENRICHMENT IDEAS:

1. Show a picture of President David O. McKay. Tell the children that President McKay taught us that "to be trusted is a greater compliment than to be loved." If we are trustworthy, we will be honest and true.

2. Sing related songs such as "Stand for the Right" (p. 159), "Choose the Right Way" (p. 160), "Dare to Do Right" (p. 158), "Do What Is Right" (Hymns, no. 237), and "Choose the Right" (Hymns, no. 239).

3. Have a child read D&C 136:20: "Seek ye; and keep all your pledges one with another."

4. Share with the children an incident or story of a child who has been honest and true.

5. Ask the children to discover the words sung on the repeated notes as you pitch lead the song. [pledge—my, self—to, good—the, keep—my, faith—and, hon—or, ev—ry, thing—I]

6. A melody picture could be prepared to show the words sung on repeated notes.

I WILL BE VALIANT

MESSAGE: I will be a valiant servant so the Lord can depend on me to do his work.

ENRICHMENT IDEAS:

1. Tape a large "V" on the shirts of several children at the beginning of Primary. During Singing Time ask the children what they think the "V" represents. Discuss the meaning of the word "valiant" and then ask each "V" child to tell something he or she could do that is valiant.

2. Show the picture (2000 Young Warriors 62050) and have a child read Alma 53:20-21. Explain that Helaman and his two thousand stripling warriors were valiant servants and they entered into a covenant to protect their liberty. The Lord could depend on them to keep the commandments and live righteously.

3. Have a child read John 13:13-17 or Matthew 25:34-40. Discuss the principle that those who serve their fellowmen are valiant.

4. Have the children march to the rhythm while singing.

5. Show the picture (The Prophet Joseph Smith 62002) and tell the children that Joseph Smith was a valiant servant. Ask the children to name other valiant servants. These are servants that the Lord can really depend on.

6. Smaller children may wish to point to themselves with both thumbs on the words "The Lord can depend on me."

7. You could ask the Valiant class to sing this song—their class song—for the children. Make a large Valiant class shield and attach cut-out pictures to represent ideas in the song.

♪ *About the Song*

In 1981, new class manuals were prepared for the Sunday consolidated schedule. Vanja Watkins wrote "I Will Be Valiant" for the Valiant class song. There was some concern about putting words in children's mouths—so it was changed to "I CAN . . ." Sister Watkins felt that it was good for children to sing about something they will promise to try and be. So now the words are as she wrote them originally.

MATERIALS:

The "Help-wanted" section of the newspaper.

Mystery Word cards: WHAT KIND? WHO? WHAT CAN I DO? HOW? WHAT? HOW? WHAT? WHO?

ATTENTION-GETTER:

- *I brought this "Help-wanted" section of the newspaper with me today. It lists the kinds of jobs that need to be done. Employers need secretaries, truck drivers, car salesmen, telephone operators, baby-sitters, and construction workers. But I don't see a single ad for the most important job in the world. Listen, and tell me what kind of job I'm talking about. [A servant of the Lord]*

LISTENING AND SINGING EXPERIENCES:

Display the mystery words. Sing the song several times, encouraging the children to listen by using questions and statements similar to those listed below. As children discover answers, invite them to sing that part of the song with you. Add one phrase at a time to the ones already learned. Consider starting with the last question and working forward.

- *WHAT KIND of servant does the Lord need? [Valiant] Valiant means to be brave and true. A servant is a person who works for someone else.*

- *WHO needs us to do his work in the latter days? [The Lord]*

- *WHAT CAN I DO to be his valiant servant? [Follow the teachings of Jesus and serve his people]*

- *HOW should we serve other people? [In a loving way]*

- *WHAT can I keep valiantly? [My covenants (promises)]*

- *HOW did we say I should keep them? [Valiantly]*

- *WHAT two things do we stand for when we are valiant servants? [Truth and right]*

- *WHO can the Lord depend on? [Me]*

- *What a great blessing it is to be the Lord's valiant servant and to have him depend on me! Let's strive to serve and follow Jesus and to truly be his valiant servants.*

I AM LIKE A STAR

MESSAGE: I am like a star shining brightly, doing and saying happy things because I know Heavenly Father loves me.

MATERIALS:

Cut a star-shaped hole in a posterboard (approximately 10" x 10"). Cover the hole with yellow cellophane or fabric. At the appropriate time, shine a flashlight through the back of the star.

ATTENTION-GETTER:

Shine the flashlight through the cellophane or fabric to light the star.

- *This star is a special star. It is shining for the world to see. We can be like a star. When we remember that Heavenly Father loves us, we smile and do happy things. We look bright and shiny.*

Turn the flashlight off. *When we forget that Heavenly Father loves us, we don't do happy things, we don't feel like smiling, and we don't shine brightly.*

Turn the flashlight back on. *Jesus talked about this in the Bible.* Have a child read Matthew 5:16, *"Let your light so shine before men, that they may see your good works, and glorify your Father which is in heaven."*

LISTENING AND SINGING EXPERIENCES:

Sing the song for the children, asking the following questions. When they answer, sing that phrase for the children and then have them join you. Begin at the end of the song and work towards the first, adding one phrase at a time until the whole song is learned.

This song says someone loves me. As I sing it for you, see if you can discover who that is. [Heavenly Father.]

- *What does the song say I can do and say? [Happy things each day.]*
- *Why can I do happy things each day? [Because I know Heavenly Father loves me.]*
- *What do we do for the world to see? [Smile.]* (A common mistake is for the children to sing "shining for the world to see." Emphasize the word smiling.)
- *What does the song say I am like? [A star shining brightly.]*
- *When we remember that Heavenly Father loves us, we can be like stars and shine brightly for those around us to see. We can do this by smiling and doing happy things every day. This week, remember that Heavenly Father loves you, and be like a star that shines brightly by doing happy helpful things for your family and friends.*

ENRICHMENT IDEAS:

1. Make a large poster board star with a hole cutout for a child's face to show through. Have a child come to the front and keep a straight face while the children sing the song until the word "smiling." Or ask a child to keep a straight face until he feels that the children are singing their best.

2. Make four melody-pictures to indicate where the melody goes for each phrase of the song. This is easily done by drawing a musical staff very lightly and marking where the melody goes with stick-on stars. Put the first phrase up and show the children how to follow the melody. Show the other three charts and ask the children which chart goes next.

   Example: (1st Phrase)

3. Encourage the children to pitch lead the song with their bodies. Begin in a sitting position and stoop or stand as the melody moves higher and lower.

4. Make simple line drawings for each phrase (see illustration). Let children hold the drawings as they sing the song. Consider putting pictures out of order, letting children correct them as they sing.

♪ *About the Song*

Pat Graham wrote this song for four and five-year-olds. The tune "Twinkle, Twinkle Little Star" naturally came to her mind. She played it high on the piano to sound like a music box with an Alberti bass, and had her five-year-old son, Matt, sing her ideas.

Later, while on assignment, Pat observed one music leader say, after leading this song, "Did you feel that, boys and girls? You sang so sweetly you brought the spirit of our Heavenly Father into our Primary."

"I will never forget the sweetness of those little children as they followed the direction of their sensitive music leader. We were all moved by the singing, but moved even more by a Priesthood leader who explained the presence of our Heavenly Father's Spirit to the children."

I WILL FOLLOW GOD'S PLAN

MESSAGE: My life is a gift from Heavenly Father and has a purpose. I will follow God's plan for me by holding fast to his word and his love. Then I will be happy on earth and in my home above.

ENRICHMENT IDEAS:

1. In random order, post word cards: GIFT, PLAN, PURPOSE, HEAVEN, CHOICE, EARTH, SEEK, FOLLOW, HOLDING, WORK, PRAY, WALK, HAPPY, HOME. Challenge several children to put them in order as the song is sung. Sing again to check the order.

2. Show the children a musical staff with two notes drawn a third apart. Demonstrate by singing the intervals of thirds for the children. Challenge them to discover the words in this song that are sung on thirds. ["I _will work_, and I _will pray_, I _will always_ . . ."]

3. Have fun with the dynamic markings by singing them opposite from the way they are written. Then sing as written and ask the children which way they feel is appropriate to the words.

4. Invite the Merrie Miss girls to sing this—their class song—as a special number or to introduce the song.

MATERIALS:

Prepare a beautifully wrapped package in which you have placed a paper with the words MY LIFE written on it.

ATTENTION-GETTER:

Show the wrapped gift.

• _Inside this box is a most precious gift. All the money in the whole world can't buy it, yet we each have one. Listen as I sing, and discover what this precious gift is. [My life]_

Open the box and show the paper. Point out that our lives are precious gifts from Heavenly Father.

LISTENING AND SINGING EXPERIENCES:

Sing the song for the children several times, directing their listening by asking questions. As they discover the answers, invite them to sing those phrases with you.

• _Where did my life begin? [In heaven]_
• _What was my choice? [To come to this lovely home on earth]_
• _For what will I seek? [For God's light to direct me from birth]_
• _What can I follow? [God's plan for me]_
• _What two things will I hold fast? [His word and his love] To hold fast means to hold on tightly._
• _I will work and I will pray, and where will I always walk? [In his way]_
• _Then how will I feel on earth and in my home above? [Happy]_

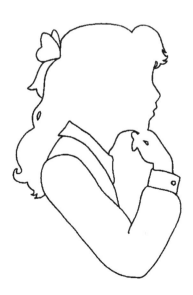

A YOUNG MAN PREPARED

MESSAGE: I am preparing myself to receive the sacred priesthood of God by living a clean life and using the scriptures as my guide.

MATERIALS:

Word card: TREPOSHIDO (the word "priesthood" scrambled).

ATTENTION-GETTER:

Display the word card. Ask the boys to solve the riddle (unscramble the word) by listening as you sing.

LISTENING AND SINGING EXPERIENCES:

- *What are you boys preparing to receive when you turn twelve? [The priesthood]*
- *Preparing yourselves to receive the Priesthood is the important message in this song. The word "prepare" or "prepared" is sung many times. Listen as I sing and count how many times I sing these words. [Four]*
- *Though you appear as a boy now, what will you soon be? [A man]*
- *How will you prepare and live clean? [In every thought, word, and deed]*
- *If you prepare and live clean, what will you be worthy to hold? [The sacred priesthood of God]*
- *You can prepare yourself by serving someone. Whom will you serve? [My fellowmen]*
- *What will you need to be armed with? [The truth, with the scriptures my guide]*
- *The last two phrases have the same words: "I'll go forward, a young man prepared." Listen very carefully and see if the melody is exactly the same. ["I'll go" is sung an octave higher the second time] Encourage the boys to sing the octave interval correctly.*
- *To receive the priesthood is a great blessing, for the priesthood is the power to act in behalf of Heavenly Father here on the earth. I encourage you to live clean lives and to study the scriptures so that you will be prepared to receive the sacred priesthood of God.*

ENRICHMENT IDEAS:

1. Point out that a dotted rhythm is used throughout the song. Tap the rhythm to the last phrase and invite the boys to tap it with you. Ask them to tap the rhythm as they sing the song with you.
2. Invite the Blazer class to sing this song for the other children.
3. Invite a guest to share an experience when the priesthood blessed his life.
4. March in place to the rhythm as you sing this song.
5. Use the alternate words "I'm a blazer", as suggested on the song page.

♪ *About the Song*

As a young boy in Idaho, Dan Carter was often moved to tears by the beautiful music of the Tabernacle Choir at conference time. He said, "I always yearned to be able to share my testimony and feelings of the gospel through music."

When he was asked to write a song to help prepare boys to receive the priesthood, he worried about his ability to write something that boys would enjoy singing. "After several weeks of working and rewriting, an idea for the music came, and I felt sure that this song could help boys." In an effort to extend the use of the song to Deacons, the words "I'm a Blazer" are optional.

GO THE SECOND MILE

MESSAGE: When there is a task to do, do it with a smile. Go the second mile by doing more than you are asked to do.

ENRICHMENT IDEAS:

1. Make a musical visual aid by drawing the melody picture (illustrated below) on four separate sheets of paper. Show the children how to follow the melody picture. Post the four melody pictures out of sequence and have the children place them in the correct order as they sing the song. Ask the children to discover what words occur at * on each pattern.

2. Have the children tell about times when they have gone the second mile.

3. Have two older children read Matthew 5:41 and 3 Nephi 12:41. Explain to the children that this must have been a very important principle of the gospel, because it was given to the people in Jerusalem and also to the people on the American continent. Challenge the children to go the second mile this week.

4. Have a child play the melody on a violin, flute, small xylophone or with piano accompaniment as an introduction and between verses.

5. Have the children pitch lead the melody of this song by stretching or stooping as the melody moves up and down.

MATERIALS :

Letter cards: G-T-S-M

Wordstrip: Go the second mile

Melody pictures:

Charts A and B

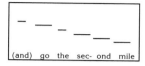

(and) go the sec- ond mile

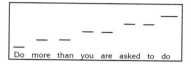

Do more than you are asked to do

ATTENTION-GETTER:

Post the letter cards G-T-S-M.

• *These letters stand for a principle that Christ taught to his followers. Raise your hand when you know what it is.*

• *When Christ was on earth, the people of Palestine were ruled by the Romans. There was a law that allowed a Roman soldier passing through an area to demand that a man carry his baggage for one mile.*

• *In the Sermon on the Mount, Christ told his listeners that they should be willing to carry the baggage a second mile. The first mile was required, but the second was a kind service they could give.* (See Bruce R. McConkie, Doctrinal New Testament Commentary, vol. 1, p. 228–29)

• *Do you know what G-T-S-M mean now?* Without further comment, sing the entire song for the children and display the wordstrip "Go the second mile."

LISTENING AND SINGING EXPERIENCES:

Sing the song several times, encouraging the children to listen by using questions and statements similar to those listed below. As children discover answers, invite them to sing that part of the song with you.

Verse One:

• *What are you doing when you do more than you are asked to do? [Going the second mile]* Show melody picture A and pitch lead, helping the children notice how the melody goes down the scale.

Practice tapping the uneven rhythm in the last phrase.

Show melody pictures B. *What are the words on the repeated notes that go up the scale? [Do more than you are asked to do]*

Pitch lead, showing how the melody rises after each repeated note.

• *When there is a task to do, how should we do it? [With a smile]*

• *We should go the second mile when there is a job to do. But in this song, a job is called something else. What is another word for a job? [Task]*

Verse Two:

• *When you go the second mile, what will you find? [You'll be happy]*

• *When are two times you should try it? [In your work and in your play]*

• *Each of us can have the satisfaction or good feeling that comes when we do more than we are expected or asked to do.*

Referring to the letter cards and wordstrip challenge the children to G-T-S-M: GO THE SECOND MILE.

I WANT TO BE A MISSIONARY NOW

MESSAGE: While I am young, I can be a missionary by sharing my testimony with my friends, by telling them about the Church, and by living the gospel.

MATERIALS:

Pictures: (Children Looking at Spring Flowers 62270), (Waiting Our Turn 62316), (Sharing the Tricycle 62317), (Jumping Rope 62523), (Missionaries Tracting 62611)

ATTENTION-GETTER:

- *What do you want to be when you are grown?* Let the children respond.
- *With most professions, you have to wait until you are grown. But you can be a missionary now as well as when you are grown. How can you be a missionary while you are young?*

Show the pictures of the children.

- *Which of these children is a missionary? (The only way to know is by what they say and what they do.)*

Help the children understand how important their actions, words, and example are in "preaching the gospel," even as they play.

LISTENING AND SINGING AND EXPERIENCES:

Sing the song for the children, using questions and statements similar to the following:

Clap the word "missionary" with the children. Help them notice the four parts (syllables) to the word. Ask them to listen for another word in the song with the same number of parts as missionary. (Hint: It is something you need before you can be a missionary.) [Testimony]

Notice how the melody bounces in long/short sounds on the word testimony and in the last line. Sing the last line again for the children to notice. Invite them to tap the last line as you sing; then invite them to sing the last line with you.

- *Is the first line similar to or different from the last line? [Same except for the pick-up notes]* Invite the children to sing the first and last lines with you while you sing the entire song.
- *Most of the song is made of long/short/long sounds. But there are five notes that are even, rather than long/short/long. What are the words on those notes? [I want to share the gospel.]*
- *The line with the even notes has the highest tone in it. What word comes on the highest tone? [Young]*
- *That same line has the lowest tone. What word comes on the lowest tone? [I]*
- *That line of music is like climbing a hill, beginning with a low tone and going to the highest tone. But in the middle of the phrase, the melody drops down as if to get a second start. What word do we sing when we drop down? [The]*

Invite the children to sing that line with you, being careful to sing the low tones accurately.

- *What word in the song is opposite of "young"? [Grown] Is grown on a high note or low note? [Low]*

As the children listen, help them notice that the music doesn't match those two words: "grown" is sung on a low note, and "young" is sung on a high note.

Ask the children to sing the entire song with the accompaniment.

ENRICHMENT IDEAS:

1. Invite a child to come forward. Have him stand up on a chair, and put a man's suit coat and a name tag on him. Place scriptures in his hands. Point out that the child may look more like a missionary now, but he doesn't have to be wearing missionaries' clothes to be a missionary now.

2. *When we say "I want" something, our voices naturally go up. When we say "I don't want," our voices go down. Listen for how many times we sing "I want." Does the melody go up or down? [Up] How many times do we sing "I don't want"? [One time] Does the melody go up or down? [Down] The composer made the music go the same way our voice goes when we speak.*

3. Sing related missionary songs such as "I Hope They Call Me on a Mission" (p. 169), "The Things I Do" (p. 170), and "We'll Bring the World His Truth" (p. 172).

♪ About the Song

Because Grietje (Greet-sha) Rowley is a convert to the Church, missionary work is very important to her. She said, "I love the children and know that Heavenly Father expects them to do great things. I wrote 'I Want to Be a Missionary Now' to show children how they can bring happiness to others." She thinks that the songs we learn in Primary can bring us joy and comfort forever.

Sister Rowley serves on the General Music Committee. She simplified, transposed, offered helpful suggestions, and proofed the notation of the words, markings and notation of every song in the *Songbook* THREE times! She believed that the *Children's Songbook* was important to our Father in Heaven and that he would help all the workers to do it in the best way.

I HOPE THEY CALL ME ON A MISSION

MESSAGE: I am eager to be a missionary when I grow up, so I can serve the Lord by sharing the gospel with others.

ENRICHMENT IDEAS:

1. This song could be taught using mystery word cards: V.1: WHO, WHEN, WHAT; V.2: WHAT, WHO, WHAT, HOW

2. Show the picture of missionaries teaching the gospel (62611) as you ask the children how they are preparing for missionary service. [Saving money, reading scriptures, praying, attending meetings]

3. Have the children learn an adult version of the song and sing it for a retired couple who are going on a mission. Change the following words:

   V.1, line 2 . . . I've retired a year or two

   V.2, line 2 . . . with whom I'll spend my time

   V.2, last word . . . prime

4. Make a "missionary boy" visual mounted on a large piece of poster paper that "grows a foot or two." Use it as a singing thermometer to encourage everyone to participate.

5. Other references: The Friend, October 1985, p. 15. Coloring Songbook, I Hope They Call me On a Mission, Aspen Books © 1991.

MATERIALS:

Props: Man's suit, tie, missionary name tag, Bible, Book of Mormon, Yardstick

Word cards: TEACH, PREACH, WORK

ATTENTION-GETTER:

Bring a young child forward and ask the other children if this child looks like a missionary. They may give responses such as:

"He isn't tall enough." (Have the child stand on a chair.)

"He isn't wearing a dark suit and tie." (Help the child into a man's suit coat and tie.)

"He doesn't have a name tag." (Pin an "Elder" name tag on the child.)

"He doesn't have the scriptures with him." (Hand the child a Bible and Book of Mormon.)

Help the children conclude that the child does look like a missionary, but he'll need to grow a foot or two taller before he can go on an official mission.

- Today we are going to learn a song called "I Hope They Call Me on a Mission." Listen as I sing, and tell me how much I'll have to grow before I can go on a mission. [A foot or two]

Show the children an estimated measurement of two feet by measuring with the yardstick twenty-four inches above the child's head.

LISTENING AND SINGING EXPERIENCES:

Sing the song several times, encouraging the children to listen by using questions and statements similar to those listed below. As the children discover the answers, invite them to sing that part of the song with you. Add one phrase at a time to the ones already learned.

Verse One:

- What do I hope by the time I go on my mission? [I will be ready]

- What three things do I want to be ready to do? [Teach, preach, work as missionaries do] Display the word cards to help the children remember the correct order.

Have them sit up tall so they can correctly sing the interval "to teach." Tell them this is an octave, or eight-note, jump.

Invite the children to feel the lively beat and syncopation by tapping the rhythm—and to notice that the rhythm changes to a steady beat on the phrase "to teach and preach and work."

Sing the first phrase, "I hope they call me on a mission," and ask the children to find other words sung on that same melody. [I hope by then I will be ready]

Invite the children to sit up like tall missionaries and sing the song with enthusiasm.

Verse Two:

- What do I want to share? [The gospel]

- Whom do I want to share it with? [Those who want to know the truth]

- I want to be a missionary and do what? [Serve and help the Lord.]

- I want to serve the Lord as a missionary while I am young. What words in the song mean "while I am young"? [While I am in my youth]

THE THINGS I DO

MESSAGE: I am too young to be called on a full-time mission, but I can spread the gospel by being a good example.

MATERIALS:

Dark food coloring and a clear jar filled with water

ENRICHMENT IDEAS:

1. Ask the children if they notice something besides the even rhythm in verse three that makes it sound different. [It is higher and the melody is a bit different.]

2. Consider standing up on all verses with the long-short rhythm and sitting with arms folded on the verse with the even rhythm.

3. Consider using all of the rhyming words as key words to aid in review.

ATTENTION GETTER:

• *How many drops do you think are in this jar of water?*

• *If you were one drop of water, could you make a difference to the rest of the water in the jar?*

Illustrate how one drop can influence all the others by adding one drop of dark food coloring to the water and noticing how it flows through the whole jar. Help children see that the things they do can influence others and help to spread the gospel. Sing the song for the children.

LISTENING AND SINGING EXPERIENCES:

Teach one verse of the song at a time, directing the children's listening and singing by asking a question each time you sing the song to the children.

Verse One:

• *How does the song say I can show that I know the word of God is true? [By the things I do]*

• *The song says I am too young to go away on a mission. What word does it use that means far away? [Abroad]*

• *This long-short-long rhythm* ♩♪♩ *is repeated over and over again. Tap it with me as I sing verse one again.* Invite the children to sing verse one with you.

Verse Two:

• *When a neighbor sees me, how will he judge the gospel? [By how I act]*

• *What word do we sing on the highest note? [Act]*

• *Find the two sets of rhyming words. [Neighborhood—good, play—day]*

Sing verse two with the children.

Verse Three:

• *How will my friend know that church is a sacred place? [By my reverence and my happy face]*

• *How will I act in church? [With dignity]*

• *How does this verse sound different than the other two? [The rhythm is smooth—more like a hymn. It's church-like]*

Sing verse three with the children.

Verse Four:

• *In everything I do, my friend will see that I am a Latter-day Saint, just as I say I am. But the song uses another word for "say." What is the word? [Profess.]*

• *If I am a good example, what might happen when the missionaries knock on my friend's door? [He'll say, "Come in and tell me more."]*

• *Find the two sets of rhyming words in this verse. [See—be, door—more]*

Invite the children to sing verse four with you.

WE'LL BRING THE WORLD HIS TRUTH

MESSAGE: We have been taught the gospel, and we want to do as the Lord commands. We will be the Lord's missionaries and take the gospel to all the world.

ENRICHMENT IDEAS:

1. Use the pictures listed below, adding key words. Remove word cards as the song is learned.

   Chorus: (2,000 Young Warriors 62050); V.1, (Nephi Subdues His Rebellious Brothers 62044), (Family With a Baby 62307), (Class Prayer 62200); V.2, (A Mother, a Little Girl, and a New Baby 62340), (Family Home Evening 62521), (President Hunter 64329), (Missionaries Tracting 62611); V.3, (Boy Being Baptized 62018), (Both Books Testify of Christ 62373),(Bedside Prayer 62217), (Missionaries Tracting 62611)

2. Put key words on "feather" headbands.

3. Read 1 Nephi 1:1 and see if the children can guess what song you are going to sing next. This could be done with any song, using the scripture reference listed below each song.

4. Stand and shift body weight from left to right on the first word of each measure as you sing the chorus.

5. Refer to the *Friend,* May 1986, p. 37.

♪ About the Song

There are three entries in the index for this song—first line, title, and sub-title (the way the children identify the song). Song titles were occasionally adjusted to state the message or subject of the song.

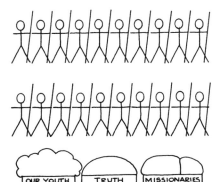

MATERIALS:

Draw one hundred stick figures on a sheet of paper. Make nineteen copies of this sheet and tape them together, edge to edge. Fold the sheets behind each other so that only the original sheet shows.

ATTENTION-GETTER:

Plan ahead to have a presentation about Helaman's army of two thousand warriors. The song will have more significance to the children if they know these stories.

Show the original sheet of stick figures. Discuss how many people one hundred is. Then unfold the other sheets of stick figures to illustrate the two thousand young men in Helaman's army. Emphasize that not a single young warrior was killed in war because of their faith and willingness to obey the teachings of their parents.

LISTENING AND SINGING EXPERIENCES:

Use questions and statements as you teach the song. Sing the song or parts of the song and then invite the children to sing that part with you. Sing the first verse and the chorus to the children when asking the first question or two. Then sing just the chorus until it is well-learned.

Chorus:

- *What will we bring the world? [His truth]*

- *Whose missionaries will we be? [The Lord's]* As children give the answer, sing the last phrase again. Invite the children to sing it with you.

- *What important word comes on a high note in the last phrase? [Lord's]* Help the children notice how the composer began the last phrase low, allowed the melody to climb up to the important word "Lord," and then had the melody jump back down again.

- Sing the chorus again. *What other words occur on the same tune as "We will be the Lord's missionaries"? [We are as the army of Helaman]*

- *When have we been taught? [In our youth]*

Verse One:

- *What must we do? [As the Lord commands]*

- *The song mentions that we have been born to goodly parents, just like a prophet of old. Which prophet? [Nephi]* Have a child read 1 Nephi 1:1: *"I, Nephi, having been born of goodly parents, therefore I was taught somewhat in all the learning of my father..."*

Hum the tune to the first phrase and ask what other words come on that tune. [We have been taught and we understand.]

- *What do we understand? [That we must do as the Lord commands]*

Questions for other verses might include:

- *Why have we been saved for these latter days? [To build the kingdom in righteous ways]*

- *What words did our prophet declare? [Let each who's worthy go forth and share.]* Show a picture of our prophet.

- *How will we increase our knowledge? [Through study and prayer]* Show a picture of the scriptures (62373) and of a child in prayer (62310).

- *How often will we learn until we are called? [Daily]*

- *Where will we be called to take the gospel? [To all the world]*

CALLED TO SERVE

MESSAGE: We are called to serve our Heavenly Father, to be a witness for his name, and to gladly proclaim his love far and wide.

MATERIALS:

Pictures: (Missionaries Tracting 62611), (Class Prayer 62200), (Mother Praying 62309), (President Hunter 64329)

Rhythm charts: (A) ♩ ♩ ♩♩   (B) ♫ ♫ ♩♩

Scriptures: D&C 4:2–3

ATTENTION-GETTER:

- *I am a part of a very special army.* Hold up pictures of priesthood leaders, missionaries, Primary teachers, and parents.
- *These people have all been called to serve in this army as well.*
- *You have also been called to serve in this special army. Listen as I sing and tell me who we are called to serve?* Sing the song to the children.

LISTENING AND SINGING EXPERIENCES:

- *Who are we called to serve?* [Heavenly Father]
- *What two names are used for Heavenly Father?* [Heavenly King of Glory, Father]
- *The song sounds like a majestic march. One of the reasons is because of this rhythm pattern.* Show the children rhythm chart A as you clap it.
- *Clap that pattern with me. Listen as I sing, and tell me how many times that pattern occurs.* [Three times in verse one]
- *What words occur on that pattern?* [Called to serve Him, Chosen e'er to, Far and wide we] As I sing the verse, please sing those words when they come.
- *There is a word on the even rhythm part that means "ever" but the V is left out. What word do we sing that means "ever"?* [E'er]
- *In two of the three places where the even rhythm occurs, Walter G. Tyler, the composer, used another technique for creating a majestic sound. He made the melody jump up one octave, like this.* Demonstrate by singing "loo," on the melody of the words "Called to." *What words occur on that jump?* [Called to and Far and.] Invite the children to practice singing those two places, noticing how it feels to sing such a big melodic jump.
- *In between those even rhythms, the composer wrote uneven sounds. Clap the rhythm of chart B. Discover what words come on the uneven rhythm.* [Heav'nly King of glory, witness for his name, tell the Father's story, Far and wide his love pro-. . .]

When children know the verse, divide them into two groups. Ask one group to sing only when the even rhythm occurs, and the other to sing only when the uneven rhythm occurs. All join together to sing the last line.

Chorus:

- *The words "onward" and "forward" are sung over and over again in the song. How many times is each sung?* [Onward—four times, forward—three times] Sing those words with me as I sing the chorus.
- *What kind of song do we sing?* [A triumph song]
- *Who is our strength?* [God—our Heavenly Father]

Read D&C 4:2–3. Discuss the importance of serving the Lord, and how the composer of the song created music to emphasize this importance. Invite the children to feel the beat of this march by patting their laps, alternating left and right hands as they sing.

ENRICHMENT IDEAS:

1. Small children may enjoy marching to the song as they hear you sing. Consider having the children pat the beat on their laps during the verse, and standing and marching when the chorus comes. Challenge the children to listen so they will know when to stand. As the verse begins again, have them sit and pat their laps.

2. Use rhythm sticks to emphasize the march-like feeling of the song. Simple rhythm sticks can be made by using chopsticks or unsharpened pencils.

♪ *About the Song*

The power of this song was felt when a group of missionaries from the Missionary Training Center marched into the Assembly Hall on Temple Square, carrying the flags of different countries and singing this song. The impact was so great that the song was added to the 1985 Hymnbook. For the *Children's Songbook*, the alto and the accompaniment were simplified.

TELL ME, DEAR LORD

MESSAGE: I pray to the Lord for guidance to understand what he would have me do.

ENRICHMENT IDEAS:

1. To aid in review, ask questions such as:

- *What do we ask the Lord to help us understand? [Thy word]*

- *What do we ask the Lord to teach us? [To know and love thy will]*

- *When are we asking for the Lord's help? [Today]*

- *In what way does the Lord tell us his will? [Thine own way]*

2. Use hand actions for the younger children: "Tell me" (point to mouth); "way I pray" (fold arms); "what thou wouldst have" (put arms up as if to question); "say" (point to mouth); "teach me to know" (point to head); "love" (point to heart); "understand" (point to head); "word" (mouth).

3. What two words are sung on the two highest notes? *[O, help]*

4. Challenge the children to enunciate the words clearly, especially the "D's" on "Lord" and "word." Have them watch you carefully so that they will end the phrases together.

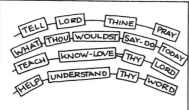

MATERIALS:

Picture: (Joseph Smith 62002)

Bible, Chalk

Word cards: Print each set on a different color paper. Set 1: THOU, THY, THINE, WOULD'ST; Set 2: TELL, WHAT, TEACH, HELP; Set 3: PRAY, TODAY, LORD, WORD; Set 4: LORD, SAY-DO, KNOW-LOVE, UNDERSTAND

ATTENTION-GETTER:

V.1: Show the picture of Joseph Smith and briefly review his story by reading James 1:5: "If any of you lack wisdom, let him ask of God, that giveth to all men liberally, and upbraideth not; and it shall be given him." Joseph was confused but wanted to do what was right. Like Joseph, we can know Heavenly Father's will for us if we will pray and ask him.

V.2: Ask a child to follow your commands: *Walk toward me, turn around, bend over, etc.*

- *Heavenly Father gives us commands (commandments). As I sing, listen to discover what we should do with Heavenly Father's commandments. [Obey them]*

LISTENING AND SINGING EXPERIENCES:

Verse One:

- *We use some respectful words that start with "th" when we pray to Heavenly Father. Listen as I sing, and discover what these words are. [Thou, thy, and thine]*

- *This song has another unusual word in it. Listen as I sing the song again, and discover the word. [Wouldst]* Explain that it means "would."

Draw four phrase markings on the chalkboard—large enough to post the word cards on the phrases. (See illustration.)

As you sing again, follow the four phrase lines carefully with your hand. Then challenge four children to post the word cards (Set 1) where they belong on the lines.

Pass out the word cards in Set 2 to four children. Challenge them to put them on the phrase lines as you sing again. Repeat this same procedure with the remaining two sets of word-cards until the phrase lines are completed as shown.

Invite the children to sing the song, referring to the phrase lines. With each repetition, invite a child to remove several of the word cards.

Verse Two:

- *What would I be guided by? [Thy loving hand]*

- *What would I hear? [Thy voice]*

- *We are guided by the Lord's hand and hear his voice as we feel the Spirit. We do not need to fear when we know the Lord is watching over us.*

- *There is a word that means that the Lord will take away our fears. Listen as I sing, and tell me the word. [Banish]*

- *There is another word that means that the Lord will give us strength when we obey his commandments. Listen as I sing, and tell me the word. [Impart]*

- *When do I want to know that Heavenly Father is near? [Each moment]*

TEACH ME TO WALK IN THE LIGHT

MESSAGE: Teach me to walk in the light so I can return to my Father in Heaven. We thank him for showing us the way. We are glad to walk in the light.

MATERIALS:

A piece of black paper and a piece of bright yellow paper.

ATTENTION-GETTER:

• *How many of you children have ever been in a cave? Some caves are very big and dark, so dark that you can't see your own hand in front of your face.*

• *A story is told of travelers who went into a cave. The lights were turned off. It was very, very dark. They were asked to point in the direction they would go to get out. When the lights were turned on, everyone was pointing in a different direction. Each day that we live here on earth, we have many choices we can make—and many directions we can go. Some choices lead us to darkness, or unhappiness.* Hold up a dark piece of paper. *And some choices lead us to light, or happiness.* Hold up a bright yellow piece of paper.

• *It is very important that we learn to make good choices and learn . . .* Sing the last phrase. Then teach that phrase to the children.

LISTENING AND SINGING EXPERIENCES:

Sing the song several times without accompaniment, encouraging the children to listen by using questions and statements similar to those listed below. As children the discover answers, invite them to sing that part of the song with you. Add one phrase at a time to the ones already learned.

Verse One:

• *Listen for how many times I sing "teach me." [Five]* Bring the children in on "to walk in the light."

• *What do I want others to teach me to know? [The things that are right]*

• *To whom do I want to learn to pray? [My Father above]* Point out the descending scale.

• *We sing "Teach me to walk in the light of his love." Whose love is this? [Heavenly Father's and Jesus']*

• *Walking in the light, or in other words, in the ways of the Savior, will bring us much happiness and will make it possible for us to return to our Father in Heaven. The scriptures tell us, "Come ye, and let us walk in the light of the Lord" (Isaiah 2:5). Invite the children to sing verse one with you.*

Verse Two: (To be sung by parents or teachers to the children.)

• *What will we learn together? [Of his commandments]*

• *Why do we want to learn his commandments? [That we may return home to his presence]*

• *We want to return home to his presence to live where? [In his sight]*

• *What will we always do? [Walk in the light]*

Verse Three: (To be sung by parents, teachers, and children together.)

• *Who are we thanking? [Father in Heaven]*

• *What are we thanking him for? [Loving guidance to show us the way]*

• *What do we praise him with? [Songs of delight]*

• *What will we "gladly, gladly" do? [Walk in the light]*

• *What does "grateful" mean? [Thankfully]*

ENRICHMENT IDEAS:

1. Put the following word cards in a bowl: LOVE, KINDNESS, HELPFUL, OBEDIENT, LYING, GRUMPY, DISOBEDIENT. Let the children pick the word cards out of the bowl and decide under which piece of paper (the dark one or the light one) that word belongs. Help them discover that the words under the light paper are the things our Father in Heaven wants us to do, and they are the things that bring us happiness.

2. Older children may enjoy singing a two-part harmony on the last line, "walk in the light," by singing a third above the melody or by singing the alto part as written.

3. Consider using pictures for review:

   V.1: (Class Prayer 62200), (Morning Prayer 62310), (Both Books of Scripture Testify of Christ 62373); V.2: (My Dad Loves Me 62552), (Passing the Sacrament 62021), (The Second Coming 62562); V.3: (Family prayer 62275), (Family Home Evening 62521), (Family With a Baby (62307)

4. For verse three: Hold up a "G" on a piece of paper. Have the children listen for four important "G" words in this verse. [Guidance, grateful, gladly, gladly]

♪ *About the Song*

While Sister Clara McMaster was on the Primary General Board, she was asked to write a song for children and parents to sing together at a special program in the Salt Lake Tabernacle. She wrote this song through much study, fasting, and prayer. Sister McMaster said, "When I was writing 'Teach Me to Walk in the Light,' I turned to the scriptures. I read a passage many, many times about walking in the light. It seems that is the way we have to walk and the way children must learn to walk—in the light of His love."

TEACHER, DO YOU LOVE ME?

MESSAGE: Teacher, I need your love and your light to show me how to be like Jesus. Child, I love you and I'll teach you. The Savior's love will lead us safely home to Heavenly Father.

ENRICHMENT IDEAS:

1. Substitute the word "father" or "mother" for "teacher," and sing this song as a special number for Father's Day or Mother's Day.

2. Use key words written on hearts for review. Challenge the children holding the key words to stand in the right order.

3. Ask the children to find the word sung on the highest note in the chorus. [Love]

♪ *About the Song*

In 1986, Primary had an opportunity to prepare a satellite fireside. It was suggested that a song could be used under the storyline and would be helpful in restating the theme of the fireside. To explain what was needed and ask who might be given this assignment, the Primary music committee met with Michael Moody, the General Music Chairman. He said he would like to think about it overnight. The next day, he returned with the first draft of this tender song.

ATTENTION-GETTER:

- *What do you remember about your life in the spirit world before you were born? [Nothing] That's right. When we are born, our infant minds remember nothing of our lives as spirits, and so we have much to learn.*

- *Heavenly Father knew that we would need helpers. Who are some of the people who help us learn?* Lead a brief discussion to include Jesus, parents, school teachers, and Primary teachers.

- *These teachers are very important because their love, example, and guidance will help us return to our Father in Heaven.*

Invite special guests—a teacher and a Primary child, or a parent and a child—to come forward and sing this number for the children.

LISTENING AND SINGING EXPERIENCES:

The song is written in two parts. The first is written for the children to sing to their teachers or parents. Then in response, the teachers or parents sing the second part to the children.

Sing the children's part several times, directing their listening by asking questions such as the following. Have them sing that part back to you. Teach the song in three sections, as listed.

Verse One:

- *What two important questions do I ask my teacher? [Do you love me? Do you care for me?]*

- *I want my teacher to love me still, even if I do what three things? [Turn away, disobey, go astray]* Tap the long-short-long rhythm ♩♪♩ on the words "even if I turn away." Have the children tap and sing that part with you.

Verse Two:

- *I ask my teacher to teach me and help me do what? [Choose the right.]*

- *What might I not always understand? [The Lord's command]*

- *I ask my teacher to please take my hand and what? [Lead me safely with his (the Lord's) light.]*

Chorus:

- *What two things do I need? [Your love, your light]*

- *What will my teacher's love and light (example) show me? [How to be like Jesus]* Tap the dotted rhythm pattern. ♩♪♪

- *The Savior's love will light the path (show the way) that will lead me where? [Safely home]* Explain that home means Heavenly Father's home.

Teacher's Part:

Consider teaching this part in the same manner to your teachers, or you may want to write the phrases or key words in Enrichment Ideas that you could remove as the song becomes familiar to them.

HOW DEAR TO GOD ARE LITTLE CHILDREN

FOR LEADERS

MATERIALS:

Picture: (Family with a Baby 62307)

When introducing this song to the leaders, read 3 Nephi 17:21-25 (the account of Jesus Christ blessing the Nephite children). Emphasize how very dear little children are to God.

Before giving copies of the music to the Primary leaders, sing (or ask someone else to sing) the song for them.

- *Listen for what three things are priceless. [Children's security, their innocence, and their purity.]*

- *Sing the second verse. Listen for the four things that Heavenly Father expects parents and leaders to do for the children. [Guide, teach, protect, and love.]*

Give copies of the song to the leaders and teachers. Teach them the beautiful three-part harmony.

ENRICHMENT IDEAS:

1. "How Dear to God Are Little Children," p. 180 (Appropriate for Leaders)

2. When introducing this song to the leaders, read 3 Nephi 17:21-25 (the account of Jesus Christ blessing the Nephite children). Emphasize how very dear little children are to God.

3. Before giving copies of the music to the Primary leaders, sing (or ask someone else to sing) the song for them. Listen for what three things are priceless. (*Chidlren's security, their innocence, and their purity*)

4. Sing the second verse. Listen for the four things that Heavenly Father expects parents and leaders to do for the children. (*Guide, teach, protect, and love*)

5. Give copies of the song to the leaders and teachers. Teach them the beautiful three-part harmony.

HOW WILL THEY KNOW?

ENRICHMENT IDEAS

♪ *About the Song*

Early plans for this book included a few songs for leaders about the importance of teaching children. As Pat Graham sat with her music committee in April Conference, 1987, they heard the Tabernacle Choir sing a SATB arrangement of "How Will They Know?" They all looked at each other as they felt the same prompting—that song should be in the *Children's Songbook*. When a song is already in print, it is sometimes difficult to obtain permission to change it, and they needed a much simpler arrangement. Pat contacted Sonos Publishing and was told that Natalie Sleeth was in poor health. It was suggested that they submit an arrangement for her approval. Laurence Lyon agreed to prepare an SSA simplification which was sent to Mrs. Sleeth in Denver. She revised it and gave permission to include it in the songbook as long as making copies would be prohibited. That notice is at the bottom of the song, and we are all blessed to have use of it.

Natalie Sleeth is well-known for "Joy in the Morning," "Baby, What You Goin' to Be?" and many other choral pieces. She wrote "How Will They Know?" when she and her husband were ill. It occurred to her that it was very important for her children and grandchildren to know what they believed in. Her husband has since passed away.

MATERIALS:

Picture: (Bedside Prayer 62217) or (Class Prayer 62200)

(Making copies of this song is prohibited. Have the leaders and teachers use songbooks—or purchase needed copies of this song at a music store.)

Display a picture of a praying child and read D&C 68:28: *"And they shall also teach their children to pray, and to walk uprightly before the Lord."* As teachers and leaders, we are responsible to help parents teach their children to pray and to walk uprightly before the Lord.

• *This song is a series of important questions about children. Carefully consider the questions as we sing.* Note the answers given in the song.

Have them sight-read the music—perhaps all singing the melody the first time through. *How will our children know the answers to these important questions? [Only if we show them and teach them so]*

Teach one verse at a time, reviewing each part until all parts are secure. Consider having a few sopranos sing the optional descant on the second verse.

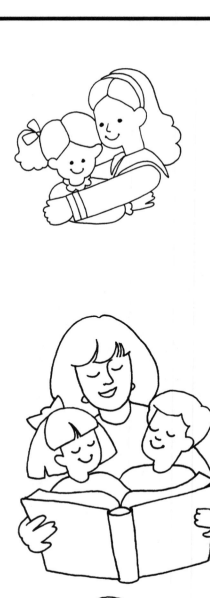

Home & Family

Rounds, descants, and two-parts songs have been included in this section to challenge and appeal to the older children in Primary. Songs about the family, grandparents, mothers, and fathers. Alternate words (i.e. mother—father) to extend the use of the song and hopefully allow relevance for children with a single parent.

FAMILIES CAN BE TOGETHER FOREVER

MESSAGE: Through the blessings of the temple, my family can be together for all eternity.

MATERIALS:

Quart jar filled with sand

Picture: (Family Fun 62384)

ATTENTION-GETTER:

Show the jar filled with sand.

- *How many grains of sand do you think are in this jar?*
- *Imagine how many grains of sand are on all the beaches in all the world. If every grain represented a year of time, eternity would still be longer. It goes forever! Listen as I sing, and tell me how long families can be together.*

LISTENING AND SINGING EXPERIENCES:

Chorus:

With each repetition, ask the children one of the following questions:

- *For how long can families be together?* [Forever]
- *Families can be together because of whose plan?* [Heavenly Father's] Heavenly Father planned for us to come to earth and live as a family.
- *Who do I always want to be with?* [My own family] Post the picture of a family.
- *Find the word in this phrase over which a fermata or hold sign has been placed.* [Fam-i-ly] This emphasizes the important word "family."
- *What has the Lord shown me?* [How I can always be with my own family.]
- *How did the composer emphasize this important message?* [She repeated it twice.]

Verse One:

- *I have a family here on earth. How do they treat me?* [They are so good to me.]
- *What do I want to share with them through all eternity?* [My life]

Verse Two:

- *When will I prepare most carefully?* [While I am in my early years]
- *Why will I prepare most carefully?* [So I can marry in God's temple for eternity.]
- *I know that if we prepare, marry in the temple, and keep all the commandments, we will have this great blessing of being together as a family through all eternity.*

ENRICHMENT IDEAS:

1. Put key words on puzzle pieces. As the children are learning the song, tape the pieces to the back of the poster (Life Eternal 67076). When the puzzle is assembled and the song is learned, reverse the puzzle to show the picture of a family in front of the temple.

2. Make a tape recording of the children singing. Play it and let the children sing with the tape.

3. Make a poster using the following pictures: (Family with Baby 62307), prepare (Class Prayer 62200), (Family Prayer 62275), temple marriage (use your local temple).

4. Lead a brief discussion on the ways we can prepare to go to the temple.

5. Be sensitive to the children who don't have a full family circle or those whose parents haven't been to the temple.

♪ *About the Song*

While Ruth Gardner was serving as music chairman on the Primary General Board, she was asked to help write a sacrament meeting presentation about temples for 1981. She likes to read and write poetry and stories, and work crossword puzzles. As she began thinking of all the things children should know about temple work, her words became a poem. Vanja Watkins, a former Primary General Board member, was asked to set the words to music. She said, "The Lord blessed me as I worked." Because it is also in the hymnbook, it was simplified by the composer and the introduction was deleted. (*Friend,* Oct. 1985, p. 14)

FAMILY PRAYER

MESSAGE: Let us kneel in prayer with our family and thank Heavenly Father for our many blessings.

ENRICHMENT IDEAS:

1. Use the chalkboard or pictures as the children suggest what we may thank Heavenly Father for. You could use pictures drawn by children. Put the pictures in random order and have the children arrange them correctly after singing the song.

2. Cut a posterboard into a large circle; write the words "Family Prayer" in the circle; and place simple pictures around the edge of the poster. Use this poster as you learn or review the song.

3. Invite the children to sing the last phrase, pitch leading to help them sing intervals in the next-to-last measure accurately.

4. Divide the children into two groups. Have the groups alternate singing every other phrase. Trade parts and repeat.

MATERIALS:

Chalk and chalkboard

A stick-figure drawing of a family kneeling in family prayer, the figures forming a circle.

Picture: (Family Prayer 62275)

ATTENTION-GETTER:

Show your drawing of the stick-figure family kneeling in prayer. What is this family doing? *[Kneeling in family prayer]*

• *As I sing the song, listen for how the family gathers for family prayer. [In a circle]* Draw a circle around the family when you sing the word "circle."

Show the picture of a family kneeling. *It doesn't matter if we are in a circle, but it is important that we gather together as a family and thank Heavenly Father for our many blessings.*

LISTENING AND SINGING EXPERIENCES:

Verse One:

• *Listen to discover what we are thanking Heavenly Father for. [The blessings we all share]* Sing that line with the children.

• *There are some magical notes in that phrase. If we hold three of the notes, we will have a beautiful chord.* Divide the children into three groups. One group holds the word "for" [Eb], another the word "the" [G], and the third group the word "bless" [Bb].

• *See if you can hear those same three notes in the first line.* Let the children sing the entire line and then repeat the chording as above. Rotate the assignments so that each group gets to hold each note: "let" [Eb], "us" [G], "gath-er" [Bb].

• *What two things do we do as we gather in a circle. [Kneel in family prayer and thank our Heavenly Father.]*

• *The melody in the song is lowest when we sing about kneeling. That helps us understand the idea of humbling ourselves before our Father in Heaven.* Have the children sing that line with you and continue to the end.

Challenge the children to help their family gather for prayer each day.

Verse Two:

• *As I sing verse two, listen for six things we thank our Heavenly Father for.* As the children discover the answers, post pictures. Use the pictures to help the children remember the correct order.

Verse Three:

• *How may we always serve him? [In thought and action too]*

• *What do so many families do at prayer time? [Humbly kneel in prayer]*

LOVE IS SPOKEN HERE

MESSAGE: Words of love are spoken in our home to each other and in prayer. I feel love in our home as I hear and watch my mother and father.

MATERIALS:

Pictures: home (Family Prayer 62275), father blesses son (Administering to the Sick 62342), father and mother teaching their family (Family Home Evening 62521), (Jesus the Christ 62572)

ATTENTION-GETTER:

- *There is a happy place where we can eat, sleep, and have family prayer and family home evening. What is this place called? [Home]* Post a picture of a home.

LISTENING AND SINGING EXPERIENCES:

Each time you sing, ask one of the following questions and have the children listen for the answer; then have the children sing that phrase several times.

Verse One:

- *As I sing this song, I would like you to discover why I am thankful. [Because love is spoken here]*
- *Listen for something that I see that tells me there is love in our home. [My mother kneeling with our family each day]* Post the picture Family Prayer.
- *Tell me something I hear in my home. [The words she whispers as she bows her head to pray]* Point out that the melody of the first two lines is almost the same. The last note is different.
- *How does her plea make me feel? What does it do? [It quiets all my fears.]* A "plea" is a prayer. It is sung on the high note of the verse which helps us feel how earnestly our mother prays for us.

Verse Two:

Help the children be aware of the melody change and how it seems to indicate strength and power.

- *What is my home blessed with? [Priesthood power]* Post the picture Administering to the Sick.
- *Priesthood power is the authority and power to act in the name of God.*
- *Who is leading the way? [Father and mother]*
- *What are they teaching me? [How to trust and obey]* Post the picture Family Home Evening. Be sure to accurately sing the C# in the phrase "Teaching me how to trust and obey."

Help the children notice that the rhythm pattern on "Father and mother leading the way" and on "teaching me how to trust and obey" is the same by asking them to tap the rhythm as they sing.

- *What are two words that mean "very easy to understand"? [Crystal clear]*
- *What can we feel when love is spoken in our homes? [The Savior near]* Post the picture of the Savior. This phrase is sung as a second ending in a two-part harmony, helping to strengthen the message.

Conclude by expressing gratitude for your home. Have the children sing the song gently, softly, and unhurried.

ENRICHMENT IDEAS:

1. When the children have learned the song well, divide them into two groups and have them sing the two verses as a duet. Have Group 1 sing the first verse; then have Group 2 sing the second verse while Group 1 hums the melody. Then have both groups sing the second ending in harmony.

2. Invite two children or teachers to sing the verses and then to lead the others in singing the two verses together.

3. Make a poster with a picture of a home drawn on it. Make pictures to fit inside a large window of the home. As the song is sung, place appropriate picture in the window.

4. Show the pictures in a three-dimensional home as instructed in the *Sharing Time Resource Manual*, p. 103, "The Prayer House." Or draw an outline of a house on one side of a large box. Cut slits on the vertical sides of a large window. Draw pictures on a roll of paper that can be pulled through the window slits as the song is sung.

5. Challenge the children to find the rhyming words.

MESSAGE: Home is where we feel the love of Heavenly Father and family members.

ENRICHMENT IDEAS:

1. Sing related songs such as "Love Is Spoken Here" (p. 190), and "Love at Home" (*Hymns,* no. 294).

2. Prepare a home-shaped poster as illustrated to review this song.

3. Invite the children to conduct the song with you leading beats per measure.

4. Be very sensitive to the family situations of each child as you teach this song.

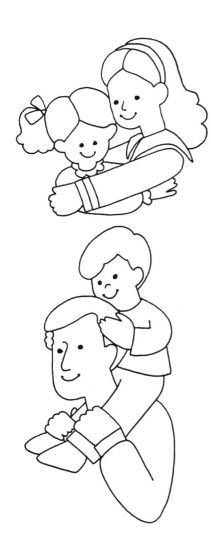

MATERIALS:

Pictures: V. 1, (Family Fun 62384), (Family Home Evening 62521); V. 2, father (Boy Being Baptized 62018), mother (Mother Praying 62309), children (Sharing the Tricycle 62317), family (Family with a Baby 62307), single mother (A Mother, a Little Girl, and a Baby 62340), single father (My Daddy Loves Me 62552), grandparents (Helping Grandmother Bake Cookies 62365)

ATTENTION-GETTER:

Invite a child to come forward. Ask the following:

· *(Child's name), can you hold your arms out in front of you?*

· *Can you raise them above your head?*

· *How about putting them behind your back?*

· *I know a song that tells us a wonderful place to put our arms. Listen as I sing and find where that is.* Sing the song with actions: Hands on heart, arms open, give child a big hug.

LISTENING AND SINGING EXPERIENCES:

Verse One:

· *Where did my arms go? [All the way around]*

· *This time as I sing, please do the actions with me.*

· *Listen for a word that rhymes with "around." [Abound]* The phrase "warmth and love abounds" means that love surrounds you.

Display the pictures Family Fun and Family Home Evening. Sing verse one again with the children.

Verse Two:

· *Who are the family members in this home? [Father, mother, children]* Post pictures.

· *What does father have? [Strength and wisdom true]*

Invite the children to sing verse two with you.

Verse Three:

· *In this verse we are singing about Heavenly Father. Where does Heavenly Father live or dwell? [In heaven above]*

· *How does our Father guide us? [In the way we live]*

· *What does he let us feel? [His love]*

Show pictures of different family settings. Not all families consist of a mother, father, and children. Some children live with their mothers, or fathers, or grandparents or others. Whatever your family situation is, your home is a place where you can feel the love of Heavenly Father and the love of family members.

SING YOUR WAY HOME

Songbook
193

MESSAGE: Singing and smiling help us to be happy.

MATERIALS:

Doctrine and Covenants

Pictures of times for singing, such as: birthdays, family nights (Family Home Evening 62521), while at work (A Family Working Together 62313) or at play (Family Fun 62384), while helping Grandma (Helping Grandmother Bake Cookies 62365), and in church.

Prepare three large, brightly colored musical notes and draw one large smile.

Melody shape:

Melody pictures:

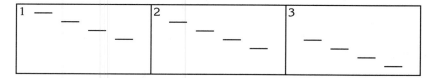

ATTENTION-GETTER:

- *When do you like to sing?* Let the children respond. Show pictures listed below. Read D&C 25:12, "For my soul delighteth in the song of the heart; yea, the song of the righteous is a prayer unto me, and it shall be answered with a blessing upon their heads.

- *Our family likes to sing when we are in the car, especially on a vacation. It is so much fun and helps the time pass quickly.*

Sing the song for the children, posting a musical note each time you sing "sing your way home." Post the smiley face for "smile every mile." Teach these phrases first. Sing the song several times, asking questions and inviting the children to sing these phrases as you indicate.

LISTENING AND SINGING EXPERIENCES:

- *If you sing your way home what will it "brighten" and "lighten?"* [Brighten your road, lighten your load]

- *Sometimes we feel discouraged or grumpy. When you sing your way home, it seems to brighten your day and help you feel happy.* The words "brighten" and "lighten" are often reversed. To help the children remember the order, point out that they are in alphabetical order: "Brighten" comes before "lighten" in the dictionary.

Show the melody shape. Point out that the pitches on "sing your way home" and "smile every mile" are the same.

Show the descending melody pictures and point out the sequence pattern in the last three short phrases. Show the cards and sing each one.

- *What are we told to do wherever we roam?* [Smile every mile] Explain that "wherever you roam" means "wherever you go."

- *Name something else that happens when you sing your way home.* [It will drive the shadows away.] This means singing will help sadness leave.

ENRICHMENT IDEAS:

1. Divide into two groups using the three descending melody pictures. Have one group hum the melody on cards 1, 2, and 3. Have the other group hum 1, 2, and 1, creating harmony.

2. For variation, teach the older children an ostinato harmony by singing the word "sing" on the first beat of each measure and sustaining it for three counts. Use the following pitches: (measure 1) G, (2) D, (3) F#, (4) D, (5) F#, (6) D, (7) G, (8) D. At measure 9 ("Smile every mile") sing in unison to the last measure, then divide again on "sing your way home," a third above the melody, as written.

3. Use finger cymbals or chimes as you sing the phrase "sing your way home."

4. Make simple line drawings on the chalkboard to represent key words in the song, or mount drawings (illustrated below) on craft sticks. Pictures could be out of sequence, and the children could place them in the correct order as they sing the song.

5. Invite one class to stand and sing just the word "sing" (then sit down) each time it comes in the song. (Three times.) Rotate the assignment to other classes.

<aside>210</aside>

MESSAGE: When our family shares happy times together, it seems that nothing could possibly go wrong.

ENRICHMENT IDEAS:

1. Challenge the children to tap the long-short-long rhythm as they sing the whole song.

2. Show a picture of a fermata and ask the children to listen for the word over which a fermata has been placed. *[Song]* Encourage the children to watch you so they will know how long to hold the word "song." Exaggerate the length of time. Hold up the fermata visual aid on other words in the song to encourage the children to watch you closely.

3. Have children take turns leading this song (2-beat pattern) and holding the fermata.

4. Sing other songs about the family, such as "Family Night" (p. 195) and "A Happy Family" (p. 198).

MATERIALS:

Sack with popcorn, storybook, and songbook inside

ATTENTION-GETTER:

- *What does your family like to do when you get together for a fun family night?*
- *Some of your ideas are mentioned in a song I know. I put three of these ideas in this sack. Listen as I sing, and see if you can discover what activities I have hidden in this sack. [Popcorn, a storybook, and a songbook].*

LISTENING AND SINGING EXPERIENCES:

Challenge the children's thinking with the following questions and statements.

- *When does the family get together? [After evening work is done].*
- *What do we learn as we're popping corn and having fun? [To know each other]*
- *Who tells a story? [Our father]*
- *Who leads us in a song? [Our mother]*

Sing and tap the rhythm of the third phrase, asking the children to notice the long-short-long rhythm pattern. Invite the children to sing and tap the rhythm with you.

- *What other words are sung to the same melody as the third phrase? [The first phrase except for the last note]*
- *Which of those two phrases ends with the highest pitch? [The third phrase]*

Ask the children to sing the first and third phrases as you sing the whole song. Encourage them to sit tall and listen carefully so they can sing the highest tone accurately.

- *When we're together for family night, what does it seem like? [That nothing in the world could possibly go wrong]*
- *The author of the words, Sister Mabel Jones Gabbott, said that the words for this song were written for her family after family home evening. She thinks one of the children gave her the idea that when they were all together as a family, nothing could go wrong.*

FAMILY NIGHT

MESSAGE: Family night is a special time because we hear stories, play games, and learn about the gospel with our family.

MATERIALS:

A storybook; a game; the scriptures; the Family Home Evening Resource Manual; flannel board pictures of father, mother, daughter, and son; and a treat

ATTENTION-GETTER:

Display the items on a table. *What do you think all of the things on the table are for?* *[Family night]* Hand each of the items to a different child. As you sing the song, have the children stand in the correct order. Repeat until they are correct.

LISTENING AND SINGING EXPERIENCES:

- *As I sing the song, listen for two words that rhyme with the word "for."* [Store and more]
- *One of those words is sung twice. Which is it?* [More] *Let's sing the first two lines.*

Sing the first line of the song again explaining to the children that the melody in this line is repeated in another place in this song. Sing the entire song, asking the children to raise their hands when they hear the same melody as the first line. *[Third line]*

Pitch lead and sing "Stories and games for everyone," helping the children notice the descending melody line. Invite the children to lead and sing that part with you.

- *The next part of that line has the same pattern, but it begins a little lower.* Invite the children to lead and sing that part with you.

Help the children notice that the direction of the last phrase also moves down the scale. With the children, pitch lead and sing "Together on family night."

Sing the entire song with accompaniment.

ENRICHMENT IDEAS:

1. Sing the first measure on "loo" and challenge the children to find all the words we sing on that melody. *[The first measure of every line]*

2. Divide the children into four groups. Have each group sing and hold one of the first four notes of the first measure to form a chord. [G E G C (omit the B)] The children could do this on "loo" or by using the words "This is the night" or "Stories and games." You could also do this on the words "always a treat" or "every family" [night].

3. Have the children look for the words that rhyme with fun. *[every-one, son]*

4. Have the children share their favorite memories of family night.

5. Challenge the children to organize and carry out a family night for their families, including a treat.

MESSAGE: Saturday is a special day for us to make preparations for Sunday.

ENRICHMENT IDEAS:

1. Younger children may enjoy pantomiming the actions of this song.

2. As the song is sung, unroll a long piece of newsprint or butcher paper with pictures of the actions. Pictures could be drawn by the children or cut from magazines or from coloring books.

3. Possible key words: CLEAN, SHOP, CLOTHES, SHOES, NAILS, HAIR.

MATERIALS:

Print or glue large cut-out letters from the word S-A-T-U-R-D-A-Y on the front of eight lunch sacks. Inside each bag, place an actual object depicting an activity mentioned in the song, such as a duster, a cereal box, the word MONDAY, a clothes brush, shoe polish, the words "get-the-work-done-day," a nail file, and shampoo.

ATTENTION-GETTER:

• *Heavenly Father gave us Sunday as a day of reverence and worship. He gave us another day to prepare for Sunday.* Give the sacks to eight children. As you sing the song, have them pull the objects from the sacks. Then have the eight children stand in the correct order with their props.

• *What day in the week was made for us to get ready for Sunday? [Saturday]*

LISTENING AND SINGING EXPERIENCES:

Sing the song several times, asking one of these questions with each repetition:

• *There are three days of the week mentioned in this song. What are they? [Saturday, Sunday, Monday]*

• *In this song, we call Saturday by a different name. What is it? [Get-the-work-done day]*

Sing the song for the children and leave out the last word of each phrase. Let the children sing the missing word.

Using the props will help the children remember the sequence of the words. Practice the large interval jumps.

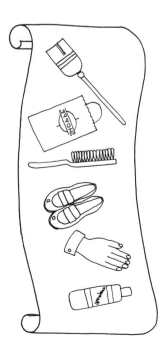
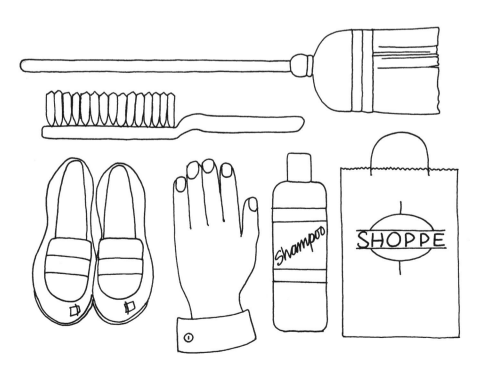

A HAPPY HELPER

MESSAGE: I feel happy when I help others.

ATTENTION-GETTER:

Ask the children to guess what you are pantomiming as you sing the song and pantomime sweeping the floor or washing dishes.

LISTENING AND SINGING EXPERIENCES:

Verse One:

Ask the children to pantomime the actions with you as you sing the song again. Let the children take turns acting out ways they help as you repeat the song.

- *When I help someone, there is someone else I am helping as well. Who is it? [Me] When we help others, we are helping ourselves by learning how to do things well and by feeling good inside.*

Verse Two:

- *I feel happy when I work. Sometimes I hum, and sometimes I sing . . .* (Go right into the "tra-la-las" of the second verse and sing to the end.)

Invite the children to sing the "tra-la-las" with you as you sing the verse again.

- *Listen and tell me how many times I sing the word "helping." [Two]*

- *Listen again and tell me why I am happy when I am helping others. [For then I'm helping me]*

Sing the entire song with the accompaniment.

ENRICHMENT IDEAS:

1. Make a small sign that reads "A Happy Helper" to hang around a child's neck. Ask a child to come forward and wear the sign. Have him choose a "helper" activity that he can lead the children in pantomiming as they sing the "tra-la-las." Repeat with other helpers.

2. For variety, change the "tra-la-las" to "do-do-dos" or humming. Suggest that the "tra-la-las" is a thinking time when you think of what you can do to help someone.

3. Write helping words (dusting, washing windows, etc.) on slips of paper and put them in a bag. Ask a child or a team to select a slip of paper and act out the action while the other children sing the song. At the end of the song, guess the answer and select a new child or team.

4. Lead a brief discussion of various ways that the children can help at home, school, play, and church. Pictures may be helpful: (Helping Grandmother Bake Cookies 62365), (Sharing the Tricycle 62317), (Waiting Our Turn 62316), (A Family Working Together 62313).

MESSAGE: My parents and Heavenly Father know what is best, so I will obey them quickly.

ENRICHMENT IDEAS:

1. Have the children sing this song as a round, with the second group starting after the first line.

2. Teach all the children to sing the ostinato. Invite a few of them to sing it while the other children sing the song. (The ostinato is not appropriate for verse three.)

3. The shape of the melody can be followed with body actions, i.e., stooping, standing on tip toes, etc.

4. Prepare four melody pictures as shown. "Loo" the melody as you point to the shape of the first card. As you sing again, challenge the children to put the remaining cards in the correct order.

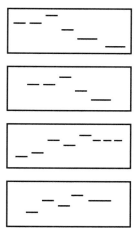

5. Have a child read Colossians 3:20 "Children, obey your parents in all things: for this is well pleasing unto the Lord." *Who are we asked to obey in this scripture?* [Parents] Then invite another child to read John 14:15, *"If ye love me, keep my commandments."* Who are we asked to obey in this scripture? [God]

6. Create a poster as illustrated.

♪ *About the Song*

Because the older children may lose interest in songs directed toward younger children, an ostinato was added to this song to challenge them. The words of the second phrase were revised to be the same in all verses, which makes the song easier to teach and also allows parents to be human (originally, "For mother knows just what is best," etc.).

MATERIALS:

Bible

Word cards: WHAT? HOW? WHY? WHEN?

ATTENTION-GETTER:

Prearrange with a child to do exactly as you direct quickly and happily.

• *John, will you please bring me the hymnbook that is on top of the piano? Thank you.*

• *I liked the way John obeyed me so quickly and happily. I liked the smile on his face.*

• *The Lord has said: "Children, obey your parents in all things: for this is well pleasing unto the Lord" (Col. 3:20).*

LISTENING AND SINGING EXPERIENCES:

• *I know a song about being obedient. Post: WHAT? HOW? WHY? WHEN? I have posted some mystery words. As I sing this song, see if you can discover the answers to these questions.* After each answer is given, sing that phrase for the children and then have them join you in singing it again.

Verse One:

• *WHAT should I do when mother calls me?* [Obey]

• *HOW should I obey?* [Quickly]

• *WHY should I obey Mother?* [I want to do just what is best]

• *WHEN do I want to do just what is best?* [Each and every day]

Verse Two:

• *The second verse is the same as the first, except we are obeying someone else. Who is it?* [Father]

Verse Three:

• *WHO is another person we should obey?* [Heavenly Father]

• *WHAT two things does Heavenly Father do?* [Loves me and blesses me each day]

A HAPPY FAMILY

MESSAGE: We are a happy family because we love each other.

MATERIALS:

Simple costuming: mother—apron or big necklace, father—necktie, sister—hair ribbon, brother—baseball cap

ATTENTION-GETTER:

Dress up four children to look like the four family members in the song, without saying who they represent. Ask the children to listen as you sing to find out who these children represent.

LISTENING AND SINGING EXPERIENCES:

Invite the children to listen as you sing again to make certain the children are lined up according to the order they are mentioned in the song.

As you sing the whole song, have the children sing "mother," "daddy," "sister," and "brother," pointing out that the name of each family member is sung on the same tone.

Ask the children to sing the song with you, listening to hear what words are sung on the highest notes. *[He loves.]* Pitch leading will help them discover the answer.

- *Love is an important word in the song. Because we love each other, what kind of family can we be? [A happy family]*

ENRICHMENT IDEAS:

1. Prepare the visual aids illustrated below. Have children place their faces in the cut-out faces.

2. Prepare simple faces on paper plates with craft sticks attached for handles.

3. Put a puzzle together with a family member on each piece.

4. Invite a family in the ward to be your visual aid.

WHEN WE'RE HELPING

MESSAGE: Helping mother makes us happy because we love her so much.

ENRICHMENT IDEAS:

1. Let the children dramatize how to help mother as they sing the "tra-la-la" of verse two.

2. Help the children enjoy the rhythm of the German folk song by clapping one-two-three, one-two-three, accenting the first beat of each measure.

3. For additional verses, change the word "mother" to "father," "grandma," "grandpa," "sister," or "brother." Ask the children to dramatize how they might help these people as they sing "tra-la-la-la."

4. For review, use pictures:

   (A Family Working Together 62313), helping mother (62340), helping father (62552), helping grandma (62365)

♪ *About the Song*

Wallace F. Bennett is a bass soloist, and his wife, Frances, plays the piano. In the 1940s, Brother Bennett served on the music committee of the Primary and the Sunday School General Boards. For a children's program, he wrote the words "When We're Helping" to a familiar tune. For many years he served as ward choir director and as a United States senator from Utah.

MATERIALS:

In a sack, put pictures or items relating to what the children might do to help their mothers: doing dishes (spoon), picking up toys (toy), etc.

ATTENTION-GETTER:

- *What are some ways you help your parents?* Show items in the sack as children give suggestions.

LISTENING AND SINGING EXPERIENCES:

- *Why do we like to help mother? [For we all love her so]* Sing the song to the children.
- *What do we do when we help mother? [We sing as we go.]* Repeat the song.
- *This rhythm pattern* ♩♩♩ *occurs several times in the song. Listen as I sing and tell me how many times you hear it. [Four times]*
- *What words occur on that rhythm pattern? [When we're help(ing); And we sing; And we like; For we all]*

Invite the children to sing the entire song.

I HAVE A FAMILY TREE

MESSAGE: I have a family tree with grandmas, grandpas, uncles, aunts, and cousins. When it's reunion time, we have a happy day together.

ATTENTION-GETTER:

- *I have a very wonderful tree. It has branches by the dozens. But it doesn't grow outside and it isn't green. You all have one, too! Listen as I sing, and tell me what this wonderful tree is.*

Sing the song several times to the children, using actions and asking one of the following questions with each repetition.

LISTENING AND SINGING EXPERIENCES:

- *What kind of tree do we all have?* [A family tree]
- *Who are some of the people in my family tree?* [Grandpas, grandmas, uncles, aunts, and cousins]
- *What is the name of the time when we all get together?* [Reunion time] Reunion time is fun, no matter what the weather is like.

Invite the children to stand up and sing.

ENRICHMENT IDEAS:

1. Bring a pedigree chart and briefly explain how we list our relatives' names. Turn it vertically to show how it does look like a tree with many branches. These ancestors are part of our family tree.

2. Draw a poster-size family tree with five main branches. As the song is sung, place leaves on the tree with pictures of relatives mentioned on each individual leaf. You might add a clock, a rain-filled cloud, a sun, and a picture of a family having a good time together.

3. Sing related songs such as "Genealogy— I Am Doing It" (p. 94) or "Families Can Be Together Forever" (p. 188).

4. See *Friend*, June 1983, p. 28, for an activity on family trees.

GRANDMOTHER

MESSAGE: I love my grandmother. She does so many nice things for me. I wish every child in the whole world had a grandmother just like mine.

ENRICHMENT IDEAS:

1. Ask the children: How many of you have living grandparents? How many live far away? How many have grandparents who live in the same city? We are very blessed to have grandparents. We can learn many things from them as we try to follow their example.

2. Substitute other family members in place of grandmother: grandfather, kind mother, great father, nice sister, fun brother.

3. To review the verses of this song, prepare a poster using pictures of grandmothers doing things with their grandchildren. V.1: kiss, hug, cheerful act of kindness (taking flowers to grandma). V.2: reading to grandchild, singing together, whispering "I love you;" V.3: cheerful act of kindness (carrying groceries), doing dishes together, whispering "I love you."

♪ *About the Song*

Nonie Sorensen, who has eleven children of her own and many wonderful grandchildren, was asked to write this grandmother song. A rocking chair rhythm was suggested. You can feel the rocking chair finally stop at the end of the song.

Sister Sorensen likes to write musical theater based on true stories. For the past six years, she and her husband have spent the summer on a mission to Nauvoo where she prepares short musicals that are given daily in the visitor's center.

MATERIALS:

Picture: (Helping Grandmother Bake Cookies 62365)

ATTENTION-GETTER:

- *I'm thinking of a very special person who does many nice things for me. As I sing about some of these nice things, see if you can guess who that special person is. Hint: It's someone who probably doesn't live with you.* Sing the entire song, but hum the word "Grandmother."
- *Who is this special person? [Grandmother]* Display the picture of a grandmother.

LISTENING AND SINGING EXPERIENCES:

Verse One:

- *Listen as I sing again, and tell me what I wish. [I wish every child in the whole wide world had a grandmother just like you.]* Sing and tap that phrase with the children. Practice the large skip going down on the word "grandmother." Be sure to hold the word "just" long enough.
- *What does Grandmother do when she sees you? [Smiles]*
- *What one-syllable word gets two notes? [See] This phrase steps right up the scale. What word goes down instead of up? [Too]*
- *What two things does your grandmother give you to show her love for you? [A kiss and a hug]*
- *Listen to this part again and tell me if the phrase "You give me a kiss" sounds exactly like "you give me a hug." [Yes]*

Verse Two:

- *How does Grandmother tell you she loves you? [She whispers that she loves me, too.] What one-syllable word is sung on two tones? [Love]*
- *What other two things does she do to show her love? [She reads me a book and sings me a song.]*

Verse Three:

- *What will I whisper back to grandmother? [I love you, too.]*
- *I'll try to be good, and what will I do? [I'll do as I should.]*

WHEN GRANDPA COMES

Songbook
201

MESSAGE: It's always fun when Grandpa and Grandma come to visit.

MATERIALS:

Picture: a grandpa

ATTENTION-GETTER:

Sing the song with accompaniment, omitting the word "grandpa," and see if the children can guess the missing word. Then sing, "It's always fun for everyone when grandpa comes." Teach that phrase to the children with pitch leading, while displaying a picture of a grandpa.

Ask the children to sing that phrase with you on each repetition of the song.

LISTENING AND SINGING EXPERIENCES:

Sing the song several times, encouraging the children to listen by using questions and statements similar to those listed below. As children discover answers, invite them to sing that part of the song with you. Add one phrase at a time to the ones already learned.

- *What does Grandpa say? [The kindest things]*
- *How does he say the kind words? [In the kindest way]*
- *Listen for a word that is a happy cheer. [Hooray!]*
- *Find two words that describe his smile. [Wrinkly, twinkly]*
- *When is grandpa happy? [All the day]*

Invite the children to tap the lively rhythm as they sing the entire song.

ENRICHMENT IDEAS:

1. Sing, "Its always fun when grandpa comes," and ask the children to listen for other words on that same melody. *["He has a wrinkly, twinkly smile."]*

2. Let the children share special memories or one nice thing about their grandpa or grandma.

3. To interest older children, obtain pictures of the children's grandparents from their families. Have the children match the grandparents to the grandchild.

4. Sing the song, posting key words in order: FUN, HOORAY, KINDEST THINGS, KINDEST WAY, SMILE, HAPPY. Remove key words as the children learn the song.

5. See if the children can find two words that rhyme with hooray! *[Way, day]*

6. Have the children clap all the repeated notes.

♪ *About the Song*

The Mormon Youth Chorus recorded this song for an album with the word change "hooray!" rather than "we're gay," which has taken on negative connotations since the song was written in 1949. The same change was made in the 1989 songbook.

I OFTEN GO WALKING

MESSAGE: The blossoms of springtime remind me of my mother, because she has taught me to love the beauties of nature.

ENRICHMENT IDEAS:

1. Display a beautiful bouquet of wild or garden flowers and tell the children these flowers remind you of your mother. Or show the picture (Children Looking at Spring Flowers 62270).

2. Review the song by singing the first half of each phrase and inviting the children to sing the second half.

3. Present the beautiful melody or harmony of this song with a violin and piano accompaniment.

4. Challenge the children to pitch lead with their bodies, following the rise and fall of the melody in the last two lines.

5. Prepare simple pictures to represent each phrase. Mount them on craft sticks for the children to hold.

♪ *About the Song*

Phyllis Luch, the major artist for the *Children's Songbook*, wrote the words for this song.

MATERIALS:

Two baskets

Blossoms of blue made from colored paper or posterboard

ATTENTION-GETTER:

Tape blue flowers around the room before singing time. Give two children the baskets and invite them to walk and gather the blossoms as you sing the first verse. Ask the children to listen to discover who the blossoms remind you of. *[Mother]*

LISTENING AND SINGING EXPERIENCES:

Sing the song several times and direct the children's listening by asking one of the following questions with each repetition:

Verse One:

- *Where do I often go walking? [In meadows of clover]*

Notice the octave skips that occur on "I often" and "in meadows" in the first two phrases. Encourage the children to sing the intervals accurately by conducting pitch levels.

- *What do I gather when I go walking? [Armfuls of blossoms of blue]*
- *Where do I gather the blossoms? [The whole meadow over]*

Challenge the children to find two sets of rhyming words. *[Clover—over, blue—you]*

Add the accompaniment and invite the children to sing verse one.

Verse Two:

- *What do I give my mother with each flower? [My love]*
- *How long does my love give forth sweet fragrance? [A whole lifetime through]*
- *What three things have I learned to love? [Blossoms and meadows and walking]*
- *From whom do I learn to love them? [Dear mother, from you]*

MY MOTHER DEAR

MESSAGE: My mother is like the sunshine, the springtime flowers, and the happy songs of bluebirds.

MATERIALS:

Pictures: mother, sunshine, flowers, and birds

ATTENTION-GETTER:

- *What comes to your mind when you think of a beautiful spring morning? [Birds singing, flowers, and sunshine] Do these things make you feel happy?*
- *I will sing a song about someone who makes us feel happy and full of love. As I sing this song, listen to see who that person is?* Sing the song, but leave out the words "mother dear" and hum those notes.

LISTENING AND SINGING EXPERIENCES:

- *About whom was I singing? [My mother]* Post a picture of a mother. Sing the last line again; then invite the children to sing that line with you as you pitch lead.
- *As I sing the song, listen to discover three springtime objects that remind us of our mothers. [Sunshine, flowers, birds]* Post pictures of each item as answers are given.
- *What is it about our mothers that is like the sunshine in the morning? [She awakens day from night.]*
- *How are our mothers like flowers in the springtime? [They are so colorful and bright.]*
- *How are our mothers and the happy songs of bluebirds alike? [They fill the air with cheer.]* Point out how the melody of this phrase is exactly like the melody of the "sunshine" phrase.

Invite the children to sing the song as the accompaniment is added.

ENRICHMENT IDEAS:

1. Invite the children to sing the first half of each phrase, and you complete each phrase. All join together for the last line. Trade parts.

2. Enlarge the pictures below and mount them on craft sticks.

3. Teach deaf signing after the song is well learned.

4. The first three phrases are similar, with a descending melody line. Invite the children to find the words on the two large interval jumps in the fourth phrase. [*Lovely and mother*]

♪ *About the Song*

This sweet message was often overlooked as a Mother's Day song because of the first line title, so the last two measures became the new title.

MOTHER, TELL ME THE STORY

MESSAGE: Mother, tell me the story that I love to hear of heaven and why I came here. Tell how you love me and then I'll go to sleep. Child, I am here. Go to sleep, and I'll watch over you and protect you through the night.

ENRICHMENT IDEAS:

1. Invite the teachers, a mother, or a father to sing the second part with the children.

2. Use the alternate word "Daddy" in place of "Mother."

3. For younger children, prepare a book cover out of posterboard with a picture of Jesus on the front and pictures with key words in the inside. (Family with a Baby 62307), mother (A Mother, a Little Girl, and a New Baby 62340), (Christ and the Children 62467), (Jesus Healing the Nephites 62541)

MATERIALS:

A scripture storybook

ATTENTION-GETTER:

Hold up the scripture storybook.

- *When I was a little child, I loved to have my mother sit very close to me and read me a story. Usually story time was just before she tucked me in bed for the night. It made me feel so safe and warm inside.*

- *Listen as I sing, and notice what children love to hear their mother tell them before going to sleep.* Sing the first verse for the children.

LISTENING AND SINGING EXPERIENCES:

Verse One: (Child)

- *I want my mother to tell me many things. What is the first thing that I love to hear?* [The story]

- *I want my mother to tell me of heaven and something else. What is it?* [Why I came here] Tap the rhythm of the first two lines, pointing out the similarities in the rhythm.

- *I want my mother to tell how she loves me. And how do I want her to speak? Here's a clue: it's on the highest note of the song.* [Gently]

- *After my mother tells me all these things, what will it be easy for me to do?* [Go to sleep]

Verse One: (Mother)

Teach this part to the mother(s) separately. Sing parts alone, then combined for a program number. You could have a mother and child sing this song as a duet and then repeat it with teachers and the children.

Optional Verse Two: (Child)

Post on the chalkboard the words to the second verse leaving off the key words: JESUS, NEAR, LOVES ME, FEAR, HIS SPIRIT, COMFORT, PEACE, and SLEEP. Challenge the children to fill in the blanks as you sing. Repeat as needed.

When the children have filled all the blanks with the key words, invite a child to erase a couple of phrases, leaving the key words on the board. Repeat until only the key words are left.

MOTHER DEAR

MESSAGE: I love Mother with her happy face and shining eyes. I will try to please our Father in Heaven to show I am grateful that he gave me my mother.

ATTENTION-GETTER:

Tell the children you know a song about a very special person. Challenge them to find out who that person is as you sing the words of each verse, substituting the words "loo-loo" for "Mother dear."

LISTENING AND SINGING EXPERIENCES:

Teach the children the phrase "Mother dear, I love you so," inviting them to sing those words with you at the beginning of each of the three verses.

Ask the children to listen for answers to questions like those below. Invite them to join you in singing the answer as they learn the phrases.

Verse One:

- *What two words describe Mother's face? [Happy, smiling]*
- *Mother's happy, smiling face makes home what kind of place? [Lovely]*

Verse Two:

- *What two words describe mother's eyes? [Lovely, Shining]*
- *What are mother's eyes like? [Stars that twinkle] Mother's eyes seem to sparkle when she is happy.*

Verse Three:

- *What will I try all day to do? [Please our Heavenly Father] You are pleasing Heavenly Father when you honor your parents and do nice things for them. Read Exodus 20:12, "Honour thy father and thy mother: that thy days may be long upon the land which the Lord thy God giveth thee."*
- *Why will I try to please Heavenly Father? [To show him that I'm so glad he gave me you]*

ENRICHMENT IDEAS:

1. Post pictures to visually portray the sequence of the verses: V.1: a mother smiling and a home. V.2: eyes and stars. V.3: children doing things that please Heavenly Father, such as praying (Bedside Prayer 62217), being kind (Sharing the Tricycle 62317), helping (A Mother, A Little Girl, and a New Baby 62340), learning the gospel (Family Home Evening 62521), and having family prayer (Family Prayer 62275).

2. Invite a class of children to draw pictures of their happy mothers. Display them as you sing.

3. Display photographs of several mothers and let boys and girls try to match children with mothers' pictures.

4. For variety, have the accompanist play the song an octave higher for a music-box effect.

5. To shorten the song, you could omit verse two, since the message is complete in verses one and three.

DEAREST MOTHER, I LOVE YOU

MESSAGE: My mother uses gentle words and helps me every day. I love her.

ENRICHMENT IDEAS:

1. To introduce the song, use pictures of mothers or photographs of the children's mothers. Challenge the children to decide whose mother each picture is.

2. Display illustrations the children have drawn to represent the key words of this song.

3. Tell the children that mothers love surprises. Challenge the children to learn this song as a surprise for their mothers and to sing it to them at home.

4. As an incentive for the children to sing well, place a cutout of a mother on one side of the flannel board and a cutout of a child on the other side. Bring the two figures together when all the children know all the words and sing beautifully.

MATERIALS:

Key words printed on the chalkboard: HEAR, HANDS, KIND AND TRUE, DEAREST

ATTENTION-GETTER:

• *I'm going to sing a song about a dear person I love. Listen, and tell me who it is. [Mother] Sing the song leaving out the word "Mother."*

LISTENING AND SINGING EXPERIENCES:

• *Who is this very dear person that I love? [Mother] Sing the song again.*

Tell the children our mothers love to hear us tell them we love them. Sing the song and have them join you on the last phrase, "Dearest mother, I love you." Pitch lead to help the children notice how the melody moves down on the phrase "I love you."

Ask the questions listed below, encouraging the children to listen as you sing to discover the answers. For older children print key words listed above on the chalkboard and erase one or two with every repetition. Younger children may enjoy imitating your actions as you sing:

"Gentle words": place forefinger on lips.

"Hear you say": cup hand behind ear.

"You're my mother": point away from yourself, then point to yourself.

"Dearest mother, I love you": hug yourself.

• *What do I hear? [Gentle words]*

• *What helps me each day? [Your kind hands]*

• *What two words describe mother? [Kind and true]*

225

MOTHER, I LOVE YOU

MESSAGE: Heavenly Father sent me to my mother. Because I love her, I want to make her happy.

MATERIALS:

Word cards: V.1, LOVE, individual letters spelling M-O-T-H-E-R; V.2, HELP, MINE, FIND, HAPPY, SMILING

ATTENTION-GETTER:

Pass out the letters spelling M-O-T-H-E-R to six children. Have them bring the letters to the front and try to spell the name of someone we love very much. [Mother] Tell the children you know a song about loving mother. Post the words M O T H E R and LOVE.

LISTENING AND SINGING EXPERIENCES:

Sing the song to the children several times, encouraging them to listen by using questions and statements similar to those listed below.

Verse One:

• How many times did I sing the word "love"? [Five]

• What did Father in Heaven do? [He sent me to you]

• What do I love to hear Mother sing? [That you love me too]

Sing the first two measures on "loo" as you pitch lead. Explain that this little melody is repeated.

Sing the entire first verse, asking the children to count how many times they hear the repeated melody. [Four]

Invite the children to sing the phrases that go with that melody in each of those four places. [Mother I love you, Mother I do, When I am near you, I love to hear you.]

Sing the last line, asking the children to listen for the word on the highest pitch. [Love] Encourage the children to sit tall and sing that high note on pitch.

• What two words are the most important? [Love and mother] Refer to the words posted.

Add the accompaniment and invite the children to sing the song with you.

Verse Two:

Teach this verse using key words: HELP, MIND, FIND, HAPPY, SMILING.

ENRICHMENT IDEAS:

1. Help the children discover the two places where the melody goes up the scale. Let them determine the appropriate dynamics to emphasize the importance of the words "sent" and "you" by showing them a crescendo visual aid (◄). Explain that when a composer places this mark above a phrase, he wants it to increase in sound. If we reverse this, we have a decrescendo sign (►). Point out that this means we should get softer. Then have the children experiment by singing the ascending scale with the decrescendo, then the crescendo. Help them feel the natural swell of the ascending scale.

2. Divide the children into two groups and let them alternate phrases as you indicate. All sing the last phrase together.

3. Use library pictures: (A Mother, a Little Girl, and a New Baby 62340).

4. Draw a melody picture on the chalkboard, illustrating the ascending scale on "Father in Heaven has sent . . ." and "Singing so softly that you. . . ." Challenge the children to fill in the words that we sing on this melody.

5. Have the children count the number of times they sing the word "you." [Seven]

6. Alternate the word "daddy" for "mother."

THE DEAREST NAMES

MESSAGE: The dearest names to me are Mother and Father.

ENRICHMENT IDEAS:

1. Briefly discuss how mothers are "tender, kind, and true" and how fathers are "noble, brave, and true."

2. Plan ahead and secure pictures of some of the children's parents to display. Let the children tell why they love their parents.

3. Have the children do simple actions for "listen," "whisper," and "I love you."

4. Divide the children into three groups. Have each group hold one of the three notes on the words "I love you" on the third line. Two chords can be formed—C, E, G, and C, F, A. The same could be done with the words "I know a name" in the first measure (C, F, A).

5. Teach the harmony notes on the last two measures to a group of older children.

WORDSEARCH

```
T O B R A V E P Y F T
L J H H T M C F U Y H
R I C N O B L E N B E
I T E N D E R F H A P
A C G L O R I O U S S
I L O V E Y O U T Z G
X R D E A R E R P I P
T R U E U L F K I N D
P P W H I S P E R Q Z
Z M O T H E R S A K T
F A T H E R K G I G F
```

MATERIALS:

Prepare an enlargement of the Word Search, as illustrated.

ATTENTION-GETTER:

• *Today we are going to use a Word Search to find key words that will help us learn a new song. I'll give you clues to a word by asking you a question and then singing the song to help you discover the answer. Listen carefully.*

As children discover answers, circle the word in the Word Search and invite them to sing that part of the song with you. Add one phrase at a time to the ones already learned.

ATTENTION-GETTER FOR YOUNGER CHILDREN:

Bring a child to the front and sing the first two lines to the children. When you come to the word "Mother," whisper it in his ear. Have the other children guess the word you whispered. Let the child in front tell when the correct answer is given.

LISTENING AND SINGING EXPERIENCES:

Verse One:

• *I know a very dear name. What is it? [Mother]* Have the children join you in singing the phrase "It is the name of mother."

• *There is one word describing the name of "mother" that is sung on three notes. What is that word? [Glo-ri-ous]* Pitch lead for emphasis.

• *In the song, we say: "Listen I'll tell the name to you." What word is used instead of "tell"? [Whisper]*

• What three words do we sing that describe Mother? *[Tender, kind, and true]* Sing as needed to discover the answers.

• *What special words do we say to Mother? [I love you]*

Invite the children to sing the song with you and to count how many times we sing "I love you." *[Three]*

Verse Two:

Sing this verse, humming the word "Father" all three times.

• *Who is this verse about? [Father]*

• *What are the three words that describe Father? [Noble, brave, and true]*

FATHERS

MESSAGE: My father, my bishop, and my Heavenly Father all love me. These special fathers protect us and guide us so that we can live with our Heavenly Father one day.

MATERIALS:

Word cards: FATHERS, WATCH, PROTECT, GUIDE, DIRECT

ATTENTION-GETTER:

Post the word FATHERS on the board.

- *Fathers are so special. They bless our lives by protecting us and teaching us the best way to live. We have many fathers. One is our earthly father. Who are some of our other fathers?*

Lead the discussion to include Heavenly Father, our bishop (the father of our ward), grandfathers, step-fathers, and the father of our country.

- *You see, we have many fathers. As I sing, listen to tell me which of these fathers I am singing about.* Sing the verses for the children.

LISTENING AND SINGING EXPERIENCES:

Sing the song several times. Encourage the children to listen by using questions and statements similar to those listed below. As children discover answers, invite them to sing that part of the song with you. Add one phrase at a time to the ones already learned.

- *Which fathers did I sing about? [The father of our home, the father of our ward, the Father of us all]*

Chorus:

- *What four things do our fathers do for us? [Watch us, protect us, guide us, and direct us.]* Post the answers as they are given and then sing again to see if they are in the correct order.

- *To where do they guide us and direct us? [Back to our home above]* This means that our fathers teach us how to live so that we can be together with our families and Heavenly Father forever.

Sing the chorus until the children have learned it well.

Verse One:

- *The father of our home leads our family with what? [Wisdom's light in all that's right]*
- *How does my father treat me? [My father's good to me.]*

Verse Two:

- *How does the father of our ward tend each members needs? [With loving care, with kindly deeds]*

Verse Three:

- *What will we reverently recall? [The Holy One who gave his Son]*
- *"The Holy One" is another name for Heavenly Father. He loves us so much that he gave his Son, Jesus Christ, to die for us. He is the Father of us all because he is the Father of our spirits.*

ENRICHMENT IDEAS:

1. Invite the bishop to sit at the front of the room as the children sing verse two for him.
2. Make a poster as illustrated.

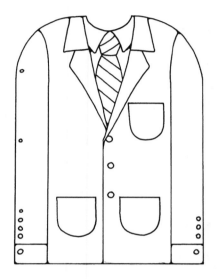

DADDY'S HOMECOMING

MESSAGE: I'm glad when Daddy comes home.

ENRICHMENT IDEAS:

1. Show a fermata visual aid and exaggerate the hold on the word "what" on the last line. Encourage the children to watch you so they will hold the word long enough.

2. Substitute the words "mother," "grandpa," and "grandma" for "daddy."

MATERIALS:

Picture: (My Daddy Loves Me 62552)

ATTENTION GETTER:

- *I'm thinking of a very special person. This person is a member of your family, works very hard, and is a man in your family. Who is it? [Daddy]*

Show a picture of a child loving her father. Be sensitive to children who do not have fathers living with them. Show how this song applies to others, such as mother, grandpa, and grandma.

- *Name some fun things you do to show that you are happy when Daddy comes home.* Have the children respond.

LISTENING AND SINGING EXPERIENCES:

Sing the song for the children, using suggested actions:

Clap hands, cup hand around mouth, hands on knees, arms around own neck, pat cheek, throw a kiss.

Young children love doing actions and will want to repeat the song several times with the actions. Do not expect all the children to sing the first day you present the song. They will begin to sing when they have heard the song several times.

MY DAD

MESSAGE: My daddy is my favorite pal. I know he loves me, and I want to be like him.

MATERIALS:

Chalk and chalkboard

ATTENTION-GETTER:

Write the letters:
D
A on the chalkboard.
D

Who can read this word? That's right. It also stands for a game I know: "Do As Dad."

Write the words:
Do
As on the chalkboard.
Dad

Prearrange for a father to come and play this game. Have him and his son or daughter come forward. Have the father do simple actions, such as praying, reading scriptures, hammering, tossing a ball, etc. Ask the child to imitate the dad in whatever he does. Thank the two for playing "Do as Dad."

LISTENING AND SINGING EXPERIENCES

- *I know a song about something else our dads teach us.* Invite the children to listen for the answer as you sing this song to them. *[Teaches honesty]*

Invite the children to sing that phrase with you. Explain what honesty means.

- *What does the song say I want? [To be like him in every way]*

- *When do I help my dad? [Every day]*

- *I like the very last phrase the best. It's about something very important that we know. What is it? [He loves me.]*

Invite the children to sing the song with you, and encourage them to watch you so they will all cut off the "d" together ending the word "dad" on the last line.

Have the pianist distinctly emphasize the starting pitch for the children so they will not have trouble finding it.

ENRICHMENT IDEAS:

1. To introduce the song another week, invite children to do a pantomime of something their father does. Have the other children guess what the action is.

2. Show a fermata and explain that when this sign is above a note, the music leader can hold out that note as long as he or she wants. Let them discover on what word the composer placed a fermata by holding the note on "Dad" for an exaggerated length of time.

3. Let the children take turns holding up the fermata to sustain singing as long as they want.

4. Have the children tap their laps on all the repeated notes. (They often come on the second and third beats of the measures.)

5. Challenge the children to sing the words or phrases that you choose to leave out.

6. Use pictures of fathers (62307, 62384, 62521, 62552, 62275, and 62379) to reinforce the message of this song.

♪ *About the Song*

The composer, Carol Gunn, said, "I wrote this song originally for my children when they were small. My little boys loved their dad and wanted to be with him every chance they got."

Heritage

There are eleven pioneer and patriotic songs in Section V, the smallest section in the book. The songs tell an important part of church history and our pioneer heritage.

PIONEER CHILDREN SANG AS THEY WALKED

MESSAGE: Pioneer children sang as they walked hundreds of miles.

MATERIALS:

Key words written on pioneer stick figures: WASHED, WORKED, PLAYED, CAMPED, READ, PRAYED

ATTENTION-GETTER:

Set the mood by having the children close their eyes. Create a mental picture of what it would be like to take a very long walk; having very tired feet; and being hot or cold, hungry, and possibly sick but having to continue. Explain that long ago there were many children who had this experience.

Sing the song for the children, having them discover who these children were and what they did as they walked. *[Pioneer children sang]* Consider having two children dressed in pioneer clothes enter and stand in front of the room to surprise the children as they open their eyes.

LISTENING AND SINGING EXPERIENCES:

Sing again having the children count the number of times you sing the word "walked." *[Thirteen]*

• *Perhaps the composer put that word in so many times because it was a very long walk.*

Teach the first line and point out that the second line is very similar only a little higher.

• *On the first and second lines we sing "walked" four times. How many times do we sing "walked" on the last line? [Five]*

• *Discover if the last line melody is the same as the first line or second line. [First]*

• *What's different about first and last lines? [The last line has one more "walked."]*

Post the key words written on stick figures in random order: WASHED, WORKED, PLAYED, CAMPED, READ, PRAYED. Invite the children to listen to the song and then put the words in order. You may need to sing the song more than once to get all words in correct order.

Point out that the things the pioneer children did on Sunday were much different than the things they did during the week.

ENRICHMENT IDEAS:

1. Smaller children may enjoy walking slowly around the room, following the leader as they sing.

2. Explain that a "pioneer" is one who prepares the way for others to follow.

3. To introduce the song another time, use pictures of pioneers walking (62493, 62528, 62608).

4. Consider singing this song with a guitar accompaniment.

5. Observe the "softer" marking when singing about Sunday, and the "slower" marking in the last measure to help the children feel how tired the pioneer children were at the end of the day.

6. Other references: Coloring Songbook, *Pioneer Children Sang as They Walked,* © 1991, Aspen Books.

♪ *About the Song*

The composer, Elizabeth Fetzer Bates (who lost her eyesight as an adult), shares these thoughts: "We are all pioneers—none of us has been in this day before. Earlier pioneers had no automobiles, railroads, airplanes, telephones, electricity, radios, or television, but they sang as they walked and walked. We can sing as we walk through today, or we can grouch every step of the way and be miserable." (*Friend*, Jul. 1982, p. 36)

PIONEER CHILDREN WERE QUICK TO OBEY

MESSAGE: Pioneer children were quick to obey and to help the best they could. We, too, can be pioneers by being willing, cheerful, and obedient.

ENRICHMENT IDEAS:

1. Have two children dress in pioneer costumes and invite them to pantomime the first two verses.

2. Draw pioneer costumes on posterboard. Cut out the face. Children "wear" the costume by holding it up to their face.

3. To teach word sequence, make a poster with a picture representing each phrase.

4. Tap the rhythm of the first measure and have the children count how many times they hear that rhythm. *[Four]*

5. As the children sing, show them how to sway back and forth and walk in place to give them the feeling of walking by the wagon.

6. Useful pictures: (Handcart Company 62528), and crossing the plains (62608, 62493, 62233).

ATTENTION-GETTER:

- *Today we will play the game "Guess Who." I will sing some clues for you. When you can guess who I am singing about, raise your hand. [Pioneer children] Sing the first two verses of the song, humming in place of the words "pioneer children" and "wagon."*

LISTENING AND SINGING EXPERIENCES:

Continue teaching by singing the song, asking questions, and then inviting the children to join you on the last line with each repetition.

Verse One:

- *What were the pioneer children quick to do? [Obey]*
- *Where were the pioneer children walking all day? [By the wagon] (Clap the rhythm, drawing attention to the dotted quarter notes*
- *Where did the pioneer children kneel to pray? [In the firelight]*

Teach the children the last line by pitch leading. Practice the three repeated notes and the descending scale at the end.

Verse Two:

- *This verse tells us four chores the children did as they traveled. Can you name them? [Carrying water, gathering wood, building a campfire, cooking the food] Sing as many times as necessary to obtain all four answers.*
- *What two things were the pioneer children doing the best they could? [Learning and helping]*

Verse Three:

- *Children today can be pioneers, too, by being what? [Willing and cheerful in all that we do]*
- *As we walk our pathway, what should be in view? [Heaven]*
- *As we walk our pathway or go through life, we should live each day so that we can be worthy of living in heaven with Heavenly Father.*
- *I hope that each of you will be like the little pioneer children by being willing, helpful, and cheerful in all you do.*

233

LITTLE PIONEER CHILDREN

MESSAGE: Pioneer children felt joy and happiness in crossing the plains.

MATERIALS:

Pioneer bonnets, scarves, and baskets

ATTENTION-GETTER:

Begin singing the song without accompaniment as you tie pioneer bonnets and scarfs on a few of the children and have others hold baskets *(for gathering berries)*. Invite these children to come to the front of the room with you to help pantomime the words as you sing the song again. Children can imitate simple pantomiming of action words.

LISTENING AND SINGING EXPERIENCES:

Sing the song several times, encouraging the children to listen by using questions and statements similar to those listed below. As the children discover answers, invite them to sing that part of the song with you.

Verse One:

- *What were the little pioneer children gathering? [Berries for food]* Check to make sure they sing gath-ring on two syllables only.
- *What were they hunting for? [Chips for wood]* These were buffalo chips, used as wood, that burned easily in fires.
- *Why were the pioneer children happy? [They gladly helped each other.]*
- *What's another word in the song that means "happy?" [Merry]*
- *Name two things they were doing on their way? [Walking along, moving along]*

Verse Two:

- *What could you hear the pioneer children doing all day? [Singing]*
- *After all their work was done, there was still time for what? [Play]*
- *What would they often do to show how merry and happy they were? [Singing and dancing]*

While the children learn the song, the pianist could play the melody line alone. Add the lilting accompaniment when they are secure with the melody.

ENRICHMENT IDEAS:

1. Listen for rhyming words, and post them as key words.

2. Have a flute or violin play the top line accompaniment.

3. Use appropriate pioneer cutouts, objects, or artifacts to add interest.

4. Other resources: D&C 136:28. Library pictures: (Handcart Company 62528), crossing the plains (62608); (Primary Visual Aid Cutouts Set 7, 33247).

5. Sing as a round. Divide into two to four groups. The first group sings four measures and then the next group begins. If space permits, children could walk around the room as they sing.

♪ About the Song

Laurence Lyon, the composer, writes: "I think the joy of 'round singing' has been nearly lost. I hope this song will encourage this kind of singing." Brother Lyon suggests that the round musically illustrates following each other as the pioneer children might have done with their parents when they crossed the plains. (*Friend*, Jul. 1982, p.36; Jul. 1984, pp 36–37)

WESTWARD HO!

MESSAGE: The pioneers faced many dangers and great hardship. But as they traveled westward to the land of promise, their hearts were aglow and eager.

ENRICHMENT IDEAS:

1. Define "weary" (tired), "laden" (burdened), "woe" (grief), "a-glow" (eager).

2. Discuss the effectiveness of using a minor key to portray the weariness and uncertainty of the pioneers. Yet show that the rhythm expresses their constant determination.

3. You may want to post the key words out of sequence and challenge the children to arrange them correctly as the song is sung.

4. Make wordstrips for the first half of each line of all three verses. Give each class one of the wordstrips and let them sing their line in turn, with everyone singing the "westward ho's" together.

5. Display a map and show the children that Utah is on the western side of the United States. You might draw the pioneer trail and move a wagon toward Salt Lake Valley as an incentive for the children to sing well.

6. Teach a small group of children the optional ostinato. Have them come to the front and sing it as the other children sing the melody.

7. Invite the girls to sing the first "westward ho" and the boys to sing the second. (You may have one side of the room sing the first and the other half the second.)

8. Plan the dynamics to build in volume to the last line, ending with a strong, repeated "westward ho."

9. Pictures: (Exodus from Nauvoo 62493); (Handcart Company 62528); crossing the plains (62608).

MATERIALS:

Word cards written on simple line drawings of covered wagons: WINDING TRAIL, DANGERS, WEARY AND LADEN, AHEAD, MOUNTAINS AND PRAIRIES, PROMISE

ATTENTION-GETTER:

Who can name the four directions on a compass or map? [North, south, east, west] The pioneers moved in one of these directions as they crossed the plains. Listen as I sing, and tell me in which direction the pioneers traveled. Sing all three verses for the children.

LISTENING AND SINGING EXPERIENCES:

- *In which direction did the pioneers travel? [Westward]*
- *The words "westward ho" were words of encouragement meaning "going west."*

Pitch lead and teach the four "westward ho" measures. Help the children to sing the octave intervals correctly.

Sing the song again, bringing the children in on all "westward ho" measures. As you sing each verse, display words you have written on the covered wagons. As the children become familiar with the words, begin removing the key words.

TO BE A PIONEER

MESSAGE: To be a pioneer, you don't have to walk miles and miles across the plains. But you do need to have courage and faith and to work with might for a cause that's right.

MATERIALS:

Picture: (Mary Fielding and Joseph F. Smith Crossing the Plains 62608 or 62575)

ATTENTION-GETTER:

Show a picture of Joseph F. Smith and relate this story.

• *One evening after a little company of pioneer wagons had made camp for the day, a group of drunken men rode into camp on horseback, cursing and swearing and threatening to kill any Mormons. Joseph F. Smith happened to meet these mobbers first; most of the other men had hidden in the brush nearby. When he saw them, his first thought was to hide with the others. But then he thought, "Why should I run from these fellows?" He marched boldly up to one of the ruffians who was cursing and declaring that it was his duty to kill every "Mormon" he met. And pointing a gun at Joseph F. Smith's head, the man demanded in a loud angry voice, "Are you a Mormon?" Without a moment of hesitation, and looking the ruffian in the eye, Joseph F. Smith boldly answered, "Yes siree; dyed in the wool; true blue, through and through."*

• *Was Joseph F. Smith a courageous man? [Yes] In fact, his answer was given with such courage and without fear that the man grasped him by the hand and said, "Well, you are the pleasantest man I ever met! Shake young fellow. I am glad to see a man that stands up for his convictions!"*

• *Joseph F. Smith showed great courage. But do you know . . . (Sing "You don't have to push a handcart. . . ." Sing entire song.)*

LISTENING AND SINGING EXPERIENCES:

Verse One:

• *The first verse tells us three things that we DON'T have to do to be a pioneer. What are they? [Push a handcart, leave your family, walk a thousand miles or more]* Repeat singing the first verse until all responses are given.

Sing again for the children so they discover the correct order; then invite them to sing verse one with you.

Verse Two:

• *The second verse tells us what we DO need to have and do to be a pioneer. What are they? [Great courage, faith, work]* Sing until all answers are given.

• *Why do we need faith? [To conquer fear]*

• *What do we work with might for? [A cause that's right]*

Sing both verses with the accompaniment.

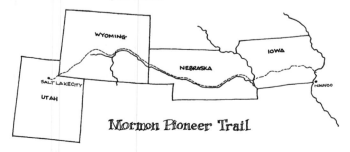

Mormon Pioneer Trail

ENRICHMENT IDEAS:

1. When both verses are well learned, teach some singers the optional descant. Then divide the group in half to sing the two parts. Trade parts.

2. Make a melody picture depicting the descending line on "marching onward, ever onward" in the descant. Have the children listen and raise their hands when they hear that melody picture. Practice just that line several times to sing the notes accurately.

3. Challenge the children to find the words in the verse where the melody goes up the scale two repeated notes at a time [Walk—a, thou—sand, miles—or] and then back down the scale [Be a pi-o-neer.]

4. Invite the children to march in place or around the room as they follow their leader and sing.

5. Relate an example of a modern-day pioneer. Challenge the children to be a pioneer by showing courage and faith, and by working with might for a cause that's right.

6. Post word cards DON'T and DO. As you sing the song, discover three things you don't have to do to be a pioneer, and three things you do have to do to be a pioneer.

DON'T	DO
1. Push a handcart	1. Have great courage
2. Leave you family	2. Have faith
3. Walk 1,000 miles	3. Work

7. Pictures: (62528, 62608, 62233, 62493, 62606, and 62554)

♪ *About the Song*

To simplify this number, the melody was written into the accompaniment. The round creates harmony in thirds.

THE OXCART

MESSAGE: The ox pulls the cart, and the wheels creak as the cart moves slowly along.

ENRICHMENT IDEAS:

1. Point out how the first line of the accompaniment sounds like strong oxen moving slowly but steadily across the plains. The second line sounds like the wooden wheels of the oxcart turning around and around.

2. Divide the singers into three groups. Have each group sing one phrase and all groups join together for the last phrase. Alternate groups.

3. Sing slowly to emphasize the slowness of the oxcart.

4. Cut out spaces between the spokes on a picture of a wheel. Place a second circle behind and fasten with a brad on the bottom circle. Write different ways to sing the song. Let a child spin the wheel to see how they will sing as you review the song.

   Let the children turn the cutout wheel as the song is sung.

6. Chant the words of the song as the accompaniment is played.

7. Emphasize the second note of each beat (the dotted eighth ♪.) when you sing "creak creak."

MATERIALS:

Cardboard cutout wheel that may be turned slowly

Picture: an oxcart

ATTENTION-GETTER:

- *Listen as I sing this pioneer song to hear what the song of the wheels is. [Creak creak . . .]* Turn the wheel very slowly as you sing the song for the children. Invite them to sing the last four "creaks" until well learned.

LISTENING AND SINGING EXPERIENCES:

Sing the song several times, encouraging the children to listen by using questions and statements similar to those listed below. As children discover answers, invite them to sing that part of the song with you. Add one phrase at a time to the ones already learned.

- *As I sing, listen to discover how many times we sing the word "creak." [Five]*
- *What kind of wheels are on the cart? [Wooden wheels]*
- *What animal pulls the cart? [Ox]*
- *This two-wheeled cart was given the name oxcart because it is pulled by an ox. An ox is a very strong, hardy animal.* Show the picture of an oxcart.

Let the children tap the rhythm with you as you sing with the accompaniment.

THE HANDCART SONG

MESSAGE: As the pioneers moved westward, they sang as they pushed and pulled their handcarts.

MATERIALS:

Picture: (Handcart Company 62528)

ATTENTION-GETTER:

- *Have you ever tried to open a heavy door or move something that is very heavy? Do you think it is more easily moved if you push it or pull it? When the handcart pioneers needed to move their heavy carts across the plains, without the help of oxen or horses, do you think they pushed or pulled their handcarts? Listen as I sing "The Handcart Song" to see what the pioneers did.* Sing the entire song to the children.

LISTENING AND SINGING EXPERIENCES:

Sing the song several times to the children, directing their listening by asking questions.

- *Did the pioneers push or pull their handcarts?* [Some pushed and some pulled.]

Show the picture of a handcart.

- *Some pioneers walked and pushed or pulled handcarts, because they had no other way of bringing their food and belongings with them.*
- *The pioneers weren't unhappy at what they had been asked to do. What did they sing on their way to the Salt Lake Valley?* [Merrily on our way we go until we reach the valley-o.]
- *When the pioneers moved to the West, with what did they meet their test?* [Courage strong]
- *As they pushed their handcarts, what did they do?* [They sang this song.]

Invite the children to tap the rhythm of the last two lines with you as you sing. Then ask them to sing that part with you.

Point out that the rhythm of the first part of the song is exactly like what they just sang. Ask them to tap the first two lines and to listen as you sing to see if the melody is also the same. [Yes]

Invite the children to sing the song with you and find two words over which a fermata has been placed. [Song, valley-o]

ENRICHMENT IDEAS:

1. Teach the optional descant to the children. When they have learned it well, divide the children into two groups. Have one group sing the descant while the other group sings the song. Trade parts.

2. Ask the younger children to stand facing a partner and hold hands. As they sing, have them push and pull their partner's arms back and forth.

3. Challenge the children to find pairs of rhyming words: *west—test, long—song, go—valley-o.*

4. Invite the children to imagine that they are sitting around the campfire after a long day of pushing and pulling their handcarts. Lead them in singing "Come, Come, Ye Saints" (Hymns, no. 30) or other favorite pioneer songs.

5. Enlarge picture as shown. Prepare as a poster or cut out each individually. Color and assemble on a flannel board.

6. Tell the children some interesting facts about the handcart pioneers:

a. It took a handcart company only eighty-five days to go from Winter Quarters to the Salt Lake Valley, while it took a covered wagon company 111 days to complete the same journey.

b. A total of 3,193 people came across the plains pushing handcarts.

c. Each cart was limited to one hundred pounds. Limits were twenty pounds of clothing and bedding per person.

♪ About the Song

The original words to the "Handcart Song" were written in the missionary journal of John Daniel Thompson McAllister. He said he composed the song to motivate the Saints of Ireland to emigrate to Utah. He later served as president of the Manti Temple. Lucile Reading, former editor of the *Friend* magazine, wrote the present verse for the children of today. The words of the chorus are the original.

COVERED WAGONS

MESSAGE: Day after day, the wagons roll along taking us safely to our new home. At night we sit around the campfire and sing songs that remind us of home.

ENRICHMENT IDEAS:

1. Print key words to the verses or simple drawings of wagon wheels. Teach a verse at a time by passing out the wheels for that verse to the children. Challenge them to stand in the correct order as you sing and to join you on the refrain. Sing again to check the order. Have the children sing with you on each verse several times before going on to the next one.

2. You may wish to vary the verses by asking the girls to sing the first verse, boys the second verse, and the entire group the third verse and chorus.

3. Cut a large wheel out of cardboard, or use a real one if available. Invite several children to come forward and roll the wheel from child to child.

4. Enlarge the pictures below and mount on poster board as shown. Connect the covered wagon with fishline so that it will "roll along" from one side of the poster to the other.

5. Young children will enjoy rolling their arms on the refrain.

6. See D&C 136:1-11.

7. Pictures: pioneer (33247, 62233, 62493, 62608); Primary Visual Aids Cutouts, Set 7.

ATTENTION-GETTER:

- *Have you ever thought about what a wonderful invention the wheel was? The wheel made it possible for people to move from place to place, because their vehicles could roll along. What kinds of vehicles can you think of that have wheels?* Let children respond. *Think back to the pioneer days to what people used as their means to travel. [Covered wagons]*

Invite the children to listen as you sing to find out where the pioneers wanted their covered wagons to take them.

LISTENING AND SINGING EXPERIENCES:

- *Where did the pioneers want their covered wagons to take them? [Safely to their new home]*

Sing the refrain again challenging the children to find two one-syllable words that are sung on two notes. *[Take, our]*

Invite the children to sing the refrain with you, listening to the piano to envision the wagon wheels rolling along.

(One of the following questions could be asked for each verse.)

- *Day after day, the wagons are rolling. Which direction must they roam? [Westward]*

- *As we sit night after night by the campfire, what do we sing? [The songs that remind us of home]*

- *When we someday reach the land of our dreaming, where will we settle and build? [On some land of our own]*

WHENEVER I THINK ABOUT PIONEERS

MESSAGE: I would like to have been a pioneer child and to have had all the exciting adventures they had.

MATERIALS:

A one-minute timer

ATTENTION-GETTER:

- *When I think about pioneers, I think of covered wagons. How many other "pioneer things" can you name in just one minute? Use the timer and let the children respond.*

LISTENING AND SINGING EXPERIENCES:

Sing the song each time you ask the children to answer the statements or questions. After their responses, invite them to sing that phrase with you. Add each phrase to those already learned.

Verse One:

- *Listen as I sing, and tell me what I would like to have been. [A child then]*
- *Listen to that phrase again, and tell me which word gets two notes. [Child]* Invite the children to sing the last phrase with you.
- *What word comes on the highest note in the song? [Like]*
- *After the high note on the word "like," the melody goes down the scale to an important word, "remember." Then the melody jumps back up to another important word. What is that word? [Children]* When the answer has been discovered, invite the children to sing that phrase until the end of verse one.
- *Who came besides the children? [Brave women and men]*

After the children have discovered the answer, invite them to feel the delightful bounce of the rhythm of that phrase by tapping it with you as you sing it again.

Invite the children to sing the entire verse with you. Teach verse two in the same manner at another time.

Verse Two:

- *When did the pioneers sleep? [When each day's measured journey was done]*

Discuss how they measured their journey—see Valiant B Manual, Lesson 21 and picture #18, The "Roadmaster."

- *Where did they sleep? [Under bright starry skies]*
- *What word rhymes with "done?" [Fun]*

Invite the children to tap the rhythm to verse two, noticing that the last half of the verse uses the same short-short-long pattern ♪♪♩ over and over. They may enjoy trying to discover how many times that pattern occurs. *[Seven times in the last half of the verse]*

Verses Three and Four:

Notice that the words are nearly the same on verses three and four because they may be sung together as a duet.

- *With whom would I like to have sung? [The pioneers]*
- *How did their voices ring out? [Loud and strong]*
- *What words of praise did they sing when they found their new home? [Hosanna, Hosanna]* Hosanna is a joyous expression of praise.
- *What two emotions filled their song? [Joy and thankfulness]*

ENRICHMENT IDEAS:

1. This song can be a two-part duet. Each part must be well-learned before combining. When the duet is performed, the pianist plays the verse three accompaniment. To help the children become more secure singing the duet, try recording the children singing verse one, and then play the tape as the children sing verse two. Repeat with verses three and four.

2. The melody line of the first verse rises and falls, much like the mountains and valleys the pioneers crossed. Ask the children to identify words that occur at the tops of the melody mountains, at the bottoms, along the flat plains, etc.

3. Singing was very important to the pioneers. Each night they gathered around the campfire and sang songs to help keep their spirits high. Have the children imagine that they are pioneer children singing to raise their spirits.

4. Challenge the children to sing the word "child" in one syllable, even though we sing it on two notes (verse one, line three). (Not chi-uld.)

5. Post the letters P-I-O-N-E-E-R on seven individual papers and pass them to the children in random order. Tell them that you will sing clues for a mystery word. See if they can stand in the correct order before you finish singing the song. (Hum the word "pioneer.")

♪ *About the Song*

The composer, A. Laurence Lyon, said: "[Most pioneer children] had very little sense of danger or hardship, . . . To most children, the crossing of the plains was one big adventure, according to historians."

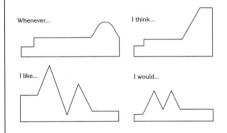

MESSAGE: I love my country where my home and loved ones are found. All that I do should help to make my country mighty, noble, and true. May it always be a land where my people are honest and free.

ENRICHMENT IDEAS:

1. As you post the flag of your country, invite the children to stand. Express the pride you feel for your country when you see the flag. Ask them to remain standing as they sing this song.

2. Invite the children to march in place as they sing. If you have a small group, consider having them march around the room behind a leader holding your flag.

♪ *About the Song*

"My Country" has a new musical setting written by Newel K. Brown with the same energy and enthusiasm he put into "I Hope They Call Me on a Mission."

We belong to a worldwide church, and children everywhere will be singing these next two patriotic songs. They are "generic," or written so that they will be appropriate regardless of the degree of political freedom of a country. Love of liberty and homeland exist everywhere, and can be shared through the universal language of music.

MATERIALS:

World globe or map

Pictures or wordstrips: desert with sand dunes; mountains with pine trees; land surrounded by ice

Word cards: *MIGHTY, NOBLE, TRUE, PEOPLE, HONEST, FREE.*

ATTENTION-GETTER:

Display a world map or globe. Ask a child to find your country on the map or globe.

- *It's a big world, isn't it. But right here* (point again to your country) *is where our homes and loved ones are found.* As you point to your country, sing the first verse with enthusiasm and pride.

LISTENING AND SINGING EXPERIENCES:

Verse One:

- *As I sing again, listen to tell me how I sing this song about my country.* [With pride]
- *Listen for a phrase that moves down the scale. Sing, "I sing it with pride."* As you pitch lead, invite the children to sing with you.
- *Countries can look very different. Some have many lakes and trees. Others have desert and sand. All are beautiful. Listen to find words that describe what some countries look like.* Post pictures or word strips as answers are given. [Desert with sand dunes, mountains with pine trees, land surrounded by ice]

Sing again, challenging the children to put the pictures or word cards in the correct sequence.

Sing, "Whether it's desert, sand-duned and wide" and ask the children to listen carefully to see if the next phrase sounds the same or different. [Same]

- *What is found here in my country?* [My home and my loved ones]
- *Who are your loved ones?* [Family, friends, neighbors, etc]

Invite the children to sing verse one.

Verse Two:

- *This is my country, and all that I do should make it what?* [Mighty, noble, and true] Post word cards: *MIGHTY, NOBLE, TRUE.*
- *I love my country. What do I hope it will always be?* [A land where my people are honest and free] Post word cards: *PEOPLE, HONEST, FREE.*
- *We don't sing "I hope it will always be." What words do we sing that mean the same.* [Long may it be]

Sing the song several times, removing word cards with each repetition.

Tell the children that wherever they live is the best place to live because it's where your home and family are found.

MY FLAG, MY FLAG

MESSAGE: I love to see our country's flag wave because it represents the brave people who fought for our liberty and for the freedoms we enjoy.

MATERIALS:

The flag of your country

ATTENTION-GETTER:

Display your country's flag. Briefly share with the children the story of how your flag came to be and what the colors or symbols represent.

- *Have you ever seen our flag waving in the breeze and felt happy and grateful to be a citizen? When has that happened to you? Perhaps while viewing the Olympics or on a national holiday. These feelings of patriotism will become stronger as you grow older. I have grown to love . . .* "My flag, my flag, my country's flag. . . ." Sing the entire song for the children.

LISTENING AND SINGING EXPERIENCES:

Sing the song several times, directing the children's listening by asking a question similar to the following with each repetition.

Invite the children to hold up a finger every time they hear you sing the word "flag." *[Seven times]*

- *I love to see my flag wave. Count the number of times I sing the word wave by raising your fingers. [Five times]*
- *What is another word for "flag?" [Banner]*
- *Our flag is the banner of whom? [The brave, the free]*
- *Our flag is also a banner symbolizing freedom. But the song doesn't say freedom. What word do we sing? [Liberty]*

Invite the children to stand in respect for their flag as they join you in singing this song.

ENRICHMENT IDEAS:

1. To set the mood, have Scouts or Cub Scouts present the flag and lead the children in the pledge of allegiance.

2. Discuss the brave ancestors who fought for the freedom and liberty that we enjoy today. Explain what freedoms we have because of them.

3. Talk about the earliest flag we know about in the scriptures. You might tell the story of Moroni's flag which was called the "Title of Liberty." (See Alma 46:12-27. See also Book of Mormon Reader, pp.76-79.) Picture: (62051).

4. Ask the children to listen for three things our flag represents: the brave, the free, liberty.

5. Define: "banner" (flag or piece of cloth with a design on it), "brave" (having courage, not being afraid), "free" (not controlled by others), "liberty" (freedom from another government's rule).

6. Prepare a copy of your flag for the children to take home and color.

7. Smaller children might enjoy marching around the room as they sing, following the leader holding the flag.

8. Use one or more flags for the children to hold as they sing the song. Have the children wave the flags as they sing.

9. Write key words or rhyming words on flags to aid in review: *wave—brave; free—liberty.*

Nature and Seasons

The songs in Nature and Seasons help us appreciate the beauty and wonder of our Heavenly Father's creations, and to recognize his hand in the world around us. Some of the timeless favorites, such as "Give, Said the Little Stream" and "Little Purple Pansies," help to bind us to our parents and grandparents. Someday our children will sing those songs to their children.

MY HEAVENLY FATHER LOVES ME

MESSAGE: I know Heavenly Father loves me, because he created this beautiful world for me. He gave me my life, my mind, and my heart. I thank him reverently for all his creations of which I'm a part.

MATERIALS:

Room freshener (lilac or rose)

Lilac branch or rose

Pictures: V.1: bird, blue sky, rain on face, wind, velvet rose, lilac tree, beautiful world;

V.2: eyes, ears, life, mind, heart

ATTENTION-GETTER:

Lightly spray the room freshener. *What does this fragrance remind you of?* [Flowers]

Show the children a lilac branch or rose. Let them touch the "velvet" petals.

• *Every time I touch a velvet rose or walk by our lilac tree, it reminds me just how much Heavenly Father loves me.*

LISTENING AND SINGING EXPERIENCES:

Verse One:

Post pictures out of order, or place them previously under the chairs of several children. Challenge the children to put the pictures in the proper sequence as you sing. Sing with the children again to check order.

Remove several pictures with each repetition.

Invite the children to sing verse one with the accompaniment.

(Teach verse two the following week.)

Verse Two:

• *Last week we sang about how much Heavenly Father loves us. He gave us many beautiful creations. You are one of his greatest creations. He has given you your eyes, your ears, your life, your minds, and your heart.* Post pictures to represent each of these as the next questions are asked.

• *Listen as I sing, and tell me what I might see with my eyes?* [The color of butterfly wings]

• *What might I hear with my ears?* [The magical sound of things]

• *What are three other things that Heavenly Father has given me?* [My life, my mind, my heart]

• *For what do I thank him reverently?* [For all his creations, of which I'm a part]

• *What do all of these things help me to know?* [That Heavenly Father loves me]

Bear your testimony of the many evidences of Heavenly Father's love and just how much he loves each one of his children.

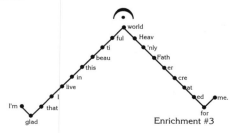

Enrichment #3

ENRICHMENT IDEAS:

1. Make a mural on a roll of butcher paper. Each class could draw a picture depicting a phrase of the song. Have the children unroll the paper as they sing the song.

2. Place cutouts of key words or pictures on head bands to be worn by children.

3. To teach the optional harmony, post a melody picture of the last four measures, as shown below. As you indicate where the melody rises and falls, have the children sing those measures with you, discovering which word is sung at the highest point on the picture.

♪ *About the Song*

The melody for "I'm glad that I live in this beautiful world. . ." appeared to be an ascending scale, with an alto part below. Originally, Clara McMaster, the composer wrote the melody as it now appears. Small cue notes help to make that more obvious. The cue notes are optional and may be sung by several high voices or simply played by the piano (see "How to Use the Songbook" p. 303). Sister McMaster is a vocalist and has performed countless times with her husband. That explains the natural harmonies that exist in her writing—the songs she has written have memorable melodies and are easy to harmonize (i.e. "Reverently, Quietly," and "Teach Me to Walk in the Light"). The beginning pitch of this song was raised an octave to help children sing in their head voice.

Clara W. McMaster, the composer, said: "I'm grateful that as a child we had an orchestra, and a chorus in our family. It was easy because we had no radios, TV, or movies. I was born on a farm, and I knew the sounds in the barnyard. When I was called to the Primary General Board, I was told that the children needed a song to teach them that their Heavenly Father loves them. I didn't really know how to do that. The Lord answered my prayers through the song of a bird. All I would have to do to write this song was to bear my testimony. This was my way of saying to the children that my Heavenly Father loves me. It wasn't my song. It was something brought into my heart many years ago. I'm grateful that the children still want to sing my song." (BYU Music Workshop, 1984)

GOD IS WATCHING OVER ALL

MESSAGE: God is watching over all of his creations. He remembers every child and will teach you what to do.

ENRICHMENT IDEAS:

1. Imitate a music box by playing the accompaniment an octave higher.

2. Divide the children into three groups. Each group sings one phrase. All join together for the last phrase.

3. Write on three slips of paper: sky with stars, world, bird. Ask three children to choose one of these papers and to draw an illustration of the word on the chalkboard.

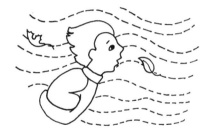

MATERIALS:

Pictures: sky, stars, a small bird, (The World 62196), (Creation—Living Creatures 62483)

ATTENTION-GETTER:

- *Can you name some of the things God has created?* Let the children respond. Post creation picture.

- *Now listen as I sing to discover four more of God's creations. [Sky, stars, worlds, sparrows]* As each response is given, hand a child a picture of that "creation."

Sing the song again and challenge the four children to stand in the correct order as their "creation" appears in the song.

LISTENING AND SINGING EXPERIENCES:

Verse One:

- *What is God watching over? [Over all]* Teach the last phrase through pitch leading.

Sing the song again, referring to the pictures. Point out how the melody pattern of the first phrase is repeated, but each repetition begins on a lower pitch. Bring the children in on the last phrase.

Add the accompaniment and invite the children to sing the first verse with you.

Verse Two:

- *Name four times when God is watching over you. [Night and day, at work or play]* This means he watches over you all the time.

- *What will he teach you? [What to do]* Heavenly Father teaches you by answering your prayers, through scriptures, through Church leaders, and through parents.

Challenge the children to find the rhyming words. *[Day • play, do • you]*

Invite the children to sing the rhyming words at the end of each phrase as you sing.

Invite the children to join you in singing verse two.

Bear testimony that God watches over every child.

I THINK THE WORLD IS GLORIOUS

MESSAGE: I sing my thanks to God for this glorious world and for parents and teachers who love me.

MATERIALS:

Six paper music notes, with one word of the song title written on each note.

Word cards: GLORIOUS, LOVELY, BIRDS, BEES, BLOSSOMS, LOVE, JOY, THANKS.

Melody picture:

I SING,			
	AND SING,		
		AND SING,	
			AND SING

ATTENTION-GETTER:

Tape the paper music notes under six different chairs. Invite the children to look for a note under their chair. Ask the six children with notes to bring them to the front and discover the title of the song by standing in the proper order. .

- *What special message is on these notes? [I Think The World is Glorious.] I would like to sing a song that will tell you how I feel about this beautiful world Heavenly Father has created.* Sing the first verse and chorus.

LISTENING AND SINGING EXPERIENCES:

Verse One:

- *What two words describe the world? [Glorious and lovely]* Display the word cards. Explain that "glorious" means "wonderful or beautiful."
- *What are three words that begin with the letter "b" that bring sweet messages to me? [Birds, bees, blossoms]* Post word cards. Explain that sweet messages are happy thoughts.

Invite the children to sing the song with you, referring to the word cards. With each repetition, remove a word card or two.

Chorus:

- *Count how many times you hear the word "sing."* Hold up your fingers as you count. *[Eight times]*

Display the "I SING" melody picture to point out the descending melody. Refer to it for both lines of the chorus.

- *What kind of a song do I sing? [A song of joy and love]* Post word cards.
- *What do I give to God above? [My thanks]* Post word cards.

Verse Two:

Teach in the same manner, posting pictures and word cards as needed.

- *Which phrase is the same as one we sang in the first verse? [I think the world is glorious and lovely as can be.]*
- *What kind of teachers do I have? [Kind and true]*
- *What does the song say about my parents? [They love me.]*

Clap the rhythm, noticing the short-long rhythm that is repeated throughout the song. ♪♩

- *The composer, Brother Alexander Schreiner said, "The world is full of many things, some good, some bad, some happy, some sad. Let us find the good things in the world to make us happy."*

ENRICHMENT IDEAS:

1. Display charts of the four musical slurs in this song, and explain that a slur is where two notes occur on one word. Practice singing the slurs.

2. Invite the children to stand up. As you sing the phrase "I sing and sing and sing and sing," place your hands high over head, on your shoulders, on your waist, and then on your toes. Point out how the melody skips down.

3. Show a picture of President Heber J. Grant. Tell the children that President Grant wanted to sing so much that he practiced and practiced and finally learned to sing all the hymns. He loved to "sing and sing and sing and sing." Sing the chorus enthusiastically.

4. As a variation on the chorus, divide the children into four groups. Have the first group sing the first "I sing" on "D" and hold, the second group sing "B" and hold, the third group sing "G" and hold, and the fourth group sing low "D." This makes a full chord.

5. Cut a large circle like a world. Around the world, place pictures of birds, bees, and blossoms, children singing, teachers, and parents.

ALL THINGS BRIGHT AND BEAUTIFUL

MESSAGE: All the beauties of the world were created by the Lord God.

ENRICHMENT IDEAS:

1. The refrain may be repeated following each of the verses. Or you could shorten the song by singing the refrain at the beginning and end only.

2. Define the words or phrases that may be unfamiliar to the children: purple-headed mountain ("a mountain seen from far away"), greenwood ("a forest green with foliage"), and rushes (willowy plants growing by water).

3. Using the chalkboard or a large piece of butcher paper, have some children draw as many beauties of the earth as they can while others sing the song. Or have them draw the pictures in the correct order on a roll of butcher paper. Have the children unroll the paper as they sing the song.

4. As you sing, post key words. Cover key words with cutouts of flowers or birds to test the children's memory, or take key words down a few at a time.

5. Change the dynamics from phrase to phrase, encouraging the children to watch you carefully. You may wish to direct with puppets or pictures of a lion (full voice) and a mouse (tiny voice).

Open Sack Puppets

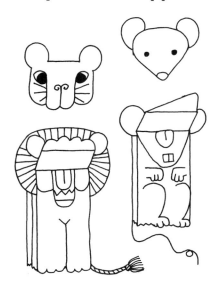

MATERIALS:

Pictures: (Children Looking at Spring Flowers 62270), (Creation—Living Creatures 62483), Isaiah, a "wise" prophet (62339), a flower, a bird

Wordstrips: bright and beautiful, great and small, the Lord God, glowing colors, tiny wings

ATTENTION-GETTER:

Post pictures around the room to represent each phrase.

• *The world is filled with "all things bright and beautiful." Listen as I sing about these bright and beautiful things. When I have finished, see if you can put the pictures in the correct order.* Sing the refrain and verse one.

LISTENING AND SINGING EXPERIENCES:

With each repetition of the song, invite the children to listen for the answer to one of these questions and then to sing that phrase with you.

Refrain:

• *What two words begin with the letter "b"? [Bright and beautiful]* Post wordstrips on the corresponding picture. Point out the descending scale of these words as you pitch lead.

• *What words describe all creatures? [Great and small]* Practice the interval on creatures (C to E) and post wordstrip.

• *Who made them all? [The Lord God]* Post wordstrip.

• *Is the melody of lines one and two the same or different? [Same]*

Verse One:

• *What did the Lord make for the little flowers that open? [Their glowing colors]* Post wordstrip by picture.

• *What did he make for each little bird that sings? [Their tiny wings]* Post wordstrip and practice the interval on "made their."

Invite the children to tap the rhythm with you as you sing, and then to join you in singing this verse.

• *The prophet Nephi said: ". . . There is a God, and he hath created all things, both the heavens and the earth, and all things that in them are. . ." (2 Nephi 2:14). We are so blessed to live in such a bright and beautiful world. Heavenly Father loves us very much!*

Verses Two, Three and Four:

Continue teaching by asking questions the children can answer by listening to the song.

BEAUTY EVERYWHERE

MESSAGE: I see the work of my Heavenly Father all around me. I am thankful for all he gives to me.

MATERIALS:

Pictures: V.1, skies, leaves on tree, flowers swaying in a breeze, happy children working and playing, God (The Resurrected Jesus Christ 62187)

Chorus: smiling face of a child

Music Sign: ⌢ fermata

ATTENTION-GETTER:

Ask six children to hold the pictures, with the wrong side to the audience. Ask the children to listen to the song as you sing and then guess what they think the pictures are. As they respond, have the child holding that picture turn it over. Sing the verse more than once if necessary.

LISTENING AND SINGING EXPERIENCES:

Verse One:

When all the pictures are displayed (out of order), ask the children to arrange them correctly as they listen to you sing again. Repeat until the pictures are in the correct order.

Invite the children to join you in singing the verse as you convey the joyful enthusiasm of these first four lines.

Tap the rhythm of the first six notes. Help the children notice that every phrase of the verse begins with that same rhythm.

Chorus:

The chorus changes meter. The lilting feeling of the verse changes to a more majestic, yet reverent, 4/4. Exaggerate these feelings to the children as you teach. Sing, asking the following questions:

• *Whose work do I see? [God's]* Explain that Jesus is the creator and God of this earth.

• *In what three things do I see the work of God? [Sky, land, river]* Invite the children to sing that line.

• *Which word is sung on the highest note? [Thanks]* Sing the line with the children, encouraging them to listen so they can sing the word "thanks" on pitch.

• *Which word is held the longest? [Thanks]* Show the fermata sign and exaggerate the hold on "thanks." *To give thanks is very important. The composer put the word "thanks" on a high note and marked it with a fermata to emphasize its importance.*

Share your love of and appreciation for the beautiful world God has given us. Add the accompaniment and sing the entire verse and chorus with the children. Teach Verse Two in a similar way.

ENRICHMENT IDEAS:

1. Have the children join you in conducting the 3/4 time. See if they can feel the change to 4/4 time.

2. To help reinforce the message, sing "My Heavenly Father Loves Me" (p. 228).

3. Have the children sing or stop singing by playing "Stop and Go." Have the children sing only the last word of each phrase as you indicate with an open hand. A closed fist indicates when you will sing.

4. Challenge the children to listen for pairs of rhyming words: *trees—breeze, play—day, see—me.* Listen again to determine which of the rhyming words is sung on the highest note. *[Breeze]*

5. Let a child raise the fermata sign two or three times as the children sing the song. Direct the children to hold the note as the sign is raised.

THE WORLD IS SO LOVELY

MESSAGE: I'm glad that I can be on earth and see all the lovely things in our world.

ENRICHMENT IDEAS:

1. Put the pictures out of order; then invite the children to put them in the proper sequence.

2. Post the two musical pictures as shown to point out where the melody climbs and falls. Ask the children to decide which chart comes first.

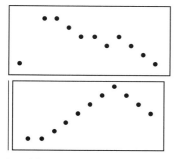

3. It is a blessing to live in this beautiful world that the Lord created for us. Challenge the children to name as many beauties of the world as they can while the accompanist plays the song through completely.

MATERIALS:

A world globe

Pictures: V.1, world, smiley face, beautiful creations; V.2, sunshine, flowers, stars, home, family

ATTENTION GETTER:

Show the children the globe. *Our world is such a beautiful place.*

• *We can go anywhere in the world and find beautiful creations. Listen as I sing, and discover another word describing the world that means beautiful. [Lovely]*

Post picture.

LISTENING AND SINGING EXPERIENCES:

Verse One:

• *I am as happy as I can be. Listen for another word for "happy." [Glad]* Post picture.

• *For what am I glad as I can be? [All that the Lord has created for me]*

Point out the ascending and descending melody pattern on the last phrase by moving your hand clockwise around the globe. Invite the children to sing verse one and to trace their imaginary globe on the last phrase.

Invite the children to sing the first verse with the accompaniment.

Verse Two:

• *What three lovely things can I see? [Sunshine, flowers, stars]* Post pictures of each.

Challenge the children to sing the second verse, listening to find the words that follow the melody as it goes up the scale and back down. *[A home where I live, and a family I love]* Post pictures of a home and family.

Express gratitude for being on the earth and seeing all the lovely things in our world.

BECAUSE GOD LOVES ME

MESSAGE: Because God loves me and wants me to be happy, he has given me this beautiful world, a family, a cheerful heart, and eyes to see.

MATERIALS:

Pictures: V.1, day, night, darkness, light, sky of blue, sunshine, V.2, family, cheerful heart, eyes, happy face

ATTENTION-GETTER:

- *Close your eyes and picture what it would be like if Heavenly Father had planned for us to have a brown sky and brown grass. Imagine that he had planned for the sun to be so far from us that we were always cold and it was never bright outside. It would be a gloomy place to live, wouldn't it?*

But because he loves us, he planned for us to live in a beautiful world.

LISTENING AND SINGING EXPERIENCES:

- *The song mentions ten different beauties of the world that God has given us. Listen to discover what these ten blessings are. [The day, the night, the darkness, the light, the sky of blue, the sun so bright, a family, a cheerful heart, eyes to see, happiness.]* Post pictures.
- *Listen again to see if we put these pictures up in the exact order that they appear in the song.*
- *Why does the song say God created all of these beauties of nature for us? [Because he loves us]*

Teach phrase by phrase, referring to the pictures. Have the children echo the phrases back to you.

- *I know Heavenly Father has given us many blessings because he loves us and wants us to live here happily.*

ENRICHMENT IDEAS:

1. Use pictures drawn by the children.
2. Briefly tell the children the story of the Creation. Then ask them to listen as they sing to see how many creations mentioned in the scriptures are also mentioned in the song.
3. Tape the pictures illustrated below under the chairs of several children. Invite the children to discover the pictures and bring them to the front of the room. As the song is sung challenge them to stand in the correct order.
4. Cutout pictures could be used and placed on craft sticks, magnetic board, or flannel board.
5. Teach the simple harmony of the second ending to the children.

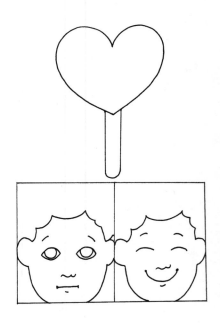

THE WORLD IS SO BIG

MESSAGE: God loves us all and has blessed us with a world filled with his creations.

ENRICHMENT IDEAS:

1. On a large poster-size circle, sketch a line drawing of the world. As the children sing the song, place simple line drawings or pictures on the world. Or draw on the chalkboard.

2. Place pictures or line drawings on individual cutouts of the world and mount them on craft sticks. Invite several children to hold the pictures in random order. As they sing, have them discover the correct order.

3. Invite several children to the front to lead the actions of the song.

4. Invite a child to come to the front and read 1 Nephi 17:36.

5. Use the illustrations below for "animals big" and "animals small." Use the pictures on p. 241 to illustrate "mountains and valleys" and on p. 249 to illustrate the "sun and stars."

LISTENING AND SINGING EXPERIENCES:

Verse One:

Teach the song through repetition, using these suggested actions:

1. Arms in a big circle

2. Hands in the shape of mountain peaks

3. Hands low to make a valley

4. Hands over head for tall trees

5. Hands shoulder-height for a big animal

6. Hand knee-height for a small animal

7. Arms in a big circle

8. Arms outstretched

• *Our world is so big and round. Listen for two other words that rhyme with "round." [Found, abound.] The word "abound" means "to have many." When we sing our blessings abound it means that we have many blessings.*

• *How many times do you hear the words and melody of the first phrase: "the world is so big and oh so round." [Two times]*

Have the children sit very tall when they sing "God's love" to make sure this octave interval is sung on pitch.

Verse Two:

Teach in the same manner, using simple actions:

1. Wiggle fingers for twinkling stars.

2. Raise hands high in circle for the sun.

• *Heavenly Father loves all of us and has blessed us with a beautiful world filled with all of his creations. The mountain, valleys, trees, animals, sun, and stars are just a few. His greatest creation was you.*

"GIVE," SAID THE LITTLE STREAM

MESSAGE: Even if we are small, there is something we can give to those around us.

MATERIALS:

Word card: GIVE

ATTENTION-GETTER:

Play the "Who Am I?" game by giving the following clues. I hurry down the hill. I'm small. But wherever I go, the fields grow greener. Who or what am I? [Little stream]

- *This little stream makes the fields grow green because it gives precious water to those fields. I know a song about this little stream and that very important word "give."* Post the word card GIVE.

LISTENING AND SINGING EXPERIENCES:

- *The word "give" is so important that it is sung many times. Listen as I sing and count the number of times I sing the word "give." [Ten times in the first verse and chorus]*

Repeat to check the answer, having the children hold up a finger every time they hear the word "give."

Chorus:

- *The chorus of this song is very joyful. It tells us that giving can make us feel like singing all the day. Listen as I sing the phrase "Singing, singing all the day," and tell me if the melody is the same or different each time I sing it. [Same]*

Have the children join you on those two phrases as you sing the chorus, and then to join you in singing the complete chorus.

Verse One:

Start at the end of the verse and work toward the beginning, using the following questions. Add each phrase to those already learned and bring the children in on the chorus each time.

- *What happens to the fields? [They grow greener.]*
- *What does the little stream know? [He's small, but the fields grow greener wherever he goes.]*
- *What did the little stream say as it hurried down the hill? [Give.]*

Verses Two and Three:

- *Where did the rain fall? [Upon the flowers]*
- *What did the rain do for the flowers? [Raised their drooping heads again]*
- *Who is our example of giving in the third verse? [Jesus]*
- *What does the song say we can all give? [Something]* **Give examples.**
- *What are we told to do? [Do as the streams and blossoms do.]*
- *The little stream gives to the fields so they can grow and live. The rain gives so the flowers and blossoms can live. We, too, should give to all around us.* **Have the children listen for this beautiful message in the third verse.**
- *Our Father in Heaven and Jesus live and love us. They give to each one of us every blessing that we have.*

ENRICHMENT IDEAS:

1. Have the older children learn the beautiful harmony.
2. Have the children pitch lead the chorus with their hands and then with their bodies as they go from a sitting to a standing position as the melody indicates.
3. Make a string poster with a flower that can grow, a stream, and raindrops. As the children learn the song, make the flower grow. (See illustration and p. 40 for instructions.)
4. Cut out five notes and five raindrops and give to the children. Each time the word "give" is sung in the song, the children holding raindrops stand up, then sit down. When they hear the word singing, the children holding the notes stand up, then sit down. Let several groups of children have a turn holding the notes and raindrops as you repeat the song.

♪ About the Song

What word finishes this sentence from the song? "I'm small, I know, but wherever I go The _____ grow greener still." If you said "grass" you are wrong! Every earlier printing of the song said "fields." Where did grass come from? Perhaps the saying "The grass is greener on the other side." This is not a word change, but obviously has been sung without looking at the words.

The 1979 Edition of the Guinness Book of World Records lists the author, Fanny Crosby (Mrs. Frances Jane Van Alstyne) as the world's most prolific hymnist. Although she had become blind as a baby, she wrote more than 8,500 hymns.

THE PROPHET SAID TO PLANT A GARDEN

MESSAGE: We will obey the prophet by planting and harvesting our garden to feed our families and share with our neighbors.

ENRICHMENT IDEAS:

1. Let the children share experiences they have had in planting and harvesting their gardens.

2. Make a string picture as shown below to help teach the words of the song. Pull each picture into view as you sing about it. (See *Friend*, March 1982, p. 45.)

♪ *About the Song*

Mary Jane Davis wrote stories and poems for children. Sometimes the poems became songs. For many years, she was bedridden, but she continued to write for children. One year, her Primary built a float for the Days of '47 Children's Parade. The leaders wanted a song for the children to sing while they walked in the parade, so Mary Jane wrote "The Prophet Said to Plant a Garden." A small tractor pulled a "garden" and all the children were dressed as vegetables.

MATERIALS:

Picture: (Spencer W. Kimball 62575)

ATTENTION-GETTER:

Show the picture of President Spencer W. Kimball. *When Spencer W. Kimball was our prophet, he felt very strongly that all members of the Church should learn to work together as families and take care of their own needs. Many times in general conference talks, he would tell us of the importance of learning to plant and harvest a garden. I'm so thankful that . . .* (Sing first verse).

LISTENING AND SINGING EXPERIENCES:

Sing the song several times, asking the following questions to encourage the children to listen and then to sing each phrase with you. As you pitch lead, point out repeated notes, descending melodies, and internal jumps.

Verse One:

- *What did the prophet say to do?* [Plant a garden.]
- *What three things has God given us?* [Rich brown soil, the rain, and sunshine too]
- *What two things will we have to do to grow a garden?* [Plant the seeds just right and tend them carefully.]
- *What will happen before we know it?* [Good things will grow to feed our family.]

Verse Two:

- *Why will we plant the seeds?* [To fill our needs]
- *Then what else will we plant?* [A few to spare]
- *How will we show we love our neighbors?* [With the harvest that we share]
- *What do we want others to do?* [Plant a garden too.]
- *What joy does a garden bring to happy girls and boys?* [Health and love]

Heavenly Father has provided us with everything we need to grow a garden. And we can be kind and show our appreciation by sharing what we grow with others. Our care of a garden will help the vegetables grow. We will grow, too, as we learn about gardening.

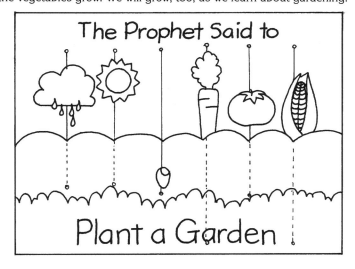

SPRINGTIME IS COMING

MESSAGE: We know springtime is coming when robins return and begin to build their nests.

MATERIALS:

Music Sign: ♩ (staccato note)

ATTENTION-GETTER:

- *Something wonderful is happening outside. Do you know what it is?* Help the children conclude that springtime is coming. *What are some of the clues that help you know that springtime is coming?* Let children respond. *As I sing this song, listen for the clue that helped me know that springtime is coming.*

LISTENING AND SINGING EXPERIENCES:

Verse One:

- *How do I know springtime is coming? [I heard a robin.]*
- *Who was the robin calling? [Her]* "Her" refers to the springtime. Invite the children to sing the last line with you.

Show the children the staccato note. Explain that when this mark is placed on a note, we sing it short and crisp. As the accompanist exaggerates those notes, challenge the children to find the words with the staccatos. *[Who was calling.]*

Verse Two:

- *Listen for another clue I have seen that tells me springtime is coming. [Robins are building a nest.]*
- *Where are they building their nest? [High up in a tree]*
- *Which phrase has the staccatos in this verse? [Are as busy]*

ENRICHMENT IDEAS:

1. Show the children a real bird's nest or one purchased at a craft store. Discuss how the birds make their nests.

2. Explain that this tune is an old Alsatian (German-French) folk tune.

3. Place cutouts of two robins and a nest on a poster-size tree as illustrated.

4. For an incentive to encourage good singing, mount the picture of a robin on poster paper. Prepare a poster-size tree with a nest high in the tree. Make the robin fly to its nest for good singing. This can be done by mounting the robin on transparent thread. See p. 40 for instructions.

5. Challenge the children to sing the entire song staccato.

BECAUSE IT'S SPRING

MESSAGE: My heart sings with gladness because of the many beauties of spring.

ENRICHMENT IDEAS:

1. Let the children find the rhyming words: clear—dear, bright—light, today—away, sing—spring.

2. Hold up a blue paper on the first line, yellow (representing the sun) on the second line, green on the third line, and red (representing the heart) on the last line. Invite the children wearing the color you hold up to sing that line with you. All children join in singing "only because it's spring!"

3. Use pictures that the children have drawn and colored.

4. As the children sing the song, they could build a nature scene with flannel board cutouts or pictures.

5. Put a picture on a craft stick to represent each phrase. Have the children put the pictures in the correct order.

MATERIALS:

Word card: WHY (written on a big question mark)

Pictures: a blue sky, robin, sun, earth, green field, clouds, and a heart with a music note on it

ATTENTION-GETTER:

Post the big question mark and tell the children you are going to sing a riddle—a series of questions or clues that lead to an answer.

Ask them to listen carefully to the clues in order to solve the riddle. Sing the complete song, except the phrase "it's spring!" Let the children answer the riddle. Teach them the phrase "only because it's spring."

LISTENING AND SINGING EXPERIENCES:

Pass out the pictures to seven children. As you sing have them try to line up in the right order. Or have another child arrange the children correctly. Or have the children post the pictures by the question mark in the right order. Sing the song several times until the order is correct. Each time you sing, bring the children in on "only because it's spring!" Let the children remove the pictures one at a time until they have learned the song.

Challenge the children to correctly sing the interval from G to B on the phrase "the earth" (second line).

Sing the first line again and ask the children to find what other phrase we sing on that same melody. *[Why are the fields so green today?]*

Invite the children to tap the rhythm with you to discover over what word a fermata ⌢ has been placed. *[Sing]*

IN THE LEAFY TREETOPS

MESSAGE: In the leafy tree tops, the birds see the sun first and sing "Good morning." In the garden, the flowers are nodding to say, "How do you do?"

ATTENTION-GETTER:

• *In the springtime, the very first sound I hear outside my window in the morning is the sound of birds singing. Have you noticed that sound outside your window? Is it a sad sound or happy sound?* **Have the children respond.** *Listen to see if you can find out what makes the birds so happy. [They're first to see the sun.]*

LISTENING AND SINGING EXPERIENCES:

Sing the song to the children, asking them to listen for the answer to the following questions:

Verse One:

• *What do birds sing in the leafy tree tops? ["Good morning."]*
• *How many times do you hear those words and that melody in this verse? [Twice]*
• *Who must the birds tell? [Everyone]*

Have the children join you in singing the first verse as you pitch lead.

Verse Two:

• *What are the flowers doing? [Nodding]*
• *Where are the flowers nodding? [In my pretty garden]*
• *What do the flowers say? ["How do you do? How do you do today?"]*

Express your gratitude for the blessings of springtime and invite the children to sing verse two with you.

ENRICHMENT IDEAS:

1. Prepare a poster-size tree, bird, sun, and flower with a hole in the middle through which the children's faces can show. Invite four children to place these props in front of them as they sing the song.

2. Make a bird and a flower sack puppet for the children to move as they sing the song.

3. Have several children hold pictures of trees, birds, and flowers, or display colorful flannel board pictures.

4. Divide the children into groups. Ask one group to pretend to be the birds and the other group the flowers.

BIRDS IN THE TREE

MESSAGE: Birds care for the eggs in their nest.

ENRICHMENT IDEAS:

1. Bring a real nest to show the children.

2. Let the girls sing the first verse and the boys the second.

ATTENTION-GETTER:

• *How many of you have seen a real bird's nest? I have, too, and I've watched the mother and father birds peck worms from the ground to feed their baby birds. The little birds make a lot of noise when they are hungry, don't they? "Cheep, cheep, cheep," they say. But all is very quiet before the baby birds hatch out of their eggs. Listen as I sing to find out where we can find a little nest. [In the branches of a tree]* Sing the song for the children, using suggested actions that are given in the *Children's Songbook.*

LISTENING AND SINGING EXPERIENCES:

Verse One:

• *This time as I sing, follow me in doing the actions.*

Invite the children to sing with you. They will learn it quickly with the actions. Repeat several times.

Verse Two:

• *How many eggs is the mother bird sitting on? [Three]*

• *What is father bird doing? [Flying round and round to guard his family]*

RAIN IS FALLING ALL AROUND

MESSAGE: Rain falls everywhere.

ATTENTION-GETTER:

Have the accompanist play the music an octave higher, using staccato notes.

- *I hear raindrops, do you? Are they falling on the housetops? On the ground? Oh, they're falling on my nose! And on my head and hands and toes!*

LISTENING AND SINGING EXPERIENCES:

Sing the song to the children, fluttering your fingers to imitate raindrops falling and pantomiming where the raindrops fall. Invite the children to imitate your actions.

- *Listen to the song again and tell me where the raindrops are falling. [On the housetops; on the ground; on my nose, head, hands, and toes]*

Help the children notice that the melody goes down on the words "head," "hands," and "toes" by touching these body parts as they sing.

- *We need rain. Grass, trees, flowers, and children could not grow without water. Rain is a blessing from Heavenly Father.*

ENRICHMENT IDEAS:

1. Divide the children into two groups. One group whispers "pitter-patter" as the other group sings the song without accompaniment.

2. For seasonal variety, refer to the alternate phrases listed in the *Children's Songbook*: "Sun is shining," "Wind is blowing," "Leaves are falling," and "Snow is falling."

3. With alternate words and a little imagination, this song can be made relevant to any season. It can also be a rest song: "Matt is stretching; jumping; dancing" or a positive reinforcement such as "We are quiet; we can tiptoe; we are happy." Encourage the children to suggest something that you could sing. This extends the use of the song.

4. Since no scripture reference was given for this song it would be appropriate to end your presentation by expressing gratitude.

POPCORN POPPING

MESSAGE: The blossoms on the apricot tree remind me of popcorn.

ENRICHMENT IDEAS:

1. Explain that apricots are a small orange-colored fruit; the blossoms are white and look like popcorn. If desired, substitute the name of a local flowering tree.

2. An effective visual aid is a blossoming branch of an apricot tree. Or you could glue large pieces of popcorn to a tree branch.

3. Consider letting the children smell both the blossoms of a fruit tree and freshly popped popcorn. Let them choose which they like the best.

4. Other references: Coloring Songbook, *Popcorn Popping*, © 1991, Aspen Books.

♪ *About the Song*

One spring when the orchards in Magna, Utah, were blossoming, Georgia Bello's young son said, "Oh, look, Mother . . . popcorn's popping on the apricot tree!" In the springtime some years later, Sister Bello looked out her window and saw the apricot blossoms. Her son's words came back to her, and she wrote the song that has since become the number one favorite of Primary children. She did not have a piano at the time and used her daughter's toy piano to find the melody—that is why it is all on white keys. She was a Primary music leader and asked her friend, Betty Lou Cooney, to write down the melody and provide a left hand accompaniment so that she could teach the song to the children of her ward.

ATTENTION-GETTER:

Tell the children the following true story:

• *One day, a four-year-old was playing outside when he noticed that spring had brought him a surprise. He ran into the house, excitedly telling his mother that there was popcorn on their apricot tree.*

Recite the words to the song as a poem in an enthusiastic way, as if you just saw this exciting springtime event.

LISTENING AND SINGING EXPERIENCES:

Sing the song several times, encouraging the children to listen by using questions similar to those listed below.

• *I looked out the window, and what did I see?* [Popcorn popping on the apricot tree]

• *What had spring brought me?* [A nice surprise]

• *What was popping right before my eyes?* [Blossoms] Be sure to sing "blossoms" not "popcorn."

• *I could take an armful and make a treat that would smell as sweet as what?* [A popcorn ball]

• *What seemed to be, but wasn't really so?* [Popcorn popping on the apricot tree]

This song can be taught using simple actions such as:

1. "Looked out the window": put hands above eyes.
2. "Popcorn popping" and "blossoms popping": open and close hands in rhythm.
3. "I could take an armful": make large circle with arms.
4. "Smell so sweet": sniff at imaginary ball of popcorn.
5. "It wasn't really so": shake head for no.
6. "But it seemed to be": nod head for yes.

LITTLE SEEDS LIE FAST ASLEEP

MESSAGE: The sun helps the seeds to grow.

MATERIALS:

A package of seeds and a small potted plant

ATTENTION-GETTER:

- *What does a seed need in order to grow into a beautiful plant? [Soil, sunlight, and water.]*
- *Let's pretend we are little seeds lying fast asleep in a row of warm soil. As I sing, follow my actions.* Improvise actions as suggested by the words.

LISTENING AND SINGING EXPERIENCES:

As you teach each verse separately, use the actions with each repetition.

Verse One:

- *Listen to hear how many times I sing the phrase "in a row." [Twice]*
- *Now listen to hear how many times I sing the phrase "wake up." [Three times]*

Invite the children to sing verse one with you.

Verse Two:

- *The little seeds didn't all wake up at the same time. How did they wake up? [One by one]*
- *They stretched up towards the sun and began to do what? [To grow]*

Invite the children to sing verse two with you. Then sing the entire song.

ENRICHMENT IDEAS:

1. You may wish to teach this song using the following actions:

   Verse One:

   First line: Bend head towards your left shoulder and rest it on your folded hands.

   Second line: Make a circle above your head with your arms—representing the sun.

   Verse Two:

   First line: Rise quietly.

   Second line: Stretch high and make a circle above your head with your arms.

2. Create a poster as illustrated with seeds and flowers attached to transparent thread. Invite a child to plant the seeds and to help the flowers grow as the children sing the song. See page 40 for instructions.

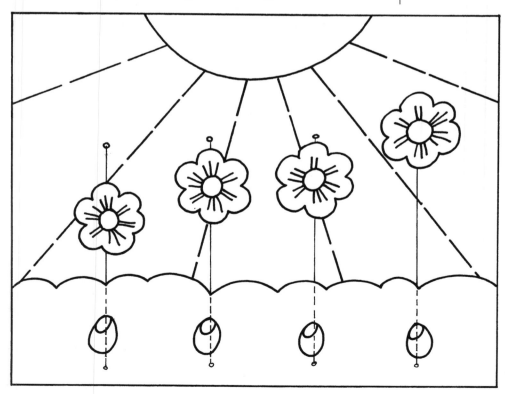

LITTLE PURPLE PANSIES

MESSAGE: Just as the little purple pansies brighten a garden and bring us gladness, we, too, must try to bring gladness to others.

ENRICHMENT IDEAS:

1. Children may enjoy holding several large pansies made from poster paper, with a hole cut in the center so the children's smiling faces may show through.

2. Challenge the children to finger tap the dotted rhythm in the first measure of each line and to clap their laps on the even rhythm of the second measure of each line.

♪ *About the Song*

There was some question as to whether "you and I" was correct in the last line, or whether it should be "you and ME." But right or wrong, the song could not be changed—it simply had to rhyme with the message of the song, which is to "try, try, try" to make the place where we are happy. The accompaniment was lightened to match the mood of the song. This lilting tune is timeless and attracts one generation after another.

ATTENTION-GETTER:

- *How do you feel when the cold and stormy winter weather finally comes to an end and you notice that first little flower peeking through the soil?* Have the children respond.

- *That one little flower brings cheer to my whole garden and gladness to me. Listen as I sing, and tell me the name of this special flower.*

LISTENING AND SINGING EXPERIENCES:

Direct the children's listening by asking questions as you sing.

Verse One:

- *What are the special flowers that bring me gladness? [Pansies]*
- *What color are the little pansies? [Purple, touched with yellow gold]* If possible, show some fresh purple pansies with yellow centers.
- *Where are the pansies growing? [In one corner of the garden old]*
- *Even though the pansies are very small, what must they try, try, try to do? [Gladden just one spot]*

Tap the rhythm of the first line and ask the children to tap with you and see if this rhythm is repeated through the entire song. *[It is.]*

Invite the children to tap and sing verse one with you.

Verse Two:

- *Where do the pansies grow? [In whatever corner]*
- *Find two words to describe how the wind may blow? [Cold, or warm]*
- *What two words describe how the day may be? [Dark (stormy), or sunny]*
- *Even though the pansies may be growing in an unnoticed corner, the cold wind may be blowing, and the day may be dark, what must the pansies try, try, try to do? [Gladden just one spot]*

Challenge the children to try to gladden those around them even though they, too, are small. Then invite them to sing the second verse with you.

OH, WHAT DO YOU DO IN THE . . .

MESSAGE: There are many fun things for you and me to do in the summertime.

MATERIALS: Paper or flannel cutouts. Mount on craft sticks or post on a flannel board.

Pictures: V.1, fishing, dreaming; V. 2, Swimming, swing in a tree; V. 3, Marching in parades, drinking lemonade, counting stars.

ATTENTION-GETTER:

Sing a question: *"Oh what do you do in the summertime, when all the world is green?"* Then say, *"What do you do, John?"* Ask several children to respond.

LISTENING AND SINGING EXPERIENCES:

Ask individual children questions from the song as you sing. For example: *"Jim, do you fish in a stream? Debbie, do you lazily dream on the bank as the clouds go by? Karen, is that what you do? So do I!"*

Pass out the pictures for all three verses. Ask the children to post them in the correct order as you sing again.

Teach the children the first phrase and then have them sing that much as you sing the rest of the song to check the order of the pictures.

Invite the children to sing all three verses. Then begin removing the pictures with each repetition until the song is learned and all the pictures are removed.

ENRICHMENT IDEAS:

1. Invite the children to pantomime the activities mentioned in the song. Others might guess what they are pantomiming.

2. Tell the children that in some parts of the world, the foliage is green only in the summertime, when it is warm. In other countries, the weather is warm and the grass is green through all the seasons. Invite all children wearing green to stand and sing.

3. Consider teaching the children how to conduct two beats to a measure. (See p. 300 of the *Children's Songbook* for beat patterns.)

4. Make up verses about autumntime and wintertime. For example:

"Oh, what do you do in the wintertime,
When all the world is white?
Do you ride on a sleigh,
go skating all day,
or watch snowflakes fall from the sky?
Is that what you do? So do I!"

Oh, what do you do in the autumntime,
When harvest days are nigh?
Do you rake leaves all day,
Play football, hooray!
Carve pumpkins and then bake a pie?
Is that what you do? So do I?

MESSAGE: Brightly colored leaves are falling all around the town because it's autumntime.

ENRICHMENT IDEAS:

1. Post a tree (trunk and branches only) on a flannel board, adding yellow, red, and brown leaves as you teach the song.

2. Display a beautiful bouquet of autumn leaves.

3. Flutter paper autumn leaves by dropping them as the children flutter their fingers.

4. Pitch lead with the children, pointing out the descending melody patterns that give us the feeling of falling leaves.

MATERIALS:

Cutouts: yellow, red, and brown leaves

ATTENTION-GETTER:

- *Today I'm going to give you a riddle. When you know what the answer is, raise your hand. I am thinking of some things that are very beautiful. They come in many colors, and they are crisp and crunchy. They are everywhere you go this time of year. Sometimes I go for a ride all around the town just to see them. They fall from the trees. What am I thinking of? [Autumn leaves]*

- *There is only one special season when you can see them. What is it?* Sing both verses of "It's Autumntime."

LISTENING AND SINGING EXPERIENCES:

Sing the song several times, encouraging the children to listen by using questions and statements similar to those listed below. As children discover answers, invite them to sing that part of the song with you. Add one phrase at a time to the ones already learned.

Verse One:

- *How many times did I sing "It's autumntime?" [Four]*

- *Where are the leaves falling? [Down]*

- *Where is autumn all around? [The town]*

Verse Two:

- *What color of leaves are mentioned? [Yellow, red, and brown]* Post these three colors of autumn leaves cut from colored paper to help the children with the proper order.

- *What can be found? [Bright colors]*

- *This is such a beautiful time of the year. The things that make it so beautiful are the colorful autumn leaves falling.* Invite the children to sing both verses.

AUTUMN DAY

MESSAGE: We are glad for the beautiful gifts of autumn that are all around us. We will remember that these gifts were given to us by God.

MATERIALS:

A wrapped gift box

Pictures: autumn scene, red and yellow apples, a tree loaded with fruit, and a boy praying (62218). Attach pictures to the sides of the wrapped gift box.

ATTENTION-GETTER:

Show the gift box and express the idea that *"God gives richest gifts today."* We can *"look on every side and see pleasant things for you and me."*

Invite the children to listen as you sing to discover what autumn gifts Heavenly Father has given us. Rotate the box to illustrate the autumn gifts as you sing. Let the children respond. *[Beautiful autumn leaves, red and yellow apples, fruit trees]*

LISTENING AND SINGING EXPERIENCES:

Sing the song several times, encouraging the children to listen by using questions and statements similar to those listed below. As children discover answers, invite them to sing that part of the song with you. Add one phrase at a time to the ones already learned.

- *These are gifts God has given to us to bless our lives. Who should we not forget?* *[God, who gives]* Pitch lead, pointing out the descending scale.
- *Each child should be happy with all that lives. The song doesn't use the word happy. What word do you hear?* *[Glad]*
- *What does God give us when autumn comes our way?* *[Richest gifts]* Invite the children to tap the rhythm of the first two lines.
- *If we look on every side, what will we see?* *[Pleasant things for you and me]*
- *We sing six words that describe the apples. What words do you hear?* *[Red, yellow, round, juicy, sweet, mellow]* Repeat until all answers are given.
- *Round, juicy apples load the trees until the trees do what?* *[Bend over and their branches brush the clover.]* Explain that clover is a type of green grass.

As the children join you in singing the song, have them listen for the reverent mood change on the last line. Notice that the time signature changes from 3/4 to 4/4.

Have a child read James 1:17, *"Every good gift and every perfect gift is from above, and cometh down from the Father."* Express your gratitude to your Father in Heaven that autumn has come our way with all its gifts. Challenge the children to notice these autumn gifts on their way home today.

ENRICHMENT IDEAS:

1. Invite the children to listen for the rhyming words.
2. Teach a group of older children the alto line.
3. Cut large autumn leaves out of brightly colored posterboard. Attach appropriate pictures to help with the word order.
4. Display a horn of plenty filled with fruit. Sing the song again and discuss all the wonderful gifts God gives us during the autumn season.
5. Children could snap, clap, and clap their laps on the three beats in each measure—then fold arms on the last line.

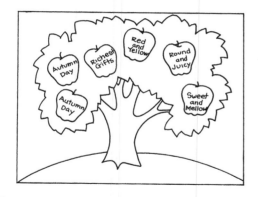

FALLING SNOW

MESSAGE: See the snow falling gently down, covering the ground below?

ENRICHMENT IDEAS:

1. Challenge the children to pitch lead the melody of this song with their bodies, standing and stooping as the melody indicate.

2. Show the children pictures of snow scenes and children having fun in the snow.

3. Explain that snow is not found in all parts of the world. Help the children discover the beauty and wonder of snow.

4. Have three children play tone bells on the repeated notes (C, A, F) for the words "falling down, gently down."

MATERIALS:

Cutouts: small snowflakes

ATTENTION-GETTER:

As you sing the song for the children, drop the snowflakes to the floor.

LISTENING AND SINGING EXPERIENCES:

· *How is the snow falling down? [Gently]*

· *What can we see? [The softly falling snow]*

· *What words are repeated? [Falling down, gently down]*

· *What is the snow doing as it gently falls down? [It is covering the ground below.]*

As the children sing, have them raise their arms and wiggle their fingers as their arms move slowly down.

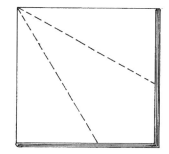
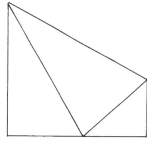

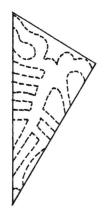

ONCE THERE WAS A SNOWMAN

MESSAGE: It is fun to build a snowman tall, tall, tall, and then to see him melt small, small, small.

MATERIALS:

Cutouts: flannel circles to form a snowman and a sun

ATTENTION-GETTER:

Begin singing the song as you build a flannel board snowman. Add the sun and remove the circles to indicate the melted snowman.

LISTENING AND SINGING EXPERIENCES:

Sing the song again, having the children imitate you. Gradually stand as you sing, *"tall, tall, tall."* Crouch down as you sing, *"small, small, small."*

Invite the children to sing with you, imitating the snowman. Remind the children to do this activity quietly because snowmen are very quiet.

ENRICHMENT IDEAS:

1. Let the children take turns "building" the flannel board snowman mentioned above.

2. Mount a large posterboard snowman on a paint stick. Have a child raise and lower it behind a flannel board during the song.

3. Have fun with dynamics by observing a crescendo on "tall, tall, tall," and a decrescendo on "small, small, small." Reinforce the dynamics with a "growing" snowman.

4. Ask the children how many times they hear a five-note scale going up. [Four] Help the children discover that the melody of the first measure on each line is the same. The children might enjoy playing the melody on resonator bells.

5. Ask older children why the ascending melody on "tall, tall, tall," and the descending melody on "small, small, small" fits the words so well.

6. Divide the children into four groups. Assign each group one of the following words and have them count the number of times they sing that word: snowman (4), tall (3), melted (4), and small (3).

♪ *About the Song*

Moiselle Renstrom was a teacher who had the gift of becoming as a little child. Thirteen of her many songs are included in *Children's Songbook* (see Authors and Composers, *Children's Songbook*, p. 306 for page numbers). She wrote simply and in the right range for children's voices. (*Friend*, Oct. 1985, p. 14.) This is one of the top twenty-five Primary songs, and is a favorite even in Tahiti where there is no snow!

Fun & Activity

In this section, there are songs about Primary and friendship,
songs with actions, and birthday songs.

LIFT UP YOUR VOICE AND SING

MESSAGE: Singing will brighten and lighten your day.

MATERIALS:

A pill bottle

ATTENTION-GETTER:

Show the children a pill bottle and tell them that you have a prescription for each one of them. Read from the label, Proverbs 17:22: *"A merry heart doeth good like a medicine."* Tell the children you are going to sing a song that suggests something that can make their hearts merry. *It can help you feel better when you are having a bad day.* Sing the song.

- *What can you do to cheer yourself up? [Lift up your voice and sing.]*

LISTENING AND SINGING EXPERIENCES:

Repeat the song several times, encouraging the children to listen by asking questions about the message. Invite them to sing the part of the song that answers the question.

- *How many times did I sing "Lift up your voice?" [Five]*

Tell the children that each repetition of "lift up your voice" on the last line begins one tone higher. As the melody goes higher, observe a crescendo to emphasize each repeated phrase and make a nice ending to the song.

- *What two things will music do? [Brighten the day and lighten the way]*

To teach the order of the phrases, point out that B (brighten) comes before L (lighten) in the alphabet.

- *What should I start? [A glad song]*
- *What should we let the song do? [Let it float, let it ring.]*

To emphasize that "a song is a wonderful kind of thing," read what the Lord says about a song. "For my soul delighteth in the song of the heart; yea, the song of the righteous is a prayer unto me, and it shall be answered with a blessing upon their heads" (D&C 25:12).

ENRICHMENT IDEAS:

1. Have fun with dynamics. Begin the last line softly and then crescendo to the end as you sing the last two measures. As you sing "Lift up your voice," make a circle with your fingers; the second time make a larger circle with your hands; and the last time, make a hoop with your arms. Invite the children to join you.

2. Make a crescendo visual aid. For fun, reverse the visual and sing a decrescendo beginning loud and getting softer. Let the children decide which dynamics better fit the message.

3. Tell the children that the first phrase of the refrain begins "we shall" and the second phrase begins "music will." The melody pattern is similar, so be careful to sing the words correctly.

4. Invite the children to pitch lead the last line with their bodies, stooping, standing, and then stretching to match the pitch.

5. Make a sock puppet as illustrated using a styrofoam ball, a wooden dowel, yarn, etc. Children will enjoy making the doll "grow" as they lift up their voices and sing.

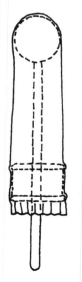 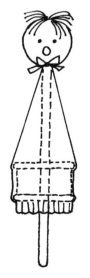 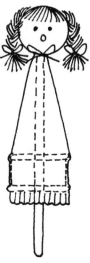 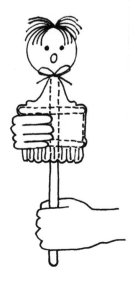

SING A SONG

MESSAGE: I like to sing a song.

ENRICHMENT IDEAS:

1. Challenge the children to sing the song in their minds. Post the word "sing" and see if the children can sing all of the words except the word "sing." You may want to choose an easier word to sing in inner hearing at first and work up to the word "sing."

2. Divide the children into four groups. Have each group sing one chart and repeat their part while the others add on.

3. Plan a body action that matches the pitch of the melody. For example, for "Sing, sing, sing," you could stand, stoop, and stand; "I like to sing" could be touch shoulders twice, touch waist and knees. Sing the song with actions in groups or all together. Begin very slowly and increase the tempo for a rest exercise.

♪ *About the Song*

The composer, Ingrid Gordon, is a beautician and a vocalist. One day when she was cutting Pat Graham's hair, she told her how much fun she had helping with music at her children's elementary school. She had wanted to begin her lesson with a song about singing—something simple the children could hear once and easily join in. As she thought about what she wanted, a little idea popped into her mind and she taught it to the children. She asked Sister Graham if she could write it down and make an accompaniment. As they sang it together, they realized that it could be sung as a round. Because rounds were needed to involve older children, Sister Graham took it to the Primary General Board committee and it was approved. To her surprise, Ingrid is now a composer! Most successful songs have been written this way—by pondering a particular need for a particular group of children for a particular occasion.

MATERIALS:

Melody pictures: charts of the melody in words.

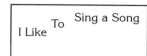

Sing   Sing
     Sing
	I Like
	     To
	       Sing

I Like To Sing a Song	Sing
	    Sing
	      Sing

ATTENTION-GETTER:

• *I know a song that has only six words. Listen carefully and tell me what these six words are. [I, like, to, sing, a, song]* Sing again if needed.

LISTENING AND SINGING EXPERIENCES:

• *Count how many times I sing the word "sing."* [Eight]

Post the four melody pictures as shown and challenge the children to put them in the right order as you sing again.

Point out that two charts have the same words, but that the melody is different. Invite them to sing with you to make sure that these two charts are in the right order.

Invite the children to pitch lead as they sing, referring to the charts.

When the children are familiar with the song, divide them in two to four groups and sing the song as a round.

FUN TO DO

MESSAGE: Singing a song is fun.

MATERIALS:

A large number seven on a chalkboard

ATTENTION-GETTER:

Display the large number seven. Tell the children you know a song that only has seven words in it. Ask the children to discover what the seven words are as you sing the song.

LISTENING AND SINGING EXPERIENCES:

Ask the children to listen to discover what word is sung on the highest note in the song. *[Is]* Sing it again, asking them to raise their hands when they hear that high note.

Invite the children to stand up when they hear a place in the song where the melody goes right down the scale. *[Last phrase]*

As you sing that phrase with the children, have them pitch lead with their bodies, going lower with each note and ending up sitting in their chairs.

Invite a child to choose something he thinks is fun to do. As you sing the song, do the actions suggested by his choice. Choose another child and repeat.

You might want to end singing time by saying, *"All of these things are fun to do. I know what is fun to do at Primary."* Sing the song, substituting one of the following: *"Folding our arms," "greeting our friends," "learning the gospel,"* or *"sitting up tall."*

ENRICHMENT IDEAS:

1. Conduct the song in a two-beat pattern. To help the children feel the two beats, have them tap their laps on the first beat and snap their fingers on the second beat. Have them join you in singing the song.

2. Tell them that not only does this song have only seven words, but we can sing it seven different ways—softer, louder, faster, slower, higher, lower, or staccato. Have fun with these different ways to sing.

3. We can also sing about doing seven different things. Hold up a box or sack containing several objects, such as a book, ball, crayons, or pictures suggesting fun activities. Invite a child to select an item from the box and sing the song about the suggested activity. Refer to suggestions at bottom of song.

4. Encourage the children to be more observant and attentive by playing the "Watch Me Game." Tell the children you are going to trick them by changing the speed or volume of the music. Then hold a note longer than usual or speed up or slow down a line.

HELLO, FRIENDS!

MESSAGE: We are happy being here and helping our friends in Primary.

ENRICHMENT IDEAS:

1. Invite the children to shake hands with each other as they sing.

2. Challenge the children to find two words that rhyme with Primary. *[Be, me]*

ATTENTION-GETTER:

Repeat the song several times as you walk among the children shaking their hands and patting their shoulders. After several repetitions, the children will be ready to sing the song with you as you ask questions similar to the following:

LISTENING AND SINGING EXPERIENCES:

- *Where is it nice to be? [Here with you in Primary]*

- *If I help you and you help me, how will we feel? [Happy as can be]*

- *This song has two lines in it. Listen carefully to see if the two melody lines are exactly the same or slightly different. [Slightly different]*

To point out the difference in the last measure of each melody line, divide the children into two groups. Have group one sing the first line on "loo" and group two sing the second line on "loo." Sing both lines together to create a two-part harmony on the last measure.

OUR DOOR IS ALWAYS OPEN

MESSAGE: We are always glad to welcome a friend.

LISTENING AND SINGING EXPERIENCES:

Divide the children into two groups. Teach each group a line of the song by singing and tapping the rhythm. Make sure the first group is secure in their part before moving on to the next group.

Sing the entire song, with each group singing their part in turn. Then trade parts.

When the children know the song well, sing it as a round.

MESSAGE: Come with me to Primary.

ENRICHMENT IDEAS:

1. Divide the children into four groups. Have them sing the song as a round, bringing in a new group at each number marked in the music. Use no accompaniment.

2. For variety, use alternate words:

    Oh, bring a friend to . . .

    Oh, be on time to . . .

    Oh, sing a song in . . .

    Oh, learn the truth in . . .

MATERIALS:

Make an invitation that says "Come with me to . . ." on the outside and "Primary" on the inside.

ATTENTION-GETTER:

Show the invitation to the children.

- *Isn't it fun to receive an invitation? Sometimes we get invitations to weddings, but more often we receive invitations to birthday parties. Let's find out where we are being invited to in this invitation.*

Open the invitation and begin singing the song for the children as if you are reading the invitation.

LISTENING AND SINGING EXPERIENCES:

- *Where are we being invited to come? [To Primary] Show the children the inside of the invitation revealing the word "Primary."*

- *Now listen as I sing again to find out how many times I sing "Come with me to Primary." [Three]*

As you pitch lead have the children listen for the words sung on the fast repeated notes. *[Ever in the world]*

Invite the children to sing as you pitch lead to help them reach the interval "oh, come" on the last line.

WE WELCOME YOU

MESSAGE: We welcome you to Primary. We gather here to learn the gospel, sing, pray, and share with each other.

MATERIALS:

Wordstrips: *To do his part, to use good manners, be polite, to love the Lord, choose the right, learn the gospel, sing, pray, share with all who come that day*

ATTENTION-GETTER:

Walk among the Primary children, shaking their hands and happily singing verse one. If possible, have the Primary presidency or teachers walk among the children singing as well. Repeat until all children are recognized with a friendly handshake.

LISTENING AND SINGING EXPERIENCES:

Part One

As each phrase is taught, invite the children to sing it back to you.

Tap the rhythm of the first phrase as you sing. Challenge the children to enunciate the quick words clearly while tapping.

- *As I sing the second phrase, find the words that are sung on an octave interval that sounds like this.* Have the accompanist play C to C on "for you."

- *As I sing the next phrase, notice how the melody on "Pri-ma-ry" is the same pattern as "like to be," only a little lower.*

- *The next phrase has another octave jump. This time the jump goes from high to low like this.* Have the accompanist play high C to middle C on "for you." *Find the words on this octave. [For you]*

As the children sing, invite them to shake hands with the person on either side of them.

ATTENTION-GETTER:

- *Over one hundred years ago, 224 children were gathered in the first Primary in a little rock chapel in Farmington, Utah. Sister Aurelia Rogers, the first Primary president, was the mother of twelve children. She had felt a need for an organization where children could be taught "everything good and how to behave." Today children all over the world go to Primary just like you do.*

Part Two

- *The song mentions five things that Primary children were taught. Listen to discover what they were. [To do his part, to use good manners, be polite, to love the Lord, choose the right]* Post answers in the order given and sing as many times as necessary to get all five answers.

Sing part two through "choose the right" to check the order of the responses. Rearrange if necessary. Point out that we learn the same things today that the children learned long ago.

- *Now every week in Primary what do we gather to do? Find four answers. [Learn the gospel, sing and pray, and share with all who come that day.]* Post answers as given and then sing again to check order.

Invite the children to sing all of part two and then to continue to sing part one to the "fine" marking.

ENRICHMENT IDEAS:

1. Use verse one of this song to welcome a new child to your Primary or to welcome in the new Sunbeams.

2. When celebrating the birthday of the Primary on August 25, substitute the alternate verse given below the song.

3. Dress as Sister Aurelia Spencer Rogers and tell about the first Primary. (See *Friend*, Aug. 1986, pp. 10 and 11.)

4. The Primary was first organized in August of 1878. Help the children discover how old the Primary is going to be this year.

   Other references: *Friend*, Aug./Sep. 1983, p. 34; Aug./Sep. 1985, p. 44; Aug. 1986, p. 10; Picture of First Primary).

♪ *About the Song*

There are two copyright dates on the words of this song. It was first published in 1978 as "A Happy Birthday to the Primary," to celebrate Primary's centennial year. Some on the committee felt that the song was not needed, as one of the known birthday songs could be used, and that the organization of Primary may not be of significance to a child. On the other hand, this song could motivate leaders to talk about Aurelia Rogers and the rock chapel and how the Church has grown.

In order to make the song more versatile, Ruth Gardner, the author, was asked to write additional words which could be sung anytime—perhaps as a welcome song—and keep the original words as "alternate" for celebrating the August 25 birthday of Primary. Because of the changes, the song also has a 1987 copyright.

The first part of the song can now stand alone and could be sung when a new child moves into the ward, the nursery children come into Primary, or the bishop visits. A bit of history was saved.

OUR PRIMARY COLORS

MESSAGE: Our Primary colors are red, yellow, and blue. Red symbolizes courage to do what is right. Yellow stands for service, and blue is for truth in thought and deed. We will be happy when this is our creed.

ENRICHMENT IDEAS:

1. Have children who are wearing red, yellow, or blue stand and sing the phrase corresponding to their color.

2. Prepare three banners on sticks in the Primary colors. Write "courage," "service," and "truth" on the banners and display them as the song is sung.

3. Make three colored headbands in the Primary colors with the corresponding key word written on them for three children to wear as the song is sung.

4. Make a simple melody picture. Ask the children to listen carefully as they sing and find the words that match this melody. [We will be happy when this is our creed.]

5. Ask the children to find the word that comes at the highest and lowest points on the chart. [Highest is the word "we." Lowest is the word "is."]

♪ *About the Song*

The 1985 *Primary Handbook* stated that the Primary colors are red, yellow, and blue, and that blue represented "truth." The song said blue is for "purity in thought and deed." Inasmuch as "truth" is probably more concrete to children, the song was changed to match the handbook. One scripture reference is given for each symbol.

MATERIALS:

Sheets of colored paper (red, yellow, blue)

Marking pen

ATTENTION-GETTER:

- *Heavenly Father has blessed us with many beautiful colors. Our country's colors are on our flag. What are they? Our Primary also has colors. Listen for the Primary colors as I sing.* Sing the entire song.

LISTENING AND SINGING EXPERIENCES:

Sing the song several times for the children, asking questions to direct their listening.

- *What are our Primary colors? [Red, yellow, and blue]* Post a sheet of colored paper in each color.

Sing the first four measures again and ask the children to find another phrase with the same melody. [Each one has a message for you and me.]

- *Each color does have a message for you and me. Each is a symbol of something very important. Listen to discover what red symbolizes. [Courage to do what is right]* Write "courage" on the red sheet and pitch lead that phrase.

- *What does yellow stand for? [Service from morning till night]* Write "service" on the yellow sheet and teach that phrase.

- *What does blue stand for? [Truth in our thought and our deed]* Write "truth" on the blue sheet and teach that phrase, explaining that deeds are our actions.

- *When will we be happy? [When this is our creed]* Explain that our creed is our belief. When we make courage, service, and truth our creed, we will be happy.

WE'RE ALL TOGETHER AGAIN

MESSAGE: Here we are singing all together again.

ATTENTION-GETTER:

Introduce the song by singing it and asking the children to listen for how many times they hear you sing "We're here." *[Six]* Sing again to check answer.

LISTENING AND SINGING EXPERIENCES:

Invite the children to sing "We're here" each time it occurs in the song.

Invite the children to tap two beats per measure as you sing, once again having the children sing "We're here" each time.

Invite the children to sing the song with you, tapping just the rhythm to "together again" as they sing.

ENRICHMENT IDEAS:

1. Divide the singers into two groups. Have one group whisper chant "we're here" while the other group sings the rest of the song. Alternate groups. (See *Children's Songbook*, p. 304.)

2. Invite the children to march to the two-beat rhythm pattern.

HELLO SONG

MESSAGE: We are glad to welcome you to Primary and happy that you came to share our Primary day with us.

ENRICHMENT IDEAS:

1. Point out that we slow down as we sing "very special way" in the third line and draw attention to the ritard (slower) and the fermatas ⌒ that we hold on the word "way." Hold up a fermata sign when the words "way" and the last "hello" are sung.

2. Have fun with the "hellos" by dividing into two groups—one to begin and one to echo. Change often so the children will "follow the leader."

3. Add variety by having children stand and sit each time they sing "hello."

4. Explain that Jesus was the greatest example of love and friendship. He told us to love one another as he loved us. If we show that kind of love to others, everyone will feel welcome and want to be with us again.

ATTENTION-GETTER:

Begin by saying "Hello." Tell the children that it is polite to say "Hello" back when someone says it to you. It makes people feel welcome. *"Let's try that again. Hello!"*

Sing the first hello, with the piano playing the echo. Repeat. *That piano is echoing me. Why don't you be the echo this time!*

LISTENING AND SINGING EXPERIENCES:

Sing the first two hellos with the children singing the echo. Hello! (Hello!) Hello! (Hello!)

• *There is another place where the echo is repeated. Listen as I sing to discover what phrase it follows. [We welcome you today.]*

Sing the song again, asking the children to discover if the melody on those phrases is the same or different. *[Different]* Teach the two phrases by pitch leading.

• *Now listen for two reasons why we're glad you came our way. [To share with us our Primary day and be our friend in a very special way]*

Invite the children to sing the song with you and choose children to sing the echoes.

HERE WE ARE TOGETHER

MESSAGE: Here we are together in our Primary.

ATTENTION-GETTER:

Begin singing the song as you gesture outward to the children. As you name children, shake hands with or gesture toward them as you sing each name. On the last line, open your arms to include the whole group.

LISTENING AND SINGING EXPERIENCES:

For variety, bring four children to the front. Have everyone sing the song, inserting the names of the four children as you indicate. Then let the four children choose four others to come forward and repeat the activity as everyone sings the song.

ENRICHMENT IDEAS:

1. Instead of inviting four children to come forward, bring four teachers or special guests present that day.

2. Choose four children to stand and sing their name alone as everyone sings the song.

3. Let the children shake each other's hands while singing.

4. Use the alternate words listed below the song to fit particular days and occasions.

FRIENDS ARE FUN

MESSAGE: It is fun to have a friend, but to have a friend you must be a friend, too.

ENRICHMENT IDEAS:

1. Read Proverbs 17:17 "A friend loveth at all times." Have the children recite it back to you.

2. Divide the children into groups (boys and girls, older and younger, right and left side, teacher and child) and have them sing the phrases as you indicate. Bring them together for the last phrase.

3. Put key words on paper dolls that are holding hands.

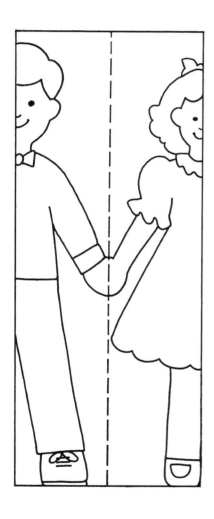

Accordian fold along
outside edges

MATERIALS:

Word cards: PLAY, STAY, LIFE

ATTENTION-GETTER:

- *Friends are fun! What do you like to do with your friends?* Let children respond. *It is fun to have a friend who will play with you. But to have a friend, you must do something very special. Listen as I sing to discover what you must do to have a friend.* Sing the first verse.

LISTENING AND SINGING EXPERIENCES:

Verse One:

- *What must you do to have a friend? [You must be a friend, too.]* Sing the last two measures again while pitch leading, then invite the children to sing that phrase with you. Bring them in on this phrase with each repetition.

- *The song tells two things that your friends do with you. Listen to discover the answers. [Play with you, stay with you]*

- *It is fun to make a friend for how long? [For your whole life through]*

Ask the children if they noticed which word is sung on the highest note of the song. *[Whole]*

Post the word cards PLAY, STAY, AND LIFE to help the children remember the sequence of phrases.

Using careful pitch leading, invite the children to join you in singing the first verse. Pay close attention to make certain the interval jumps are sung correctly.

Verse Two:

- *If you want a friend, what must you show? [That you care]* Invite the children to sing this last phrase with each repetition.

- *If you want to play a game, how should you play it? [Fair]*

- *If you want a piece of cake, what must you learn? [To share]*

- *If you do these things, what would you have if you should need a friend? [You would have one there.]*

Express your feelings of gratitude for your friends and challenge the children to remember the importance of being a good friend.

WE ARE DIFFERENT

MESSAGE: We are different, but we love and help each other.

MATERIALS:

Word cards: KNOW, DIFFERENT, HELP, LEARN, LOVE, REACH

ATTENTION-GETTER:

Bring a child to the front and turn to face him or her. Sing the song using simple actions:

"I know you,	*and*	*you know me."*
(Point to child.)		(Point to yourself.)

"We are as different as the sun and the sea."
(Grasp hands with child.)

"I know you,	*and*	*you know me."*
(Point to child.)		(Point to yourself.)

"And that's the way it is supposed to be."
(Give the child a handshake or a hug.)

LISTENING AND SINGING EXPERIENCES:

Verse One:

Repeat the above with several other children.

Invite the children to pair off and sing the song with a partner, using the actions.

Verses Two and Three:

Invite six children to hold the word cards. As you sing the entire song, have another child arrange the children in the proper sequence. Have the children sing verse one and the last line of verses two and three with you.

Add the accompaniment, and have the children sing the entire song using the word cards.

You could play a wood block on beats one, three, and four (follow the left hand piano line).

ENRICHMENT IDEAS:

1. For younger children, teach verses two and three with actions.

2. For older children, focus on the key words in the first line of each verse—KNOW, HELP, AND LOVE. You could make a match with the key words of the second line—DIFFERENT, LEARN, and REACH.

3. Challenge the children to tap the rhythm with you. Consider using rhythm instruments.

4. For variation sing lines one and three using a "stop and go" method with music leader singing "I know you" and indicating to the children to sing "and you know me."

5. When the song is well learned, sing using sign language.

6. Other references: *Friend,* Apr. 1987, p. 34; Sept. 1987, p. 12.

♪ *About the Song*

The composer said, "People have trouble initially with the syncopation and should play the song slowly and count out loud. This is how it is with anything that is different—at first we are uncomfortable, but with time, the differences become the attraction."

MESSAGE: No matter what the weather, many of God's creations join in singing a happy song.

ENRICHMENT IDEAS:

1. Place the pictures on craft sticks or on a flip chart. Or make them into sack puppets.

2. Divide the children into three groups, one for each of the first three lines, with all singing the last line together.

3. Tape record the sounds of ducks, hens, birds, wind (by blowing into a microphone), and children singing. Challenge the children to guess what the "mystery" sounds are and then to sing the song together.

4. Invite the children to finger tap the playful rhythm as they sing.

MATERIALS:

Pictures: a duck, a hen, a bird, and wind in the treetops

ATTENTION-GETTER:

- *Can you name some of the sounds you hear when you go for a springtime walk?* Let children respond. *Many of Heavenly Father's creations actually sing. As I sing this song for you, listen to discover which of these creations sing "a happy song."*

LISTENING AND SINGING EXPERIENCES:

Sing the song several times for the children, directing their listening by using the following questions and statements.

Verse One:

- *Which of God's creations sing "a happy song"?* [Ducks, hens, birds, and wind]

As the children mention each creation, display the pictures in random order.

Sing the song again and invite the children to put the pictures in the proper sequence.

Point out that the words "a happy song" are sung on a descending scale. Ask the children to sing those words as an ostinato while you sing the entire song.

- *What do all of these creations join in singing?* [A happy song]

Invite the children to sing the song with you, adding the accompaniment.

Verse Two:

- *What are children singing?* [A happy song]
- *How long do they sing together?* [The whole day long]
- *When we sing together, what don't we mind?* [The weather]

BE HAPPY!

MESSAGE: Be happy all day long, and others will be, too!

ATTENTION-GETTER:

- *There is something very magical about being happy! Watch this! Bring a child forward and look him right in the eye. Give the child a big smile. Did you see the magic? My happiness spread to (child's name)! Listen as I sing the song "Be Happy" to discover what happens when we are happy all day long.*

LISTENING AND SINGING EXPERIENCES:

Sing the song several times, directing the children's listening by asking questions.

- *Being happy is contagious—it spreads to others. When we are happy all day long, what happens? [Others will be, too]*

- *How many times do I sing the word "happy" in the first verse and chorus? [Four]*

- *When we are happy all day long, what will we find out? [That he whose heart has joy and song gives joy to others too.]* Have the children sing that line while tapping the short-long-short-long rhythm. ♪ ♩ ♪ ♩

Ask the children to tap the rhythm of the whole song to see if that rhythm is almost constant. [Yes]

Ask the children to be happy like the little birds as they sit up tall and sing the song with you.

Challenge the children to try the magic of being happy all day long.

ENRICHMENT IDEAS:

1. Make a happy face on posterboard as illustrated. As the children smile and sing, pull the transparent thread attached to the center of the mouth, turning the face into a happy face.

2. Ask the children if they have grandparents who are over seventy years old. Point out that this song was written in 1914 before some of their grandparents were born. Being happy was important in their time, too.

3. Display happy self-portraits that the children have drawn.

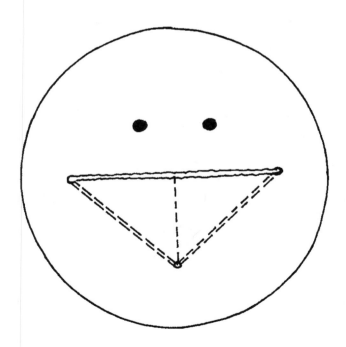

IF YOU'RE HAPPY

MESSAGE: If you're happy and you know it, then your face will surely show it.

ENRICHMENT IDEAS:

1. Invite the children to choose alternate action words. There are unlimited possibilities.

2. Sing an alternate phrase and then sing the phrase used the time before "tap your toes (tap, tap) clap your hands (clap, clap)." See how many additional phrases the children can remember in sequence. You could have a child lead each phrase.

ATTENTION-GETTER:

- *The look on our faces tells other people how we feel. Show me your mad face. Let children respond. Oh, you look like you're mad. Now show me your sad face. Let children respond.*

- *You look so sad. If our faces show when we are mad and sad, then what happens to our faces when we are happy? Let children respond. If you're happy, "your face will surely show it!"*

- *Sometimes when we're very, very happy we want to jump for joy or sing a song or shout "hurray!" Listen as I sing a fun song to see what we'll do when we're happy and we know it. [Clap our hands]*

LISTENING AND SINGING EXPERIENCES:

- *Count on your fingers how many times I sing, "If you're happy and you know it."* [Four]

Invite the children to do the actions with you as you sing the song for them. Then invite the children to join you in singing with actions.

SMILES

MESSAGE: When you smile, you make the world a better place.

ATTENTION-GETTER:

Introduce the song by asking all the children to frown. Have them trace their frown with their fingers, then show in the air with their fingers how a frown is shaped ⌒. Next, ask them to smile and trace a smile in the air ⌣. Sing both verses of the song for the children, frowning and smiling in the appropriate places.

LISTENING AND SINGING EXPERIENCES:

Sing the song again, asking the children to listen and discover the answers to the following questions.

Verse One:

• *What should you do if you meet a frown? [Do not let it stay and quickly turn it upside down.]*

Verse Two:

• *What happens to the world when you smile? [It is made into a better place.]*

• *Who likes a frowny face? [No one]*

• *This song makes us feel happy. Let's sing it together just for fun!*

ENRICHMENT IDEAS:

1. Have two children stand back-to-back interlocking arms. One child smiles, the other frowns, and they turn as the song indicates.

2. Make a large, round cardboard face that can be turned upside down to change a frown to a smile. (See illustration.) Have a child hold the face and turn it as the words indicate. Invite the children to frown and smile in the appropriate places as they sing.

3. Have two assistants hold a large piece of butcher paper with several small holes cut in it just the size of a mouth. Invite several children to stand behind the paper with their mouths up to the holes. Ask the children to smile or frown where indicated as the song is sung.

A SMILE IS LIKE THE SUNSHINE

MESSAGE: A smile is like the sunshine, for it brightens up our day.

ENRICHMENT IDEAS:

1. Hold up a ⌢ card and explain it to the children. Challenge them to listen to discover which word is held a little longer. [Twinkle]

2. Challenge the children to sing the entire song with detached, crisp staccato notes.

3. Invite the children to tap the rhythm as they sing.

4. Cut a sun out of yellow posterboard. Make the mouth by threading yarn through two holes and tying in back. Attach transparent thread to center of mouth and through a hole below mouth. As the children sing, pull the transparent thread from behind to change the frown into a smile.

ATTENTION-GETTER:

- *How many of you like magic tricks? I have learned a magic trick that is simply amazing. It can turn a frown into a smile.*

Bring a child to the front and ask him to show a frowning face. Look him right in the eye and let a cheerful smile slowly appear on your face. The children will see how the child couldn't resist smiling himself.

- *Did you see how my smile chased away his frown? A smile is like a magic trick. Listen as I sing this song to find what else a smile is like.*

LISTENING AND SINGING EXPERIENCES:

As the children discover the answers to these questions, invite them to sing that phrase with you.

- *What is a smile like? [The sunshine]*
- *What does a smile brighten? [It brightens up the day.]*
- *What does a smile give the eye? [A twinkle]*
- *What do smiles chase away? [Frowns]*

Have the children sing the song with you, listening for the word on the highest tone. [Twinkle]

TWO LITTLE EYES

MESSAGE: All of the parts of my body make me.

ATTENTION-GETTER:

Blink your eyes for the children. *Were my eyes blinking or winking?*

- *Let's all try to wink one of our eyes. Now let's blink our two little eyes. It is a little easier to blink than to wink, isn't it?*

- *I know a song about blinking our eyes. Every time I sing "blink, blink, blink," would you blink your eyes with me?* Sing the entire song for the children, using the actions indicated by the words.

LISTENING AND SINGING EXPERIENCES:

Continue using the actions throughout the presentation.

- *The song mentioned my "two little eyes that see." As I sing the song again, listen for what other things make me. [Head, shoulders, knees, and toes]*

Pitch lead the first two measures and sing the second line again. Invite the children to pitch lead with you, then sing that line together.

Sing the first two lines with the children.

- *In the song there are some happy words that don't mean anything. Listen as I sing to find them. [Tra-la-la] Those are such fun words to sing!*

Sing the third line, tapping the rhythm on the tra-la-las, and have the children join you.

- *There is a place in this song where we slow down or ritard. Listen as I sing and raise your hand when you think you have found the ritard.* Invite the children to sing the first three lines. Explain that when you point to yourself, they should stop singing and listen to you. Emphasize the ritard so they can find it easily. Have them sing the last line with you.

Invite the children to stand and sing the song from the beginning.

ENRICHMENT IDEAS:

1. Challenge the children to sing the words "blink, blink, blink" in a detached, crisp way.

2. Challenge the children to clap their hands on the rests that come on the last measures of lines two and four. (Clue: listen for the word "me" and the high chord on the piano before clapping.)

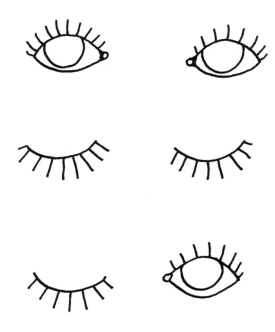

I HAVE TWO EARS

MESSAGE: I thank Heavenly Father for giving me a body. I'll try to use it wisely in all I do.

ENRICHMENT IDEAS:

1. Refer to the visual aids and ask the children which part of their bodies they wouldn't mind giving up. Take down each one of the pictures and discuss how hard it would be to do without that part of your body.

2. Make a ⌒ Explain that when that mark is over a note, the conductor can hold that note as long as she wants. Ask the children to listen for the fermata. Exaggerate it so it can be found easily. Explain that it feels good to hold the words "Heavenly Father" longer because they are very important words.

3. Divide older children into three groups. Have each group hold one of the three notes on "Father" (F major chord, F, A, C).

4. Use actions indicated by words.

MATERIALS:

Drawings of ears, eyes, feet, lips, and hands

Pictures depicting a child at work, at play, and smiling

ATTENTION-GETTER:

- *Heavenly Father has given us wonderful bodies. Our bodies are made up of many parts and we have two of some parts. Can you name some of these?* Let children respond.

- *As I sing, listen to find some pairs that we may have missed.* Sing entire song.

Post the pictures in random order and challenge the children to post them in the correct order as you sing again. Sing once again to check the order of the pictures.

LISTENING AND SINGING EXPERIENCES:

Help the children discover the special purposes of these body "pairs" by repeating the song several times and asking questions as listed below. Pitch lead and repeat each phrase as the answer is discovered.

Verse One:

- *Why were we given two ears? [To hear the truth]* Make certain that the children are confident with the E♭ on "to" before going on.

- *Why were we given two eyes? [To see the good]*

- *Why were we given two feet? [To carry me to places where they should]*

- *When should we use our bodies wisely? [In work and play]* Point out that this means all the time.

- *Whom do we thank for making us this way? [Heavenly Father]*

Verse Two:

- *Why do we have two lips? [To speak kind words]*

- *Why do we have two hands? [To work for me]*

- *What is another name for these special pairs Heavenly Father has given us? [Loving helpers]*

Ask if anyone has ever had a broken arm, sprained ankle, or eye patch. Explain that we especially appreciate our special pairs or "loving helpers" when one isn't working quite right. They are wonderful gifts from Heavenly Father.

TWO HAPPY FEET

MESSAGE: I have two happy feet that can make noise, but in my Heavenly Father's house I walk so softly that you can't hear my feet at all.

ATTENTION-GETTER:

Invite a child to come forward. *I'm sure your two happy little feet can run.*

- *What else can they do?* Let children respond. *When we do some of these things, our feet make noises don't they? I know a song about something our feet can do that doesn't make any sound at all.*

Sing the song for the children.

LISTENING AND SINGING EXPERIENCES:

Sing the song several times for the children, directing their listening by asking questions.

- *What can our feet do without making any noise?* [Walk in our Heavenly Father's house.]
- *The song mentions three other things our feet can do that sometimes makes a noise. What are they?* [Take me where I go, hop me, skip me.] Sing as needed to get the three answers.

Sing the first line again pointing out the melody. Then sing the entire song asking the children to raise their hands when they hear other words that are sung on that same melody. [But in my Heavenly Father's house so softly do they fall.]

Through pitch leading, show how the melody goes up and down the scale.

Invite the children to pitch lead the song with you to see how the whole song follows this same pattern of moving up and down the scale.

Repeat again, inviting the children to sing with you.

ENRICHMENT IDEAS:

1. Divide the children into two groups and have them take turns singing the phrases as you indicate. As you point to each group, challenge them to stand and sing without making any noise at all with their feet.

2. Challenge the children to pitch lead with their bodies, standing and stooping to the rise and fall of the melody.

3. Use lion and mouse puppets to indicate the volume. The first two lines are sung in full voice. See how quietly the children can sing the last two lines.

4. Sing the last two measures very slowly. Exaggerate the slow tempo and encourage the children to watch you closely.

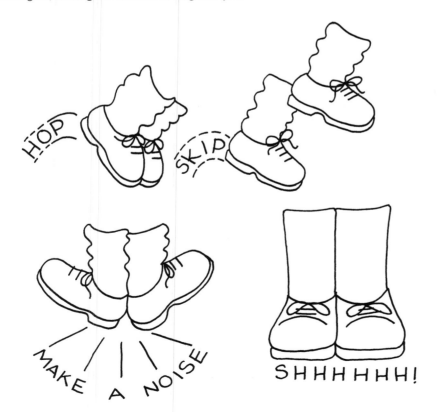

I WIGGLE

MESSAGE: By wiggling, I get rid of the wiggles in me so I can sit quietly.

ENRICHMENT IDEAS:

1. Challenge the children to sing the song leaving out the words fingers, toes, shoulders, and nose, but continuing the actions as suggested by the words.

2. Vary the song by substituting words for other parts of the body.

ATTENTION-GETTER:

- *We have lots of body parts that we can wiggle. What are some of them?* Let children respond. As they do, have children wiggle those parts.

- *How about your nose? That one's not so easy. Listen as I sing this wiggle song to find out what other body parts I can wiggle.* Sing the song for the children, using actions indicated by words.

LISTENING AND SINGING EXPERIENCES:

- *This time as I sing it, wiggle along with me. On the last line fold your arms or your hands.*

- *This song has a fun melody. It keeps getting higher and higher, and then at the end it gets low and quiet. Watch as I pitch lead to see how it gets higher and higher with each wiggle. Then tell me what words we sing on the low quiet notes. [I will be still, as still as can be.]*

Invite the children to stand and sing with you, using the actions indicated by the words. Listen to make certain they are singing the intervals and rhythm correctly.

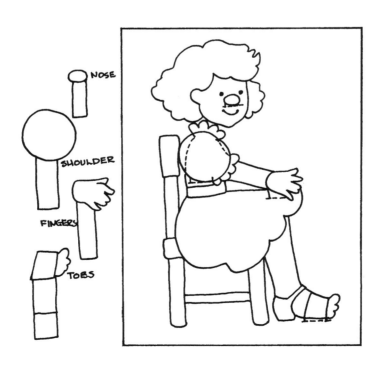

I HAVE TWO LITTLE HANDS

MESSAGE: I am thankful to Heavenly Father for my hands, for, though they are small, they know how to do many good things and how to obey.

ATTENTION-GETTER:

Bring a small child to the front and compare his hands with yours. Point out that his hands are much smaller than yours. Ask questions such as: *"My big hands can pick up toys, can your little hands?"* Then point out that small children can do many helpful and obedient things, even though they have two little hands.

LISTENING AND SINGING EXPERIENCES:

Verse One:

- *Listen as I sing to discover how my two little hands are folded. [Snugly and tight]*
- *Find two words that describe how little my hands are. [Tiny and weak]*
- *Though my hands are tiny and weak, what do they know? [What is right.]*

Hum the melody of the first line, and ask the children to find other words that are sung on this melody. *[During all the long hours till daylight is through]*

- *During the day, what is there for my two hands to do? [Plenty indeed]*

Verse Two:

- *How do we address Heavenly Father when we thank him for our two little hands? [Kind Father]*
- *What do we ask him? [To bless them till each understands]*
- *What do we want to understand? [That children can only be happy all day when two little hands have learned how to obey]*
- *It is so important to use our hands to help others and to obey Heavenly Father.*

ENRICHMENT IDEAS:

1. Challenge the children to find the rhyming words.
2. Lead a discussion on the many things the children can do even though their hands are little.
3. "Lap tap" the strong first beat of each measure and "finger tap" beats two and three.
4. Invite the children to sway back and forth as they sing.

MY HANDS

MESSAGE: Though I can move my hands all about, see how quiet they can be.

ENRICHMENT IDEAS:

1. Let a child be the leader for all to follow.

2. Try singing the song very slowly and speed up the tempo with each repetition.

ATTENTION-GETTER:

- *Let's pretend there is a mirror between us. When you look in the mirror, the person does everything that you do. As I sing this action song, be my reflection and copy me exactly. Everyone stand up and watch closely.* Sing the song using actions. Fold your arms on the last measure.

LISTENING AND SINGING EXPERIENCES:

Sing the song again, having the children imitate you.

Sing the song again, leaving out the words that tell where to place your hands *(head, shoulders, waist, side, etc.).* Let the children sing the missing words as you pantomime the actions.

Challenge the children to sing the song using the actions and to sing the last measure in their very softest voices.

ROLL YOUR HANDS

ATTENTION-GETTER:

- *How many of you can roll your hands like this? Show me. Can you roll them slowly? Swiftly?*
- *Can you fold your arms like me? You've just learned all the actions to our new activity song.*
- *As I sing, do the actions just like me.* Sing the song three times to include all actions.

LISTENING AND SINGING EXPERIENCES:

- *As I sing the song again, see if you can match my actions exactly.* Don't move too "swiftly" on verse two.

Invite the children to sing the song with you and do the actions.

- *As we sing again, listen to see if there are any long notes in the phrase about folding our arms. [No, it moves right along.]*

ENRICHMENT IDEAS:

1. Use alternate actions: rolling thumbs, feet, or head.
2. Substitute other word phrases, for example: Pick up all the toys; Let's all sing this song; Stand up straight and tall.

HEAD, SHOULDERS, KNEES, AND TOES

ATTENTION-GETTER:

Ask the children to say the name of the body part that you touch. This is my (head), my (shoulders), my (knees), and (toes), (eyes), (ears), (mouth), and (nose). You have just said every word in a fun song I know.

LISTENING AND SINGING EXPERIENCES:

- *This time I'll sing the words, and you do the actions with me.*

Invite the children to sing with you as you sing it again.

ENRICHMENT IDEAS:

1. Sing this song using different tempos.
2. Have older children try singing the body parts backwards: "Toes, knees, shoulders, head." For the last part sing, "Nose, mouth, ears, and eyes." This will be a real challenge, but fun.
3. Sing very slowly and wiggle each body part.
4. Show the pages 250-51 in the *Children's Songbook*. Let the children guess the song the children are singing in the picture.

TO GET QUIET

ENRICHMENT IDEAS:

1. Challenge the older children to find where the melody repeats itself. [Each line begins the same.]

2. Let the children pitch lead the two descending scales with you. You may wish to body pitch lead.

3. Point out how the rising notes help you feel like stretching and following the rise and fall of the melody line.

ATTENTION-GETTER:

- *I like to count, don't you? I'm sure all of you can count to ten. Let's try it. Everyone count your fingers. I know a song that has some numbers in it. Listen and tell me what is the highest number in this song. [Four]* Do the actions indicated by the words as you sing for the children.

LISTENING AND SINGING EXPERIENCES:

Have the children stand and follow you in doing the actions as you sing it again.

- *It feels so good to stretch. Let's stretch up even higher this time.* Invite them to follow you again as you sing.

- *Let's try it all together. Let's make our singing voices as soft as we can when we get to the very end.*

DO AS I'M DOING

ENRICHMENT IDEAS:

1. For variation, try suddenly changing tempo or dynamics throughout the song. Challenge the children to follow you closely.

2. Select a child to act out one way he helps at home. As the other children follow the action, have them guess what it is that the child does to help.

3. Play follow the leader and walk around the room as you do the actions.

4. Help the children feel the syncopated rhythm by tapping their knees to the rhythmic pattern as they sing the beginning of the first, second, fourth, and fifth lines. ♪ ♩ ♪ ♩

ATTENTION-GETTER:

Prearrange the following activity with a child or leader.

Ask the children if they can discover who you are imitating as you copy the actions of the selected person. Then invite the children to see how well they can copy you as you sing the song with the actions.

LISTENING AND SINGING EXPERIENCES:

Sing the song again, using a different action.

Invite the children to sing the song with you and to choose the action for all to imitate.

Invite a child to come forward and be the leader as you sing again.

HINGES

MATERIALS:

A stick that can be easily broken

A box with hinges

ATTENTION-GETTER:

Show the children the stick and explain to them that, because this stick has no hinge, it will crack in two if we try to bend it. (Crack it.) Then show them a box with a hinged lid and demonstrate how easily it will open because it has hinges.

- *Our bodies have hinges, too, even though we can't see them. They are all hidden under our skin. These hinges make it easy for us to bend. Can you name some places where you think we have a hinge?* Let children respond.

- *As I sing, listen to hear what would happen to me if I didn't have hinges.* Sing using actions listed with each repetition.

LISTENING AND SINGING EXPERIENCES:

- *What would happen to me? [I would crack.]*

Invite the children to join you in doing the actions as you sing once again.

Challenge the children to sing the last word of each phrase when you stop singing. The actions will help them.

Invite them to sing with you. Challenge them to get every action just right.

Suggested actions:

Flex hands and elbows; Bend knees; Touch top of neck; Touch toes; Bend forward at waist; Straighten up; Bend both elbows and knees; Straighten up or clap

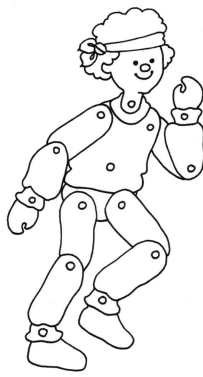

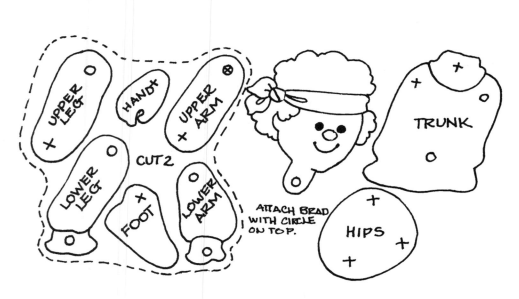

STAND UP

ENRICHMENT IDEAS:

1. As the song ends and the children sit down, you may want to fold your arms along with the "sit down" action so the children will end quietly.

2. Point out that the melody rises as we stand up and touch our head and falls as we bend down to touch the floor.

ATTENTION-GETTER:

Today we will play a game called "Follow the Leader."

Invite the children to answer your questions by doing the suggested actions.

- *Can you stand up when "stand up" is said?*
- *Can you place your hands on top of your head?*
- *Can you bend down low and touch the floor?*
- *Can you shake your hands one-two-three-four?*
- *Can you put your hands on your hips?*
- *Can you turn around?*
- *Can you give a smile and then sit down?*

LISTENING AND SINGING EXPERIENCES:

Sing the song, following the actions suggested by the words.

Invite the children to do the actions with you several times before inviting them to sing with you.

OH, HOW WE LOVE TO STAND

ENRICHMENT IDEAS:

1. Consider using the alternate actions and words as suggested below the song.

2. Select a child to come to the front and lead an action. Use the child's name and follow the actions he or she does.

3. For variety, speed up the tempo slightly each time you repeat the song.

ATTENTION-GETTER:

- *Oh, how I love to stand when I've tried so hard to sit quietly for a long time. When my body is really tired from sitting, sometimes I like to sing to this song.*

Sing the song for the children, doing the actions.

LISTENING AND SINGING EXPERIENCES:

Sing the song again, asking the children to listen for how many different actions are mentioned. *[Five]*

Have the children do the actions with you and listen for what is best of all. *[Sit down.]*

Invite the children to join you in singing the song and doing the actions.

HEALTHY, WEALTHY, AND WISE

MESSAGE: Going to bed, and getting up early, makes us healthy and ready to learn.

ATTENTION-GETTER:

Briefly tell the children that Benjamin Franklin was a great man in the early days of the United States. He did and said many wise things. One of the wise things he said has become a song. Ask the children to listen as you sing for what going to bed early and getting up early will do for a person. *[It makes a man healthy, wealthy, and wise.]*

LISTENING AND SINGING EXPERIENCES:

As you teach this song, draw attention to the rise and fall of the melody by clear pitch leading. Sing the first phrase and ask the children to listen for other words that we sing on that same melody. *[Makes a man healthy and wealthy and wise.]*

- *How does the second phrase resemble the first? [It moves the same way, but begins on a higher pitch.]*

Have the children listen carefully to discover how the third phrase differs from the other. *[It has a higher melody, and even rhythm.]*

Emphasize the eighth notes on the third count of each measure on phrases one, two, and four by lightly tapping the rhythm as you sing the melody line. Instead of singing the words, you might sing instead "Slow-slow-quick-quick," or "One-two-three-ee," to match the rhythm.

Invite the children to sing the song with you.

ENRICHMENT IDEAS:

1. To sing as a round, follow the instructions given below the song.

2. To direct the rise in melody of each phrase, pitch lead by holding your hand on the level of the beginning tone of each phrase.

3. Challenge the children to body pitch lead by holding the pose showing the beginning pitch of each line.

296

THE WISE MAN AND THE FOOLISH MAN

MESSAGE: The wise man built his house on a firm foundation, and the winds and rain could not destroy it. The foolish man built his house on sand, and the winds and rain destroyed it.

ENRICHMENT IDEAS:

1. When children know the song well, begin omitting one action word each time through the song (*rock, rains, floods, sand, washed away*). Repeat the song over and over until all action words are sung silently.

2. Besides the actions listed in the songbook, you might add:

   wise man: circle eyes with fingers to look like glasses

   house: fingers of each hand slant up and touch at tips like a roof

   foolish: point finger to head and shake head to say no

3. Invite an older child to read Matthew 7:24-27 aloud. Give each child the scripture reference so they can read it at home with their family.

MATERIALS:

A rock large enough to stand on

A box with sand

ATTENTION-GETTER:

Show the children the rock and the sand and discuss which is more sturdy to stand on.

- *I know a song about a rock and sand. Listen to see which is better to build a house on.* Sing the song all the way through, doing the appropriate actions as suggested below the song.

- *The words to this song are taken from a parable that Jesus gave in his Sermon on the Mount and again when he appeared in ancient America.* Briefly explain the parable *(See Matt. 7:24–27; Hel. 5:12).*

- *This parable teaches us to build our testimonies on a firm foundation, which is Jesus Christ.*

- *If we do this, then when storms or problems come into our lives, our testimonies will be strong enough to withstand them.*

LISTENING AND SINGING EXPERIENCES:

Sing the song all the way through, inviting the children to do the actions with you.

Sing the song again with the children.

Tell the children to remember this week to build their testimonies on a firm foundation. Our testimonies of Christ can be like a rock to help us be strong even when temptations and problems come our way.

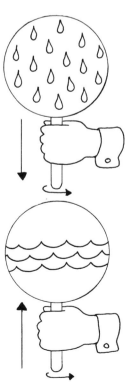

FELIZ CUMPLEAÑOS

MESSAGE: We can say "Happy birthday" in many other languages, but any way you say it, it means happy birthday to you.

MATERIALS:

Four large birthday cards, each with "Happy Birthday to you" written in one of the languages mentioned.

Word cards: SPANISH, GERMAN, NORWEGIAN.

ATTENTION-GETTER:

- *I have some birthday cards that I'd like to share.* Pass the cards out to three children, keeping the English card for yourself.
- *Here's what mine says, "Happy Birthday to you."*

Ask the children to open their cards and read the message inside.

LISTENING AND SINGING EXPERIENCES:

Sing the song to the children as you gather the cards and post them in random order. Then sing the song again to see if the cards are posted in the correct order.

Choose three children to match the country with the birthday card by posting the word cards as you sing.

Sing "Feliz Cumpleaños" and have the children sing it back to you. Repeat until they are comfortable with the pronunciation. Do the same with the words "Fröhlicher Geburtstag" and "Gratulerer med dagen."

Invite the children to sing just the Happy Birthdays as you sing the rest of the song.

- *No matter which way you say it, each way means "Happy Birthday to you."* Invite the children to sing the song with you.

Teach verse two in a similar manner.

ENRICHMENT IDEAS:

1. Prepare poster-size costumes, using the pictures shown. Cut the faces out so a child could put his own face through the cutout hole.

2. Prepare the pictures as shown and pass out to the children in random order. As you sing the song, challenge them to come to the front and arrange themselves in the correct order before you finish singing the song.

3. On a world map, connect a string from the picture of each child to the correct country and say "Happy Birthday" to each one in their language.

4. You could use an opaque projector to teach verse two. Have the children read the phonetic pronunciation and observe the rhythm of the extra syllables.

♪ *About the Song*

Prompted by the expansion of the Church, the *Children's Songbook* Committee felt the need to add a second verse which could include non-European countries. The Translation Department provided the words "Happy Birthday" in all 18 major languages, including the phonetic pronunciation and accent markings. With only three note adjustments for additional syllables, the committee was able to include Samoan, Japanese, and Korean in a second verse. We contacted the author/composer, Maurine Ozment, and received permission to add a verse.

YOUR HAPPY BIRTHDAY

MESSAGE: This month is a special one because it's your birthday. We'll celebrate your happy day by singing Happy Birthday to you.

ENRICHMENT IDEAS:

1. Print key words on candle-shaped cutouts. Place the candles on a posterboard cake. Remove the candles one by one as the children become familiar with the words.

2. Invite all children with a birthday this month to come to the front as the children sing to them.

3. Follow this song with the familiar birthday song, "Happy Birthday to You."

♪ *About the Song*

The 1979 *Guinness Book of World Records* claims that "Happy Birthday to You" is the most often sung song in the world. It was written by two sisters, Mildred and Patty Hill, who were kindergarten teachers in Kentucky at the turn of the century. Patty Hill also composed "Once within a Lowly Stable."

ATTENTION-GETTER:

- *[Name of month] is an important month to me because it is the month of my birthday. In what month is your birthday?* **Let children respond.** *All of these months are very special because they are the months of our birthdays.*

LISTENING AND SINGING EXPERIENCES:

- *As I sing this birthday song, listen for two words that are fun to sing, but don't really mean anything! [Zip-a-dee-ay and heigh-dee-ho.]* Invite children to sing that phrase back to you while tapping the rhythm.

- *What would we really like to celebrate with you? [Your happy day]*

- *What is something we can do to celebrate with you? [We'll sing a song that we all know, Happy Birthday to you.]* Point out the descending scale through pitch leading, and invite the children to sing this phrase.

- *Listen as I sing again to find the word with a hold sign ⌒. [Know]* Exaggerate for emphasis.

Invite the children to sing the song with you.

HAPPY, HAPPY BIRTHDAY

MESSAGE: If I had just one wish, it would be to wish you a happy birthday and happy days all year long.

ATTENTION-GETTER:

From the newspaper, read a few names of babies born on the day of the birthday child. Add the child's name to the list and say, *"And on this day, eight years ago, [child's name] was born."* Call the child up to the front.

LISTENING AND SINGING EXPERIENCES:

• *Listen as I sing this birthday song to [name of child] and find one joyful word that is repeated several times.* Invite the birthday child to sit down.

Ask the children to hold up a finger every time you sing the word "happy" as you repeat the song. *[Five]*

• *If I could have only one wish, what would it be? [To wish you a happy, happy birthday to you from me]*

• *Sing the song with me this time and tell me what two words we sing when our voices go from a low note to the highest note in the song. [Wish—then]*

Bring the birthday child forward again and have the children sing their very best for him.

ENRICHMENT IDEAS:

1. Construct a large birthday cake from posterboard. Display a picture or the names of each birthday child honored that day.

2. Have the children sing the words in the last measure staccato (in a crisp, detached way), as indicated on the music.

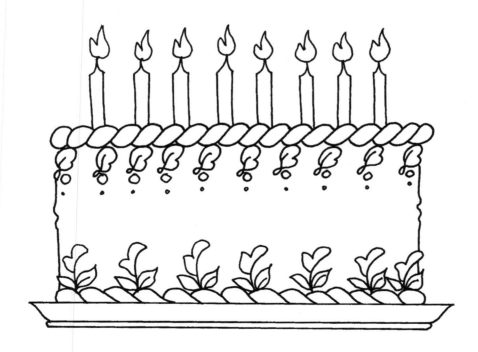

HAVE A VERY HAPPY BIRTHDAY

MESSAGE: Have a very happy birthday and a year filled with joy, gladness, and the love of friends.

ENRICHMENT IDEAS:

1. Divide the children into four groups. Let each group stand and sing one of the four phrases to the birthday child.

2. To help the children hear the quick sixteenth notes ♪, invite the children to tap and sing as you post cards as illustrated. Draw attention to the one card that is different from the others.

ATTENTION-GETTER:

- *What is your favorite day of year? (Let children respond.) My birthday is one of my favorite days, too. I always feel excited inside when my friends and family sing "Happy Birthday" to me. Listen as I sing to see what I would like your birthday to be filled with. [Sunshine everywhere.]*

LISTENING AND SINGING EXPERIENCES:

Sing the song again, asking one of these questions with each repetition.

Verse One:

- *I wish for the year to bring you three things. What are they? [Joy, gladness, and the love of friends who care.]* Sing as needed to get all the answers. Invite the children to tap the short-short-long ♫ ♩. rhythm that begins each phrase as they sing verse one.

Verse Two:

- *This time we don't sing "a very happy birthday" to you. What do we wish you? [A most exciting birthday.]*
- *With whom could you share a smile? [Someone new.]*
- *To whom could you say a kind word? [Your neighbor.]*
- *Who could you let him know? [A happy you.]*

Verse Three:

- *What is another way to wish a very happy birthday? [Have a very special birthday.]*
- *What should we add to your cake? [A candle.]*
- *What two things can we share on our birthdays? [Our cake and friendship.]*

YOU'VE HAD A BIRTHDAY

MESSAGE: We want to sing happy birthday to you.

ENRICHMENT IDEAS:

1. Show the children a quarter rest sign 𝄽. Explain that this sign represents one beat where we are silent and don't sing. Ask them to tap the rhythm as they sing and watch you closely as you snap your fingers on the rest. Invite the children to tap and snap as they sing.

2. When well-learned, sing as a round as indicated on the music.

ATTENTION-GETTER:

Begin singing the song as you walk to the child who is having a birthday this week. Take the child by the hand and bring him to the front as you finish singing the song. Repeat with each birthday child.

LISTENING AND SINGING EXPERIENCES:

As you sing again, invite the children to join you on the words hooray and happy birthday to you as you indicate.

Invite the children to join you and to find the octave interval (C to C) on the words too happy. Make sure the children sing the interval correctly.

GLOSSARY

Explanation of Symbols and Terms (Also see *Children's Songbook*, p. 300-4)

Body Pitch Leading—Moving your whole body up and down according to the pitch of the melody.

Chest Voice—Singing in the speaking register.

Descant—An optional voice part (higher than the melody) with words of its own; can also be played as an instrumental part (see *Children's Songbook*, p. 304).

Dynamics—Volume and tempo markings which create the mood of the song (*p*–soft; *f*–loud; cresc.–increasing volume gradually; *dim.*–decreasing volume gradually). The tempo is indicated by the metronome marking (♩=100) and descriptive words (with energy).

Fermata—A pause or hold ⌒ usually at least half again the note value (see *Children's Songbook*, p. 303).

Finger Tap—Lightly tap index fingers together to the beat or to the rhythm. This is preferable to clapping, which often becomes boisterous.

Form—An outline showing which lines or phrases of the song are alike or different (i.e., AABA, ABAC, ABAB). This can be decided by sentences, lines, or musical phrases.

Inner Hearing—Thinking the words or melody of a song rather than speaking or singing them; actually imagining the sound in your mind.

Legato—Smooth, connected singing or playing.

Listening Experience—A question that causes the child to listen to the song to find the answer.

Melody Picture—A visual representation of the pitch of the melody. This can be shown with dots, lines, other objects i.e., stars, notes, etc. or as a graph. See p. 22 (Part One).

Obbligato—An optional instrumental part above the melody (see *Children's Songbook*, p. 304).

Phrase—A musical thought similar to a sentence. A phrase is often two or four measures and should be sung legato (connected) to give meaning; the end of a phrase usually provides a natural breathing place.

Phrase Chart—A line representation of musical thoughts or breathing places in the song.

Pitch Lead—Conducting by showing the pitch of the melody; also may represent the length of time the is held.

Rote Learning—Learning by listening rather than reading.

Staccato—Light, detached singing or playing.

Standard Beat Patterns—Patterns for conducting music (see *Children's Songbook*, p. 304.)

Whisper-singing—Singing in your softest voice as though whispering.

Word Slurs—Two pitches on one syllable.

Alphabetical Listing of Song Titles & Lesson Plans